# Jury Selection Procedures

## Our Uncertain Commitment to Representative Panels

# Jury Selection Procedures

## Our Uncertain Commitment to Representative Panels

Jon M. Van Dyke

Ballinger Publishing Company • Cambridge, Massachusetts
A Subsidiary of J.B. Lippincott Company

International Standard Book Number: 0-88410-237-8

Library of Congress Catalog Card Number: 76-43342

Printed in the United States of America

**Library of Congress Cataloging in Publication Data**

Van Dyke, Jon M.
　Jury selection procedures.

　Bibliography: p.
　Includes index.
　1. Jury—United States. I. Title.
KF9680.V35　　　347'.73'75　　　76-43342
ISBN 0-88410-237-8

# Contents

## Introduction: The Jury— Impartial, Independent, and Representative

The North Carolina jury took only seventy-five minutes to find Joan Little not guilty of killing her jailer, who (she stated) had tried to assault her sexually. The defense team had spent ten days in July 1975 to question 150 prospective jurors in an effort to find a panel it considered sympathetic to the young black woman's plea of self-defense. The ten-day examination—similar to others involving significant political and social issues—was the culmination of the nine-month-long Joan Little Fair Trial Jury Project, an undertaking that cost nearly forty thousand dollars, most of it spent on a seven-member team of professional sociologists, psychologists, and pollsters. The project involved over a thousand telephone interviews, the use of a computer to correlate attitudes and demographic data, and detailed questioning of prospective jurors—with a psychic and body-language expert on hand to be sure that nonverbal clues would not be missed[1] —in order to decide which jurors to remove from the panel through challenges. The forty thousand dollars were only part of the total defense cost of $325,000, most of it raised from citizens around the country in a sophisticated direct-mail campaign.

Is this what it takes to assemble an impartial jury in the United States today? What is the likelihood that a young black woman would find her "peers" on a jury without such an effort? Procedures like those used in the Little trial—and employed in the defense of Angela Davis, John Mitchell and Maurice Stans, the Harrisburg Seven and others—have been called by some a new form of jury tampering.[2] Not all judges permit attorneys to conduct wide-ranging questioning and challenging, and not all attorneys approve of it. Some critics believe that the challenge efforts employed in some recent well-publicized cases have perverted the process of jury selection, and that the objective of impaneling an impartial jury is more remote than ever when one side can marshall extensive resources to "shape" the jury to its desires.

But whether or not such procedures go "too far"—an issue that warrants consideration and is discussed below[a]—is a question that must be seen in light of the reason they take place. Every defendant in a criminal trial in the United States has the right, according to the Constitution, to trial by an "impartial jury."[3] Extensive questioning of prospective jurors is aimed at eliminating bias in a jury panel, and it would not be necessary if panels could be presumed impartial in the first place. But in many cases they are not. In cases that generate a high level of emotion, as did the Watergate cases, the trials of antiwar activists, and the Joan Little and Patricia Hearst cases, many prospective jurors have formed opinions about the guilt or innocence of the defendant beforehand, and some effort must be made to ascertain such possible prejudice. This problem has been compounded in some highly volatile cases by the government's use of the Federal Bureau of Investigation to investigate prospective jurors and provide information to help the prosecution exercise challenges to "shape" the jury the way it desires. An F.B.I. informer was a member of the defense team assisting with jury selection in the "Attica Brothers" trials that followed the 1971 uprising and armed assault in the state prison at Attica, New York, and apparently reported defense strategy regularly to the F.B.I.[b,4] Even when such methods are not used, the government's clerks supervise jury selection and thus the government has greater control over who is called in the first place. The application of sophisticated social-science methods to jury selection may be an overreaction, casting new doubts about the jury's impartiality, but it was originally, at least, a response to government actions in the opposite direction.

In the more common, unpublicized cases, jury selection is a less sophisticated contest but still can result in imbalances that, inten-

---

[a]See Chapter Seven, p. 177.

[b]Sociologist Jay Schulman, who assisted in jury selection for the defense in this trial, the Joan Little trial, the Harrisburg Seven trial, and several other major political trials, said in an affidavit following the public testimony of the F.B.I. informer at Attica that he "was amazed at the unfailing correctness" of the prosecutor's peremptory challenges (because of access to defense records). "In every prior case on which I have worked," he continued, "prosecution strikes have never achieved this degree of correctness." *New York Times*, April 13, 1975, p. 50 (city ed.).

tional or not, threaten the jury's impartiality. Jurors are supposed to be drawn at random from the community. When they are not, the jury may overrepresent some segments of society and underrepresent others, an imbalance that raises the specter of bias. The concept of the jury requires that neither side exert pressure on the jury, directly or indirectly. Juries today are selected in ways that go much farther toward ensuring fairness than did those of the past, but the issue of impartiality is very much alive.

Mistrust of the jury system has lately been expressed by many observers and participants. Defendants and victims of crime sometimes doubt the fairness of verdicts, arguing that jurors act out of emotion rather than reason, or that jurors are prejudiced to begin with. Professionals in the judicial system criticize inefficiencies and have recommended major changes, including reducing the size of juries and eliminating the requirement for unanimity, to speed up selection and deliberation and to save money. Many citizens feel that jury trials are largely an inconvenience, merely postponing the day when criminals are taken off the streets. And people called for jury duty have attacked the system because of the long waits, low pay, bureaucratic confusion, and occasional abuse by attorneys and judges.

These criticisms have serious consequences for our judicial system, because the jury plays such a unique and important role. The cases that go to a jury are the exceptional, generally serious ones, such as murder cases or cases in which there is genuine controversy about the facts. Every person accused of a crime that can lead to imprisonment even for a day has the right to a jury trial under the Constitution, but most defendants waive that right. In most jurisdictions only between 5 and 15 percent of all criminal cases ever reach a jury; most of the others are settled through plea bargaining. Although plea bargaining has been widely criticized as well, it remains the most prevalent means of settling criminal cases, mainly because it has certain benefits for both sides if the defendant is guilty—and most persons who pass through the stages of arrest, investigation by a district attorney, and formal accusation by a grand jury or judge after a preliminary hearing are guilty. Once indicted, such a defendant is better off pleading to a lesser charge than facing a jury that is likely to convict on a greater charge, and the prosecution saves the court costs by not going to trial. Whether society is better off by such plea-bargaining is a major question presently being debated both within and outside the criminal justice system.

In the complicated cases when a defendant does choose a jury trial, or the serious cases in which the prosecution is not willing to plea-bargain, the jury has the power to deprive the accused of his or her freedom—a very serious step in our society. The jury hears and assesses the evidence in a case and makes the final judgment on guilt or innocence. It has immense power and a profound responsibility. For this reason, although the jury is used in relatively few cases, its integrity is one of the keystones of the judicial system. If the jury's decision is not accepted as impartial, respect for the whole system breaks down.[c] Why then use a jury? Why entrust ordinary people with such sensitive decisions in such important cases?

The jury—a group of ordinary people assembled for a limited period to decide a given case—is considered the fairest instrument of justice because of a belief that the danger of bias is even greater when "experts" are used: the means to counter the inevitably somewhat subjective view of a single person is to call on twelve to do the job. It is a tenet of our system that although a governmental bureaucracy may be necessary to monitor the day-to-day affairs of the community, the sensitive decisions of justice are likely to be reached with a greater wisdom by persons unconnected with the centers of power. In the United States, as in England where the jury originated, community participation is the choice over decision-making by "experts."[d] Only when the decision-makers come from the popula-

---

[c]Cynicism about the justice of plea-bargaining has had this effect in some quarters.

[d]It should be noted here that we are talking in this book primarily about criminal juries, rather than civil juries or grand juries. Both these juries are currently under fire: grand juries for being tools of the prosecution and for operating in secrecy without legal safeguards to protect witnesses and potential defendants; civil juries for being inefficient, time-consuming, and not sufficiently qualified to deal with complex cases. The pros and cons of continuing to use grand juries and civil juries are too complex to be discussed adequately here. Some of the observations about the makeup of criminal juries can also be applied to these juries, and some examples of these juries are used to illustrate the discussion of criminal juries, but the case for these juries is not the same. Continued use of the grand jury may depend largely on the elimination of abuse. For my thoughts on the subject of the grand jury, see Van Dyke, Wolinsky, Broder, Elliott, and Reilly, "*Quadra v. Superior Court of San Francisco*: A Challenge to the Composition of the San Francisco Grand Jury," *Hastings Law Journal* 27 (1976): 565-636; and Van Dyke, "Grand Juries: Representative or Elite?" *Hastings Law Journal* 28 (1976):37. Two significant differences exist between the civil and the criminal jury: the possible penalty that a civil jury can impose is less—only the transfer of property—than that of a criminal jury, which can deprive a person of freedom, and the case for "expert" decision-making and efficiency is somewhat stronger in the case of civil juries, because the stakes are smaller. The United Kingdom has ended the use of juries in civil cases other than libel, and in the United States a similar movement has taken some types of litigation out of the civil courts, through devices such as workmen's compensation and no-fault insurance. Some civil cases do, however, involve difficult social questions (suits for damages resulting from police brutality or illegal wiretapping, for instance), and a strong case can be made for having a representative jury decide these cases even though they are "civil" in nature.

tion at large, and return to it, will their decisions reflect the collective conscience of the community and be accepted by the community.

As G.K. Chesterton, the English novelist, poet, and essayist of the early twentieth century, put it after serving as a juror:

> And the horrible thing about all legal officials, even the best, about all judges, magistrates, barristers, detectives, and policemen, is not that they are wicked (some of them are good), not that they are stupid (several of them are quite intelligent), it is simply that they have got used to it. . . .
>
> Our civilization has decided, and very justly decided, that determining the guilt or innocence of men is a thing too important to be trusted to trained men. If it wishes for light upon that awful matter, it asks men who know no more law than I know, but who can feel the things that I felt in the jury box. When it wants a library catalogued, or the solar system discovered, or any trifle of that kind, it uses up its specialists. *But when it wishes anything done which is really serious, it collects twelve of the ordinary men standing round.* The same thing was done, if I remember right, by the Founder of Christianity.[5]

The jury may have weaknesses—lack of efficiency and expertise are those most commonly cited—but these shortcomings are also the source of its strength, its legitimacy as the collective conscience of the community. That conscience is summoned in an ingenious way. No individual is totally objective; all people have their own personal views and expériences. That is why the decision of a group of twelve is considered more reliable in sensitive cases than that of one person, even a person well-versed in the law. The jury is an attempt to minimize the bias in all of us by drawing a group of persons from the community and trusting that the combination of differing perspectives will balance out. This is the closest approximation to impartiality we can get, and it works most of the time.

The impartiality thus built into the jury system—and protected by the Constitution's Sixth Amendment guarantee of trial by "impartial jury"—can, however, be threatened. In order to be impartial, and be viewed as impartial (and hence the legitimate vehicle of justice—a critical aspect of the jury system), a jury must also be independent. Freedom from outside influence is necessary to preserve impartiality. If jury members seem to be hand-picked by one side or the other, the jury's impartiality and hence its integrity will be suspect. It may be—or may seem to be—biased because of its makeup. The jury, then, must be chosen in a way that leads to its acceptance by the community as independent.

The jury's impartiality and independence must be ensured, in turn, by its representativeness. In a complex society such as ours, a jury that is the true "conscience of the community" must include a fair cross-section of the groups that make up the community. Each person comes to the jury box as an individual, not as a representative of an ethnic, racial, or age group. But since people's outlooks and experiences do depend in part upon such factors as socioeconomic status, ethnic background, sex, or age, to ignore such differences is to deny the diversity in society as well as the fundamental character of the "community" whose voice is to be heard in the jury room. So, although each juror's individuality must be respected (in fact, the system counts on jurors trying to overcome their prejudices to judge a case on its own merits), the juror's identification with certain demographic groups must also be respected.

As the jury strives for impartiality because it balances the biases of twelve different individuals, so a jury in a heterogeneous society must approximate impartiality by balancing the different elements in society. The jury's power rests in the capacity of individuals with diverse viewpoints to reach a common decision that can be accepted as the community's verdict and will carry weight with a diverse community. A jury representing the broad spectrum of society is a jury whose independence and impartiality need not be suspect, and whose legitimacy is thus protected.

Steps that threaten the jury's impartiality by impeding its independence and representativeness should be viewed with great suspicion, and signs of waning respect for the jury should be considered seriously. Selection systems should ensure that fair, independent panels can be assembled and that the opportunity for bias is thus minimized. The social-science techniques described at the opening of this Introduction are the exceptional methods used for the exceptional trial, procedures that illuminate some of the problems of jury selection but are not the only significant area of concern. Our courts have made great progress in recent years toward assembling juries that more accurately represent the community, that are more independent and thus more likely to be impartial, than in the past. But we still retain attitudes, legal standards, and procedures that have the effect of producing juries that are less impartial than they can and should be.

We shall examine some of these problems in this book, with a view to protecting the jury's integrity in a judicial system that has been losing the respect of its citizens. The jury, often the last resort when sensitive decisions must be made, is itself a sensitive instrument, whose role, character, and potential must be understood if it is to regain the respect of those who come in contact with it, and of the public at large.

## NOTES

1. This material is taken from Edward Tivnan, "Jury by Trial," *New York Times Magazine*, Nov. 16, 1975, p. 30.
2. *Ibid.*
3. *U.S. Constitution, Sixth Amendment.*
4. *New York Times*, April 13, 1975, p. 1 (city ed.).
5. G.K. Chesterton, "The Twelve Men," *Tremendous Trifles* (12th ed.; New York: Sheed and Ward, 1930), p. 55 (emphasis added).

## NOTES

1. 

2. 

3. 

4.

# Acknowledgments

The information in this book has been assembled with the assistance of many colleagues and friends. Professor Alan Scheflin of the University of Santa Clara Law School, helped with the writing of Chapters Seven and Eight, and with the Postscript on Jury Nullification, and his assistance in helping to formulate ideas and arguments pervades the entire book. Sherry Broder, now staff attorney for the Hawaii Correctional Legal Services, also helped immeasurably by discussing the ideas that are analyzed here and by providing inspiration.

Among the students at San Francisco's Hastings College of the Law (of the University of California) who worked long hours in computing percentages, interviewing jury commissioners, and researching arguments are Shelton Baxter, Jeff Bradley, John Carrico, Margaret Cooley, Deborah Coutin, Seth Dawson, Douglas Elliott, Edmundo Espinoza, Harold Feder, Dan Grimmer, Jim Hassan, Julie Kesler-Goeltz (who undertook the historical research that appears in Chapter Six), Ted Kruger, Edward Levinson, John Poole, Gregory Ricca, and Dennis Weaver. Three non-law-students who also provided this type of assistance are Gordon Abbott, Jo Ann Bell, Pam Calef, and Lynne Terry.

Too many jury commissioners, judges, and court officials provided me with help to list all of them, but I can certainly say that the overwhelming majority of the judges and civil servants that I contacted were eager to help with this project. Many people in the academic and legal worlds assisted me with information and guidance, and I would particularly like to thank Marvin J. Anderson

(Dean of the Hastings College of the Law, University of California), Ruth Astle (an attorney in San Francisco), Professor Edward Beiser (of Brown University's Political Science Department), Rhonda Copelon (of New York's Center for Constitutional Rights), Charles Garry (the San Francisco-based attorney who pioneered the practice of carefully questioning potential jurors to expose racial bias), Ann Fagan Ginger (of the Meiklejohn Library in Berkeley and author of the excellent book, *Jury Selection in Criminal Trials* (Tiburon, Calif.: Lawpress, 1975)); David Kairys (a Philadelphia attorney), Tom Munsterman (of Bird Engineering-Research Associates, Vienna, Va.), Professor Peter Sperlich (of the University of California (Berkeley) Political Science Department), Jim Wisley (of California State University, Fullerton), the Hon. Frederick Woleslagel (District Judge in Lyons, Kansas), Sidney Wolinsky (of Public Advocates in San Francisco), Professor Hans Zeisel (of the University of Chicago Law School), and Professor Matthew Zwerling (of the University of San Francisco Law School) for their generous help. My parents, Stuart and Eleonora Van Dyke, gave me useful advice and loving encouragement during the time that I was working on this book. And a special thanks to Charlotte and Irving Broder for their help.

This research was funded by the Twentieth Century Fund in New York City, and Carol Barker, John Booth, M.J. Rossant, and Richard Rust of that organization all provided an unusual amount of assistance throughout the project. Finally, but certainly not least important, the manuscript was carefully edited and helpfully reorganized by Carol Weiland, of New York City. Sincere thanks to all of you!

## Chapter One

# A Jury of One's Peers

The jury is the most democratic of our institutions. The idea itself—that ordinary citizens without experience in judicial decision-making should be impaneled to decide issues of great importance—is an unusual one in the world today. The jury developed as part of a long struggle against centralized power in Britain and later in those countries that inherited the British traditions of justice. But the jury is unusual even in democracies. Most institutions of democratic governments draw their power from the people, who elect their representatives to the decision-making bodies, but in the courtroom it is the people themselves, as jurors, who make the decisions. No wonder, then, that the jury continues to be the object of controversy.

In most countries, legal experts—judges—rather than ordinary citizens weigh the evidence and render verdicts, even if the laws are enacted by democratically elected legislatures. Some European nations, including France and Germany, borrowed the jury as a fundamentally democratic institution in the late eighteenth and nineteenth centuries, but they modified it profoundly so that today their main heritage of experiments with the jury is the participation of lay persons along with judges in rendering verdicts. Many democratic countries, Israel for example, have never used juries; instead they rely on judges to resolve civil disputes and to determine guilt or innocence in criminal cases.[1]

The democratic features of the jury have evolved slowly, and when juries first began to be used in Britain and the United States, they were not selected according to the democratic principles that hold sway today. The jury has been affected by changes in society and has helped change society as well. After almost a millenium of experience with the jury, we see a jury trial as the right of every defendant accused of a serious crime and the jury as a body properly including a cross-section of the community, randomly selected. But the jury was originally a creation of the crown and made up of landowners. Concepts of its form and function have evolved over the centuries along with democratic government.

## ENGLISH ORIGINS

The roots of the jury date back to Anglo-Saxon England, but its modern development began with William the Conqueror, who determined the countryside's wealth and population through "inquests" or "inquisitions" (a system also employed by the Roman emperors). The king sent his barons to the villages and townships, where they summoned the important men from the neighborhood, placed them under oath, and questioned them about the community's financial affairs. The sworn men were fundamentally witnesses, supplying the information to the royal officers that eventually produced the Domesday Book, a massive census completed between 1081 and 1086. They were primarily interested in financial affairs but occasionally examined criminal matters as well.

Henry II, who ruled from 1154 to 1189 and was concerned with strengthening the crown's presence in the countryside, can probably be credited more than any other single individual with laying the foundation for the modern jury. He developed the system of inquests begun by William into the direct ancestor of the grand jury, by impaneling men to consider criminal cases and accuse those suspected of committing crimes. These procedures were institutionalized in 1166, at the Assize of Clarendon, with the rule

> that inquiry shall be made in every county in every hundred by the twelve most lawful men of the hundred and by the four most lawful men of every vill, upon oath that they shall speak the truth, whether in their hundred or vill there be any man who is accused or believed to be a robber, murderer, thief, or a receiver of robbers, murderers or thieves since the King's accession. And thus the justice and sheriffs shall enquire before themselves.[2]

It was up to the sheriff or justice to decide what to do next. Most civil disputes over land ownership were decided by assizes, in which a group of carefully selected men studied the case and gave a verdict.

In criminal cases, guilt or innocence was usually determined either by trial by battle or trial by ordeal, an ancient and brutal form of settling controversies, which was supervised by the clergy to give divine sanction to a decision. The most common ordeals in England, where they existed before the Norman Conquests, were the Ordeal of the Hot Iron and the Ordeal of Cold Water. In the first type, a man accused of a crime was obliged to carry a heated iron in his hands for a distance of nine feet, after which his hands were bandaged for three nights and examined. If the wounds healed, the accused was pronounced innocent, but if "unhealthy matter" was found, he was judged unclean.[3] In the Ordeal of Cold Water, a man was bound and dropped into a body of water. If he sank to a distance greater than the length of his hair, he was guilty; if he floated, innocent.

In trial by battle, which was introduced by the Normans and was a precursor of the duel, ligitants—or, later, specially trained "champions,"—did battle to determine who would win a dispute. Another method of adjudication was the Wager of Law or Proof by Compurgation, in which the accused was required to assemble a group of persons—usually twelve—who would swear that the accused's oath was trustworthy. When oath-taking failed to acquit an accused, he or she was subject to the ordeal.

The jury was used erratically and was the crown's prerogative until 1215, when a group of barons exacted from King John, in the Magna Carta, the promise that:

> No free man shall be taken or imprisoned or [dispossessed] or outlawed or exiled or in any way destroyed . . . except by the lawful judgment of his peers and the law of the land.[4]

The jury of 1215 was still more like our modern grand jury than a trial jury because its role was to decide whether the evidence justified further proceedings against a defendant, further proceedings in the nature of an ordeal. But in the same year as the Magna Carta, Pope Innocent III prohibited participation by priests in trials by ordeal, and the way was opened for trials by jury to take their place. A decline of religious values had in any case already brought into question the validity of the oaths taken in ordeals as well as the motives of the clergy, who were found to manipulate some of the ordeals and to profit from fees collected from them.[5,a] The thirteenth century thus saw a gradual shift from trials by ordeal to trials by jury.

---

[a]Proof by compurgation was already in some disfavor as early as 1166 because it was clearly susceptible to abuse, but merchants, particularly in London, clung to the procedure, and it was used to settle commercial disputes for some time. As late as 1364, a statute was passed ensuring to merchants the right to "wage law" as a defense to debts that were claimed on the evidence of a merchant's books. Proof by compurgation was not finally abolished in England until 1833.

In the first half of the fourteenth century, the trial jury and the grand jury were finally separated. The trial jury began to be recognized as a body whose task was to evaluate the evidence and come up with a definitive verdict as to guilt or innocence, as differentiated from the grand jury, which had brought the charges. In 1352 a statute was passed stating explicitly that grand jurors could not also sit on the trial jury.[6] After that date, when one of the king's traveling justices arrived to hear disputes, the local sheriff would choose twelve men[7],[b] from the immediate surrounding community to serve as jurors, and then would select an additional group of twenty-four men (usually knights) from a larger area to serve as an accusing body for the entire county. These twenty-four eliminated one member so they could act by majority vote, investigated incidents, and soon took over the entire burden of filing indictments.[8]

As the concept of the trial jury emerged, so did the rule of unanimity. For a time, decisions reflecting an eleven-to-one split were accepted, with the dissenting juror fined for perjury on the theory that he must have been wrong if the eleven others disagreed with him. Another technique involved adding additional jurors when the original twelve were split until a group of twelve could be assembled that would agree on a verdict. But these alternatives did not satisfy the true purpose of the jury—to provide a reliable decision reflecting the view of the community in as authoritative a manner as trial by ordeal had earlier reflected the views of the divinity. Nothing short of a unanimous verdict would supply this level of reliability.[9]

Although the Magna Carta had taken the right to use a jury out of the hands of the crown and given it to the barons, the crown retained considerable control over the jury's decisions for several more centuries. Until the early 1500s, jury verdicts could be overturned by a larger, specially selected, and generally more elite "jury of attaint." The original jurors were then frequently imprisoned and their lands confiscated by the crown, on the assumption that they committed perjury in returning an "erroneous" verdict. After juries of attaint were discredited because of the harshness of their penalties, verdicts were still sometimes rejected by a judge, and jurors could still be imprisoned or fined.

---

[b]It is not known for certain why juries of twelve developed. Theorists frequently refer to the twelve prophets or the twelve disciples and to the Proof by Compurgation which had frequently called on twelve men. The real reason probably was that 12 is a number large enough to ensure some reliability and impartiality (see below, Chapter Eight) and yet small enough to function with some degree of efficiency. In any case, by the middle of the fourteenth century the requirement of twelve was fixed.

In the late seventeenth century, the supremacy of the jury's verdict, and thus its independence, was finally established in a celebrated case involving William Penn and William Mead. Penn (who was then 26) and Mead (another young Quaker activist) were charged in 1670 with conducting an unlawful assembly after they had held a meeting of Quakers in London that had been disrupted by others. The jury refused to return a guilty verdict, even though the judges pressured them heavily for several days to do so. Edward Bushell, leader of the dissenting jurors, was soundly scolded by the magistrate. After a series of deliberations and verdicts that were rejected by the court, the jury eventually found Penn and Mead not guilty. The magistrate then imposed a stiff fine on the jurors and ordered them imprisoned until they paid off.

The undaunted jurors, insisting on their right to return a verdict free from judicial coercion, applied for a writ of habeas corpus. Two-and-a-half months later, Chief Justice Vaughan, speaking for himself and ten other sitting appeals judges of the Court of Common Pleas, freed the jurors and stated decisively that jurors cannot be punished for their decision. Vaughan's historic opinion in Bushell's case emphasized that the purpose of the jury is to obtain persons from the location of the alleged crime so that they can evaluate the evidence according to their own understanding, reasoning, and conscience.[10] Why, he asked, insist on careful selection procedures— to ensure that jurors come from the site of the incident and are unbiased—unless the verdict of the jury is to stand as the final decision on the question? The Vaughan decision articulates a principle we now fully accept: that if the jury is to play its intended role as an impartial fact-finder, expressing the community's decision, it must be independent. Otherwise, it is not really the community's voice but the voice of the crown (or state), and the entire rationale for using a jury is erased.

In 1681, eleven years after the trial jury's independence was established in Bushell's case,[11] a grand jury asserted the same power. In that year a London grand jury refused to return an indictment against the Earl of Shaftsbury, who was accused of treason. After hearing the prosecution's witnesses and questioning them in private, the grand jury returned the bill presented by the prosecutor with the word "ignoramus" written on its back. The royal authorities then presented the same evidence before the Oxford grand jury, which apparently did not share the politics of its counterpart in London. It indicted the earl.[12] Despite the Oxford action, the principle that a grand jury could stand between the king and the accused was established, and the London grand jurors were not punished.

## THE AMERICAN JURY

The independence of the jury from the crown was also an important aspect of the North American drive for independence from Britain in the eighteenth century. The people who settled in the original thirteen colonies considered jury trial a fundamental right, as indeed it had been in England for centuries. Most of the colonies specifically guaranteed trial by jury in their charters, although the methods of selection, size of the vicinage (the area from which jurors are selected), and the extent of use differed from colony to colony, and even within some colonies in different periods.

The colonists recognized the importance of trial by jury perhaps even more than their English forefathers because in colonial America it was the public prosecutor—an arm of the state—who initiated most proceedings, whereas in England at the time virtually all trials, including criminal cases (except for treason), were suits between private parties (civil suits).[13] A shortage of lawyers and the considerable distances within colonies as settlement spread westward necessitated the use of public prosecutors in America. The prevalence of these prosecutors meant that the accused "faced a government official whose specific function it was to prosecute, and who was incomparably more familiar than the accused with the problems of procedure, the idiosyncracies of juries, and . . . the personnel of the court. The balance would continue to be weighted in favor of the Crown unless extreme vigilance was practiced to safeguard the precarious privileges" of the accused.[14]

The First Continental Congress in 1774 stressed the importance of the jury by declaring that "the respective colonies are entitled to . . . the great and inestimable privilege of being tried by their peers of vicinage, according to the course of [common] law."[15] The Declaration of Independence specifically included among grievances against the king deprivation "in many cases of the benefits of trial by jury." One such deprivation was an edict by the governor of colonial New York in 1765 that jury verdicts could be appealed to the governor and his council and overruled by them if deemed incorrect.[16] Such a claim obviously ran counter to the recognition of the jury's independence in William Penn's case a hundred years earlier. Another deprivation was the Port Bill of 1773, which gave the royal governor of Massachusetts the power to transfer trials to another colony or back to England[17]—a move that denied the accused a jury from the community, which also had been recognized in the Penn controversy.

The importance of jury trial was also expressed in the constitutions of the thirteen original states. Many employed phrases similar to Maryland's, which declared that "the trial of facts where they arise, is one of the greatest securities of the lives, liberties and estates of the people," among whose rights is "a speedy trial by an impartial jury, without whose unanimous consent he ought not to be found guilty."[18] Some state constitutions borrowed language from the Magna Carta in their provisions on jury trial.

The great variation in practice among the thirteen colonies probably explains why the only provision relating to jury trial in the original 1787 Constitution was in Article III, Section 2, which states that "the trial of all crimes, except in cases of impeachment, shall be by jury; and such trials shall be held in the state where the said crimes shall have been committed." The vagueness of this provision was one reason for opposition to the Constitution during the ratification period, 1787-1789. Many people expressed fears that jury verdicts might be reversed by appellate judges,[19] that the vicinage requirement was too broad (calling for juries drawn within a state, rather than from smaller areas), and that no provision specifically guaranteed the right to challenge prospective jurors. The right to be tried by a jury of one's peers in one's neighborhood, which had been abridged in the Port Bill, was seen as insufficiently protected. As Patrick Henry declared at the Virginia Convention for ratification of the Constitution:

> [T]his great privilege . . . is prostrated by this paper. . . . Juries from the vicinage being not secured, this right is in reality sacrificed. All is gone. . . . Why do we love this trial by jury? Because it prevents the hand of oppression from cutting you off.[20]

These fears were largely answered by the Bill of Rights, adopted as the first ten amendments to the Constitution in 1791, which refer to trial by jury in three different places: (1) the Fifth Amendment declaration that no person can be criminally charged "unless on a presentment or indictment of a grand jury"; (2) the Sixth Amendment guarantee that persons so accused shall have the right to a trial "by an impartial jury of the State and district wherein the crime shall have been committed"; and (3) the Seventh Amendment guarantee of the same right in civil cases: "In suits at common law, where the value in controversy shall exceed twenty dollars, the right of jury trial shall be preserved, and no fact tried by a jury, shall be otherwise re-examined in any court of the United States, than according to the rules of the common law." The Constitution thus firmly established an individual's right to demand the community's sanction—expressed in the jury's verdict—before he or she can be convicted of a crime and denied freedom.

To an accused person, the jury constitutes a barrier between the individual and the state, preventing oppression by government. As such, it is one of the foundations of liberty and was called by Thomas Jefferson "the only anchor ever yet imagined by man by which a government can be held to the principles of the Constitution."[21] Or as Lord Justice Patrick Devlin has said of the English jury:

> Each jury is a little parliament. The jury sense is the parliamentary sense. I cannot see the one dying and the other surviving. The first object of any tyrant in Whitehall would be to make Parliament utterly subservient to his will; and the next to overthrow or diminish trial by jury, for no tyrant could afford to leave a subject's freedom in the hands of twelve of his countrymen. So that trial by jury is more than an instrument of justice and more than one wheel of the constitution: it is the lamp that shows that freedom lives.[22]

The meaning of the constitutional protection of trial by jury was summed up by Justice Byron R. White in a 1968 U.S. Supreme Court ruling:

> The guarantees of jury trial in the Federal and State Constitutions reflect a profound judgment about the way in which law should be enforced and justice administered. *A right to jury trial is granted to criminal defendants in order to prevent oppression by the Government.* Those who wrote our constitutions knew from history and experience that it was necessary to protect against unfounded criminal charges brought to eliminate enemies and against judges too responsive to the voice of higher authority. The framers of the constitutions strove to create an independent judiciary but insisted upon further protection against such arbitrary action. *Providing an accused with the right to be tried by a jury of his peers gave him an inestimable safeguard against the corrupt or overzealous prosecutor and against the compliant, biased or eccentric judge.* If the defendant preferred the common-sense judgment of a jury to the more tutored but perhaps less sympathetic reaction of a single judge, he was to have it. Beyond this, the jury trial provisions in the Federal and State Constitutions reflect a fundamental decision about the exercise of official power—a reluctance to entrust plenary powers over the life and liberty of the citizen to one judge or to a group of judges. Fear of unchecked power, so typical of our State and Federal Government in other respects, found expression in the criminal law in this insistence upon community participation in the determination of guilt or innocence.[23]

The question how specifically to achieve "community participation" in a jury has not, however, been answered with the kind of unanimity expressed for the principle itself. Juries have not always been chosen simply from "twelve of the ordinary men standing around," as Chesterton wrote. Two fundamental requirements have governed jury selection throughout the last millenium. The Magna Carta said that jurors should be "peers" of the accused, a term that appears again in colonial and state constitutions in America. From the time of Henry II, juries were drawn from the immediate vicinity of the crime, and a strict definition of "vicinage" was a central concern of the Founders. But the universally accepted principles of "peer" and "community" have been variously defined.

The jury's legitimacy has always rested in its capacity to express fairly the community's conscience; what has changed over the centuries is *how* a jury best expresses the community's conscience. Different definitions of "peer" and "community" are therefore not just of academic interest but help determine how well the jury can fulfill its role. Ensuring the jury's integrity may necessitate different approaches in today's complex society than in medieval England or colonial America.

## PEERS AND COMMUNITY

The U.S. Supreme Court defined "peer" in the 1880 case of *Strauder v. West Virginia,*[c] when Justice William Strong wrote: "The very idea of a jury is a body of men composed of *peers or equals* of the person whose rights it is selected or summoned to determine; that is, of his neighbors, fellows, associates, *persons having the same legal status in society as that which he holds.*"[2,4] In the sense that all citizens above the age of eighteen who have not been convicted of a felony are legal equals, all Americans are peers of all other Americans. Thus it ought to be fairly simple to decide who should sit on juries. But disagreement nonetheless exists, disagreement that must be analyzed in terms of both the purpose of the jury—to render a reliable judgment that will be accepted by the community—and the social and political character of that community today.

The notion that a jury should be composed of the defendant's "peers" originally meant that an accused person had the right to be tried by members of his or her class, and some people have argued that this idea should be reinstituted now. Many see the United States as composed of fairly distinct socioeconomic and racial classes and believe it is unrealistic to consider all persons equally appropriate to serve as jurors in all cases. For example, prior to the 1970-71 New

---

[c]The *Strauder* decision actually permitted many exceptions—women, for example—that we no longer accept. For a fuller discussion of this case, see Chapter Three, p. 51.

York Black Panther Trial, defendant Joan Bird declared at a public rally that "a peer is a person from the same economic, social, and religious background, meaning you black people here in Babylon."[25] One apparently "class"-oriented type of jury was used in the District of Columbia, where "condemnation juries," assembled to pass on the value of property to be condemned, were until 1970 composed exclusively of freeholders because they were presumably "peers" of the owners of the property.[26] This practice can be traced back to the earliest juries, in which knights—who owned property—were included on all juries hearing land disputes.

Those who advocate a class-conscious jury have argued that the economic and social conditions of the black community, for instance, cannot be understood except by persons who live there, and hence that black defendants should be judged by all-black juries.[27] An identical argument can be made on behalf of young defendants in recent years, especially when the crime involves an issue more common and more accepted among many young people, such as political demonstrations or drugs. The data that are analyzed in Chapter Two indicates that jurors tend to be more sympathetic to litigants of their own racial or socioeconomic background, and so a jury without any persons from the racial or socioeconomic group of the defendant would probably not be so understanding of the defendant's position as a jury that contained persons like the defendant.

Historical precedent certainly exists for impaneling juries from only one segment of the society. The knights who forced King John to sign the Magna Carta in 1215 obtained, thereby, the right to be tried by a jury composed exclusively of knights. "Specialized" juries have been used throughout Anglo-American history to bring jurors together who might have particular insights into the issues to be tried. The English impaneled special juries of merchants to adjudicate commercial disputes until 1971,[28] and had occasionally convened juries of cooks, for instance, to try persons accused of selling bad food. In this country, Native Americans are permitted to adjudicate in their own manner many of the local disputes that occur on reservations,[29] and the armed services have exclusive jurisdiction over most crimes that occur on military bases through courts-martial, with other members of the military acting as jurors.

The problem with a jury drawn only from a narrow group—from the community of knights if the accused is a knight, for example, or from the black community when the defendant is black—is that such a jury fails to recognize adequately the concept of community. The jury's role is not only to protect the accused but to represent the public that has been victimized. A jury composed entirely of members of the defendant's racial or socioeconomic group would certainly be able to understand the defendant's point of view but might not be able to understand the perspective of the victim. In contemporary society, selection of a jury must take into account the fact that the victim may come from another part of the community than the accused. For this reason, "community" must be broadly defined. The point of view of the victim's community would not be represented in a "specialized" jury consisting only of the defendant's peers. Only in a situation that is truly self-contained, such as a minor crime on Native-American land, would a jury drawn from only one group serve as an impartial arbiter representing all the competing factions.

An approach that would take into account the "communities" of both victim and accused is impaneling a mixed jury, for which ample historical precedent also can be found. In thirteenth-century England, juries composed of equal numbers of Jews and Christians resolved disputes between a Jew and a Christian.[30] During the late seventeenth century, the Plymouth Colony (in Massachusetts) regularly added a number of "Indians" to join with the English settlers in juries that passed on disputes or crimes involving the natives.[31] Until the nineteenth century, juries composed of six aliens and six citizens were used both in England and in North America when aliens were accused of a crime.[32] In some districts in the Canadian provinces of Quebec and Manitoba today, the sheriff is required to return panels of jurors composed half of French-speaking persons and half of English-speaking persons. A defendant who can speak only one of the two languages may request a jury composed entirely of persons speaking that language, and the judge will normally comply "unless the ends of justice are better served by impaneling a mixed jury."[33]

Such juries recognize that peers of both the victim and the accused should have the chance to hear a case and thus go further toward ensuring impartiality through representativeness than the "specialized" jury. But if each jury is to be constituted to include representatives of the accused and the victim, the "community" of each would have to be defined for each crime, creating enormous administrative and philosophical problems. Such juries would be administratively impossible to achieve in today's society, which includes many more than two identifiable groups and where the groups relevant to the case might differ according to the crime. (For example, a black woman who had been raped might consider her "community" in this case to be women; while if she had been robbed by a white, she might consider it to be blacks, both men and women.) Like the "specialized" juries, such "mixed" juries narrowly define "community" by identifying only two groups that are affected, and would result in an undesirable compartmentalization of justice.

In our heterogeneous society, the jury's impartiality can be achieved only if it reflects, as accurately as possible, a broad range of views consonant with those of the larger community—defined necessarily as the judicial district responsible for the case. Society as a whole is affected by a crime, and the justice rendered should legitimately express the judgment of society as a whole. If a jury is weighted to reflect the values of a particular group—be it only of the accused or of both the accused and the victim—its impartiality and, hence, legitimacy will be questioned. A jury drawn on parochial lines cannot meet the necessary test of expressing the conscience of the community. Only a verdict reached through deliberation of twelve diverse individuals will carry weight with society as a whole, as well as its parts. The difficulty in reaching such a verdict is more than justified by the legitimacy of the verdict so reached. To ensure that the jury, this most democratic of our institutions, is performing its democratic tasks properly, it must represent a cross-section of society.

Ample historical precedent also exists for the "cross-section-of-the-community" jury, going as far back as the thirteenth century. Juries—which were then accusatory bodies—were frequently assembled by summoning equal numbers of men from different villages, with each group giving its version of the events. Implicit in the decision to summon such a jury is a belief that those living in different areas may see things differently and that fairness can best be attained by collecting a wide range of views. The assumption is not that people will necessarily judge the case at hand on the basis of views or experiences directly related to area or class. The justification for a jury representing a cross-section of the community is instead the realization that people do have their own perspectives—based on their different lives—and that only by balancing these perspectives can we hope to achieve impartiality. Including a fair cross-section is the best way of protecting the jury's integrity.

A jury that includes a representative cross-section fulfills the needs of impartiality, reliability, and legitimacy essential to the jury system. Such a jury provides a modern definition of "peer" and "community" by recognizing that no one should be excluded from jury service on the basis of poverty, race, sex, age, nationality, or religion, and by insisting that all persons be equally represented on jury panels to ensure their impartiality and independence. The Supreme Court first recognized the importance of such a jury in

1940,[34] and it reaffirmed its position in 1975 when it declared that "selection of a petit jury from a representative cross-section of the community is an essential component of the Sixth Amendment right to a jury trial."[35] Realization of this principle has, however, been impeded in some courts that still use selection methods tending to alter the "cross-section."

## THE ELITE JURY

Our commitment to representative juries has been undermined in some areas by continuing sentiment for the "blue-ribbon" or "elite" jury, composed of the most "competent," "better educated," or "responsible" members of the population. Such criteria have been allowed by the U.S. Supreme Court, most recently in 1970, when Justice Potter Stewart wrote for the Court in the case of *Carter v. Jury Commission*:

> The States remain free to confine the selection [of jurors] to citizens, to persons meeting specified qualifications of age and educational attainment, *and to those possessing good intelligence, sound judgment, and fair character.*[36]

The inclusion of all segments of society on juries chosen in this way is inevitably a secondary consideration, although Justice Stewart in *Carter* insisted that persons specially selecting jurors did have an obligation to seek "qualified" members from all segments of the community.

Elite juries have a long tradition. The English have generally combined an insistence on representation from the local area with some requirement for competence or standing in the community. In the twelfth century, jurors were selected on the basis of their loyalty to the crown and their reputed honesty as well as for their familiarity with local conditions. At the time, only freemen, and not serfs (who outnumbered freemen by about ten to one), were permitted to serve on juries.[37] In land disputes, juries had to include four knights as well as twelve freemen, with a majority of twelve required for a verdict.[38] Blue-ribbon or elite juries of landowners handled appeals from other juries and cases considered particularly complex. Until 1972, an individual had to own property to serve as a juror in England.[39] The concept of "peer" clearly had to be bent to accommodate such requirements.

Many colonial courts, for example those in the Carolinas, had strict property requirements for jurors as well. Some colonies required only a minimal amount of property but had their jurors chosen by the sheriff, who tended to select—especially for grand juries—the large landowners of the area.[40] Both Massachusetts and Virginia had some experience with jurors selected somewhat randomly or elected from their town meetings. In both situations, the crown's representatives became distressed with the citizen justice thus being meted out, and they countered with a requirement that the royal sheriff pick jurors and grand jurors from among the more affluent landowners. In Massachusetts, this edict was part of the 1773 Port Bill and was a major cause of the subsequent unrest leading to revolution. The few token colonists opposing British rule who were selected for the Massachusetts grand jury by the royal sheriff—men like Paul Revere and John Hancock's brother Ebenezer—refused to take their oath to serve.[41]

In the early days of the Republic, property qualifications existed for both voting and jury duty; limitation of jury duty to males was consistent with the exclusion of women from the voter rolls (as exclusion of serfs from juries in Norman England was consistent with the fact that serfs did not share other rights of freemen). During the 1800s, many states dropped their property requirements, although at least a dozen still retained them in the last quarter of that century.[42] Some states selected their jurors from voter rolls and some from tax rolls (which automatically limited them to propertyowners); some jurors were selected by judges, town officials, or county supervisors, and some through a "key-man" system, where jury commissioners consulted prominent members of the community ("key men") for suggestions of jurors. The federal courts impaneled elite juries through the "key-man" system until 1968, when they adopted voter registration lists as their source for jurors.[43] Most states also select jurors from voter lists now, but some—mainly in the South and New England—still carefully select their jurors from among the citizens deemed to have the best "character" and highest "intelligence."

One prominent defender of such criteria is former Senator Sam J. Ervin, Jr., of North Carolina, who spelled out his views in a 1967 article[44] on what became the federal Jury Selection and Service Act. As explained below, the federal act provides that federal jurors be selected randomly through a jury "wheel" based on voter lists. In Ervin's view, because the jury represents the conscience and experience of the community, it must be "representative of the society for which it acts." But these "representative" jurors, according to Ervin, must have "sufficient intelligence to understand the issues presented" at trials and to be able to evaluate the competing testimony. The idea that the jury should be a "cross-section of the community," as was suggested in the proposed legislation, was considered improper by Ervin because that "necessarily suggests that justice is a function of 'class' " and that the "search for truth" is a "partisan operation— there is one truth for the poor and another for the rich." Further- more, Ervin wrote, the idea that selecting intelligent jurors will discriminate against the lower economic classes is "not only false, but condescending." Ervin rejected as a goal a jury of, for instance, twelve bankers, but aimed for a jury "composed of persons of common sense and integrity who show interest and alertness, a concern for their own affairs and for society's and who will bring to the jury box the same high qualities they exhibit in their other activities."

Another proponent of special criteria in jury selection is Judge Charles W. Light of the Second Judicial District in Arkansas, who opposed a modified jury wheel bill, which passed in the 1967 session of the Arkansas Legislature, because it eliminated the requirement that jurors be "persons of good character, approved integrity, sound judgment and reasonable information." Judge Light considered both "common sense and integrity" and a representative jury "drawn from all walks of life" to be essential. "There is no conflict in these criteria," he declared. "To merit the continued respect of our communities juries must be both impartial and qualified."[45]

In theory no inherent contradiction may exist between specific qualifications and representativeness of juries, but in practice such a contradiction seems unavoidable. When decisions are made about the qualification of prospective jurors, the bias of those who make the decisions inevitably affects the outcome. The assumption that Ervin condemns as "condescending"—that selecting "intelligent jurors" will discriminate against poorer members—in fact has been the rule. As the data in Chapter Two and Appendixes F-I indicate, the under- representation on juries of some groups—lower socioeconomic groups, nonwhites, the young and the aged, and women—is one critical, but common, result of discretionary selection criteria.

The argument that "quality" among jurors is necessary, or even desirable, if jury verdicts are to carry legitimacy in the community, has been countered from many corners. In a debate in Congress with Senator Ervin over the Jury Selection Act, then Attorney General Ramsey Clark stated:

> The defendant has to have confidence, as does society, in [the jurors'] absolute impartiality, and if some particular intelligence test is used it necessarily will reflect preferences and prejudices. However hard the testing person might have tried to be selective, he will only represent his own point of view and the person standing trial might be prejudiced.[46]

Criteria such as "good character" or "intelligent and upright" are too vague to be meaningful; inevitably, they invite abuse. The Supreme Court found unconstitutional similar statutes that for years limited the right to vote to those who are "morally upright." As Chief Justice Earl Warren wrote in 1966: "The good morals requirement is so vague and subjective that it has constituted an open invitation to abuse at the hands of voting officials."[4 7] Four years later, because the problem of administrative abuse of such vague and subjective statutes was seen to be a threat to the right to vote, Congress suspended the use of all tests of "good character" for admission to the electorate.[4 8]

The jury selected by court authorities on the basis of predetermined discretionary criteria is not sufficiently insulated from government pressure and hence does not meet the test of independence and impartiality. Even if the government does not intentionally "shape" the jury, or does not in fact discriminate, the appearance of influence by the state should be enough to call such methods into question. The jury's independence, after all, was long fought for both in England and North America, and for good reason. Without it, the jury system itself is in jeopardy.

## THE REPRESENTATIVE JURY: THE RANDOM APPROACH

To ensure jury independence and impartiality, Congress outlawed special requirements for federal jurors in 1968, in a bill that directed the courts to choose jurors randomly. Judge Irving R. Kaufman of the U.S. Court of Appeals for the Second Circuit, then the head of the federal judiciary's Committee on the Operation of the Jury System (which proposed moving to a random selection scheme in 1967), defended the proposed bill before Congress:

> The principal opposition to the [new bill] is centered on the requirement that juror qualifications be determined on the basis of objective criteria only. This provision would abolish the so-called blue ribbon jury, chosen for special "intelligence" or "common sense" qualifications.
>
> The judges of my Committee considered this matter carefully and at length. We came to these conclusions: . . . long experience with subjective requirements such as "intelligence" and "common sense" has demonstrated beyond any doubt that these vague terms provide a fertile ground for discrimination and arbitrariness, even when the jury officials act in good faith. . . .
>
> . . . We have learned that at the present time a prospective juror may be considered unfit for jury service because he is not very articulate, or speaks

with an accent, or appears nervous (something all of us experience in strange or new settings). But all these considerations are arbitrary. They have nothing to do with "intelligence," "common sense," or, what is more important, ability to understand the issues in a trial. *And they are discriminatory—usually against the poor.*

The end result of subjective tests is not to secure more intelligent jurors, but more homogeneous jurors. If this is sought in the American jury, then it will become very much like the English jury—predominately middle-aged, middle-class and middle-minded. . . .

But, I submit, such a goal is not in harmony with our historic jury tradition. *If the law is to reflect the moral sense of the community, the whole community—and not just a special part—must help to shape it.* If the jury's verdict is to reflect the community's judgment—*the whole community's judgment*—jurors must be fairly selected from *a cross-section of the whole community*, not merely a segment of it.[49]

The contention of elite-jury proponents that intelligence among jurors is necessary to uphold the integrity of the jury system is met by the assertion that the jury's strength is in its capacity to reflect "the moral sense of the community, the whole community." The view that some are more qualified to be jurors than others contradicts the principle of the jury system, which is that a group of ordinary citizens is better able to resolve a dispute than is an "expert." As another federal judge who served on the Jury Committee, Walter Pettus Gewin, argued:

[C]areful study has given support to the opinions of some scholars that the so-called blue ribbon jury is not superior to one chosen by random selection. This is so because the indispensable faculty for good jury service is *judgment*, an inherent mental quality which does not perforce coincide with superior intelligence.[50]

The Federal Jury Selection and Service Act of 1968 expressed a commitment to summoning jurors from the whole community, without special qualifications, through random selection. Some people have argued that if we are truly committed to juries that are a "cross-section" of the community, we should try to structure each jury so that it is a microcosm of the community, like the "mixed" juries of earlier days, discussed above at p. 11. If we truly want a cross-section, the argument goes, why not consciously choose jurors who will represent all the different groups in our society? The Supreme Court has, however, consistently said that such "proportionate representation on each jury is not required,"[51] and good reasons exist why attempts to adapt this ancient solution to contemporary conditions should be resisted. So many identifiable interests have already emerged that the mathematical problems are almost insurmountable. The computer attempting to structure each jury would have to consider the race, sex, age, income, occupation, educational level, and religion of each juror—and perhaps other factors as well—in order to be sure that all relevant demographic characteristics would be considered. Furthermore, a juror selected under this system might feel that she or he is filling some predetermined "slot" and might attempt to give the view generally associated with those demographic characteristics rather than the juror's personal feelings about the case. The jurors might find it harder to work together as a group because they may be more conscious of their identified differences than the much stronger common bonds that unite them as people.

The logical, and desirable, way to impanel an impartial and representative jury—and the method chosen by Congress—is to put together a complete list of eligible jurors and select randomly from it, on the assumption that the laws of statistics will produce representative juries most of the time. This approach safeguards the selection process from possible manipulation and ensures the independence of the jury. Such a randomly selected jury will not necessarily be "impartial" in the strict sense of that term, because the jurors bring to the jury box prejudice and perspectives gained from their lifetimes of experience. But they will be impartial in the sense that they will reflect the range of the community's attitudes, which is the best we can do. The random approach recognizes that our "community" has enlarged because of the technological revolution that has provided us with communication links and common sources of information, but it also ensures that the diversity within our society is reflected on our juries because each population group is represented insofar as possible in proportion to its strength in the population.[d]

The jury representing a cross-section of the community, randomly selected, conforms to our commitment to a pluralistic society and a democratic government. While "peer" means one of the same rank, or an equal, we know that in fact, in most periods of the jury's history, some have been more equal than others. The founders' eloquent expressions of democracy referred to the white propertied classes, and males at that; and in many cases, only the propertied (and always only males) could serve on juries in early America. At the time of the Magna Carta, those who secured the right to a jury

---

[d]The mechanics of such a method are discussed in detail in Chapter Four, below.

trial were the barons, an elite group in our eyes; and only freemen, not serfs, could be jurors. As recently as World War II, it was easy for most Americans to consider the privilege of making important governmental decisions as the prerogative of whites (and usually males), and thus accept juries that excluded blacks and women. Only in the first postwar decade—which saw the integration of the armed forces, the first civil rights legislation, and the rejection of segregation as unconstitutional—did national policy begin to insist that blacks had the same rights as whites. The last two decades have seen increasing acceptance, intellectually if not emotionally, of that principle, and its extension to other minority groups and women. Today, it is no longer acceptable to qualify "equality" or "peer."

When we talk of a jury of one's peers in the community today, we mean a jury drawn from the whole population of the area and representing a cross-section of it. With that understanding, we can see if today's juries in fact reflect this concept, and how to change them if they do not.

## NOTES

1. Marcus Gleiser, *Juries and Justice* (New York: A.S. Barnes, 1968).

2. T.F.T. Plucknett, *A Concise History of the Common Law* (5th ed.; Boston: Little, Brown, 1956), pp. 112-13.

3. *Ibid.*, p. 114.

4. 17 John (Magna Carta), c.39 (1215); see Lloyd E. Moore, *The Jury: Tool of Kings, Palladium of Liberty* (Cincinnati: W.H. Anderson Co., 1973), pp. 49-51.

5. Plucknett, *Concise History of the Common Law*, pp. 115-16; John Profatt, *A Treatise on Trial by Jury* (San Francisco, 1877), p. 25.

6. 25 Edward III, stat. 5, c.3 (1352).

7. See Moore, *The Jury*, p. 41.

8. Frederick Pollock and Frederic W. Maitland, *History of English Law* (Cambridge, U.K.: Cambridge University Press, 1968), Vol. 2, pp. 646-47; Reeves, *History of the English Law* (3rd ed., 1814), Vol. III, p. 133.

9. See Pollock and Maitland, *History of English Law*, Vol. 2, pp. 622-28.

10. Trial of William Penn and William Mead, 6 State Trials 951, 999, at 1011-12 (1670); Bushell's Case, Vaughan 135 (Common Pleas, 1670).

11. Bushell's Case, Vaughan 135 (Common Pleas, 1670).

12. "Proceeding at the Old-Bailey, Upon a Bill of Indictment for High Treason, Against Anthony Earl of Shaftsbury," 8 Howard State Trials 759 (1681); see also "The Trial of Stephen Colledge at Oxford for High Treason," *ibid.*, p. 550.

13. Francis H. Heller, *The Sixth Amendment to the Constitution of the United States* (Lawrence, Kan.: U. of Kansas Press, 1951), p. 21.

14. *Ibid.*

15. *Declaration of Rights of the Continental Congress* (1774), Article 5; reprinted in Charles C. Tansill, ed., *Documents Illustrative of the Formation of the Union of the American States*, House Document No. 398, 69th Congress, 1st Session (Washington: Government Printing Office, 1927), p. 3.

16. Bernard Bailyn, "The Logic of Rebellion," in *The Reinterpretation of the American Revolution, 1763-98*, ed. Jack P. Green (New York: Harper & Row, 1968), p. 216.

17. Merrill Jensen, *A History of the American Revolution, 1763-76* (New York: Bobbs-Merrill Co., 1967), p. 457.

18. *Maryland Declaration of Rights*, Articles III, XVIII, and XIX, reprinted in Francis N. Thorpe, *The Federal and State Constitutions, Colonial Charters, and Other Organic Laws of the States, Territories and Colonies Now or Heretofore forming the United States of America* (Washington: Government Printing Office, 1909), Vol. III, pp. 1686, 1688.

19. Patrick Henry in the Virginia convention, June 20, 1788, in Jonathan Elliot, ed., *The Debates in the Several State Conventions on the Adoption of the Federal Constitution* . . . (Philadelphia: J.B. Lippincott Company, 1835), Vol. III, p. 540. See also Grayson's remarks in *ibid.*, p. 568; Bloodworth and Spencer in the North Carolina Convention in *ibid.*, Vol. IV, pp. 151, 154; and those of Luther Martin in *ibid.*, Vol. II, p. 381.

20. *Ibid.*, Vol. III, pp. 545-46.

21. Bloomstein, "The American Jury System," *Current History* 60 (June 1971): 361, quoting from a letter Jefferson wrote to Thomas Paine.

22. Sir Patrick Devlin, *Trial by Jury* (London: Stevens & Sons, 1956), p. 164.

23. *Duncan v. Louisiana*, 391 U.S. 155-56 (emphasis added).

24. 100 U.S. 303, 308 (emphasis added).

25. *New York Times*, July 12, 1970, p. 30.

26. Richard C. Kleindienst, "Rethinking the Jury System," *Forensic Quarterly* 45 (Aug. 1971): 338; District of Columbia Code, title 16, sec. 1312, repealed in 1970.

27. Note, "The Case for Black Juries," *Yale Law Journal* 79 (1970): 531.

28. Juries Act of 1949, sections 18 and 19, repealed in 1971, sec. 40 (I), 56, Sched II, Part I, Vol. 41, pp. 835, 836, 841.

29. See 18 *U.S.C.*, sections 1152, 1153, 1162.

30. *Select Cases, Procedure without Writ Under Henry III* (Seldon Society Series, Nos. 3-5).

31. Thayer, "A Chapter of Legal History in Massachusetts," *Harvard Law Review* 9 (1895): 1, 8, quoting from *Plymouth Colony Records*, Vol. 6, p. 98.

32. See, e.g., Francis X. Busch, *Law and Tactics in Jury Trials* (Indianapolis: Bobbs-Merrill Co., 1949), pp. 467-68; Moore, *The Jury*, pp. 60-61, 83; statute 27 Edward III, Ch. 8; statute 28 Edward III, Ch. 13, 2; statute 6 Geo. IV, Ch. 50, 547; statutes 33 and 34 Vic., Ch. 14, Sec. 5; *United States v. Cartacho*, F. Cas. No. 14,738 (D.Va. 1823); *United States v. Carnot*, F. Cas. No. 14,726 (1824); *Wendling v. Commonwealth*, 143 Ky. 587, 137 S.W. 205 (1911); *Ex Parte Virginia*, 100 U.S. 339, 369 (Field, J., dissenting).

33. Roger E. Salhany, *Canadian Criminal Procedure* (Toronto: Canada Law Book Co., Ltd., 1968), p. 110; and see Canada's *Criminal Code*, Ch. C-34,

sections 555 and 564 (1970), and the *Quebec Statutes*, Chap. 26 (Jury Act) sections 25-32, 36-39.

34. *Smith v. Texas*, 311 U.S. 128 (1940).

35. *Taylor v. Louisiana*, 419 U.S. 522, 528 (1975).

36. *Carter v. Jury Commission of Greene County*, 396 U.S. 320, 332 (1970) (emphasis added).

37. Devlin, *Trial by Jury*, p.17.

38. Moore, *The Jury*, pp. 38, 42.

39. Criminal Justice Act, 1972 (c.71), S. 25, Sched. II, Pt. I; 42 *Halsbury's Statutes* (3d ed.) 773, 778.

40. R.D. Younger, *The People's Panel: The Grand Jury in the United States* (Providence: Brown U. Press, 1963), p. 5.

41. *Ibid.*, p. 32

42. Profatt, *A Treatise on Trial by Jury*, pp. 161-62.

43. Jury Selection and Service Act of 1968, 28 *U.S.C.*, 1861-69.

44. *American Bar Association Journal* 53 (1967): 132.

45. Light, "Does Arkansas Need the Jury Wheel?" *The Arkansas Lawyer* (June 1967), p. 6.

46. Subcommittee on Improvements in Judiciary Machinery of the Senate Judiciary Committee, *Hearings, Federal Jury Selection*, 90th Cong., 1st Sess. (March 21-July 20, 1967), pp. 48-49 and 56; *New York Times*, March 22, 1967, p. 22.

47. *South Carolina v. Katzenbach*, 383 U.S. 301, 312-13 (1966). See also *Schnell v. Davis*, 81 F. Supp. 872 (S.D. Ala. 1949).

48. Voting Rights Act Amendments of 1970, Public Act 91-285, sec. 201.

49. *Hearings, Federal Jury Selection*, p. 255 (emphasis added).

50. Walter Pettus Gewin, "The Jury Selection and Service Act of 1968: Implementation in the Fifth Circuit Court of Appeals," *Mercer Law Review* 20 (1969): 349-50 (emphasis in the original).

51. *Virginia v. Rives*, 100 U.S. 313 (1880); *Cassell v. Texas*, 339 U.S. 282 (1950); *Swain v. Alabama*, 380 U.S. 202 (1965); *Carter v. Jury Commission of Greene County*, 396 U.S. 320 (1970).

## Chapter Two

# Today's Juries: Less than Representative

If juries impaneled today embodied the expressed goal of reflecting a cross-section of the community, most defendants would face juries that included at least some members of their age group, race, or ethnic group. The victims of crime would be convinced that some jurors could understand their situation. The public—which in a sense is affected by all crimes—could feel that it was fairly represented on most of the juries that try criminal cases. Because exact representation on each jury is mathematically and practically impossible, not all juries in any court can include a perfect cross-section, and not all demographic groups will be found on all juries in a district. But in the long run, juries should reflect the complex fabric of society as faithfully as possible. Only then can their decisions be accepted as fair and their verdicts as final.

Many people who come into contact with the criminal justice system do not encounter such juries. Although juries that reflect the community's diversity occur much more frequently than they have in the past, they are far from universal. Court challenges and legislative enactments regarding jury selection methods in recent years have given previously disenfranchised groups a much greater share of our jury panels. But in some areas, the defendant or plaintiff can count on a representative jury *not* being assembled. Most courts in the United States still have a long way to go before truly representative juries are the rule.

We do not have to prove that the presence or absence of certain groups affects the outcome of a jury's deliberation in order to be concerned about underrepresentation. Our democratic instincts—and the integrity of the jury system—require fair representation. As Justice Thurgood Marshall has observed:

> When any large and identifiable segment of the community is excluded from jury service, the effect is to remove from the jury room qualities of human nature and varieties of human experience, the range of which is unknown and perhaps unknowable. It is not necessary to assume that the excluded group will consistently vote as a class in order to conclude, as we do, that their exclusion deprives the jury of a perspective on human events that may have unsuspected importance in any case that may be presented.[1]

The range of viewpoints essential to an impartial jury will be circumscribed if certain groups are excluded from jury service. The jury system itself, with its provision for unanimity rather than simple majority rule, provides a special opportunity—indeed, a necessity— for interaction among jurors, for the use of reason and persuasion. The twelfth juror can make the difference.

Jurors are selected in a three-stage process: the court compiles a list of eligible jurors, grants excuses to some of those who are called, and then the competing attorneys challenge still more of them. Each stage can introduce or increase disproportions among identifiable groups. Different groups are underrepresented for different reasons. Where jury commissioners still personally select prospective jurors or ask "key men" for nominations, an opportunity for discrimination, intentional or not, clearly exists. Where voter lists are the exclusive source of names, groups that are underrepresented on these lists will be called as jurors less frequently. Members of some identifiable groups are granted excuses more liberally; some are affected by restrictions on age or residence; and some are challenged more often. The responsibility for underrepresentation through the use of certain procedures is a complex issue, with some observers blaming individuals for their failure to participate—as by failing to register to vote or by requesting an excuse—and others pointing to failures in the system that contribute to underrepresentation. These issues will be dealt with when we examine the procedures in detail in Chapters Four through Six. The results are what concern us here.

Despite recent gains, in most courts in the United States significant segments of the population are still not included on juries as often as they would be in a completely random system aimed at impaneling a representative cross-section. Blue-collar workers, nonwhites, the young, the elderly, and women are the groups most widely underrepresented on juries, and in many jurisdictions, the underrepresentation of these groups is substantial and dramatic. The data illustrating the disproportions in detail are gathered together in Appendixes F through I[a] and include surveys by the clerks of the federal courts, research by the author in state courts, court cases involving claims of underrepresentation, and surveys by other students of the jury system. Because the data come from a number of different sources, and because different courts keep different kinds of records, they are not all parallel. Some of the samples are not large enough in size to provide a definitive picture of the court's procedures. Individuals, furthermore, are too complex to be categorized neatly on charts, and our tools to measure the effects of disproportion are primitive. But the overall picture the statistics paint, allowing for shortcomings, seems clear. This is a picture of juries that are more homogeneous than the population at large. The groups that are most underrepresented on juries—blue-collar workers, nonwhites, the young, the elderly, and women—of course overlap in many cases. By isolating each of these groups, however, we can make some observations on how each group fares in comparison to the population as a whole. In some cases, the possible effects of the presence or absence of certain groups on juries have been calculated.

## BLUE-COLLAR WORKERS

Men and women who work with their hands are substantially less likely to become jurors than are their counterparts in white-collar jobs.[b] In four-fifths of the federal districts surveyed in 1971, blue-collar workers had fewer seats on juries than they would have had if they had been represented in proportion to their presence in the population. Three out of every ten federal districts underrepresented these workers by more than 20 percent—which would seem to be a "substantial" amount.[c] For example, in two divisions in the Middle District of Florida in 1971, blue-collar workers made up 57.9 percent of the Fort Myers Division's working population in the 1970 census, but just 34.8 percent of jurors among those employed (an

---

[a]See pp. 291-371.

[b]For data, see Appendix F, p. 297.

[c]"Substantial" underrepresentation of a group on jury panels has been declared by the Federal Jury Selection and Service Act of 1968 to be unlawful. For a discussion of the possible measures of "substantial" underrepresentation, see Chapter Four. Underrepresentation is computed here by the "comparative" method, in which the difference between a group's percentage of the population and its percentage of places on the jury panel is considered as a percentage of the proper proportion of places. Thus, if a group constitutes 50 percent of the population but only 40 percent of jurors, it is considered to be underrepresented by 20 percent; that is, it has 20 percent fewer seats than it should have. See Chapter Three, p. 60, and Chapter Four, pp. 94-98.

underrepresentation of 39.9 percent); in the Jacksonville Division, they were 50.6 percent of the population and just 32.7 percent of jurors. In the Eastern District of New York, blue-collar workers comprised 41.8 percent of the work force but just 27.8 percent of employed jurors, a disparity of 33.5 percent.

The courts in eleven states whose surveys of jurors' occupations are included in Appendix F show the same pattern. Every one of the nineteen counties surveyed except Suffolk (Boston), Massachusetts, indicated underrepresentation of blue-collar workers, many in significant numbers. A study of over 2,000 jurors in San Francisco, for instance, revealed that blue-collar workers hold 26 percent fewer seats on that city's jury panels than their population in the community.

The two main reasons for underrepresentation of blue-collar workers are: (1) a lower voter-registration rate, and hence underrepresentation as jurors where the voter registration list is used exclusively to select jurors; and (2) excusal from jury service (for financial reasons) at a higher rate than those who are better or worse off, because the economic hardship of jury duty often hits this group harder. These topics are discussed in detail in Chapters Four and Five.

Figures on income are much more difficult to obtain than occupation statistics (which are routinely collected by many courts when they summon people for jury service) but what data we do have suggest chronic underrepresentation. Studies of jurors' income in nine counties in the West revealed that persons making less than $10,000 were underrepresented on all their juries.

One way of measuring representation according to income is to plot, geographically, the residence of jurors. The residences of all persons who became qualified jurors in San Francisco between October 1970 and October 1971 were located and placed on a map divided into the 148 census tracts used by the Bureau of the Census. The chance of any San Franciscan becoming a juror that year was 0.397 percent, or about four in a thousand. If an individual lived in one of the 14 census tracts with a median housing value of over $50,000 and a median monthly rent of over $150, however, the chances rose to 0.612 percent (more than six out of a thousand). By contrast, if an individual lived in one of the 19 census tracts with less than $25,000 median housing value and under $100 median rent, the chances of becoming a juror dropped to only 0.192 percent (less than two out of a thousand).[2]

Another way of gauging representation of different socioeconomic groups is to examine the education levels of jurors. Surveys of eighteen state and federal districts in Appendix F indicate that those with less than a high school education are *always* underrepresented.

Although we need not document the effect of underrepresentation of any group in order to insist on a fair representation, the available studies indicate that a jury's socioeconomic profile does affect verdicts. The Chicago Jury Project, a study of jury deliberations undertaken with the financial assistance of the Ford Foundation in the late 1950s and early 1960s, discovered that persons of higher status jobs, more income, and more education were less likely to give a defendant the lenient verdict of acquittal by reason of insanity than were persons of lower socioeconomic status.[3] A researcher in Louisiana found, similarly, that higher-status jurors were more likely to return a guilty verdict than were lower-status jurors.[4]

A more recent study indicated that the greater the disparity in socioeconomic status between jurors and the accused, the greater the chances that jurors would convict.[5] In this investigation, Freda Adler, then an Assistant Professor of Psychiatry at the Medical College of Pennsylvania, reviewed the court records of 50 matched sets of jury trials in criminal cases in Montgomery County, Pennsylvania. The cases were matched in the sense that the defendants were the same age (approximately), the same sex, the same race, and were accused of committing virtually the same offense, but one of the accused in each set had been convicted and the other acquitted. Adler ranked all the defendants and all of their jurors on a standard prestige scale that ranks occupation according to societal prestige. (U.S. Supreme Court justices lead the list, and at the bottom of the scale are sharecroppers, garbage collectors, street sweepers, and shoe-shiners.) She discovered that the defendants who were convicted had a slightly lower (but not statistically significant) prestige average than the defendants who were acquitted and that the jurors who convicted had a somewhat higher prestige average (enough to be statistically significant) than those who acquitted. But more importantly, she discovered that in 41 of the 50 matched sets (82 percent) the jury that convicted had a greater gulf between its "average prestige" on the standard prestige scale and that of the defendant than did the jury that acquitted. In other words, if the jurors and the defendant were in the same socioeconomic stratum (whether it was high or low), the jurors were substantially more likely to acquit than if the jurors were in either a higher or lower socioeconomic position than the defendant.

The same point seems to be made by a study showing that civil-suit jurors rendered a larger percentage of favorable verdicts to plaintiffs in their own occupation group than to those in other groups.[6] Jury Verdict Research, Inc., an organization that provides information to trial lawyers, examined the decisions of 6,266 jurors, broke them down by occupation, and attempted to compare the preferences of each occupational group of jurors to the population as a whole. The figures in Table 2-1 indicate the percentage of cases in which jurors of various occupation groups voted for a plaintiff in the listed groups. Of the six occupational groups, four gave the highest percentage of plaintiff's verdicts to plaintiffs from within their own occupation category, and a fifth (clerical) gave a very high rating to clerical plaintiffs. Only salesmen were not favorably disposed to persons in their own occupation group.

## NONWHITES

Nonwhites are underrepresented on juries in the vast majority of courts in this country. In the federal district courts, which have collected the most complete demographic statistics through surveys of their jurors in 1971 and 1974,[d] nonwhites are underrepresented in 77.1 percent of the 166 surveys the author was able to obtain in districts with a nonwhite population of 4 percent or more. *In more than half* of the reporting districts, nonwhites were underrepresented by *20 percent or more*, which we consider a "substantial" amount and hence a violation of the federal statute (see Chapter Four, pp. 94-98). An eighth of the districts underrepresented nonwhites by *more than 50 percent*.

Appendix G (pp. 311-30) compares the results of the official surveys to the 1970 census data (which, the Census Bureau has conceded, underrepresents nonwhites by about 6 percent[7]). The federal government defines Hispanic people as "white," so the term "nonwhite" when used in these federal charts includes only blacks, Asians (who are a significant percentage in California, Hawaii, and New York City), and Native Americans.

The federal courts that showed the greatest underrepresentation were those in the southern states of Alabama, Florida, Georgia, Louisiana, Maryland, Mississippi, North Carolina, Oklahoma, South Carolina, Texas, and Virginia, although northern states such as Colorado, Connecticut, and New York also show serious underrepresentation. Typical of the most striking figures are those from the Hattiesburg Division of the Southern District of Mississippi, where blacks make up 23.3 percent of the population but had just 13.7 percent of the jury seats in 1971 and 10.4 percent in 1974—disparities of 41.2 percent and 55.4 percent. In the Southern Division of

---

dSee Appendix G, pp. 311-30.

**Table 2-1. Votes in Favor of Plaintiff, by Occupation (Percent)**

| Jurors Occupation | Plaintiff's Occupation | | | | | |
|---|---|---|---|---|---|---|
| | *Professional* | *Executives* | *Salesmen* | *Clerical* | *Skilled Tradesmen* | *Blue Collar* |
| Professional | 74 | 45 | 55 | 56 | 67 | 67 |
| Executives | 45 | 72 | 44 | 68 | 66 | 67 |
| Salesmen | 46 | 60 | 43 | 93 | 50 | 61 |
| Clerical | 67 | 48 | 46 | 69 | 79 | 69 |
| Skilled Tradesmen | 84 | 83 | 29 | 79 | 87 | 73 |
| Blue Collar | 65 | 36 | 39 | 50 | 61 | 66 |

Source: Jury Verdict Research, Inc., *Personal Injury Valuation Handbooks*, Vol. VIII, *Psychological Factors Affecting Verdicts—Jurors*, (Cleveland: J.V.R., Inc., 1969), p. x. Reprinted with permission of Jury Verdict Research, Inc.

Tennessee's Eastern District, the Census Bureau reported that blacks made up 16 percent of the over-21 population, but the federal district court's 1974 survey of its jurors found that blacks held only 10.2 percent of the places on the jury wheel and just 4.1 percent of actual seats on juries—disparities of 36.3 percent at the first stage and 74.4 percent in the jury box.

Data on black jurors in the local courts of fifteen states also show underrepresentation to be the rule. Statistics from the state courts are somewhat less systematic and have been assembled from surveys conducted by attorneys challenging jury selection in litigation, from visual observations conducted by the author and by law students, and from questionnaires distributed to jurors in some courts as they report for duty. Surveys of black representation in a few of the larger urban areas (Baltimore, Chicago, San Francisco, and St. Louis) indicate that the requisite number of blacks are being summoned for jury duty (although the census figures are probably particularly low in these cities because the black population has been rising in all of them since 1970). But the surveys from the southern states and some from the North (Brooklyn and Buffalo) show that blacks are not filling the percentage of seats on the juries that their population warrants. Studies of jury rolls in Montgomery County, Alabama, and Erie County (Buffalo), New York, for example, noted underrepresentations of 72.2 percent and 34.5 percent, respectively.

Among the reasons for underrepresentation of blacks are the exclusive reliance on the voter registration list, which still definitely underrepresents the black community; infrequent updating of juror lists, which loses a lot of black names because blacks move more frequently than whites;[8] discretionary selection that permits jury commissioners to discriminate against blacks either through conscious design or because blacks are underrepresented in the occupational classes that are preferred when selecting jurors; increased likelihood of excuses for blacks; and increased likelihood of being challenged if they do make it onto the jury venire.

Other ethnic minority groups, including persons of Hispanic origin, Native Americans, and Asians, are underrepresented even more dramatically than are blacks. Surveys from twenty courts (in seven states) with concentrations of Chicanos, Puerto Ricans, or other Latin people,[e] show a dramatic underrepresentation of Hispanic jurors, in some cases in the range of 50 percent or more. In Santa Clara, California, for example, with a Spanish-surnamed population of 13.6 percent, only 7.2 percent of those sent jury summonses and only 6.1 percent of those actually seated as jurors

eSee Table G-4, Appendix G, p. 324.

between September 1969 and September 1970 were Spanish surnamed—55 percent less than their share of the population.[9] Harris County (Houston), Texas, underrepresented Hispanics by 73.6 percent on their jury lists in October 1971, when a Spanish-surnamed adult population of 8.7 percent made up just 2.3 percent of jurors.

The federal district courts have not obtained separate demographic data on Hispanic jurors because the federal government classifies Hispanics as whites, but some scattered data from federal courts show consistent underrepresentation. An examination of the names of 529 grand jurors who served in the Northern District of California between 1969 and 1975, for instance, showed only 33 Spanish surnames, or 6.3 percent—compared with the 11.2 percent of the adult population made up by the Spanish surnamed, according to the 1970 census (or 13.8 percent if the figure is adjusted to new census estimates). The rate of underrepresentation of Hispanics on these grand juries was 43.8 percent (or 54.3 percent if the revised figure is used). (Table G-3, p. 323.)

The main reasons for underrepresentation of Hispanics are (1) the rate of voter registration, which according to the Census Bureau is only 44.4 percent, the lowest of any ethnic group; (2) the fact that many Hispanics have no proper papers of any sort and are reluctant to identify themselves to the government; and (3) that those who are called for jury duty are excused at a higher rate than usual. Even Puerto Ricans in New York (all of whom are citizens) appear on New York City juries in very low percentages.

Americans of Asian descent and Native Americans form a significant proportion of the population only in some areas, and in most of these make up less than 5 percent of the population. But in almost all of these areas—except Hawaii—they are underrepresented, often substantially. In the federal courts, which began sampling both groups in 1974, the San Francisco-Oakland-Eureka Division of the Northern District of California underrepresented Asians by 58.8 percent (5.1 percent of the adult population but only 2.1 percent of jurors), and the Southern District of California underrepresented them by 62.5 percent (1.6 percent of population and 0.6 percent of jurors). (Table G-5, p. 327.)

Native Americans were underrepresented in all districts whose surveys have been obtained, often by more than 50 percent, to the point where they play little role in our judicial system.[f] The federal court district with the highest proportion of Native Americans in the adult population—the Prescott Division of Arizona, where they constitute 25.8 percent—underrepresented this group by 81.8 per-

[f]See Table G-7, Appendix G, p. 329.

cent in 1974. In the Phoenix Division, where Native Americans are 1.5 percent of the population, none was found in a sample of 1,729 jurors.

The underrepresentation of nonwhites on juries can have a profound effect on the strength of the jury system and the criminal justice system in general. Discrimination bred by prejudice has contributed to widespread mistrust by black people of most of the (white-dominated) institutions of power, and most particularly the agencies of law enforcement. As Dr. Richard A. Cloward, a Columbia University sociologist, put it: "There is . . . much less faith, much less belief in the fairness, the even-handedness of social institutions, and, in particular, institutions of law enforcement."[10] This mistrust was described in 1967 by the Kerner Commission as follows:

> The belief is pervasive among ghetto residents that lower courts in our urban communities dispense "assembly-line justice"; that from arrest to sentencing, the poor and uneducated are denied equal justice with the affluent, that procedures such as bail and fines have been perverted to perpetuate class inequity. We have found that the apparatus of justice in some areas has itself become a focus for distrust and hostility.[11]

The jury system is supposed to establish the legitimacy of the justice rendered—to prevent such mistrust and hostility from occurring. But racially connected misconceptions and prejudice can imperil the impartiality of a jury. Only by balancing this prejudice—which jurors of all kinds feel about some issues or people—through a jury composed of a cross-section of the community can impartiality be fostered. As Dr. Cloward stated:

> [A] white juror sitting in a jury box listening to the testimony of a black witness would sift and evaluate and appraise that testimony through a screen of preconceived notions about what black people are. Now, some of those notions may be based in fact . . . and some may be notions that have some relation to fact but are greatly exaggerated, and still others of those screening biases or notions may be completely contrary to fact. None of these things would be as likely to be true of a black juror listening to and appraising and judging the same testimony. The black juror, because of more similar life experiences to the black witness would, it seems to me, appraise that testimony from a distinctively different vantage point and from a distinctively different life experience in the world and the like.[12]

Misunderstanding and prejudice subtly enter the courtroom and affect the kind of justice that is rendered. Although it is too much to expect this one institution of society to make up for the inequities in the others, we can at least attempt, by making the jury more responsive through representativeness, to increase the fairness of the criminal justice system (whose other parts also need reform). Without a jury system whose integrity can be respected, the task is hopeless.

Today, there are more blacks on juries than in 1967, when the Kerner Report was issued, but not as many as there should be. The kind of difference that black representation can make was illustrated by a black man who served as a juror in Los Angeles in 1973 and described his experience:

> It seemed like the only reason that they arrested the [black] defendant [who was charged with auto theft] was that someone in the gas station across the street looking out into the light in the dark could identify the run-of-the-mill black man from 90 to 100 feet away. They arrested him in the area of York Boulevard [a white neighborhood near Occidental College and Pasadena]. Well, we all know what being black is on York Boulevard. I was raised and born in Los Angeles so it is nothing new to me. If you are black and you're on York Boulevard at four o'clock in the morning, they are going to pick you up. They will pick me up on York Boulevard walking at four o'clock in the morning. This was the only thing that they seemed to have against the man, so we acquitted him.[13]

This juror offered the other jurors an opportunity to understand an aspect of the case they might not otherwise have had—thanks to his unique knowledge of the neighborhood and community. His presence on the jury brought a perspective without which "justice" may have turned out differently.

The experience of two cities that recently changed their methods of selecting jurors suggests that major changes in jury profiles can affect verdicts over time. In the City of Baltimore, as a result of a new statute enacted by the Maryland Legislature, jury commissioners switched in September 1969 from selecting jurors from the lists of property owners—which meant older, richer, whiter juries—to taking them randomly from the voter registration list. This change meant that instead of juries that were at least 70 percent white, juries were impaneled that were first 34.4 percent black (from September 1969 to August 1970), then 40.7 percent black (in 1971), then 45.5 percent black (in 1972) and 46.7 percent black (in 1973). The rate of conviction, which between 1965 and 1969 had averaged about 83.6 percent in Baltimore's jury trials, dropped to about 65.3 percent during the first few months after the switch and remained below 70 percent during the next several years.[g]

In every important crime category except burglary, the conviction

gSee Appendix J, p. 375.

rate in Baltimore dropped, and in most categories, it dropped substantially, particularly in the years immediately after the change. The figures for rape—perhaps the most controversial for a racially mixed southern community—showed the most dramatic change, from a conviction rate of 85.2 percent before 1969 to 48.5 percent after. Although some other factors—for example the amount of plea-bargaining or the quality of the prosecution—might account for this change, it seems likely that the difference in jury composition is at least partly the cause. This, in any case, was the assumption of critics and of the prosecution when rising acquittal rates produced controversy in the media and criticism by trial judges, to which the State's Attorney, Milton B. Allen, a black and a former defense attorney, responded that the new jurors want to see more evidence before they convict. "We find these jurors want hard evidence," Allen told the press in October 1971. "What has always been legally sufficient to convict—police testimony, oral confessions, eye witnesses—is no longer enough. The new juror wants to hold the weapon in his hand, he wants to see diagrams of the scene, he wants to see the defendant's signature on the confession." The State's Attorney's Office has responded to this increased pressure by trying to build stronger cases before going to court. All missing evidence is explained in detail, and each point of proof is covered by as many witnesses as possible.[h] The conviction rate in some crime categories is slowly rising, but whether they reach the old levels remains to be seen.[14]

In Los Angeles County, a temporary change in jury selection methods to include more blacks and Hispanics also produced a change in verdicts. In seven of the county's eight judicial districts, jurors had been selected from within the geographical confines of the district, but in the Central District—which contains Los Angeles' downtown area and poor residential districts—jurors have been selected from throughout the county. This practice was changed for an eighteen-month period between July 1970 and January 1972, when jurors were selected only from the Central District, in conformance with selection schemes in other districts. The Central District is 32 percent black and 18 percent Chicano; the nonwhite proportion in countywide juries is about 15 percent.[15]

---

[h]Consistent with the Baltimore experience is the result of a survey conducted by the *Detroit Free Press* of 500 persons who served as jurors in 1970. The jurors were asked whether they would accept the testimony of a police officer simply "because he was a policeman and policemen have no reason to lie." Twenty-three percent of the white jurors replied affirmatively, but only 10 percent of the blacks were similarly trusting. John Oppedahl and Tom Ricke, "An In-Depth Survey of What Juries Think," *Detroit Free Press*, July 25, 1971, p. 4B.

In the period during which jurors for the Central District were selected from that area alone (half of 1970 and all of 1971), conviction rates dropped sharply, rising again in 1972. According to statistics kept by the Executive Officer of the Los Angeles County Superior Court, the percentage of convictions fell from 67 percent in 1969, to 64.6 percent in 1970, to 47.2 percent in 1971 (the one full year during which jurors were called from the Central District), then up to 66.6 percent in 1972 and 61.9 percent in 1973. Informal figures from the Los Angeles District Attorney's office, kept on a slightly different basis, show a change from 67.3 percent in 1969 to 65.2 percent in 1970 to 54.9 percent in 1971 (and then a rise to 80 percent in the first six months of 1972). Comparison with rates in the other districts indicates that conviction rates in these jurisdictions did not undergo a similar drop in 1971. Some districts did record substantial drops in a few categories, but none showed a consistent decrease.[i] As in Baltimore, it cannot be proved that the change in juries caused change in verdicts, but that was the assumption of many officials.[16]

Because of displeasure with the jury verdicts under the new selection system, mainly from attorneys representing corporations in civil cases, it was disbanded at the beginning of 1972, and the Superior Court judges reinstated the countywide jury pool for the Central District. A number of prominent residents of Los Angeles, including Mayor Thomas Bradley, then sued the Superior Court judges and after extensive litigation the judges altered their rule once again so that all eight judicial districts in Los Angeles now summon jurors from throughout the county, but persons are given an automatic excuse on request if they live more than 20 miles from the courthouse to which they are summoned.[17]

## THE YOUNG AND THE ELDERLY

In every federal court surveyed and in virtually every state court for which data is available, both the young and old are underrepresented consistently and dramatically.[j] A glance at the surveys from both federal and state courts reveals that, in most jurisdictions, the groups at each end of the age spectrum are generally underrepresented, with those in the middle overrepresented. In the federal court for the Eastern District of Michigan, an almost perfect curve could be drawn, to chart the age distribution, as the percentage of jurors compared to population goes from —73.6 percent for the 21-24 year olds,

[i]See Appendix J, pp. 377, 380-81.

[j]See Appendix H, p. 331.

gradually to a high of 68.9 percent for those 45-59, then drops down steadily until those 65 and over are underrepresented once again, by —38.7 percent (see Table 2-2). This age distribution is typical of a majority of districts.

Most federal and state courts underrepresent the under-thirty population by at least 30 percent. In the federal court for the District of Massachusetts, for example, those 21-25 were underrepresented by 60.3 percent and those 26-29 by 32.1 percent. In quite a few districts, including the New York City counties of Kings (Brooklyn), Queens, and the Bronx, the underrepresentation extends to all persons under forty.

The young are found in relatively small numbers on juries for a number of reasons, including (1) the fact that nine states still require jurors to be 21 and one other has a minimum age of 19;[k] (2) the voter registration list underrepresents the young; (3) some courts, most particularly the federal courts, use out-of-date lists of voters, thus eliminating all new voters and those who move most frequently (the young fall into both categories); (4) eleven states and the federal courts have a residency requirement (usually one year),[l] which discriminates against those who move most frequently; and (5) the young are excused more frequently than the middle-aged, thus further reducing their numbers. Some of the courts in states that

**Table 2-2.   Age Distribution of Jurors, Eastern District of Michigan**

| Age | 1970 Census (Percent) | Jurors (Percent) | Rate of Error |
|---|---|---|---|
| 21-24 | 7.2% | 1.9% | −73.6% |
| 25-29 | 10.4 | 6.9 | −33.7 |
| 30-34 | 12.3 | 7.9 | −35.8 |
| 35-39 | 12.8 | 10.8 | −15.6 |
| 40-44 | 11.6 | 14.2 | +22.4 |
| 45-49 | 10.3 | 17.4 | +68.9 |
| 50-54 | 8.7 | 13.9 | +59.8 |
| 55-59 | 7.9 | 11.5 | +45.6 |
| 60-64 | 6.4 | 7.9 | +23.4 |
| 65 & Over | 12.4 | 7.6 | −38.7 |
| Number of Jurors: | 850 | | |

Source: Examination of juror questionnaires conducted by attorney Neal Bush in 1970 for *U.S. v. Sinclair*, Crim. No. 44395.

[k]See Appendix A, p. 257.

[l]See Appendix C, p. 271.

supplement the list of registered voters with the driver's license list (Colorado and North Dakota) are able to obtain close to a representative number of the young.

Underrepresentation of the young should be seen in light of the fact that a large proportion of defendants are themselves young, and chronologically at least, young people can be considered peers of these accused. In 1970, 13.8 percent of all persons arrested for major crimes throughout the country were between 18 and 20, and 18 percent of all those tried in federal courts were between 18 and 20. In 1969, the median age of all federal defendants was only 27.4 years.[18] This underscores the importance of fair representation of young people, an identifiable group, many of whose members, according to recent surveys,[19] share opinions and experiences somewhat different from their elders.

The *Detroit Free Press* survey of 500 jurors in 1970 mentioned above[20] found that young jurors differed from their elders on a number of important issues. The questions that indicate important age differences (and the answers by age) follow:

1. "When a policeman testified, I tended to believe him because he was a policeman, and policemen have no reason to lie—agree or disagree?"

|  |  |
|---|---|
| 21-29: | 10 percent agreement. |
| 30-39: | 10 percent agreement. |
| 40-49: | 18 percent agreement. |
| 50 and over: | 24 percent agreement. |

2. "Sometimes I felt the judge was being unfair—agree or disagree?"

|  |  |
|---|---|
| 21-29: | 26 percent agreement. |
| 30-39: | 13 percent agreement. |
| 40-49: | 10 percent agreement. |
| 50 and over: | 8 percent agreement. |

3. "Generally, I felt that since the police and prosecution had charged a person with a crime, he was probably guilty of something—agree or disagree?"

|  |  |
|---|---|
| 21-29: | 7.5 percent agreement. |
| 50 and over: | 21.6 percent agreement. |
| (other ages not available) | |

4. "At least once, I got bored or sleepy during a trial—agree or disagree?"

| | |
|---|---|
| 21-29: | 44 percent agreement. |
| 30-39: | 36 percent agreement. |
| 40-49: | 34 percent agreement. |
| 50 and over: | 22 percent agreement. |

5. "How helpful to forming an opinion in the case would it have been if you had been able to ask witnesses questions?"

| | |
|---|---|
| 21-29: | 58 percent said "somewhat" or "quite helpful" (as opposed to "not very helpful" or "not helpful at all.") |
| 30-39: | 30 percent said "somewhat" or "quite helpful." |
| 40-49: | 34 percent said "somewhat" or "quite helpful." |
| 50 and over: | 23 percent said "somewhat" or "quite helpful." |

6. "Sometimes I asked God to make sure that we would make the right decision—agree or disagree?"

| | |
|---|---|
| 21-29: | 13 percent agreement. |
| 30-39: | 65 percent agreement. |
| 40-49: | 61 percent agreement. |
| 50 and over: | 68 percent agreement. |

7. "I never worried about a verdict, because I knew God would not allow us to make the wrong decision—agree or disagree?

| | |
|---|---|
| 21-29: | 4 percent agreement. |
| 30-39: | 20 percent agreement. |
| 40-49: | 20 percent agreement. |
| 50 and over: | 21 percent agreement. |

The young also differ with their elders on the proper approach to the questions of drugs, other victimless crimes, abortions, and the general question of how tough society should be on persons who violate the general norms. Typical is a 1972 Gallup poll on the death penalty, which reported that among persons 18-24 48 percent favored the death penalty and 44 percent opposed it; among persons over 50, 60 percent favored the death penalty and only 27 percent opposed it.[21]

Persons over 65 are even more underrepresented in many courts than their younger counterparts. In most courts surveyed, both state and federal, people over 65 are underrepresented at an average rate of more than 50 percent, except in Arlington, Virginia; Orange County, California; and the State of New York (where persons, once put on the jury roll, stay until they are 70 or 75 and are called repeatedly). The main reasons for this disproportion are that nine states have a maximum age of service (ranging from 65 to 75) beyond which people are absolutely barred from being jurors, and another twenty states permit by statute persons beyond a given age (ranging from 60 to 70) to be automatically excused if they do not want to serve. Most jury commissioners will excuse an older person by request, even if the applicable statute does not specifically authorize such an excuse.

Many societies give the positions of greatest power to their oldest members, but we send our elderly out to pasture, rejecting the chance to find out what special insights the people that have lived the longest may have that would help us in our jury decisions. It is difficult to evaluate the contributions of the elderly based on past jury decisions because those older persons who serve as jurors now are in some sense "volunteers," having chosen not to take advantage of the opportunity to avoid jury service that is provided in most jurisdictions through virtually automatic excuses. We also have far less information about older people than about the young, whose attitudes seem to be constantly surveyed.[m] Those who choose to serve may be more civic-minded than those who seek an excuse, or perhaps a bit more bored with their retired lives.

## WOMEN

It is commonly assumed that women dominate our jury panels because they are thought to have more free time and to be more available for jury duty than men. In fact, the opposite is true in most courts, and in some states, women continue to be grossly underrepresented. The surveys conducted by the clerks of the federal district courts in 1971 and 1974 show an unmistakable pattern—88.9 percent of the 234 surveys I was able to obtain show an underrepresentation of women among those who appear for jury duty. In 30.7

[m]The Chicago Jury Project did find that although the old were somewhat less willing than the young to award the more lenient verdict of an acquittal by reason of insanity, *the old were more willing to do so than the middle-aged.* The proposed explanation was that the old have less property than the middle aged and hence are somewhat less oriented toward maintaining the status quo (and locking up all deviants) than are their more affluent juniors. Rita James Simon, *The Jury and the Defense of Insanity* (Boston: Little, Brown, 1967), p. 111.

percent of the surveys, underrepresentation is between 10 and 20 percent; another 21.4 percent show an underrepresentation of between 20 and 30 percent; and another 8.1 percent show an underrepresentation of over 30 percent. Take as an example the Western District of Missouri, which has five divisions. In four of the five divisions, women are underrepresented; in three of them by about 25 percent and in one by 17.5 percent; only one division has the same proportion of women jurors as women in the population. This pattern is typical, as a look at the tables in Appendix I will reveal; underrepresentation is the norm (pp. 349-71).

Examples of explicit and overt discrimination are becoming less common as our society moves slowly toward accepting at least the principle of political equality for women, but most courts nonetheless still use selection procedures that have the effect of underrepresenting them. Virtually all the state and federal courts grant excuses to women (usually, but not solely, in their role as mothers) more liberally than they do to men. One state (Montana) still uses tax rolls as its primary source of jurors, a list that dramatically underrepresents women because property is most frequently listed under the name of the man. California's statutes indicate that women are to be treated no differently from men, but eleven of the sixteen surveys from that state show an underrepresentation of women, as do surveys from many other states. Only a few jurisdictions—Baltimore, Maryland, and Bernalillo County (Albuquerque), New Mexico, are two examples—indicate an overrepresentation of women.

In some state courts, women make up but a small fraction of jurors. Alabama, Georgia, Massachusetts, Missouri, and Tennessee all have statutes that permit women to be excused from jury duty automatically,[n] and in each of these states, juries are heavily dominated by men. A 1972 survey of juries in Montgomery County, Alabama, revealed that women constituted only 16 percent of the jurors in that jurisdiction, a figure matched by Coweta County, Georgia, between 1969 and 1971 (16.2 percent women). Until the Supreme Court voided the state law in 1975, Louisiana called as jurors only those women who volunteered. New York State granted an automatic excuse to women until changing its law in 1975,[22] and until that time, women made up less than 20 percent of the jurors in

[n]Alabama's statute is phrased as follows: "When any female shall have been summoned for jury duty, she shall have the right to appear before the trial judge, and such judge, for good cause shown, shall have the judicial discretion to excuse said person from jury duty." Title 30, sec. 21. The other four states listed here phrase the excuse in more absolute and automatic terms, but the Massachusetts statute has recently been interpreted so that a woman must make some showing of hardship before she will be excused.

that state. Suffolk County, Massachusetts, has until quite recently followed the practice of summoning substantially fewer women than men for jury duty to avoid the subsequent problem of having to grant their request for excuse. The 1973 jury list for Boston contained only 25 percent women[23] (the figure was 36-37 percent in 1974). And in neighboring Connecticut, which, like Massachusetts, allows local civil servants to hand-pick persons for the jury rolls, the officials often leave women with children off even their preliminary lists.[24]

It should not be necessary to find any real difference in the jury verdicts of women (compared to men) in order to insist that women be adequately represented on juries. As Justice William O. Douglas said in a 1946 Supreme Court decision: "The two sexes are not fungible. A flavor, a distinct quality is lost if either sex is excluded"[25] or underrepresented on our jury panels. The exclusion or underrepresentation of any group denies to that group—and to us all—the full robust functioning of an institution basic to our democracy. But certain differences in judicial approach between the sexes can nonetheless be noted.

Despite the conventional wisdom of lawyers, women—like other groups—tend to favor their own. The data assembled from civil lawsuits by Jury Verdict Research, Inc., indicate that neither women nor men are overly influenced by the sex of the litigants in determining which side should win, but the data do indicate that once liability is established, women jurors will give a larger award to a female plaintiff (17 percent above average) and male jurors will similarly boost the figure awarded to a victorious male plaintiff (12 percent above average).[26] In examining "housewives," as opposed to working women, Jury Verdict Research found that the former tend to operate more as women than as members of their husband's socioeconomic class, in the sense that they tend to render verdicts that are more similar to those of other housewives than to those of their husbands. Housewives favor the plaintiff slightly less than average and render awards that are somewhat below the average. They seem most responsive to the plaintiff's side in product liability cases (perhaps because of their role as consumers), they are somewhat below average on work accident cases, and—surprisingly—they vote for minors as plaintiffs substantially less than average.[27]

Virtually all studies of juror behavior in criminal cases have found that women are more lenient toward the accused, or perhaps more sensitive to all factors that may be involved in the fact situation. The data on differences in verdicts rendered by women and men are in most cases so small, however, that they cannot be considered statistically significant. A study of verdicts in Multnomah County (Portland), Oregon, immediately before and after women were added to their juries (in 1922), noted a remarkable drop in the conviction rate from 62.7 percent with all-male juries to 41.4 percent during the year when women were added.[28] A similar phenomenon apparently occurred in civil decisions in South Carolina during the year immediately after women were first allowed to sit on their juries in 1967. A study of juries in 1966 and 1967 found that the new juries containing both women and men were more inclined to favor the underdog—and to award a judgment to a litigant from a lower socioeconomic status—than was the all-male jury of the year before the change.[29]

## CONCLUSION

Clarence Darrow warned criminal defense attorneys many years ago that they should avoid wealthy jurors because, next to the Board of Trade, the wealthy consider the penitentiary to be the most important of all public buildings.[30] It is difficult to prove this axiom, at least with the information at our disposal. But confirmation is not necessary in order to argue, as Justice Thurgood Marshall did, that the perspective of those in the lower socioeconomic strata and the perhaps unknown importance of their participation necessitate their inclusion in juries. Nor is it necessary to prove that blacks, Hispanics, young people, the elderly, or women will bring a particular set of attitudes into the jury room in order to urge their inclusion on juries. The information gleaned through examination of verdicts should be seen as confirming our understanding that each person brings into the jury box his or her own set of experiences and beliefs and that it is our responsibility to ensure that the variety of experiences and backgrounds is as fairly represented as possible.

The jury's processes are an art, not a science. We can identify some possible factors in a possible result, but the nature of the system is such that neither the ambitions—the thinking and judgment of each juror, and the interaction among jurors—nor the result—the verdict— can be predicted. Fulfilling the goal of impartiality requires that we provide an opportunity for the full range of views. Our ability to elicit the community's conscience on the difficult issues of justice is diminished by the exclusion of broad groups of people, and the legitimacy of the jury's verdict is thereby impaired.

## NOTES

1. *Peters v. Kiff*, 407 U.S. 493, 503-504 (1972).
2. Figures assembled by Greg and Nancy Ricca and Jim Porter, students at Hastings College of the Law, University of California (in San Francisco).

3. Rita James Simon, *The Jury and the Defense of Insanity* (Boston: Little, Brown, 1967), pp. 106-10.

4. J.P. Reed, "Jury Deliberations, Voting, and Verdict Trends," *Southwestern Social Science Quarterly* 45 (1965):361-74; see generally Cookie Stephen, "Selective Characteristics of Jurors and Litigants: Their Influences on Juries' Verdicts," *The Jury System in America: A Critical Overview*, ed. Rita James Simon (Beverly Hills: Sage Publications, 1975), pp. 95-121.

5. Freda Adler, "Socioeconomic Factors Influencing Jury Verdicts," *New York University Review of Law and Social Change* 3 (Winter 1973):1.

6. Jury Verdict Research, Inc., *Personal Injury Valuation Handbooks*, Vol. VIII, *Psychological Factors Affecting Verdicts—Jurors* (Cleveland, J.V.R., Inc., 1969).

7. Jacob S. Siegel, "Estimates of Coverage of the Population by Sex, Race, and Age in the 1970 Census," *Demography* 11 (Feb. 1974):1; U.S. Bureau of the Census, *Census of Population and Housing*: 1970 Evaluation and Research Program PHC(E)-4, "Estimates of Coverage of Population by Sex, Race and Age: Demographic Analysis" (Washington: Government Printing Office, 1973).

8. *Statistical Abstract of the United States* (Washington: Government Printing Office, 1973), p. 37.

9. Figures prepared by attorney Richard Such for a jury challenge in the case of the *People v. Rios*, No. 48220 (Santa Clara County Superior Court, Calif., 1970).

10. Testimony at a jury challenge prior to the murder trial of Bobby Seale and Ericka Huggins on October 15, 1970, New Haven, Connecticut (Transcript, p. 436).

11. National Advisory Commission on Civil Disorders, *Report* (Washington: Government Printing Office, 1967).

12. From the Seale-Huggins hearing, October 15, 1970, New Haven, Connecticut (Transcript, pp. 438-39).

13. Ralph Davis, "Black Jurors," *Guild Practitioner* 30 (1973):112-13.

14. This description is from interviews and correspondence with the Baltimore State's Attorney, Milton B. Allen, in 1973 and 1974.

15. See Appendix G, pp. 319 and 324.

16. Two sociological studies of jury behavior have also found that blacks are more likely to favor acquittal than are whites in some circumstances. See D.W. Broeder, "The University of Chicago Jury Project," *Nebraska Law Review* 38 (1959):744-60; and Rita James Simon, *The Jury and the Defense of Insanity*. See generally Cookie Stephen, 'Selective Characteristics of Jurors and Litigants."

17. See *Adams v. Superior Court*, 27 Cal. App. 3d 719, 730-33, 104 Cal. Rptr. 144 (1972); *People v. Taylor*, 46 Cal. App. 3d 513, 120 Cal. Rptr. 762 (1975); *Bradley v. Judges of Superior Court*, 372 F.Supp.26 (C.D.Cal. 1974) and 531 F.2d 413 (9th Cir. 1976).

18. Subcommittee No. 5 of the House Judiciary Committee, *Hearings: Federal Jury Service*, 92nd Congress, 1st Sess., Nov. 10, 1971, pp. 27, 54, 62.

19. See, for example, Gallup Opinion Index, Report No. 92 (February 1973), p. 20; No. 107 (May 1974), p. 23; also *New York Times*, May 14, 22, 26, 1974; see generally, Ginger and Powers, "Mississippi Juror Age Requirement—

Unfair to the Defendant, Unfair to the Young, and Unfair to the Public—Is It Constitutional?" *Mississippi Law Journal* 47 (1976):1-30.

20. John Oppedahl, "The Generation Gap in Court," *Detroit Free Press*, July 26, 1971.

21. Gallup Opinion Index, Report No. 90 (Dec. 1972), p. 27.

22. *San Francisco Chronicle*, February 7, 1975, p. 11.

23. My examination of that list, June 10, 1974.

24. From testimony presented in the jury challenge preceding the 1971 murder trial of Bobby Seale and Ericka Huggins, October 1970.

25. *Ballard v. United States*, 329 U.S. 187, 193-94.

26. Jury Verdict Research, Inc., *Personal Injury Valuation Handbooks*, 3676-87 (Report 71) (1966), discussed in Stuart S. Nagel and Lenore J. Weitzman, "Women as Litigants," *Hastings Law Journal* 23 (1971):171, 192-97.

27. Philip J. Hermann, "Occupations of Jurors as an Influence on Their Verdict," *Forum* 5 (1970):154; Jury Verdict Research, Inc., *PIV Handbooks*, pp. 5200-5221.

28. R. Justin Miller, "The Woman Juror," *Oregon Law Review* 2 (1922):41.

29. Snyder, "Sex Role Differential and Juror Decisions," *Sociology and Social Research* 55 (1971):444.

30. Note, "The Jury Voir Dire: Useless Delay or Valuable Technique," *South Dakota Law Review* 11 (1966):356.

## Chapter Three

## An Impartial Jury:
## The View from the
## Supreme Court

The perception that the composition of a jury affects its verdict is the basis of challenges by defendants to the makeup of juries that convicted them. The all-white jury trying a black man, the all-male jury trying a woman, the jury of the propertied judging the case of a laborer, and the middle-aged deciding the fate of a youth—all these have been challenged for not fulfilling the constitutional guarantee of an "impartial jury." It is argued in these cases that if some groups are excluded or substantially underrepresented on a jury—most importantly, the group to which the defendant belongs—then we cannot be sure that all steps were taken to prevent bias. And if the jury was biased, it is claimed, the guilty verdict should be overturned; the jury failed to provide legitimacy to the decisions reached. Because all people have their own prejudices, and the jury is not a scientific instrument, it cannot be guaranteed that bias will not play a part. But the best way to minimize bias is to impanel a representative cross-section of the community; without such a cross-section, doubts about the jury's partiality will persist.

The belief that an "impartial" jury means a broadly representative one was not always as widely accepted as it is today. It has taken a series of attacks on exclusionary practices through jury challenges, combined with increasing movements for equality in society, to come to the point where it is generally accepted that everyone has a right to serve on a jury and that the absence or underrepresentation of some groups can imperil its fairness. Over the years, many appellants failed to get from the courts the kind of interpretation of "impartial jury" that they were seeking, for only gradually did the courts expand their definition of the constitutional right to trial by a jury to include, specifically, "a representative cross-section."[1] Much of the impetus toward representative juries has been legislative in origin—the Federal Jury Selection and Service Act of 1968, for instance, which requires such juries—and judicial decisions have been restrained in their approach. The courts have long accepted the idea that the makeup of a jury is important but have historically taken a cautious approach toward the question of when corrective court action is warranted.

The Sixth Amendment's guarantee of trial *"by an impartial jury,"* probably the most important constitutional standard governing a fair trial, actually gives only the broadest contours of the nature of this right. We know that the right to trial by jury was a matter of central concern to our early leaders, who wrote, debated, and eventually ratified the Constitution and Bill of Rights. We also understand that the vague reference to jury trial in the 1787 version of the Constitution was an impetus for passage of the Bill of Rights (added to the Constitution as the first ten amendments in 1791), which specifically guaranteed the right to an indictment by a grand jury prior to criminal trials (in the Fifth Amendment) and the right to a jury trial in both criminal (Sixth Amendment) and civil (Seventh Amendment) matters. We do not know, however, precisely what is meant by these clauses; they have been subject to varying interpretations over the years.

Little attention was given to the specific meaning of the words "impartial jury" during the ratification debates, so we cannot say for certain what they meant then, but the idea that juries should be broadly representative of the populace certainly had its adherents. The Virginian Richard Henry Lee expressed the idea in elegant language in 1787 when the original draft of the Constitution was being considered by the states:

> It is essential in every free country that *common people* should have a part and share of influence, in the judicial as well as in the legislative department. To hold open to them the offices of senators and judges to fill, for which an expensive education is required, cannot answer any valuable purposes for them. . . .
> *The trial by jury* in the judicial department, and the collection of the people by their representatives in the legislature, are those fortunate inventions which have procured for them, in this country, their true proportion of influence, and the wisest and most fit means of protecting themselves in the community. Their situation as jurors and representatives, enables them to acquire information and knowledge in the affairs and

government of the society; and to come forward, in turn, as the centinels and guardians of each other.[2]

This theme was also hinted at by President Thomas Jefferson in his first inaugural address in 1801, when he stated that "trials by juries *impartially selected*"[3] was one of the principles of our government, thus indicating strongly that the writers of the Sixth Amendment were concerned about jury *selection* when they used the word "impartial." The different practices in the thirteen original states surely influenced the choice of such a general term as "impartial jury," just as those differences help explain the failure to specify rights to jury trial more fully in the original 1787 Constitution. But we can safely say that by "impartial" our country's founders meant at least a jury that was not biased in favor of the prosecution, a jury independent of outside influence, a jury that was—as far as could be ensured—fair.

It has been up to the federal courts to give meaning to the Sixth Amendment in deciding jury challenges, and they began the process of interpretation about a century ago. The Bill of Rights was originally meant to be a constraint only on the federal government— not on the state governments, which were constrained by their own constitutions—and the federal courts had only limited jurisdiction for most of the nineteenth century, generating relatively few civil liberties issues for appellate review. The U.S. Supreme Court did not, therefore, review any cases charging discrimination in jury selection until ratification in 1868 of the Fourteenth Amendment, which prohibits the states from denying "to any person within its jurisdiction the equal protection of the laws." In recent years, the Court has ruled that the Fourteenth Amendment imposes on the states most of the specific obligations of the Bill of Rights, and in 1968 the Court stated explicitly that all of the states are bound by the Sixth Amendment's requirement of trial "by an impartial jury."[4] The Court has said that an "impartial" jury must be a representative jury, but it has never laid down an explicit rule on what mathematical standards will govern jury challenges and instead prefers to deal with all the problems raised by this language on a case-by-case basis.

The Court has developed certain guidelines by which to judge jury challenges. In order to challenge successfully a method of jury selection, a litigant must show both (1) that some clearly identifiable group (or "cognizable class") has been deprived of its fair share of seats on the jury panels, and (2) that this deprivation occurred not by chance but through governmental design at some level, namely, that an "opportunity to discriminate" exists. Both of these elements of the challenge have evolved over the years, but they still remain as impressive hurdles, difficult or impossible for many litigants to overcome. What they mean, in effect, is that a group must show that without its participation a jury will not be representative (that it is a group different from the population as a whole in a significant way) and that bias against it is not only apparent but real. The challenger does not have to show that some governmental official actually intended to discriminate but does have to prove that the opportunity to discriminate existed.

Blacks are, of course, the clearly identifiable group, or "cognizable class," that has suffered the most discrimination in our society, and the Court has always accepted the principle that they could complain of discrimination in jury selection. Other groups have had to prove, however, both that they exist and that they have suffered discrimination as a group. The Court did not, for instance, recognize Hispanic-Americans as a "cognizable class" until 1954, when Chief Justice Earl Warren applied the following test to the problem:

> Throughout our history differences in race and color have defined easily identifiable groups which have at times required the aid of the courts in securing equal treatment under the laws. But community prejudices are not static and from time to time other differences from the community norm may define other groups which need the same protection. Whether such a group exists within a community is a question of fact. *When the existence of a distinct class is demonstrated, and it is further shown that the laws, as written or as applied, single out that class for different treatment not based on some reasonable classification, the guarantees of the Constitution have been violated.*[5]

Under this test, the Supreme Court has ruled that all racial or ethnic groups[6] and women[7] are "cognizable classes" and seems to have held that persons who do not believe in capital punishment form such a group.[8] But the Court has yet to rule on most other classes that logically seem to be "cognizable." In 1946, the Supreme Court ruled that "daily-wage earners" were a cognizable class,[9] but it has never extended this ruling to "the poor" in general, and lower courts have been reluctant to do so. In 1974, the Court assumed for the purpose of one argument that the young are a cognizable class but then rejected the argument raised on behalf of the young; most lower courts have refused to give the young the official status of "cognizability."[10] Occasional lower courts have classified the less educated,[11] Roman Catholics,[12] and those who do not believe in a supreme being[13] as "cognizable" groups, but the Supreme Court has not yet given its stamp of approval to any of these decisions. Thus, of the five major groups underrepresented on juries—blue-collar workers, nonwhites, the young, the old, and women—two (blacks and women) are considered "cognizable classes," one (youth) is only sometimes defined as such; some members of one group (daily-wage earners) but not the group itself have achieved such a designation; and one (the aged) has not yet presented the Court with a jury challenge.

Once the court recognizes the group in question as a "cognizable class," it examines the extent to which the class has been underrepresented on a jury or juries and whether the selection scheme used gave the selectors an "opportunity to discriminate." The Supreme Court has never allowed a jury challenge merely because a cognizable class is underrepresented. Something more is always required. Originally, the challengers were required to prove a specific "intent" to discriminate, but that high standard is no longer enforced. In recent years, the Court has sustained challenges where, for instance, the selection scheme allowed the selectors to learn the race of the potential jurors, thus giving them the "opportunity" to favor one group over another.[14]

The Supreme Court has said that either of the two methods used to select jurors today can be constitutional:[15] schemes in which jurors are selected more or less randomly from one or several presumably standard and neutral lists and those in which the selectors exercise "discretion" in deciding who should serve as a juror. But the courts have been scrutinizing the discretionary selection methods much more rigorously than the random systems because the discretionary methods always allow the "opportunity to discriminate": those who select the names of jurors always make a choice, preferring some persons over others. Faced with such schemes, the Supreme Court and the lower courts have examined the *results* of the selection process to determine whether an "impartial," "representative" "cross-section" has in fact been assembled. The courts have sometimes said quite explicitly that "figures speak and when they do, courts listen,"[16] and that seems to be the prevailing policy when discretionary selection schemes are used. If the court finds an "opportunity to discriminate," combined with figures showing a significant underrepresentation of a cognizable group, then the burden is on the selectors to justify their method of selection.[17] The courts have not demanded an actual "intent to discriminate" in these cases.

The courts have been much more reluctant to interfere with jury selection schemes that operate in a more or less random fashion, such as selection from voter registration lists and—although the governing standard is unclear—seem to require a showing of an actual "intent to discriminate" in such cases, and have only rarely allowed the figures to speak for themselves, even when they show a substantial underrepresentation of a cognizable class. Because it is extremely difficult to prove such a conscious "intent," even though the voter registration list definitely underrepresents certain groups (see Chapter Four, p. 89), virtually every Court that has passed on the exclusive use of these voter lists has approved the scheme.[18]

The somewhat schizophrenic approach used by the Court is exemplified by language in a 1976 decision, *Washington v. Davis*,[19] involving the use of statistics to demonstrate discrimination in an employment situation. The Court's majority opinion, written by Justice Byron White, discusses the jury cases for an analogy and uses language that seems inconsistent:

(A):   "Almost 100 years ago, *Strauder v. West Virginia*, 100 U.S. 303 (1879), established that the exclusion of Negroes from grand and petit juries in criminal proceedings violated the Equal Protection Clause, *but the fact that a particular jury or a series of juries does not statistically reflect the racial composition of the community does not in itself make out an invidious discrimination forbidden by the Clause.*[20]

(B):   "Necessarily, an invidious discriminatory purpose may often be inferred from the totality of the relevant facts, including the fact, if it is true, that the law bears more heavily on one race than another. *It is also not infrequently true that the discriminatory impact—in the jury cases for example, the total or seriously disproportionate exclusion of Negroes from jury venires—may for all practical purposes demonstrate unconstitutionality because in various circumstances the discrimination is very difficult to explain on nonracial grounds.*[21]

The Court has thus been unwilling to let the figures stand alone in establishing discrimination and wants to find some discriminatory "purpose" or "intent" in addition. But if the discrimination is total or "seriously disproportionate" the Court has sometimes assumed that the discrimination could not exist without a discriminatory "purpose" or "intent." Litigants challenging juries must thus operate within these uncertain guidelines.

In the century since passage of the Fourteenth Amendment, the Supreme Court has considered more than fifty challenges to juries for alleged lack of representativeness. Its interpretation of the guarantees of "equal protection" and "impartiality" as applied to jury selection has evolved over that time, as have its interpretations of representativeness and participation in other areas of our governmental process. The Supreme Court has been a conservative body for most of this period, and it is fair to say that—except for the years of the Warren Court (1953-69)—the Court has been reluctant to break new ground. It has only infrequently (and with caution) interfered with selection procedures that perpetuate the inequities of our society and that underrepresent the poor, nonwhites, women, the young, and the elderly.

The courts, perhaps particularly the Supreme Court, are not insulated from political forces, and the climate of the times has affected their rulings on jury selection. Naturally, it also affects whether certain cases are brought to the courts at all. (It is true that passage of the Fourteenth Amendment in 1868 opened the way for the Supreme Court's consideration of state-court-jury challenges, but it is more important that the issue of blacks on juries in the South was moot before emancipation. Similarly, charges of discrimination against women on juries could not be expected to receive a hearing until women obtained the vote.) A survey of jury challenges reveals a checkered history, with significant gains on the part of those charging discrimination often followed by long periods of stagnation or even reversal.

## RACIAL DISCRIMINATION

In 1880, twelve years after the Fourteenth Amendment added the equal protection clause to our Constitution, the Supreme Court declared unconstitutional a West Virginia statute that explicitly limited jury service to "[all] *white* male persons" and thus overtly discriminated against all blacks and other nonwhites (*Strauder v. West Virginia*).[22] The Court indicated in this early opinion, however, that some "standards" could be erected to exclude persons from jury service, and the "standards" they suggested would limit service to educated male property-holders. Justice William Strong wrote the following language for the Court:

> We do not say that within the limits from which it is not excluded by the [Fourteenth] Amendment a State may not prescribe the qualifications of its jurors, and in so doing make discriminations. *It may confine the selection to males, to freeholders, to citizens, to persons within certain ages, or to persons having educational qualifications.* We do not believe the Fourteenth Amendment was ever intended to prohibit this.[23]

More recent Supreme Court decisions have stated that virtually all of these "standards" serve to discriminate unconstitutionally against protected groups ("cognizable classes") in our society,[24] but the road away from *Strauder* has been slow. The Court did not, for instance, finally rule unconstitutional overt discrimination against women until 1975.[25]

During the first fifty-five years following the *Strauder* decision, the Supreme Court was not receptive to any jury challenges except in truly extreme situations. The Court reversed jury selection schemes if overt discrimination was authorized by statute or was undisputed[26] and sent challenges back to lower courts if the trial judge refused to hear arguments altogether.[27] Generally, however, the *Strauder* "standards" barred the challenge, and if racial discrimination was involved, the Court frequently discovered procedural barriers that allowed it to avoid the issue.[28] Given the tenor of the times—the end of Reconstruction, Jim Crow laws, the *Plessy v. Ferguson*[29] decision approving "separate but equal" facilities—it should probably not be surprising that the Court seemed less than eager to find opportunities to increase black representation on juries.

A typical example of the Court's approach during this period was *Thomas v. Texas* (1909),[30] which demonstrates the Court's reluctance to interfere with state court procedures, no matter how discriminatory they were. Thomas, a black charged with rape, alleged that because of racial discrimination no more than one black person ever sat on the twelve-member Harris County (Houston) grand juries and that no blacks were to be found on his jury venire, even though one-fourth of the population was black. The evidence introduced at the hearing corroborated Thomas's allegations and showed, in addition, that only about one black per week was drawn for the trial jury panel that supplied jurors for all the courts in the county. Nonetheless, the Texas appellate court ruled that no unconstitutional discrimination had taken place.[31] Their "explanation" consisted of quotations from the jury commissioners, who testified that they did not discriminate, that they were flooded with qualified white jurors, and that blacks tended to be eligible for excuses more often than whites. Despite the drastic underrepresentation of blacks on these juries, the U.S. Supreme Court affirmed the Texas decision, accepting the state court's "factual" decision on what constitutes discrimination. The deferential language of Chief Justice Melville Weston Fuller reads as follows:

> As before remarked, whether such discrimination was practiced in this case was a question of fact, and the determination of that question adversely to plaintiff in error by the trial court and by the Court of Criminal Appeals was decisive, so far as this court is concerned, unless it could be held that these decisions constitute such abuse as amounted to an

infraction of the Federal Constitution, which cannot be presumed, and which there is no reason to hold on the record before us. On the contrary, the careful opinion of the Court of Criminal Appeals, setting forth the evidence, justified the conclusion of that court that the negro race was not intentionally or otherwise discriminated against in the selection of the grand and petit jurors.[32]

The Supreme Court heard no challenges to jury selection methods between 1909 and 1935, perhaps because the stringent requirements laid down in the cases before 1909 inhibited defendants from raising the issue.

In 1935, with the case of *Norris v. Alabama*,[33] a new era in jury challenges began. In this case the Supreme Court for the first time looked more skeptically at claims by governmental officials that they did not intend to discriminate. The lawyers for Clarence Norris (a black teenager) presented a sophisticated challenge, calling elderly men to testify that in their memory no black had ever served on a grand jury in Jackson County, Alabama, where Norris was indicted, and showing that blacks were also absent from the trial juries of Morgan County, where Norris was convicted (of rape) and sentenced to death. A Jackson County clerk testified that after he made up his list of male citizens in the county, someone else reviewed the list, putting the abbreviation "col." next to the names of the colored males. Similar evidence was produced for Morgan County. The prosecution responded by presenting affidavits and oral testimony by members of the jury board—much like the evidence presented in *Thomas v. Texas*—that they simply did not consider race when compiling their lists of qualified jurors. The Alabama Supreme Court concluded that because the accused had not proved "intentional discrimination" the conviction should stand.

The U.S. Supreme Court reversed the conviction, however, this time refusing to accept the "factual" determination of the state courts on the question of discrimination. In an opinion written by Chief Justice Charles Evans Hughes, the Court reviewed the facts on its own and articulated for the first time the notion that once the accused established a "prima facie case" of discrimination, the burden of proof then shifts to the prosecution to explain the apparent discrimination. A simple statement by the jury commissioners that they did not consider race was not considered enough to nullify a showing of apparent discrimination.

Much of the litigation that followed *Norris v. Alabama* concerned the question of what constitutes a "prima facie case" of discrimination and what the government must do to rebut such a case once made. Figures are a necessary element in establishing such a case, but figures in themselves have not been enough to prove discrimination. The courts have always looked for some other factor that establishes the "opportunity to discriminate." Since 1935, the Court has decided an average of one case each year, ruling in favor of the challengers in many instances, but always requiring extensive proof on a case-by-case basis and refusing to lay down a rule that would require uniform selection schemes or that would reduce the burdens placed on litigants who feel that their juries have been selected through discriminatory methods.

*Smith v. Texas* (1940),[34] whose facts were almost identical to those of the 1909 case of *Thomas v. Texas*,[35] —but whose result is opposite—illustrates the difference in the Court's approach. Both cases occurred in Harris County, Texas, and both challenged the composition of the indicting grand jury. Texas grand jurors are selected by three to five jury commissioners, who are appointed by the presiding trial judge. They prepare a list of about sixteen names, from which the judge selects twelve (usually the first twelve on the list) to serve as grand jurors. During the years 1931-38, of 512 persons on those lists only 18 were black: 13 of the blacks were placed at the bottom of the list (number 16); 4 others were numbers 13, 14, or 15; and only 1 was put among the first 12. Of the persons who actually became grand jurors, only 5 were black (and of those 5, 3 were actually the same black man who was selected three different times) compared to 379 whites.

The jury commissioners testified that they had not intentionally discriminated, but Justice Hugo Black, writing for the Court's majority, rejected their testimony, saying that "chance or accident" could not account for the low number of blacks or the location they were given on the lists. Thus, the figures combined with the "opportunity to discriminate" (through the system of "personal selection") to make a successful challenge.

*Smith* is also important because it is the first case in which the Court explicitly stated that the jury, to be an "instrument" of "public justice," must be "a body truly representative of the community."[36] To justify this important perception, Justice Black compared jury duty to all other functions that bring citizens and the government together:

> For racial discrimination to result in the exclusion from jury service of otherwise qualified groups not only violates our Constitution and the laws enacted under it but is at war with our basic concepts of a democratic society and a representative government.[37]

This strong language was picked up two years later by Justice Frank Murphy in *Glasser v. United States* (1942),[38] where the defendants alleged by affidavit that all women on the jury venire were members of the League of Women Voters who had received lectures at which the views of the prosecution were presented. In his majority opinion, Justice Murphy writes eloquently about the importance of the jury as a "shield against oppression," quotes Justice Black in *Smith* about the notion of representativeness, says explicitly that "whatever limitations were inherent in the historical common law concept of the jury as a body of one's peers do not prevail in this country," and condemns "the deliberate selection of jurors from the membership of particular private organizations" which would make the jury "the organ of a special class" and "openly partisan." And for the first time, a majority opinion of the Court uses the words "a cross-section of the community" as the standard for jury selection:

> The officials charged with choosing federal jurors ... must not allow the desire for competent jurors to lead them into selections which do not comport with the concept of the jury as a *cross-section of the community*.[39]

But Justices Black and Murphy quickly found themselves in the minority in *Akins v. Texas* (1945),[40] a case that considered the extent of evidence necessary to establish a prima facie case of discrimination (and also in the important case of *Fay v. New York* [1947],[41] discussed below, p. 63, in which the elite or blue-ribbon jury was approved, although it clearly did not reflect a cross-section of the community). *Akins* concerned a grand jury selected in Dallas County, Texas, which had indicted a black man who was later convicted and sentenced to death for murder. Because only one black was on the indicting twelve-member grand jury, the defendant raised the claim of racial discrimination. All three of the jury commissioners testified that they consciously sought one black grand juror—no more, no less. Dallas County was then 15.5 percent black, indicating that an average of 1.9 blacks should have served on each twelve-person grand jury, but no more than one black had in fact ever been selected.

Despite the explicit testimony of the three jury commissioners, Justice Stanley Reed's opinion for the majority concluded that a "careful examination of these statements in connection with all the other evidence leaves us unconvinced that the commissioners deliberately and intentionally limited the number of Negroes on the grand jury list."[42] Justice Murphy dissented, saying, "Clearer proof of intentional and deliberate limitation on the basis of color would be difficult to produce,"[43] but he was able to gain only the votes of Justice Black and Chief Justice Harlan Fiske Stone.

Nonwhite defendants were left adrift after this opinion. Figures showing underrepresentation were apparently not adequate to establish a prima facie case of discrimination, nor were explicit statements by the jury commissioners of their intention to limit nonwhite representation.

Lower court judges were also confused because it seemed impossible to reconcile the statements in *Smith* and *Glasser* with the results in *Akins* and *Fay*. Judge Learned Hand of the U.S. Court of Appeals for the Second Circuit, in reviewing the jury selection that had preceded the major trial of the leaders of the U.S. Communist party in the late 1940s,[44] described the prevailing standards in language that recalls the "standards" given to us 70 years earlier in *Strauder:*

> It is perhaps in order to say a word about the phrase itself—"cross-section"—because the defendants so much rely upon it. It means a fair sample; and a sample drawn at random from the whole community will of course represent the distribution of wealth in the community as a whole, as it would represent the distribution of age, height, predisposition to sclerosis, or any other characteristic; but nobody contends that the list must be a sample of the whole community. Minors and the aged are excluded, as are the infirm and those of unsound mind, and practically so are all the exempt; a sample at random with any of those included would be different from that which concededly the law may and does prescribe. It is therefore idle to talk of the justness of a sample until one knows what is the composition of the group which it is to represent. As we have seen, not only does the law exclude the groups we have just mentioned, but it excludes those who do not satisfy the very modest financial minimum still retained; and those also who cannot pass an examination as to other prescribed qualities—intelligence, character and general information. . . . There cannot of course be any doubt that the resulting sample is different from what it would have been had the clerk sent out notices to all districts, based on their population, thus abandoning any effort to make any selection in advance.[45]

The words "cross-section" as thus interpreted did not mean "cross-section" of the community but instead cross-section of whatever segment of the community was legally designated for jury duty, and therefore these words placed no real limit on restrictive selection procedures.

The Court maintained this somewhat ambiguous approach through the 1960s and has only in the 1970s clarified the governing standards. The last of the ambiguous cases was *Swain v. Alabama* (1965),[46] which needs to be explained in some length because it has had a substantial influence on lower court decisions. The case involved a challenge to the jury selection procedure of Talladega County, Alabama, brought by a 19-year-old black male (Robert

Swain) who was convicted of raping a 17-year-old white female and sentenced to death. Blacks made up 26 percent of the over-21 male population of the county, but they constituted only between 10 and 15 percent of the grand and trial jury panels during the preceding ten-year period. Two blacks served on the 18-member grand jury that indicted Swain. No blacks served on his trial jury, and in fact, no black had served on a trial jury in Talladega County since 1950 because those few who were included on the jury venires were invariably challenged peremptorily or for cause in the process of selection.[a]

Constance Baker Motley, who represented Swain and is now a federal judge in New York, presented a sophisticated and carefully argued challenge to what was probably the most liberal Supreme Court ever assembled, and they rejected the challenge outright. Justice Byron R. White, after giving the facts of the case and describing the methods of selecting jurors, concluded:

> Venires drawn from the jury box made up in this manner unquestionably contained a smaller proportion of the Negro community than of the white community. But a defendant in a criminal case is not constitutionally entitled to demand a proportionate number of his race on the jury which tries him nor on the venire or jury roll from which petit jurors are drawn. . . . Neither the jury roll nor the venire need be a perfect mirror of the community or accurately reflect the proportionate strength of every identifiable group. . . . We cannot say that purposeful discrimination based on race alone is satisfactorily proved by showing that an identifiable group in a community is underrepresented by as much as 10 percent. . . . Here the commissioners denied that racial considerations entered into their selections of either their contacts in the community or the names of prospective jurors. . . . The overall percentage disparity has been small and reflects no studied attempt to include or exclude a specified number of Negroes. Undoubtedly the selection of prospective jurors was somewhat haphazard and little effort was made to ensure that all groups in the community were fully represented. But an imperfect system is not equivalent to purposeful discrimination based on race. We do not think that the burden of proof was carried by petitioner in this case.[47]

This opinion seems to be inconsistent with both earlier and later Supreme Court decisions. Although Justice White's statement that proportionate representation is not required on every jury has been the consistent view of the courts, his acceptance of disproportion *over time* contradicts the principles expressed in *Smith* and *Glasser*. According to *Swain*, a jury representing a cross-section of the community is not constitutionally required. Furthermore, although

---

[a]For a discussion of the *Swain* challenges, see Chapter Six, p. 150.

mere numbers have never been enough to prove discrimination in the courts, numerical evidence combined with the "opportunity to discriminate" were persuasive in such cases as *Norris* and *Smith.* Yet here, Justice White both gives the figures a very questionable reading and accepts statements by the jury commissioners at face value. Justice White calls the disparity between black population and representation on juries "small," referring to the underrepresentation—10 to 15 percent of jurors *versus* 26 percent of the population—as "10 percent."[48]   In fact, using the comparative method adopted by White in a later decision, blacks were underrepresented by *50 percent*—that is, 50 percent fewer blacks were on the jury venires than would have been the case if the selection process had been truly fair.[b]

The Supreme Court has handed down three significant racial discrimination opinions since *Swain* that undercut the force of the 1965 decision to a large extent.[49]   In each, the Court has been sympathetic to the challenge and has used strong language stating that selection schemes should not discriminate. But the justices have not explicitly repudiated *Swain* and still indicate that they require something more than mere numerical disparity before they will reverse a conviction.

*Carter v. Jury Commission of Greene County* (1970)[50] is important because it is the first case in which the Court permitted a group of citizens to bring suit charging that they had been denied the right to serve on a jury. (Previously, only defendants arguing that their right to a fair trial had been denied were allowed to raise jury challenges.) The Court thus recognized the "right" to equal consideration in the selection of jurors. The district court had ordered the Greene County (Alabama) jury commissioners to stop systematically excluding blacks from the jury rolls but did not—as the petitioners had wanted—declare unconstitutional the Alabama statutes giving discretion to the local jury commissioners or order the governor to appoint black jury commissioners. The Supreme Court affirmed both parts of this ruling, saying that the states "remain free to confine the selection [of jurors] to citizens, to persons meeting specified qualifications . . . and to those possessing good intelligence, sound judgment, and fair character."[51] But the Court emphasized that once the state decides to use discretionary criteria it has an affirmative duty to seek out persons from all parts of the community who meet these standards.

*Turner v. Fouche* (1970),[52] announced the same day as *Carter*, involved Taliaferro County, Georgia, which is 60 percent black but

---

bSee below, p. 60.

whose jury roll contained only 37 percent blacks. The unanimous opinion, written by Justice Potter Stewart, came close to saying that these figures alone constituted a prima facie case of discrimination:

> In the absence of a countervailing explanation by the appellees, we cannot say that the underrepresentation reflected in these figures is so insubstantial as to warrant no corrective action by a federal court charged with the responsibility of enforcing constitutional guarantees.[53]

Because the percent of underrepresentation or "rate of error" in *Turner*, using the comparative method (38.3 percent),[c] is less than the percent of underrepresentation in *Swain* (about 50 percent), it could be argued that the Court was undercutting its earlier strict *Swain* test. But the Court then proceeded to point to two additional considerations that helped establish a prima facie case of discrimination in *Turner*, thus again indicating that figures alone are not enough: (1) Of the 178 persons excused "as not conforming to the statutory qualifications for juries either because of their being unintelligent or because of their not being upright citizens," 171 were black—a clear showing of discriminatory use of discretion; and (2) 225 persons were eliminated from the jury rolls because the jury commissioners could obtain no information about them, and the Court assumed that many of these were black because the jury commissioners all were white.

In the most recent Supreme Court case involving racial discrimination, *Alexander v. Louisiana* (1972),[54] the jury selection methods of Lafayette Parish, Louisiana, were challenged. The parish had a population that was 21.1 percent black, but the returned jury questionnaires, which provided a space for "race", contained only 13.8 percent blacks. Only one out of the twenty-person grand jury challenged by the petitioner was black, and none of his trial jurors was black. Justice White's opinion for the Court said that the mathematical demonstration was persuasive but not alone decisive. Because the statistics were combined with the "opportunity to discriminate" in the selection process, however, this procedure must fall:

> This Court has never announced mathematical standards for the demonstration of "systematic" exclusion of blacks but has rather emphasized that a factual inquiry is necessary in each case which takes into account all possible explanatory factors. The progressive decimation of potential Negro grand jurors is indeed striking here, but we do not rest our conclusion that petitioner has demonstrated a prima facie case of invidious racial discrimination on statistical improbability alone, for the selection

---

[c]See below, pp. 60 and 94-98.

procedures themselves were not racially neutral. The racial designation on both the questionnaire and the information card provided a clear and easy *opportunity for racial discrimination.*[55]

It was in *Alexander v. Louisiana* that the Supreme Court first used the "comparative" method of computing underrepresentation (in which a group's percent of the jury pool is subtracted from its percent of the adult population and then that figure is divided by the percent of the population) rather than the "absolute" method employed in *Swain* (in which the percent of the jury pool is simply subtracted from the percent of the population). In *Alexander*, Justice Byron White referred to the drop-off from the black population of 21 percent to 14 percent in the jury pool as "a reduction of one-third"[56] and the subsequent reduction to 7 percent on the list of qualified jurors as a "further reduction by one-half."[57] (That is, 14 is 7 less than 21, and 7 is one-third of 21; 7 is one-half of 14.) In *Swain*, by contrast, White had examined data showing that blacks made up 26 percent of the population and 10 to 15 percent of the jury rolls and concluded that they were underrepresented by "10 percent."[58] (Correcting his faulty subtraction, we can assume he meant "11 to 16 percent" rather than "10 percent.") This proportion reflects the absolute percent of underrepresentation from a basis of 100. Using a comparative method, as White did in the 1972 case, the percent of underrepresentation in *Swain* is 50 percent. That is, blacks held half—50 percent fewer—the number of seats they would have held if the jury included a fair cross-section of the community.

The comparative computation system has gained increasing acceptance since *Alexander.*[59] Its advantages were explained by U.S. District Judge Charles B. Renfrew of San Francisco, in a recent opinion accepting a jury challenge in which the author participated as one of the attorneys for the plaintiffs:

> This calculation [the comparative method] is useful because the importance of a difference of a given amount, for example, 10%, varies depending upon the magnitude of the group's representation in the population. A disparity of 10% constitutes a far more significant underrepresentation when the group comprises 12% of the population but only 2% of the grand jury (−83%) [under the comparative method] than when the group comprises 60% of the population but only 50% of the grand jury (−20%)[60] [*sic:* should be −17%].

Because problems in statistical accuracy may arise if the population group examined constitutes less than 5 percent of the whole population, the absolute figures should be looked at as well. But given that caution, the comparative method is more revealing of the success of a selection scheme in achieving—or failing to achieve—the goal of producing a representative jury.

It is still impossible to say just what kind of a showing on mathematical grounds must be made before a litigant will be said to have established a "prima facie case" of discrimination, which shifts the burden of proof to the government to justify its method of selection.[d] The process of establishing a "prima facie" case is, however, much easier if a litigant is attacking a "discretionary" selection scheme because the "opportunity to discriminate" is obvious. Compare the following two 1974 cases.

In *Thompson v. Sheppard,*[61] a challenge was made to a selection scheme based on the voter registration list, which underrepresented blacks by 36.7 percent (30.2 percent of the adults in Dougherty County, Georgia; 19.2 percent on the 1972 jury rolls) and women by 28.1 percent (52.7 percent in the county, 37.9 percent on the jury rolls). The panel of federal appeals judges barely noticed these figures and said that the challenge should fail because the selection scheme used a random approach:

> We conclude that a jury list drawn objectively, mechanically, and at random from the entire voting list of a county is entitled to the presumption that it is drawn from a source which is a fairly representative cross-section of the inhabitants of that jurisdiction. The presumption, of course, is rebuttable but the challenger must carry the burden of showing that the product of such a procedure is, in fact, constitutionally defective.[62]

No guidance is provided on the question of what might constitute a sufficient "rebuttal" of the presumption.

In *Quadra v. Superior Court of San Francisco (II)*[63] the figures for the 1970-75 San Francisco Grand Juries, whose members were hand-picked by Superior Court judges, showed an underrepresentation ranging from 5.2 percent to 86.3 percent for nonwhites and ranging from 49.8 percent to 89.9 percent for women. Judge Renfrew found that a prima facie case had been presented, that the "opportunity to discriminate" clearly existed, and that the explanation by the Superior Court judges of San Francisco that they were trying to select a "qualified" grand jury was inadequate to meet the burden imposed upon them. Judge Renfrew concluded:

---

[d]See Chapter Four, pp. 94-98, for a more complete discussion of the level of underrepresentation or "rate of error" that will trigger judicial scrutiny of a jury selection scheme.

[T]he application of the so-called higher qualifications was done in a complete *ad hoc*, discretionary manner. In the absence of articulated standards, it is impossible for the Court to ensure that the standards are, in fact, related to the task facing the civil investigative grand jury. Similarly, it is impossible to determine what percentage of the various identifiable groups in the community have the requisite qualifications. Without that information, it is impossible to determine whether the grand jury represents "a cross-section of the population suitable in character and intelligence for that civic duty." *Brown v. Allen*, 344 U.S. 443, 474 (1953).[64]

Judge Renfrew thus saw in the disproportionate figures (which were not contested) an implicit discrimination, a failure to ensure nondiscrimination by ascertaining what proportion of members of given groups is qualified for jury service on the basis of objective standards.

This approach could easily be applied to randomly selected juries as well, imposing on the government the burden of justifying, for instance, the exclusive use of the voter registration list as the source for jurors when nonwhites and other groups are thereby clearly underrepresented. The "opportunity to discriminate" exists in this situation, too, because the voter registration list has been chosen as the exclusive source for jurors by persons with the knowledge that the choice will lead to underrepresentation of certain groups. No court has yet taken this approach, however, and at the moment, random selection methods appear to have a strange immunity from judicial scrutiny.

## ECONOMIC DISCRIMINATION

The ambiguous attitude toward racial discrimination that flared forth most dramatically in the late 1940s can also be seen in Court opinions involving discrimination against the poor. The Court ruled in 1946 that overt discrimination against a potential juror because of his or her economic status was improper, but when faced the following year with a dramatic example of a "blue-ribbon" jury selected almost exclusively from among the wealthy, the Court refused by a narrow margin (5-4) to strike down the scheme.

The first case was *Thiel v. Southern Pacific Co.* (1946),[65] in which the plaintiff challenged the policy of the clerk in the federal court for the Northern District of California of intentionally excluding from jury rolls all persons who worked for a daily wage. The clerk's stated reason for the policy was to spare such persons the financial hardship they would suffer if they served on a jury. In ordering a new trial, Justice Frank Murphy wrote: "One who is paid $3 a day may be as fully competent as one who is paid $30 a week or $300 a month." The justice affirmed the concept of a representative jury with the following language:

> The American tradition of trial by jury, considered in connection with either criminal or civil proceedings, necessarily contemplates an impartial jury drawn from a cross-section of the community. *Smith v. Texas*, 311 U.S. 128, 130; *Glasser v. United States*, 315 U.S. 60, 85. This does not mean, of course, that every jury must contain representatives of all the economic, social, religious, racial, political and geographical groups of the community; frequently such complete representation would be impossible. But it does mean that prospective jurors shall be selected by court officials without systematic and intentional exclusion of any of these groups. *Recognition must be given to the fact those eligible for jury service are to be found in every strata of society.* Jury competence is an individual rather than a group or class matter. That fact lies at the very heart of the jury system. *To disregard it is to open the door to class distinctions and discriminations which are abhorrent to the democratic ideals of trial by jury.*[66]

This statement of ideals has not, however, ended discrimination against people in lower socioeconomic strata, perhaps because most such discrimination in jury selection is more subtle than the clerk's policy in *Thiel*. Blue-collar workers are underrepresented on the jury panels of virtually all courts in the United States because they are granted excuses individually and because they are underrepresented on voter registration lists. The Supreme Court in *Thiel* seems to have given tacit approval to the practice of excusing persons for individual hardship with the following almost off-handed statement (it may not have realized the full implications of the remark):

> It is clear that a federal judge would be justified in excusing a daily wage earner for whom jury service would entail an undue financial hardship.[67]

The second case involving discrimination against socioeconomic groups was *Fay v. New York* (1947),[68] which explicitly gave constitutional sanction to the blue-ribbon jury. Although the practice has been ended in recent years, courts in New York State for many years impaneled "special juries" to decide cases of particular intricacy or notoriety. To qualify for the special jury panel, a person had to believe in the death penalty, believe in the value of circumstantial evidence (which is almost always favorable to the prosecution), and favor all the laws of the state. A survey of the 2,911 special jurors on the 1945 panel for New York County (Manhattan) indicated that only 30 were women and that of the 2,664 with classifiable occupations, 18.8 percent were professionals (compared with 12.1 percent in the Manhattan work force, according to the 1940 census), 43 percent were managers, proprietors, and administrators (compared with 9.3 percent in the work force as a whole), 38 percent were clerical and sales workers (compared with 21.3 percent in the work force), 0.2 percent were skilled craftsmen or foremen (compared with 7.7 percent in the county work force), and none at all were laborers, service workers, or operatives (even though 57.3 percent of the Manhattan work force had such occupations).[69] (A 1933-34 study, acknowledged by the Supreme Court along with the preceding data, indicated that special jurors convicted at a rate of about 82.5 percent in certain homicide cases, while ordinary juries convicted at a rate of 40 percent in comparable cases.)[70] It would be difficult to imagine a more compelling showing of an unrepresentative jury; yet the Court majority, speaking through a Roosevelt-appointee, Justice Robert H. Jackson, rejected the challenge. The Court said that purposeful and intentional discrimination had not been proved and that without such a demonstration local procedures would be accepted as constitutional.

The reasoning behind this decision has definitely been undermined by the later cases of *Carter, Turner v. Fouche, Alexander*, and *Taylor v. Louisiana*,[e] but it has been extraordinarily difficult to vindicate, through appeals, the rights of those underrepresented on juries because of their economic status. Almost all juries today continue to underrepresent blue-collar workers and the poor in large numbers, usually through more subtle methods than those challenged in *Fay*.

Challenges to underrepresentation caused by exclusive reliance on the voter registration list—on which the poor and blue-collar workers are underrepresented—are difficult, time-consuming, expensive, and traditionally unsuccessful. One sophisticated attempt, nevertheless, was made in 1973 in the U.S. District Court for the Eastern District of Louisiana (*United States v. McDaniels*).[71] After conducting an elaborate set of interviews and gathering data from many sources, the defense showed that because food-stamp recipients register to vote at a much lower rate (30 percent versus 77.8 percent for the general population) they are underrepresented on federal juries in the area by 61.4 percent. Although Judge Alvin B. Rubin indicated that he was impressed with these figures, he disallowed the challenge to the exclusive use of the voter registration list because he did not consider the poor a "cognizable class." Rubin argued that it is impossible to define the poor:

---

eSee below, p. 67.

Unlike race, religion, sex or national origin, which are determinable binarially, economic status is entirely a matter of degree. There can be little doubt that a married couple with an annual income of $2,850 and no savings would consider themselves "poor." But they are not eligible for food stamps. The division of the entire population into "poor" and "not poor" persons creates an illusion of a real dividing line where none exists in fact. For there is no national standard of who is poor and who is not poor. The classification of persons by a specific dollar income, resulting in a household of one income being in one classification, and another—with only $1.00 more annual income being in another—serves a useful function to determine who may be eligible for a public benefit, but it is entirely arbitrary if used as the sole criterion of economic status or of poverty, for jury purposes.[72]

Such reasoning is not convincing because, as Rubin noted, the poor have been defined by some government agencies and could be identified for purposes of jury service as well, even though the definition would be arbitrary. Our definitions of race (in terms of the fraction necessary to qualify as a member of a race) are also arbitrary but useful in measuring discrimination. But the Supreme Court has been reluctant to rectify discrimination based on economic status in many areas other than jury selection,[73] and Judge Rubin's opinion in *McDaniel* is consistent with the high court's recent views.[74]

## SEX DISCRIMINATION

Women, like blue-collar workers, have been underrepresented on juries primarily because of excuses: excuses on request in some jurisdictions, much more liberal granting of excuses to mothers than fathers in most other districts, and, until 1975, total exclusion from some juries of all but those women who volunteered.

The right of a woman to serve on a jury at all has not always been accepted. The Supreme Court's initial statement on sex discrimination on juries was in *Strauder v. West Virginia* (1880), where Justice William Strong wrote that courts can limit jury service "to *males*," as well as to certain other groups.[75] This view remained the governing constitutional standard for many years, and the Court did not have occasion to consider the question again until *Ballard v. United States* (1946).[76] At that time, the federal courts were statutorily required to select their jurors in the same manner as the courts of the state in which they were located. California had been seating women on its local juries, but the federal courts in California were slow to adopt this practice. When the failure of the federal courts to include women was challenged, the court reversed the challenger's conviction, with language that directly contravenes the *Strauder* opinion. Justice William O. Douglas included the following important paragraph in his opinion for the Court in *Ballard*:

> It is said . . . that an all male panel drawn from the various groups within a community will be as truly representative as if women were included. The thought is that the factors which tend to influence the action of women are the same as those which influence the action of men—personality, background, economic status—and not sex. Yet it is not enough to say that women when sitting as jurors neither act nor tend to act as a class. Men likewise do not act as a class. But, if the shoe were on the other foot, who would claim that a jury was truly representative of the community if all men were intentionally and systematically excluded from the panel? *The truth is that the two sexes are not fungible; a community made up exclusively of one is different from a community composed of both; the subtle interplay of influence one on the other is among the imponderables.* To insulate the courtroom from either may not in a given case make an iota of difference. *Yet a flavor, a distinct quality is lost if either sex is excluded. The exclusion of one may indeed make the jury less representative of the community than would be true if an economic or racial group were excluded.*[77]

Despite this far-reaching view, however, the *Ballard* decision was subsequently seen as simply interpreting the statute requiring the federal courts to follow state practice rather than establishing a constitutional standard that governed all courts.[78] State legislatures slowly began altering their rules that restricted women on juries, but independent of any federal court rulings on the matter.

The Supreme Court's view of women (or its acceptance of the changing role of women in society) has been evolving over the years, as can be seen by comparing a 1961 ruling with a 1975 decision on a similar issue. In *Hoyt v. Florida* (1961),[79] a woman convicted of killing her husband with a baseball bat complained that she had been denied her right to the "due process of law" because she had been tried by an all-male jury. Florida's practice at the time was to include on its jury rolls only those women who volunteered for jury service, a very small group (about 20 out of 10,000). The Supreme Court rejected Mrs. Hoyt's challenge, stating that Florida's legislative choice was based on a "reasonable classification." As the opinion written by Justice John M. Harlan put it:

> Despite the enlightened emancipation of women from the restrictions and protections of bygone years, and their entry into many parts of community life formerly considered to be reserved to men, *woman is still*

*regarded as the center of home and family life.* We cannot say that it is constitutionally impermissible for a State, acting in pursuit of the general welfare, to conclude that a woman should be relieved from the civic duty of jury service unless she herself determines that such service is consistent with her own special responsibilities.[80]

The Court finally reversed this view in *Taylor v. Louisiana* (1975),[81] when it overturned a Louisiana law that, like the Florida statute in *Hoyt*, limited jury duty among women to those who volunteered. Justice Byron White, writing for the majority, declared:

... [W]e agree with the Court in *Ballard*: If the fair cross-section rule is to govern the selection of juries, as we have concluded it must, women cannot be systematically excluded from jury panels from which petit juries are drawn.[82]

In reversing its stand in *Hoyt*, the Court cited statistics on the extensive employment of women outside the home.

The 1975 decision did not end the problem of underrepresentation of women on juries because the Court made a distinction between blanket exemptions for women and exemptions for "individuals in the case of special hardship or incapacity," along with those in certain important occupations. The Court stated that it was "untenable to suggest these days that it would be a special hardship for each and every woman to perform jury service or that society cannot spare *any* woman in their present duties."[83] Thus, the Court rejected exclusion of all women but upheld the principle of excuses for hardship. Of the latter, it said: "It would not appear that such exemptions would pose substantial threats that the remaining pool of jurors would not be representative of the community."[84]

*Taylor* thus seems to state that statutes allowing all women an automatic excuse or excusing all mothers of small children (although not fathers) are still permissible. All the lower courts that ruled on the issue prior to *Taylor* upheld such statutes.[85] These statutes fall within the broad category of "protective legislative," i.e., laws that purport to protect women from the rigors of society but which may in fact simply deny women a full and equal role in that society. In *Kahn v. Shevin* (1974),[86] the most recent case involving such protective legislation, the Court found constitutional a Florida statute that discriminated in favor of women by granting to widows a $500 property exemption while denying the same bonus to widowers. *Kahn v. Shevin* may stand for the proposition that all protective legislation is constitutional, but further litigation will be needed to clarify the issue.

## AGE DISCRIMINATION

The young and the aged, like women and the poor, tend to be excused from jury duty more often than the general population. In many states, persons over sixty-five are granted easy or automatic excuses, without having to show hardship or even inconvenience— merely because they are old. In such states, the older persons who actually serve as jurors—like the women in Louisiana before its restrictive statute was overturned—are really volunteers. Some courts are beginning to become sensitive to discrimination against the aged, but the idea is still a novel one. The Supreme Court ruled in 1976 that a Massachusetts requirement that state police officers must retire at age 50 was constitutional[87] thus saying that some discriminations based on age are permissible. The government's interest in a youthful police force is, however, substantially more justifiable than the government's interest in juries without young adults and senior citizens.

As yet, no explicit challenges to the jury selection schemes that underrepresent the aged have been mounted. One case that might serve as a precedent is the jury challenge that preceded the trials of the Attica defendants in 1974. Justice Gilbert H. King of the Erie County (New York) Supreme Court ruled, citing *Thiel*, that the automatic granting of excuses to students was unconstitutional because, he wrote, "Complete exclusion of a class regardless of motivation and regardless of whether there is actual hardship involved is impermissible."[88] The Supreme Court, however, has not yet expressed this view in quite such explicit language, and many courts continue to grant automatic excuses.

Most schemes that underrepresent the young on juries have been permitted to stand by the lower courts, and few challenges of the schemes have reached the Supreme Court. The lower courts have sharply divided on the question whether the young form a "cognizable class." Some courts have ruled that they do,[89] but a larger number have decided the other way.[90] The Supreme Court was faced with the problem in 1974 and "assumed, without deciding" that the young *did* form a cognizable class, but it then ruled that a showing of systematic exclusion had not been established.[91] Because the challenge was not allowed, the legal question is still open.

It is surprising that the courts have been somewhat reluctant to acknowledge that the young form a cognizable class, because logic and Supreme Court precedent both point in that direction. According to the quote from *Hernandez v. Texas* (1954) printed earlier in this chapter at page 48, a "cognizable class" is simply (1) a commonly recognized group (2) whose members hold some common perspectives because of their membership in that group, and (3) that may be subject to conscious or unconscious discrimination by government officials. The young are certainly recognized in the common vernacular as a group, the surveys discussed in Chapter Two indicate that the young do differ in their thinking from other adults, and the figures printed in Appendix H indicate that the young are substantially underrepresented on our juries. Under the prevailing standards, therefore, the young should be acknowledged to be a "cognizable class."

Judges that have reached the opposite conclusion have taken a much more restrictive view of this doctrine. Federal Judge Charles M. Metzner (of the Southern District of New York) said in the context of a challenge to the underrepresentation of the young, that "cognizable" groups must:

> (1) have a definite composition without arbitrarily chosen members; (2) be cohesive in terms of a basic similarity in attitudes, ideas, or experience; and (3) have a community of interest that cannot be adequately protected by the rest of the populace.[92]

Requirement 2 does not seem to be appropriate if strictly applied, because no racial, ethnic, or socioeconomic group has a rigorous ideological cohesiveness, and it seems to have been rejected in language used by Justice Thurgood Marshall in the case of *Peters v. Kiff* (1972), a case involving exclusion of blacks:

> *It is not necessary to assume that the excluded group will consistently vote as a class* in order to conclude, as we do, that their exclusion deprives the jury of a perspective on human events that may have unsuspected importance in any case that may be presented.[93]

Requirement 3 seems a little patronizing, in assuming that it is permissible to discriminate as long as the group discriminated against is "protected" by the majority. And Requirement 1 could not be met even by racial groups if strictly applied, because our mathematical definitions of who is a black or a Native-American, for example, are certainly arbitrary. All population groups exist along a spectrum, and a rigorous requirement of definiteness will eliminate all methods of grouping people. These overrigorous requirements are, nonetheless, illustrative of the reluctant view that many judges have taken toward acknowledging the existence of the young as a cognizable class.

One factor that keeps young people off juries in nine states is the retention of the age of twenty-one as the minimum for jury service. This exclusion seems illogical now that the voting age, and the age for virtually every other governmental function, is eighteen. Although eighteen is an arbitrary line, it is the almost universally accepted line demarking adulthood, and it has been argued that it has achieved a constitutional status of its own.[94]

The courts that have passed on the constitutionality of excluding 18-to-20 year olds on juries have not, however, accepted this analysis, and have uniformly rejected the challenges.[95] Although most judges have not explained their reasoning, Federal District Judge Charles M. Metzner's opinion in *United States v. Guzman* (1972)[96] did so by denying that the right to vote and the right to serve on a jury are similar:

> The right to vote and the right to sit in judgment of others have certain fundamental differences which cannot be overlooked. The act of voting is a personal expression of favor or disfavor for particular policies, personalities or laws. The voter is motivated by his personal self-interest, or what he considers best for the general populace. However, when one sits on a jury, he is required to accept and apply the law as the judge gives it to him, whether or not he agrees with it and no matter what his personal feelings are toward the parties in question. He must have the maturity and understanding to do what may often be an unpleasant task.[97]

This description of a juror's responsibilities is a narrow view that denies the historically important role that many courageous jurors have played in refusing to be a rubber stamp for judges and in refusing to convict defendants accused of violating unjust laws.[f] Jurors, like voters, serve to ensure that the government retains its common-sense humanity, and both are a link between the people and government.

Exclusive use of the voter registration list to select jury panels has thus far been upheld, even though it clearly underrepresents the young as well as other identifiable groups who are underrepresented on juries as a result.[g] The U.S. Court of Appeals for the Ninth Circuit, for instance, dismissed a challenge on these grounds, describing the "known propensity of younger persons" to neglect voting as a "self-inflicted" wound.[98]

The federal appellate court that reviewed (and reversed on other grounds) the conviction of David Dellinger, Tom Hayden, Abbie Hoffman, Jerry Rubin, and Rennie Davis, who were indicted after the 1968 Democratic Convention in Chicago, conceded that it would

---

[f]See Postscript: Jury Nullification, pp. 225-51.

[g]See Chapter Four, p. 89.

be "desirable" to supplement the voter lists with other lists of names because the young were clearly underrepresented and because "there are many attitudes toward life and government in which it is commonly thought that younger people generally differ from older people." But the court refused to rule that the exclusive use of the voter list was unconstitutional, because that list is so administratively convenient and the distortion that results is not "sufficient" to render the discrimination "invidious."[99]

Two additional practices serve to underrepresent the young because they are the most mobile segment of our population. (In an average year 42.6 percent of those between 20 and 24 move their residence, compared to only 9.1 percent of those between 45 and 64.)[100] One is the federal courts' practice of refilling their jury wheels only once every four years—ensuring that during the final year of each cycle no one under 21 and no one who has moved in the past three years will serve on a federal jury. Congress specifically approved this practice in 1972,[101] and every court that has passed on its constitutionality has upheld it.[102]

A second court practice with a similar effect is the requirement in the federal system and in eleven of the states that a person reside in the jurisdiction for a given period of time (usually one year) before she or he can be called for jury service. Residency requirements are one of the more peculiar anomalies of jury selection statutes because the Supreme Court has firmly denounced all residency requirements that infringe upon the related right of voting or that restrict access to other governmental activities such as welfare and publicly supported health care.

In *Shapiro v. Thompson* (1969),[103] the Supreme Court struck down a law imposing a one-year waiting period for welfare on the ground that the right to travel from state to state is a "fundamental right" basic to our scheme of government, and hence that the state cannot abridge that right unless it can demonstrate "a *compelling* governmental interest";[104] mere administrative convenience can never justify such an infringement.[h] Then, in *Dunn v. Blumstein* (1972),[105] the Court found unconstitutional Tennessee's voting requirement of one-year residency in the state and three months in the county (although a year later the Court was persuaded that a fifty-day residency requirement could be justified to meet the state's limited administrative interests).[106] Other courts have adopted this reasoning to strike down residency requirements for therapeutic abortions,[107] for employment by a state or municipality,[108] for licensing as a lawyer,[109] and for receipt of indigent hospitalization benefits.[110]

---

[h]For further discussion of this test, see pp. 72-76, below.

But no court has yet struck down a residency requirement for jury service.[111] No persuasive reasoning has been offered to justify a continuing residency for jury service when it is unconstitutional for virtually all other governmental functions. The stated reason for including a residency requirement in the federal statute was to assure "some substantial nexus between a juror and the community whose sense of justice the jury as a whole is expected to reflect."[112] That is the same kind of justification that was put forth by the state of Tennessee in the voting case and rejected by the U.S. Supreme Court. Persons new to a community are just as much a part of it as long-time residents and have a valid point of view on its activities. Those new residents selected for jury duty in fact should be seen as representing all new arrivals, who are otherwise denied their right to participate.

## JURY SERVICE IS A "FUNDAMENTAL RIGHT"[113]

The courts' consideration of jury challenges, as we have seen, began with the Fourteenth Amendment, which imposed almost all of the obligations of the Bill of Rights on the states. The courts' approach to jury selection cases has not, however, always conformed to its treatment of other Fourteenth Amendment issues. The Court has generally placed formidable obstacles in the way of those challenging jury selection schemes. If, instead, the Court applied its usual Equal Protection Clause tests to jury selection problems, it could overturn most jury selection schemes that discriminate against or underrepresent population groups.

In most situations, the Court will not disturb legislative or administrative actions that classify or categorize people if the classification scheme has some rational basis or reasonable relationship to the government's purpose.[114] But the Court alters this traditional stance of deference to the legislative judgment in two situations: (1) if the government operates a program that discriminates against persons in "suspect categories" (the suspect categories are race, national origin, alienage, and—for four justices—sex);[115] or (2) if the program is one involving "fundamental rights." In these situations, the Court will subject the scheme to a more rigorous standard of judicial review generally described as "strict scrutiny" and will strike it down unless the government can justify its result by some "compelling governmental interest."[116]

A "fundamental right" is a right so basic to our democratic government that the government must ensure the equal access of all citizens to it; all discrimination affecting access to the right must be eliminated unless justified by some "compelling state interest." The Supreme Court has explicitly recognized as "fundamental" rights the right of a criminal defendant to due process and a fair trial,[117] First Amendment rights to freedom of speech,[118] the right to vote,[119] the right to travel,[120] and the right to privacy.[121]

Whenever governmental action or inaction infringes upon citizen access to any of these "fundamental rights," the Court has struck down the scheme or called for some remedial legislation. The Supreme Court has ruled, for instance, that persons accused of crimes must be given an attorney at state's expense if they cannot afford to hire a lawyer,[122] that a poor defendant must be provided with a free trial transcript even if that transcript is made available to others only for a fee,[123] and that a poor person cannot be thrown in jail for nonpayment of a fine but must be given an opportunity to pay it off under an installment plan.[124] Other Supreme Court rulings have determined that all Americans have the right to vote without paying a fee [125] and that a state cannot limit the right to travel from one state to another by levying a tax on travelers.[126] In other words, poverty cannot be a barrier to attainment of "fundamental rights." Neither can any other status—race, sex, country of origin, and so forth—whether or not such classifications are "suspect."

The Court has never explicitly stated which standard of judicial review should govern cases involving jury selection, although such cases always raise the question whether a litigant's right to a representative jury or the right of a citizen to an equal opportunity to sit on a jury are "fundamental rights." If one or both of these questions were answered affirmatively, all court practices that have a discriminatory effect—such as residency requirements and the granting of excuses to one group more frequently than to others—would be subject to the "strict scrutiny" of the Court and struck down unless a "compelling governmental interest" could be found to justify the selection method that discriminates. If this question is answered negatively, and if no "suspect category" is involved, the selection scheme is subjected to the more lenient "rational basis" test, meaning that it will normally be permitted to stand if the government can show "some rational basis" for retaining it.

A number of Supreme Court opinions over the past twenty years express a firm conviction that trial by a jury representing a cross-section of the community *is* a fundamental right, but the Court has not yet explicitly applied the "compelling state interest" test to a problem of jury selection, and the lower courts have been reluctant to use this test. The Court has, however, made frequent reference to the "fundamental" importance of a fair jury trial. In *Reid v. Covert* (1957),[127] a case rejecting the government's assertion that the wife of an American serviceman accused of killing her husband overseas could be tried by a military court martial, Justice Hugo Black said for a majority of the Court:

> [I]n view of our heritage and the history of the adoption of the Constitution and the Bill of Rights, it seems peculiarly anomalous to say that trial before a civilian judge and by *an independent jury picked from the common citizenry are not fundamental rights.*[128]

In *Duncan v. Louisiana* (1968),[129] in which the Supreme Court ruled that the Sixth Amendment requires the states to grant jury trials to all persons facing a possible penalty of six months or more in jail, Justice Byron R. White wrote for the Court that the right to trial by jury is among those *"fundamental* principles of liberty and justice which lie at the base of all our civil and political institutions."[130]

The Court went even further in the 1975 case of *Taylor v. Louisiana*,[131] in which Justice White stated that the requirement that juries be composed of a "fair cross-section" of the community is *"fundamental* to the American system of justice"[132] and *"fundamental* to the jury trial guaranteed by the Sixth Amendment."[133] In rejecting Louisiana's argument that jury service would interfere with the "distinctive role in society" of women, he stated that "[t]he right to a proper jury cannot be overcome on *merely rational grounds. There must be weightier reasons* if a distinctive class representing 53% of the eligible jurors is for all practical purposes to be excluded from jury service."[134] Justice White thus clearly considers the "rational basis" standard of review inappropriate for problems of jury selection, and consequently, some higher standard—such as the "compelling state interest" test—must be required.

In addition to examining this problem from the point of view of the litigant—who appears to have a "fundamental right" to an impartially selected jury—it is equally important to see the perspective of the citizen who appears to have the "fundamental right" to be considered equally, along with all other citizens, for jury service. The U.S. Supreme Court unanimously recognized the right of citizens to bring actions claiming discrimination in the selection of jurors in the case of *Carter v. Jury Commission*, where Justice Stewart wrote for the Court:

> Whether jury service be deemed a right, a privilege, or a duty, the State may no more extend it to some of its citizens and deny it to others on racial grounds *than it may invidiously discriminate in the offering and withholding of the elective franchise.*[135]

The analogy of jury service to the vote is important because the right to vote has been explicitly viewed as "fundamental" in a number of recent cases,[136] and hence all allegations of discrimination regarding the vote are governed by the "strict scrutiny, compelling state interest" test. Both jury service and the vote are essential democratic links between the government and the people that must be protected against any legislative or bureaucratic discrimination.

The reasons that we rely so heavily on the jury are, as the court declared in two 1968 cases, "to prevent oppression by the Government"[137] and "to maintain a link between contemporary community values and the penal system."[138] These functions can be performed by the jury only if the jurors are selected without discrimination of any sort so that the jurors are in fact representatives of "contemporary community values" capable of preventing "oppression by the government." Thus, the selection of jurors must be protected by a standard as strict as that protecting the exercise of the vote.[i]

These ideas were restated more explicitly in the 1975 case of *Taylor v. Louisiana.*[139] In that case, the Court allowed a man to raise the issue of discrimination against women, thus eliminating an important procedural barrier to jury challenges and recognizing that the right to a representative jury is so important that it can be asserted by all persons involved with the jury system. The importance to the community of equal access to jury panels, as a means of ensuring the integrity of the system, was emphasized by the Court in *Taylor*:

> Community participation in the administration of the criminal law, moreover, is not only consistent with our democratic heritage but is also critical to public confidence in the fairness of the criminal justice system.[140]

Yet the courts have still not established clear standards that would make it easier to ensure that our juries reflect a cross-section of the community. Although it has at times spoken forcefully on the subject, the Supreme Court considers jury challenges only sporadically, and the lower courts have been reluctant to break new ground in this field. In contrast to their aggressive approach toward rectifying problems of racial discrimination in education and toward reapportioning the state legislatures, and their extensive use of statistics in these areas, the courts have been relatively passive in dealing with jury discrimination, even though this problem exists directly within their own branch of government.

---

[i]For a discussion of some of the procedural obstacles to exercising both these rights, see Chapter Four, pp. 91-93.

This reluctance might be explained by an unwillingness to change the status quo, a desire to preserve elite juries, or an inability to admit that the courts do not work as well as they should. One can postulate that the courts' deep respect for the workings of the American system of justice renders them more cautious about tinkering with it than with other institutions of government. On the other hand, it could be argued that such concern should make judges doubly sensitive to any imbalances in the system and eager to right them. But such perception depends on the judges' conception of the ideal jury.

The courts seem to be moving toward greater recognition of underrepresentation in juries and toward a commitment to make our juries truly representative. This process could be quickly completed if the courts would subject all classifications affecting jury service to a stricter level of review and overturn all classifications that cannot be justified by a compelling state interest. This would eliminate residency requirements, procedures and policies that excuse some types of people more easily than others, and the use of lists that underrepresent significant demographic groups. Most of the recent jury reforms, however, have been legislative in origin. The chapters that follow explore those changes and point to the need for continued reform.

## NOTES

1. Taylor v. Louisiana, 419 U.S. 522, 528 (1975).

2. Richard Henry Lee, "Letters of a Federal Farmer," Letter IV, October 12, 1787, in *Pamphlets on the Constitution of the United States* 316 (Paul Leicester Ford ed. 1968), quoted in a statement made by Charles Morgan in Subcommittee on Courts, Civil Liberties and the Administration of Justice of the House Judiciary Committee, *Hearings: Three-Judge Court and Six-Person Civil Jury*, 93rd Cong., 2nd Sess. (October 10, 1973 and January 24, 1974), p. 133 (emphasis added).

3. James D. Richardson, ed., *Messages and Papers of the Presidents* (Washington, D.C.: Bureau of National Literature and Art, 1876), pp. 323-24 (emphasis added).

4. *Duncan v. Louisiana*, 391 U.S. 145 (1968).

5. *Hernandez v. Texas*, 347 U.S. 475, 478 (1954) (emphasis added).

6. See also e.g., *State v. Plenty Horse*, 85 S.D. 401, 184 N.W.2d 654 (1971); *State v. Guirlando*, 152 La. 570, 93 So.796 (1922); *International Longshoreman and Warehouseman's Union v. Ackerman*, 82 F. Supp. 65 (D.Hawaii, 1943); *United States v. Fujimoto*, 104 F. Supp. 727 (D.Hawaii), *cert. denied* 344 U.S. 852 (1953).

7. *Ballard v. United States*, 329 U.S. 187 (1946); *Taylor v. Louisiana*, 419 U.S. 522 (1975).

8. *Witherspoon v. Illinois*, 391 U.S. 510 (1968).

9. *Thiel v. Southern Pacific Co.* 328 U.S. 217 (1946).

10. *Hamling v. United States*, 418 U.S. 87 (1974); for the lower court cases see notes 89 and 90, below.

11. *United States v. Cohen*, 275 F. Supp. 724 (D.Md., 1967); *United States v. Butera*, 420 F.2d 564 (1st Cir. 1970).

12. *Juarez v. State*, 102 Texas Crim. 297, 277 S.W. 1091 (1925); see also *United States v. Suskin*, 450 F.2d 596 (2d Cir. 1971).

13. *Schowgurow v. State*, 240 Md. 121, 213 A.2d 475 (1965); *State v. Madison*, 240 Md. 265, 213 A.2d 880 (1968).

14. See, e.g., *Avery v. Georgia*, 345 U.S. 559 (1953); and *Whitus v. Georgia*, 385 U.S. 545 (1967).

15. *Carter v. Jury Commission of Greene County*, 396 U.S. 320 (1970).

16. *Penn v. Eubanks*, 360 F. Supp. 699 (M.D. Ala., 1973). See also *Alabama v. United States*, 304 F.2d 583, 586 (5th Cir. 1962): "In the problem of racial discrimination, statistics often tell much, and courts listen."

17. See, e.g., *Carter v. Jury Commission of Greene County* 396 U.S. 320 (1970); *Turner v. Fouche* 396 U.S. 346 (1970); *Alexander v. Louisiana*, 405 U.S. 625 (1972); *Gibson v. Blair*, 467 F.2d 842 (5th Cir. 1972); *Preston v. Mandeville*, 428 F.2d 1392 (5th Cir. 1970); *Black v. Curb*, 422 F.2d 656 (5th Cir. 1970) and 464 F.2d 165 (5th Cir. 1972); *Salary v. Wilson*, 415 F.2d 467 (5th Cir. 1969); *United States v. Zirpolo*, 450 F.2d 424 (3rd Cir. 1970); *United States v. Butera*, 420 F.2d 564 (1st Cir. 1970).

18. See, e.g., *United States v. Greenberg* 200 F. Supp. 382 (S.D.N.Y. 1961); *Gorin v. United States* 313 F.2d 641, 644 (1st Cir. 1963); *United States v. Kelly*, 349 F.2d 720, 778 (2d Cir. 1965); *Grimes v. United States*, 391 F.2d 709 (5th Cir. 1968); *United States v. Caci*, 401 F.2d 664, 671 (2d Cir. 1968); *Camp v. United States* 413 F.2d 419, 421 (5th Cir. 1969); *United States v. Dangler*, 422 F.2d 344, 345 (5th Cir. 1970); *United States v. Parker*, 428 F.2d 488, 489 (9th Cir. 1970); *United States v. Kroncke*, 321 F. Supp. 913, 914 (D.Minn., 1970); *People v. Newton*, 8 Cal. App. 3d 359, 87 Cal. Rptr. 394 (1970); *United States v. Bennett*, 445 F.2d 638, 641 (9th Cir. 1971); *United States v. Gast*, 457 F.2d 141, 142 (7th Cir. 1972); *United States v. Guzman*, 468 F.2d 1245, 1248 (2d Cir. 1972); *People v. Sirhan*, 7 Cal. 3d 710, 749-50, 102 Cal. Rptr. 385, 497 P.2d 1121 (1972); *People v. Powell*, 40 Cal. App. 3d 107, 126-27, 115 Cal. Rptr. 109 (1974); *People v. Gibbs*, 12 Cal. App. 3d 526, 539, 90 Cal. Rptr. 866 (1970); *People v. Breckenridge*, 52 Cal. App. 3d 913, 125 Cal. Rptr. 425, 429 (1975); *People v. Keith*, 52 Cal. App. 3d 947, 125 Cal. Rptr. 676, 679 (1975); *United States v. Lewis*, 472 F.2d 252, 256 (3d Cir. 1973); *United States v. Freeman*, 514 F.2d 171, 173 (8th Cir. 1975); *People v. McDowell* 27 Cal. App. 3d 864, 870-71, 104 Cal. Rptr. 181 (1972); *People v. Murphy*, 35 Cal. App. 3d 905, 111 Cal. Rptr. 295, 303 (1973); *United States v. James*, 528 F.2d 999, 1022 (5th Cir. 1976); *Murrah v. Arkansas*, 532 F.2d 105, 106 (8th Cir. 1976).

One case in which a federal court has ordered that the voter list be supplemented by other lists is *Ford v. Hollowell*, 385 F. Supp. 1392, 1399-1400 (N.D.Miss., 1974) where it was shown that blacks in Mississippi in the late 1960s had been intimidated from registering to vote.

19. 96 S.Ct. 2040 (1976).

20. *Ibid.*, p. 2047.

21. *Ibid.*, p. 2049. Judge Walter P. Gewin of the U.S. Court of Appeals for the Fifth Circuit, who has struggled with jury selection problems over the years as a member of the federal judiciary's supervising committee argued in 1975 that courts should be more willing to allow statistics alone to establish a prima facie case of discrimination in jury selection. Gewin, "An Analysis of Jury Selection Decisions," 506 F.2d 811, 829-30 (1975).

22. 100 U.S. 303 (1880).

23. *Ibid.*, p. 310 (emphasis added).

24. See e.g., *Thiel v. Southern Pacific Ry*, 328 U.S. 217 (1946); *Turner v. Fouche*, 396 U.S. 346 (1970); *Taylor v. Louisiana*, 419 U.S. 522 (1975).

25. *Taylor v. Louisiana*, 419 U.S. 522 (1975).

26. *Neal v. Delaware*, 103 U.S. 370 (1881); *Bush v. Kentucky*, 107 U.S. 110 (1883).

27. *Carter v. Texas*, 177 U.S. 442 (1900); *Rogers v. Alabama*, 192 U.S. 226 (1904).

28. See, e.g., *Gibson v. Mississippi*, 162 U.S. 565 (1896); *Tarrance v. Florida*, 188 U.S. 519 (1903); *Brownfield v. South Carolina*, 189 U.S. 426 (1903); *Martin v. Texas*, 200 U.S. 316 (1906).

29. 163 U.S. 537 (1896).

30. 212 U.S. 278.

31. *Thomas v. State*, 49 Tex. Cr. R. 633, 95 S.W. 1069 (1906).

32. 212 U.S. at 282-83.

33. 294 U.S. 587.

34. 311 U.S. 128.

35. 212 U.S. 278.

36. 311 U.S. at 130.

37. *Ibid.*

38. 315 U.S. 60.

39. 315 U.S. at 86 (emphasis added). Ironically, however, the Court affirmed the conviction. Justice Murphy extracted a doctrine from the 1880-1909 period of judicial abstention and said that even though the affidavit alleging biased selection was not contested by the prosecution, it could not alone be accepted as true because no supporting "evidence" was offered.

40. 325 U.S. 398.

41. 332 U.S. 261.

42. 325 U.S. at 407.

43. 325 U.S. at 410.

44. *United States v. Dennis*, 183 F.2d 201 (2d Cir. 1950).

45. 183 F.2d at 224.

46. 380 U.S. 202.

47. *Ibid.* at 208.

48. *Ibid.* at 209.

49. See, e.g., *Bradley v. Judges of the Los Angeles Superior Court*, 531 F.2d 413, 416 n.8 (9th Cir. 1976); *Blackwell v. Thomas*, 476 F.2d 443, 447 (4th Cir. 1973).

50. 396 U.S. 320.

51. *Ibid.* at 332.

52. 396 U.S. 346.

53. *Ibid.* at 359.

54. 405 U.S. 625.

55. *Ibid.* at 630 (emphasis added).

56. *Ibid.* at 629.

57. *Ibid.*

58. 380 U.S. at 209.

59. See, e.g., *Bradley v. Judges of the Los Angeles Superior Court*, 531 F.2d 413, 416 n.8 (9th Cir. 1976); *Stephens v. Cox*, 449 F.2d 657 (4th Cir. 1971); *Gould v. State*, 131 Ga. App. 811, 207 S.E.2d 519, 523 (1974); *Ford v. Hollowell*, 385 F. Supp. 1392, 1399 (N.D.Miss., 1974); *Thompson v. Sheppard*, 502 F.2d 1389, 1390 (5th Cir. 1974) (John R. Brown, J., dissenting); *United States v. Grant*, 475 F.2d 581, 582 (4th Cir. 1973) (Winter, J., dissenting). Recent decisions that continue to use the "absolute" method are *Smith v. Yeager*, 465 F.2d 272, 279 n.19 (3rd Cir. 1972); *United States v. Whitley*, 491 F.2d 1248, 1249 (8th Cir. 1974); *United States v. Jenkins*, 496 F.2d 57, 65-66 (2nd Cir. 1974); *United States v. Goff*, 509 F.2d 825 (5th Cir. 1975); *Partida v. Castaneda*, 524 F.2d 481 (5th Cir. 1975); *United States v. Test*, 399 F. Supp. 683 (D.Colo., 1975). See generally, Gewin, "An Analysis of Jury Selection Decisions," 506 F.2d 811, 834-35 (1975).

60. *Quadra v. Superior Court of San Francisco* (II), 403 F. Supp. 486, 495 n.9 (N.D.Cal., 1975).

61. 490 F.2d 830, *rehearing denied*, 502 F.2d 1389 (5th Cir. 1974).

62. *Ibid.* at 833.

63. *Quadra v. Superior Court of San Francisco* (II), 403 F. Supp. 486 (N.D.Cal., 1975).

64. *Ibid.* at 498.

65. 328 U.S. 217.

66. *Ibid.* at 220 (emphasis added).

67. *Ibid.* at 224.

68. 332 U.S. 261.

69. *Ibid.* at 275.

70. *Ibid.* at 279.

71. 370 F. Supp. 298 (E.D.La., 1973), *affirmed sub nom, United States v. Goff*, 509 F.2d 825 (5th Cir. 1975).

72. *Ibid.* at 307.

73. See, e.g., *San Antonio Independent School District v. Rodriquez*, 411 U.S. 1 (1973); *United States v. Kras*, 409 U.S. 434 (1973); *Ortwein v. Schwab*, 410 U.S. 656 (1973).

74. See also *People v. Navarette*, 54 Cal. App. 3d 1064, 127 Cal. Rptr. 55 (1976), holding that blue collar workers are not a "cognizable class."

75. 100 U.S. 303, at 310 (emphasis added).

76. 329 U.S. 187.

77. *Ibid.* at 193-94 (footnotes omitted and emphasis added).

78. See, e.g., *Fay v. New York*, 332 U.S. 261 (1947).

79. 368 U.S. 57.

80. *Ibid.* at 61-62 (emphasis added).

81. 419 U.S. 522.

82. *Ibid.* at 533.

83. *Ibid.* at 534-35.

84. *Ibid.* at 534.

85. See, e.g., *United States v. Eskew,* 460 F.2d 1028 (9th Cir. 1972); *United States v. Briggs,* 366 F. Supp. 1356, 1362 (N.D.Fla., 1973); *Marshall v. Holmes,* 365 F. Supp. 613 (N.D.Fla., 1973).

86. 416 U.S. 351.

87. *Massachusetts Board of Retirement v. Murgia,* 96 S.Ct. 2562 (1976).

88. *People v. Attica Brothers,* unpublished, Erie County Supreme Court, June 27, 1974; see *New York Times,* July 4, 1974, p. 1.

89. *United States v. Duke,* 263 F. Supp. 828 (S.D.Ind., 1976); *People v. Taylor,* No. A-277-425 (Los Angeles Superior Court, Oct. 11, 1974); *People v. Fujita,* 43 Cal. App.3d 454, 117 Cal. Rptr. 757, 770 (1974) (dicta); *Simmons v. Jones,* 317 F. Supp. 397 (S.D.Ga., 1970); *State v. Holmstron,* 43 Wis.2d 465, 168 N.W.2d 574 (1969) (dicta); *United States v. Butera,* 420 F.2d 564 (1st Cir. 1970); *United States v. Sinclair* (unreported opinion by Judge Damon Keith, Crim. No. 44375) (E.D.Mich., Jan. 25, 1971); *People v. Bingham,* No. 4094 (unreported opinion by Superior Court Judge Warren Stoll, sitting in Marin County, Calif., December 1973), *reversed sub nom, People v. Pinell,* 43 Cal. App.3d 627, 117 Cal. Rptr. 913 (1975). See generally, Note, "Federal Courts, Juror Selection, Under Representation of Young Adults on Juror Source Lists," *Wayne Law Review,* 19 (1973): 1287.

90. See, e.g., *United States v. Gargan,* 314 F. Supp. 414, 417 (W.D.Wis., 1970), *affd. sub nom, United States v. Gast,* 457 F.2d 141, 142-43 (7th Cir.) *cert. denied,* 406 U.S. 969 (1972) (21-26 year olds are not a cognizable class); *United States v. McVean,* 436 F.2d 1120, 1122 (5th Cir.), *cert. denied,* 404 U.S. 822 (1971); *United States v. Kuhn,* 441 F.2d 179, 181 (5th Cir. 1971) (21-23 year olds); *United States v. Waddy,* 340 F. Supp. 509 (S.D.N.Y., 1971); *United States v. Deardorff,* 343 F. Supp. 1033, 1043 (S.D.N.Y., 1971); *People v. Hoiland,* 22 Cal. App.3d 530, 99 Cal. Rptr. 523, 529 (1971) (21-30 year olds); *Duncan v. United States,* 456 F.2d 1401, 1404 (9th Cir. 1972) (18-20 year olds); *Chase v. United States,* 468 F.2d 141, 144-46 (7th Cir. 1972) (21-24 year olds); *United States v. Ross,* 468 F.2d 1213, 1217 (9th Cir. 1972); *cert. denied,* 410 U.S. 389 (1973); *United States v. Ware,* 473 F.2d 530 (9th Cir. 1973); *United States v. Olson,* 473 F.2d 686, 688 (8th Cir. 1973), *cert. denied,* 412 U.S. 905 (1973); *United States v. Quinn,* 364 F. Supp. 432, 435 (N.D.Ga., 1973); *United States v. Ream,* 491 F.2d 1243 (5th Cir. 1974); *Wilkins v. State,* 16 Md. App. 587, 300 A.2d 411, 414, *affd.,* 270 Md. 62, 310 A.2d 39 (1973); *People v. Redwine,* 50 Mich. App. 593, 213 N.W. 2d 841, 843 (1974); *United States v. Briggs,* 366 F. Supp. 1356, 1362 (N.D.Fla., 1973); *United States v. Geelan,* 509 F.2d 737 (8th Cir. 1974) (18-20 year olds); *United States v. Diggs,* 522 F.2d 1310, 1317 (D.C. Cir. 1975).

91. *Hamling v. United States,* 418 U.S. 87 (1974).

92. *United States v. Guzman,* 337 F. Supp. 140, 143-44 (S.D.N.Y., 1972).

93. 407 U.S. 493, 504 (emphasis added).

94. See, e.g., *Oregon v. Mitchell*, 400 U.S. 112, 243-44 (1970) (Opinion of Justices Brennan, White, and Marshall).

95. See, e.g., *United States v. McVean*, 436 F.2d 1120, 1122 (5th Cir. 1971), *cert. denied*, 404 U.S. 822 (1971); *United States v. Allen*, 445 F.2d 849 (5th Cir. 1971); *United States v. Waddy*, 340 F. Supp. 509, 512-13 (S.D.N.Y. 1971); *United States v. Deardorff*, 343 F. Supp. 1033, 1042 (S.D.N.Y. 1971); *People v. Hoiland*, 22 Cal. App. 3d 530, 534-37, 99 Cal. Rptr. 523, 526-27 (1971); *United States v. Gargan*, 314 F. Supp. 414, 417 (W.D. Wis. 1970); *affd. sub nom.*, *United States v. Gast*, 457 F.2d 141, 143 (7th Cir.), *cert. denied*, 406 U.S. 969 (1972); *United States v. Duncan*, 456 F.2d 1401, 1404-405 (9th Cir. 1972); *United States v. Ross*, 468 F.2d 1213, 1215 (9th Cir. 1972); *United States v. Guzman*, 337 F. Supp. 140, 144 (S.D.N.Y.) *affd.*, 468 F.2d 1245, 1247 n.21 (2nd Cir. 1972); *United States v. Ware*, 473 F.2d 530, 537 (9th Cir. 1973); *United States v. Olson*, 473 F.2d 686, 688 (8th Cir.) *cert. denied*, 412 U.S. 905 (1973); *United States v. Osborne*, 482 F.2d 1354, 1355 (8th Cir. 1973); *Hopkins v. State*, 19 Md. App. 414, 311 A.2d 483, 485 (1973); *Burke v. State*, 19 Md. App. 645, 313 A.2d 864, 867 (1974); *State v. Stewart*, 120 N.J. Super. 409, 295 A.2d 202, 203 (1972); *Commonwealth v. Cobbs*, 452 Pa. 397, 305 A.2d 25, 27-28 (1973); *Shelby v. State*, 479 S.W.2d 31 (Tex. Crim. App. 1972); *State v. Boggs*, 80 Wa.2d 427, 495 P.2d 321, 325 (1972); *People v. Scott*, 17 Ill. App. 3d 1026, 309 N.E.2d 257 (1974).

96. 337 F. Supp. 140 (S.D.N.Y. 1972).

97. *Ibid.* at 144.

98. *United States v. Hamling*, 481 F.2d 307, 314 (9th Cir. 1973), *affd.*; 418 U.S. 87 (1974).

99. *United States v. Dellinger*, 472 F.2d 340, 365-66 (7th Cir. 1972).

100. *1973 Statistical Abstract of the United States* (Washington: Government Printing Office, 1974), p. 37.

101. 28 *U.S.C.* 1863 (b) (4), as amended by Public Law 92-269, Section 3(c), (April 6, 1972).

102. See, e.g., *United States v. Kuhn*, 441 F.2d 179 (5th Cir. 1971); *Chase v. United States*, 458 F.2d 141 (7th Cir. 1972); *United States v. Pentado*, 463 F.2d 355, 359 (5th Cir. 1972); *United States v. Ross*, 468 F.2d 1213 (9th Cir. 1972); *United States v. Gooding*, 473 F.2d 425, 429 (5th Cir. 1973); *United States v. Ware*, 473 F.2d 530, 536 (9th Cir. 1973); *United States v. Arroyave*, 477 F.2d 157, 160 (5th Cir. 1973); *United States v. Resnick*, 483 F.2d 354, 356 (5th Cir. 1973); *United States v. Ream*, 491 F.2d 1243 (5th Cir. 1974); *Hamling v. United States*, 418 U.S. 87 (1974); *United States v. Hill*, 500 F.2d 733, 738-39 (5th Cir. 1974); *United States v. Smith*, 523 F.2d 771, 781 (5th Cir. 1975).

103. 394 U.S. 618.

104. *Ibid.* at 634 (emphasis in original).

105. 405 U.S. 330.

106. *Marston v. Lewis*, 410 U.S. 679 (1973), and *Burns v. Fortson*, 410 U.S. 686 (1973).

107. *Corkey v. Edwards*, 322 F. Supp. 1248 (W.D.N.C. 1971), *vacated on other grounds*, 410 U.S. 950 (1973).

108. *State v. Wylie*, 516 P.2d 148 (Alaska 1973); *Eggert v. City of Seattle*, 81 Wash.2d 840, 505 P.2d 801 (1973).

109. *Keenan v. Board of Law Examiners*, 317 F. Supp. 1350 (E.D.N.C. 1970); *Smith v. Davis*, 350 F. Supp. 1225 (S.D.W.Va. 1972); *Lipman v. Van Zant*, 329 F. Supp. 391 (N.D.Miss., 1971).

110. *Memorial Hospital v. Maricopa County*, 415 U.S. 250 (1974); *Valenciano v. Bateman*, 323 F. Supp. 600 (D. Ariz. 1971); and see *Corr v. Westchester County Dept. of Social Services*, 33 N.Y.2d 111, 350 N.Y.S.2d 401 (1973). At least one court extended this line of decisions to residency requirements for divorces, *State v. Adams*, 522 P.2d 1125 (Alaska, 1974), but the Supreme Court held otherwise because of the state's interest in respecting the marriage and divorce decrees of neighboring states and in limiting the possibility that it might turn into a "divorce mill." *Sosna v. Iowa*, 419 U.S. 393 (1975).

111. See, e.g., *United States v. Duncan*, 456 F.2d 1401, 1406 (9th Cir. 1972); *United States v. Gast*, 457 F.2d 141, 143 (7th Cir. 1972); *United States v. Ross*, 468 F.2d 1213, 1215-16 (9th Cir. 1972), cert. denied, 410 U.S. 989 (1973); *United States v. Owen*, 492 F.2d 1100, 1109 (5th Cir. 1974); *United States v. Perry*, 480 F.2d 147, 148 (5th Cir. 1973); *Craig v. Wyse*, 373 F. Supp. 1008 (D.Colo., 1974); *Adams v. Superior Court*, 12 Cal.3d 55, 115 Cal. Rptr. 247, 524 P.2d 375 (1974) (4-3 decision); *Reed v. State*, 292 So.2d 7 (Fla. 1974) (4-2 decision); *Williams v. State*, 51 Ala. 1, 282 So.2d 349 (1973).

112. *U.S. Cong. and Admin. News*, 90th Cong., 2d Session (1968), p. 1796.

113. The ideas in this section were expressed in a somewhat different form in Van Dyke, "Jury Service Is a Fundamental Right," *Hastings Constitutional Law Quarterly* 2 (1975): 27-31.

114. See, e.g., *Williamson v. Lee Optical Co.*, 348 U.S. 483 (1955); *Railway Express Agency v. New York*, 336 U.S. 106 (1949).

115. See *Frontiero v. Richardson*, 411 U.S. 677 (1973).

116. See, e.g., *Dunn v. Blumstein*, 405 U.S. 330 (1972); *San Antonio Ind. School Dist. v. Rodriquez*, 411 U.S. 1 (1973); *Shapiro v. Thompson*, 394 U.S. 618 (1969).

117. *Griffin v. Illinois*, 351 U.S. 12 (1956); *Gideon v. Wainwright* 372 U.S. 335 (1968); *Douglas v. California*, 372 U.S. 353 (1963); *Williams v. Illinois*, 399 U.S. 235 (1970); *Tate v. Short*, 401 U.S. 395 (1971); *Mayer v. City of Chicago*, 404 U.S. 189 (1971); *Argersinger v. Hamlin*, 407 U.S. 25 (1972).

118. *Chicago Police Dept. v. Mosley*, 408 U.S. 92 (1972).

119. *Harper v. Virginia Board of Elections*, 383 U.S. 663 (1966); *Dunn v. Blumstein*, 405 U.S. 330 (1972).

120. *Shapiro v. Thompson*, 394 U.S. 618 (1969).

121. *Griswold v. Connecticut*, 381 U.S. 479 (1965); *Roe v. Wade*, 410 U.S. 113 (1973).

122. *Gideon v. Wainwright*, 372 U.S. 335 (1963); *Douglas v. California*, 372 U.S. 353 (1963); *Argersinger v. Hamlin*, 407 U.S. 25 (1972).

123. *Griffin v. Illinois*, 351 U.S. 12 (1956).

124. *Williams v. Illinois*, 399 U.S. 235 (1970); *Tate v. Short*, 401 U.S. 395 (1971).

125. *Harper v. Virginia Board of Elections*, 383 U.S. 663 (1966).

126. *Crandall v. Nevada*, 6 Wall. 35 (1867); and see *Edwards v. California*, 314 U.S. 160 (1941), and *Shapiro v. Thompson*, 394 U.S. 618 (1969).

127. 354 U.S. 1 (1957).

128. *Ibid.* at 9 (emphasis added).

129. 391 U.S. 145.

130. *Ibid.* at 148 (emphasis added).

131. 419 U.S. 522.

132. *Ibid.* at 530 (emphasis added).

133. *Ibid.* (emphasis added).

134. *Ibid.* at 534 (emphasis added).

135. 396 U.S. 320, 330 (1970) (emphasis added).

136. E.g., *Dunn v. Blumstein*, 405 U.S. 330 (1972); *Harper v. Virginia Bd. of Elections*, 383 U.S. 663 (1966).

137. *Duncan v. Louisiana*, 391 U.S. 145, 155 (1968).

138. *Witherspoon v. Illinois*, 391 U.S. 510, 519 n.15 (1968).

139. 419 U.S. 522.

140. *Ibid.* at 530.

## Chapter Four

## The First Stage:
## The Wheel

How faithfully juries reflect a community's cross-section depends on the success of a series of procedures through which jurors are chosen. The first stage of selection—compilation of a list of prospective jurors—must be designed to produce as complete a list as possible if representative juries are to be impaneled. We have made considerable progress toward this goal over the last decade, but definitely still have room for improvement.

The most important step toward making our federal juries more representative was taken in the Congress in 1968, when it passed the Jury Selection and Service Act.[1] The legislation stated at the outset that:

It is the policy of the United States that all litigants in the Federal courts entitled to trial by jury shall have the right to grand and petit juries selected *at random* from *a fair cross section of the community* in the district or division wherein the court convenes. It is further the policy of the United States that all citizens have the opportunity to be considered for service on grand and petit juries in the district courts of the United States and shall have an obligation to serve as jurors when summoned for that purpose.[2]

The next section of the bill strengthens this commitment by pledging that "No citizen shall be excluded from service as a grand or petit juror in the district courts of the United States on account of race, color, religion, sex, national origin, or economic status."[3]

In order to realize these goals, the new law provided that a master jury wheel be drawn in each jurisdiction from the list of registered voters or, where more appropriate, the list of actual voters. In addition, the statute says that—"[w]here necessary to foster the policy and protect the rights secured" in the declarations cited above—federal courts should supplement the voter lists with additional lists.[4] The voter list is used primarily because it is the most administratively convenient source for jurors. In many areas, especially cities, voter registration lists are already on computer tapes, which can be programmed to select names randomly for jury lists. Obtaining the list of potential jurors can be accomplished in a matter of minutes. Since the list is kept by a government agency, it can usually be obtained easily and relatively inexpensively.

The 1968 act established a detailed procedure for the compilation of the jury wheel and selection from it in order to ensure that the wheel is broadly representative of the district. Each district court is directed to start with its list of voters, select an "interval number" (based on the percentage of persons they will need for jury duty out of the total number of voters), and compile a "master wheel" by taking names at the chosen interval from the list. Once the master wheel is prepared, it remains unchanged and unsupplemented for four years,[5] and the court clerk randomly draws names from the master wheel from time to time to begin the process of moving persons to the "qualified wheel." The clerk sends questionnaires to those persons whose names are drawn, and if they are not disqualified, exempt, or excused, the clerk places their names in the qualified wheel to be summoned later for actual jury duty.

The Jury Selection and Service Act completely restructured the process of selecting jurors for the federal courts. Before the passage of the act, almost all federal courts chose their jurors through the "key-man" system, under which court clerks or jury commissioners consulted with prominent, well-established civic or political leaders (the "key men") for suggestions of prospective jurors. The key men were asked to propose as a juror, typically, someone "esteemed in his community as a person of good character, approved integrity, sound judgment and fair education,"[6] who also met the statutory qualifications for jury service. Because of the care with which jurors were selected, the federal courts boasted about the "quality" of their jurors. These "blue-ribbon" juries were, however, far from representative of the community and contained a disproportionately high number of middle-aged, middle- or upper-class, white men.[7]

Most state courts have in recent years made changes similar to the 1968 federal statute and now randomly select jurors from some standard list, such as the list of voters. But some have held on to the "key-man" system. Sixteen states in New England and the South still authorize the key-man system in one form or another and continue to impanel unrepresentative juries. Connecticut, Massachusetts, New Hampshire, and Vermont give their town officials discretion to submit names of persons deemed worthy for jury service, with virtually no guidance on which persons should be chosen. In many Massachusetts towns, the police conduct an annual door-to-door census to compile a list of residents, and this fairly complete census is usually the original source used by election commissioners or town selectmen in compiling a jury list. But because the law gives the local officials unguided discretion, they are able to pick and choose names from that list,[8] and they pay close attention to the name, sex, and occupation of the persons on the census list when making their choices.

In the South, Alabama, Arkansas, Florida, Georgia, Kentucky, Louisiana, North Carolina, Oklahoma, South Carolina, Tennessee, Virginia, and West Virginia all have statutes that permit local jury commissioners to exercise a great deal of discretion in choosing jurors. Some counties in these states have started using the voter list and randomly selecting from it, but most still rely on personal selection. In Alabama, each county's three-person jury commission (appointed by the governor) is instructed by statute to compile a complete list of all eligible jurors, starting from existing lists, including the voter registration list, the tax assessor list, city directories, and telephone directories,[9] and jury commissioners are supposed to survey personally the county once a year to locate persons who are not on the usual lists. In reality, however, the commissioners tend to select persons they know, namely, the "established" members of the community, and as a result, the selection processes of Alabama[10] and other southern states[11] have been a source of almost constant litigation. The South Carolina statutes—to give another example—require jury commissioners to place the names of two out of every three qualified electors on their jury lists,[12] but many of those left off have been blacks. (See Appendix G, p. 322.)

Grand juries, which have traditionally been more elite than trial juries, continue to be selected according to special criteria in many jurisdictions.[a] In most of California's fifty-eight counties, where grand juries are mainly investigative bodies (because most criminal charges are brought by "information" filed by the district attorney and presented for examination to a magistrate),[13] all grand jurors are nominated by superior court judges. Most of these grand juries are openly "blue-ribbon" bodies, and because of the inequities in this

---

[a]See Appendix B, p. 263.

procedure, several counties (including San Francisco) now select grand jurors randomly.[14] In Connecticut, where grand juries return indictments in capital cases, grand jurors are hand-picked by county sheriffs without any guidelines. In Colorado, where grand jurors are supposed to be chosen in the same way as trial jurors, in fact the people whose names are produced at random by the computer are interviewed by a judge and district attorney, who select those who will become grand jurors.[15]

Some states that no longer either select their jurors through a key-man system or give jury commissioners a free rein in making up lists, retain special criteria that provide for the continuing exercise of discretion. Arkansas, for example, recently switched from a key-man system to a modified random system that is more impartial but still preserves the opportunity for substantial abuse. The county jury commissioners are instructed to choose a fairly large number of names from the list of registered voters. It is unlikely that the commissioners can select only persons they know, but they are not instructed to be impartial. In fact, they are specifically directed by statute to choose jurors who are "temperate" and of "good behavior" and are possessed of "sound judgment or reasonable information."[16] The stated reason that dissuaded the Arkansas legislature from adopting a completely random system was the fear that democratically selected jurors would be less wise than hand-picked jurors.[17]

## THE LIST OF VOTERS

The voter registration list has been chosen as the sole source for jurors by the Congress and many state legislatures to eliminate the kind of bias introduced by the key-man system and other forms of discretionary selection. The question today, almost ten years after passage of the federal act, is how well the act's purposes of obtaining representative juries is fulfilled by an exclusive reliance on the voter lists. The answer is that federal juries are much more heterogeneous than they were under the key-man system, but that we still do not have representative juries.

The primary purpose of the 1968 act (expressed in its "declaration of policy"), that all litigants in federal jury trials have the right to juries "selected at random from a fair cross section of the community" and that all citizens have an obligation and should have an opportunity to serve on such juries, is impeded when some groups are underrepresented in substantial measure over time. Yet, as we have seen,[b] some groups continue to be substantially underrepresented on juries, and one of the causes of underrepresentation of certain groups is the exclusive use of voter lists. Members of some groups register at a much lower rate than the national average, and these groups end up being underrepresented on juries selected from voter lists.

According to surveys conducted by the U.S. Census Bureau, nonwhites, the poor, and the young register to vote at substantially lower rates than the remainder of the population. The Bureau's 1972 figures reveal the following disparities: (1) whereas 73.4 percent of whites reported that they were registered to vote, only 65.5 percent of blacks so stated and only 44.4 percent of Hispanics said they were registered;[c] (2) 58.1 percent of the country's 18-20 year olds, 59.5 percent of our 21-24 year olds, and 66.1 percent of the 25-29 year olds said they were registered, compared to percentages of at least 70 percent for all other age groups, ranging up to a high of 80.2 percent for the 55-64 age category; (3) 61.2 percent of those making less than $3,000 said they were registered, 64.1 percent of those earning between $3,000 and $4,999, and only 65.7 percent of those making between $5,000 and $7,499 were registered, compared to 77.7 percent for those earning $10,000 to $15,000 and 85 percent of those making over $15,000; (4) 61.5 percent of those with an eighth-grade education or less said they were registered, compared to 84.4 percent of those with at least one year of college; and (5) only 66.5 percent of the nation's blue-collar workers said they were registered, compared to 82.4 percent of the white-collar employees.[d,18] These data and related sociological literature were examined and summarized as follows by District Judge Jay Sullivan of Shawnee County, Kansas, in 1974, when he ruled that Kansas law requires that the voter list be supplemented by the locally compiled census list:

> Registered voters' lists include persons who are or tend to be: white, members of the Jewish, Catholic, Presbyterian and other Protestant and established religious beliefs, well-educated or higher educated citizens than average, middle-age citizens and men. As a class, citizens who are not registered voters include persons who are and tend to be: members of the

---

[b]See Chapter Two and Appendixes F through I.

[c]Some areas report even lower voting rates. Kenneth Freeman, Jr., a Native-American residing on the Fort Berthold Indian Reservation in North Dakota, alleged in his trial, apparently without contradiction by the prosecution, that only 17 percent of the eligible residents of that reservation had voted in the most recent general election. *United States v. Freeman*, 514 F.2d 171 (1975).

[d]These figures are not precise because the Census Bureau has found that 5 to 8 percent of the population say they have voted even though they have not.

minority races or ethnic background, women, members of certain fundamentalist religious orders and beliefs, persons of low economic status,
persons of low education levels, young citizens basically 18-25 years of age
and old citizens.[19]

Some observers of jury selection take the position that underrepresentations on jury panels resulting from the exclusive use of
voter lists are not improper because it is the individual's responsibility to register to vote.[20] Some argue that voter lists constitute a
natural filter separating out potentially undesirable jurors. The
assumption is that those who do vote have indicated at least some
measure of concern with (and, supposedly, understanding of) public
issues—a concern and understanding that will also be needed in the
jury box. Conversely, it is argued that those uninterested in voting
will probably not make good jurors. Judge Irving R. Kaufman of the
U.S. Court of Appeals for the Second Circuit, who was then
chairman of the committee of federal judges that drafted the earliest
version of the 1968 Jury Selection Act, testified in the Senate along
these lines:

> I call to your attention that the use of voter lists supplies an important
> built-in screening element. It automatically eliminates those individuals
> not interested enough in their government to vote or indeed not qualified
> to do so.[21]

This sentiment was also endorsed by the House Judiciary Committee,[22] which considered the bill, and by some state courts that have
spoken on the subject.[23]

This position seems illogical and unwise, however, for both
philosophical and practical reasons. The Federal Jury Selection and
Service Act disqualifies as jurors only noncitizens; those under 18;
those who cannot read, write, and understand English to the degree
necessary to fill out the qualification form; those mentally or
physically infirm; those under indictment or convicted of an offense
punishable by imprisonment of more than one year; and those who
have lived in the jurisdiction less than a year. The act includes no
intelligence test for jury service, nor is such a test consistent with the
act's purposes. But participation in the electoral process by registering to vote is in fact a prerequisite to jury service.

Such a qualification is sometimes defended on the ground that it is
an "objective" qualification, without the obvious opportunity for
bias inherent in criteria such as "competence" and "intelligence,"
which are determined by a jury commissioner or court employee

inevitably according to his or her personal viewpoint and assessment. It can be argued that as long as there are no barriers to voting on the basis of sex, race, or religion, no one is excluded from jury service.

But it seems more reasonable to argue that if explicit tests for jury service are rejected—as they were in the 1968 Act, which replaced the blue-ribbon concept with the goal of representativeness—implicit tests should also be eliminated. The criterion of being a voter should be subjected to the same scrutiny as the criteria used to impanel "blue-ribbon" juries. A failure to participate in elections does not indicate an inability to make the decisions involved in jury service. No evidence indicates that voters are possessed of better judgment than nonvoters, and a jury whose members' "quality" is determined by their registering to vote will not only have no special claim to wisdom but also will fail to represent the community as fully as it should.

If not registering to vote is indeed sometimes a sympton of alienation from the institutions of society (although it is by no means always that, as we shall see), citing this alienation as a disqualification for jury service does not serve the judicial system. The rationale of the jury system is to lend legitimacy to justice through verdicts reached by a cross-section of the community. Excluding certain people from participation in that process because, for one reason or another, they have not voted or do not want to vote contradicts the system itself. It further alienates those who may already be alienated, instead of providing them with an opportunity to participate and thus, ideally, to become more involved in society. Serving on a jury is not meant to be a reward for good citizenship; it is an opportunity and a responsibility that derives from citizenship itself. In addition, some people fail to register to vote because they want to avoid jury duty, and thus the exclusive use of the voter list as a source for jurors is in some sense a tax on the right to vote, and certainly a totally inappropriate one (see below, p. 99).

In fact, people who fail to register are not necessarily alienated. Many people do not register for reasons connected with the system of registration, not with their interest in civic matters. Some people are not registered because they move frequently, the young are registered in lower numbers because they have not had as long a chance to register; and some fail to vote because registration procedures are cumbersome.

In most American counties, it is difficult to register to vote, and because of the difficulty of registering, the United States has one of the lowest voting records of any Western democracy. Only 55 percent of eligible adults voted in the 1972 election, compared to recent figures of 94 percent in Australia, 89 percent in Sweden and Denmark, 85 percent in West Germany, 80 percent in Britain and France, 76 percent in Canada, and 74 percent in Japan.[24]

A survey of persons who had not voted in the 1972 election by Daniel Yankelovitch discovered that only 26 percent of those who had not registered had made a conscious choice not to do so. The vast majority of people did not register, according to Yankelovitch's findings, because "the road to registration . . . is an obstacle course, with roadblocks all along the way and one barrier reinforcing another."[25] A 1972 survey of 251 communities found that 77 percent offered no Saturday registration and 75 percent closed their offices at 6 p.m. or earlier which imposes a hardship on most wage earners.[26] As of 1973, only 16 states allowed registration on weekends, many of these just one weekend a year.[27]

In many areas, the registration system is simply haphazard. Missouri has six different systems for cities, depending on their size, and a seventh available to counties at their option. Iowa requires registration in its cities, but not in its rural areas.[28] North Dakota has no statewide law requiring registration, but some local areas do so at their option. In those states that do try to encourage registration, the system frequently includes registration stations at public places such as shopping centers and busy street corners but only during certain periods and not always in all neighborhoods on an equal basis. Volunteer door-to-door registration solicitation also misses certain neighborhoods.

Finally, many Americans are still discouraged from voting by local officials. Voting discrimination has existed in some parts of the United States throughout our history, and Congress's decision in 1975 to renact the 1965 Voting Rights Act and dramatically expand its coverage is strong evidence that the problem remains. The legislation now authorizes federal supervision of local elections in all or part of Alabama, Alaska, Arizona, California, Colorado, Florida, Georgia, Louisiana, Mississippi, New Mexico, New York, North Carolina, South Dakota, Texas, Utah, and Wyoming.[29] The continued need for this important remedial legislation should make judges doubt whether the exclusive use of voter lists to impanel jurors is well designed to ensure that no population group is discriminated against.

Many of the inequities that follow from use of the list of registered voters as a sole source for jurors could be lessened if the process of registration were simplified, and a drive has been under way in Congress during most of the 1970s to do just that through a system of registration by mail. Originally proposed by Senator

Edward M. Kennedy (D., Mass.) and more recently pushed by Senator Gale W. McGee (D., Wyoming) and Jimmy Carter, the bill would require that every postal patron be sent a postcard at least 30 days before each election, which she or he would be asked to fill out and mail to the designated state or local election official. The postcards would also be available at all post offices and at federal, state, and local government offices. Although the bill as written would cover only federal elections, states would be encouraged to participate for local elections as well, through payments by the federal government of up to 130 percent of the cost of processing their postcards.[30]

Because of opposition by Republicans and southern Democrats, who have argued, among other things, that it would encourage "voter fraud," that "the constitutional right of states to determine voter qualifications would be infringed,"[31] and that it would offer an open invitation for people to "steal the election of the President of the United States and Senators and Congressmen,"[32] the legislation has yet to be enacted. The emotionalism of such arguments can be countered by the evidence that postcard registration has been done in Great Britain for years, and several states—including Texas, Maryland, New York, and Minnesota—now use a postcard registration system without any noticeable fraud. Almost every other governmental function is now performed by mail—including, of course, the filing of income tax returns—in an orderly fashion. With the aid of computers, all names and addresses can be easily screened to catch those instances of fraud that may occur.

Simplifying registration procedures should mean a significant increase in the number of people who register and vote and hence of those who can be reached by courts seeking jurors through the voter lists. Until such a system of simplified registration has been adopted nationwide, and until it has been demonstrated to have eliminated discrepancies among registration rates for different groups, we must continue to search for supplemental lists that will accurately reflect all segments of the community.

## FINDING A CROSS-SECTION

The representative jury is the defendant's right, which should no more be impeded by the test of registering to vote than by any other test. As U.S. District Judge Charles Wyzanski, Jr. (of Massachusetts) forcefully wrote in a 1972 opinion:

> The defendant has a right . . . *not to have the pool [of prospective jurors] diminished at the start by the actions or inactions of public officials, nor*

*by the inertia, indifference, or inconvenience of any substantial group or class who do not choose to vote or to serve on juries.* From the viewpoint of a black, or young, or poor, or rich defendant, his interest is in having a pool with a fair proportion of blacks, young, poor, and rich. To him it is a matter of indifference as to whether a diminished pool is due to action or inaction or third persons, whether public or private. In substance, the defendant is entitled to require that the public officials charged with jury selection, including judges who excuse jurors, proceed in such a way as to compel the calling of *all eligible for jury duty* who do not have socially valid excuses. In this connection jury duty is an obligation owed to the defendant, not a privilege which at the juror's pleasure the juror may choose to exercise or forego.[33]

If we are committed to the goal, as expressed by the Supreme Court, of a "jury drawn from a fair cross-section of the community,"[34] we must continue to seek selection methods that will produce that cross-section.

The Federal Jury Selection Act states that the voters list should be supplemented by other lists whenever it does not produce a fair cross-section of the community.[35] To bolster its "declaration of intent" that defendants have a right to a jury "selected at random from a cross-section of the community," the federal act provides that "the defendant may move to dismiss the indictment or stay the proceedings against him on the ground of *substantial* failure to comply with provisions of this title in selecting the grand or petit jury."[36] The statute does not, however, give the precise measure of underrepresentation from a true cross-section, and no federal judge has yet ordered a federal court to supplement the voter lists,[37] although a federal judge did say that local jury commissioners in Mississippi should have supplemented in *Ford v. Hollowell* (1974).[38] The questions that remain unanswered are how to determine "substantial" failure to comply and what to do about it.

The legislative history provides little guidance on these questions. Representative Robert W. Kastenmeier (D., Wisconsin) discussed the matter of supplementing the voter lists during the House debates:

In the past, in some parts of the country, Negroes were largely excluded from the electoral process. The Voting Rights Act of 1965 has altered this situation significantly. Still, there are some areas where the percentage of Negroes registered to vote are much lower than that for white. In such areas, the juror-selection plan *must* prescribe sources in addition to voter lists.[39]

Representative Emmanuel Cellar (D-N.Y.) stated when he introduced the bill on the floor of the House that it would be up to the courts to decide when "substantial" deviations occurred:

The bill uses the term "fair cross section of the community" recognizing that there will be *minor* deviations from a fully accurate cross section. The voting list need not *perfectly* mirror the percentage structure of the community, but any *substantial* percentage deviations must be corrected by the use of supplemental sources. The committee would leave the definition of "substantial" to judicial decision.[40]

As we saw in Chapter Three (p. 60) the courts have thus far alternated between two main methods of computing underrepresentation, the "comparative" method and the "absolute" method.[e]

[e]Two other methods of computation have been suggested and occasionally used:

1. *The Proportion-of-Eligibles Test*, first proposed by the U.S. Commission on Civil Rights in a 1968 memorandum, measures the operation of the selection plan in terms of the percentage of different groups selected:

If analysis discloses that there is a disparity of 20% or more between the proportion of eligible minority persons selected, then steps shall be taken to remedy this disparity.

The criterion set out above is based on the view that the most meaningful and accurate measure of racial disparity in jury selection is a comparison between the proportion of voting age whites and the proportion of voting age blacks who are included in the pool drawn upon in making up the jury wheel.

Thus, for example, if names for the master jury wheel are selected from voter registration lists, the criterion can be expressed in terms of a comparison between the proportion of voting age whites who are registered, as against the proportion of voting age blacks who are registered.

The 20% disparity level expressed in the guideline above means that if 70% of voting age whites are registered, then at least 56% of voting age blacks must be registered to vote.

On its face, this racial disparity in which 70% of voting age whites, but only 56% of voting age blacks are drawn from seems indefensible. This level is recommended here, however, as an interim and experimental measure. It is an "interim" measure in the sense that once 1970 census data and more complete jury questionnaire data are available, a more rigorous standard of equality should be feasible.

(This suggestion was included in a staff memorandum prepared by the Office of General Counsel, United States Commission on Civil Rights, entitled "Assuring a Fair Racial Cross Section in the Selection of Jurors under the Jury Selection and Service Act of 1968," and quoted in Walter Pettus Gewin, "Should Guidelines be Established for Determining When District Courts Should Use Other Sources of Names of Prospective Jurors in Addition to Voter Registration Lists or Lists of Actual Voters, and, If So, What Guidelines Should Be Used," *The Jury System in the Federal Courts* (Works of the Committee on the Operation of the Jury System of the Judicial Conference of the United States, 1966-73) (St. Paul: West Publishing Co., 1974), pp. 107-108. This test is also discussed in Gewin, "An Analysis of Jury Selection Decisions," 506 F.2d 805, 818 (1975).)

This method of computation was used by Federal District Judge Alvin B. Rubin of New Orleans in a 1973 decision, and he said that using this method a 10 percent underrepresentation could be considered minor, a 30 percent underrepresentation would definitely be "substantial," and a 16.7 percent

The comparative method "compares" the percent of a demographic group on the jury to the percent in the population and computes the difference between those two figures. This difference is then divided by the group's percent of the population to determine the level of underrepresentation or "rate of error."[41] The absolute method,[42] as explained before, looks only at the difference between the percent on the jury and the percent of the population,[f] and thus makes it extremely difficult for small population groups ever to complain of underrepresentation.[43]

Several judges have grappled with these tests in recent years in an

---

underrepresentation (the one he was faced with) "strikes me as one where the weights are about evenly balanced." *United States v. McDaniels*, 370 F. Supp. 298, 304 (E.D.La., 1973), affirmed sub nom *United States v. Goff*, 509 F.2d 825 (5th Cir. 1975).

2. *The Statistical-Decision-Theory Approach*, a more statistically sophisticated test, was suggested in 1973 by B.R. Stauber to William B. Eldridge, the director of research for the Federal Judicial Center, which helps monitor the success of the 1968 Act, (see Gewin, "Should Guidelines Be Established . . . ," pp. 108-109, and Gewin, "An Analysis of Jury Selection Decisions," p. 818, and has been persuasively promoted by several commentators. (See Finkelstein, "The Application of Statistical Decision Theory to the Jury Discrimination Cases," *Harvard Law Review* 80 (1966): 338; Sperlich and Jaspovice, "Statistical Decision Theory and the Selection of Grand Jurors: Testing for Discrimination in a Single Panel," *Hastings Constitutional Law Quarterly* 2 (1975): 75.

This test would ascertain whether the proportion of various population groups vary from their size in the community by more than would be expected if the jury wheels were in fact selected in a true random fashion:

> Thus, if the population of a given area is 80% white, and a random sample of 5,000 is selected, the probability is approximately 85% that the proportion of the sample comprising white population will be between 78.9% and 81.1%. The probability is approximately 99% that the proportion of white population in the sample will be between 78.5% and 81.5%. The probability is about 1% that the proportion of the sample consisting of white races in a random sample will fall outside the latter limits. (Gewin, "Should Guidelines Be Established . . . ," 108-109; and Gewin, "An Analysis of Jury Selection Decision," p. 818.)

These figures can be easily computed according to standard statistical theory, but some policy decision on the maximum allowable limit must still be made. University of California (Berkeley) Professor Peter Sperlich and his associate Martin Jaspovice have suggested a 0.05 level of probability (i.e., a 5 percent chance that an unbiased selection scheme will be judged biased) as an acceptable compromise to balance this type of error against the error of letting a biased selection scheme pass as unbiased. Sperlich and Jaspovice, "Statistical Decision . . . ," p. 82, n. 36.)

[f]Some courts have expressed confusion over whether they should compare a group's percentage on the jury to its percentage in the population or to its percentage on the voter lists. See, e.g., *Sanford v. Hutto*, 394 F. Supp. 1278, 1280-81 (E.D.Ark., 1975). It is clear that the percentage on the jury should be compared to the percentage in the adult population, because this is the community that we are attempting to obtain a cross-section of. See *Bradley v. Judges of the Los Angeles Superior Court*, 531 F.2d 413, 415 n. 1 (9th Cir. 1976), and *Murrah v. Arkansas*, 532 F.2d 105, 108 (8th Cir. 1976).

attempt to determine what rate of error should be considered substantial, but most cases have involved federal court review of state courts still using the "key-man" selection procedure, which always contains an "opportunity to discriminate." These decisions may not, therefore be directly analogous to the problem of reviewing federal juries impaneled from voter lists. One federal judge ruled in a case involving the local courts of St. Francis County, Arkansas, that a 14 percent underrepresentation of blacks, using the absolute system, constituted substantial underrepresentation, because of the opportunity to discriminate that resulted from the use of a discretionary selection procedure.[44] A second federal judge ruled that a 63 percent underrepresentation of blacks on the juries of Calhoun County, Mississippi, using the comparative system, was unconstitutional and required that the jury commissioners supplement their efforts to find black jurors.[45] A third judge found that a 5.2 to 86.3 percent underrepresentation of blacks and a 49.8 to 89.9 percent underrepresentation of women (over a six-year period) on the grand juries of San Francisco County, California, using the comparative method, was "sufficiently substantial to establish a *prima facie* case of unconstitutional exclusion."[46]

One of the few decisions that discusses these tests fully in a case arising out of a federal jury selection is *United States v. Test*, a 1975 case from Colorado.[47] Federal District Judge Alfred A. Arraj was faced with figures showing that Chicanos in the Grand Junction Division constituted 8.89 percent of the voting-age population but comprised only 4.81 percent of the jurors in a random sample taken from the jury wheel. The rate of error, using the comparative test was thus −46 percent, but the difference in absolute terms was only 4.08 percent. Judge Arraj concluded that this underrepresentation was not "substantial" enough to require the use of supplemental lists, because it amounts to only 2 persons on a jury panel of 50, 0.9 persons on a grand jury of 23 and 0.49 persons on a trial jury of 12.[48]

This approach makes it virtually impossible for a minority group that does not constitute at least a quarter of the population ever to complain successfully about discrimination, because their numbers in absolute terms will always be small, and it thus seems to defeat the purposes of Congress in passing the 1968 reform legislation. Judge Arraj's view that an additional Chicano on every grand jury and one more on every other trial jury would make little difference also seems contrary to experience. A jury decision, as explained in Chapter Two, is always the composite of different views, and each additional perspective helps the other jurors to come to a more reasoned decision.

Some standards must be set if corrective action is going to be required in specific cases, and the intent of the federal act is to be more than a verbal commitment. My own view is that the comparative method more accurately expresses the real impact of the selection scheme on minority groups, most of whom appear in relatively small numbers in our country (which is why they need particular judicial protection).

The suggestion of the Civil Rights Commission that a 20 percent underrepresentation (or "rate of error") should trigger some attempt to supplement the voter registration list[49] seems appropriate in the usual case. If an underrepresentation is observed over two consecutive years, however, then a lower rate of underrepresentation—10 percent—would be a more appropriate standard. A particular problem arises when a group is very small—under 5 percent of the eligible population—because of the inherent uncertainties of any random draw. In the case of such small groups, a somewhat higher rate of underrepresentation should be required: 40 percent during one year, 20 percent over a two-year span, 10 percent if it holds at that steady rate of underrepresentation for three or more years. And for those very small population groups—under 1 percent—the required rate of underrepresentation should be doubled once again: 80 percent during one year, 40 percent over a two-year period, and 20 percent for three or more years. Whenever these figures are reached, the selectors should be required to supplement the list of voters with some compensating source of names.

## SUPPLEMENTATION WITH OTHER LISTS

The most important effort to obtain representative juries by supplementing voter lists is that of the Uniform Jury Selection and Service Act,[g] a model state statute drafted in 1970 by the National Conference of Commissioners on Uniform Laws, which has thus far been adopted by three states—Colorado, Idaho, and North Dakota—and experimentally by a fourth—Indiana.[h] Although patterned on the federal act, the Uniform Jury Selection Act is more aggressive in its commitment to include a cross-section of the community. Whereas the federal act *permits* each federal court district to supplement voter lists, the Uniform Act "makes such supplementation mandatory,"[50] citing the two main reasons for doing so:

---

[g]See Appendix M, p. 411.

[h]Indiana adopted the bill in 1971, but applied it only to Lake County, in the northwest corner of the state next to Chicago. The Indiana Supreme Court subsequently interpreted the bill to eliminate the requirement that the voter list be supplemented by additional lists.

Exclusive use of voter lists as the basis for selecting citizens to be called for jury service may have a chilling effect upon exercise of the franchise, particularly by wage-earners for whom jury service may be a particular economic hardship. Principally for that reason the Report of the President's Commission on Registration and Voting Participation (November, 1963) recommended that voter registration lists be used only for electoral purposes. Furthermore, voter lists typically constitute far from complete lists of the citizens qualified for jury service. Considerable filling out of the master list to be more inclusive than the voter lists is necessary to carry out the declaration . . . that "all qualified citizens shall have the opportunity . . . to be considered for jury service."

The use of voter registration lists as the exclusive source for jurors does discourage some people from voting.[51] Some people who realize that they will be put on the jury rolls only if they register, and who feel for economic or personal reasons that they cannot spare the time required for jury service, choose not to register. A penalty is thus exacted for voting. Only if people believe that all citizens are equally subject to being summoned for jury service will they accept the assignment without resentment. The exclusive use of the voter list as the source for jurors thus not only fails to produce representative juries but also discourages some people from voting, interfering with the democratic nature of both elections and jury service.

What other lists might be used to replace or supplement the voter list in order to avoid these problems? After examining the other lists that might be available, most observers have concluded that the list of holders of drivers' licenses is most convenient and best suited in most—although not all—areas to supplement the voters' list because it provides a large number of additional names of potential jurors. Taken together, the voters' list and the drivers' license list provide a much more complete list of the residents of the area than the voters' list alone, and these lists are convenient, accessible, and easy to use with the aid of computers. Some people are still missed, though, because not even in our highly automotive society does everyone drive. The poor, women, the young, and especially the old are underrepresented on the drivers' lists. Before looking at the drivers' license list, a quick review of other possible lists will help to show why this list is probably the best single choice if only one additional list can be used.

Three sources of names possessed by the federal government could theoretically increase the pool of jurors considerably, even to the point of ensuring that almost everyone had the chance of being called as a juror, but some legal and philosophical problems might be raised if we used these lists for jury selection. (1) Census lists, which include almost everyone in the country and are updated every five years, have never—so far as we know—been used for any other purpose. (2) Almost everyone at some point in life obtains a Social Security number, and these numbers are used for some other purposes. (3) Finally, most people file income tax returns, even if they earn a minimal amount of money, and use of the income tax lists plus the welfare and unemployment lists could theoretically produce the names of most Americans over 18.

The convenience of these lists is, however, just what argues against employing them to select juries. A serious and extended national debate would have to precede the use of any of these lists for another purpose. Such a debate is already under way regarding use of Social Security numbers, which—because of the 1976 federal tax bill—can be used by the states for drivers licenses and to track down runaway fathers.[52] The precedent of using these lists—even for so benign a purpose as jury selection—smacks of a "national registration" scheme that many people find alien to our traditions of freedom.[53] Many Americans rebel against the idea of the government having a complete list of all of us for fear that such a list might be misused, but such lists are now available to the government (and probably have been misused). So perhaps they might as well be used for jury selection.

In some parts of the United States where local censuses are conducted, these lists are used as a source for jurors. The cities and towns of Massachusetts conduct an annual census compiled by police officers who walk door to door asking for the names of the inhabitants. Under a bill proposed by the Chief Judge of the Superior Court in 1974 and still under relatively active consideration by the Massachusetts legislature, Suffolk County (containing Boston) would have used their police census as their exclusive source for jurors, thus providing an almost complete list of residents for their juries.[54],[i] In Kansas, the county assessors conduct an annual census, and counties have the option to use that list either in conjunction with the voter list or as the exclusive source for jurors. In Kansas City, Kansas, the two lists are combined by computer, but in more rural parts of the state, the census list has sometimes been found to be less up-to-date than the voter registration list, and so the latter is used exclusively.[55]

Some lists that have been used in certain areas instead of voter registration lists, or to supplement the voters' list, tend to under-

---

[i]These lists have in fact been used by other Massachusetts towns as a source of jurors, as noted on p. 87, but local officials have gone over the lists personally, exercising discretion in their choices, whereas in the Suffolk County proposal names would be pulled randomly from the census.

represent the same groups that are also underrepresented on voter lists and thus should be used sparingly—if at all. Prominent among these are city directories, tax rolls, telephone books, and utility company lists.

*The Polk City Directory* is published annually or bi-annually in virtually all urban areas for the use of businesses that solicit by direct mail. It is compiled from two sources: lists of employees provided by the major employers of the area and a limited amount of door-to-door canvassing. Since businesses are interested in the stable and affluent members of the community, these are the people most likely to be canvassed. Furthermore, the directories decisively underrepresent the young, even more than do voter registration lists. Despite this inherent bias, city directories have until recently been a popular source of names for jurors. The city of Denver used its city directory as the exclusive source for jurors until 1971, and Washington, D.C., used it as the exclusive source until 1973, when it was found to drastically underrepresent the poor.ʲ

Juries in Montana are still assembled exclusively from *tax lists.* This system involves an overt and obvious economic discrimination; yet it has been upheld as constitutional by some courts, under the theory that it does not constitute systematic discrimination against any cognizable group.[56] Exclusion of the poor is the most evident bias in such lists. In addition, because different types of tax rolls are sometimes used together, and because lists such as the real estate rolls will list a property owner separately for each piece of property, they are highly repetitive and inefficient..

A number of jury commissioners in California counties and elsewhere have from time to time used *the telephone book* as a source for names, but it has proved to be inadequate because it includes many businesses, has multiple listings for some people, and

ʲOf the 500 questionnaires sent in 1971 by the clerk's office for the District of Columbia District Court to names listed on the District's master wheel, which was assembled exclusively from the Polk City Directory, 134—26.8 percent—were returned by the post office as undeliverable, indicating that the directory is out-of-date and inaccurate. Of those who did respond, only 56.2 percent were black, compared to the citywide percent of 72.4 black (an underrepresentation of 22.4 percent). A comparison by the D.C. Public Defender's Office of three lists of the poor to the Polk list found that 76 percent of the D.C. residents on the list of disadvantaged job applicants in the Manpower Administration files were omitted from the Polk Directory; 59 percent of the Washington residents who applied for legal assistance at the federally funded Neighborhood Legal Service offices were omitted from the list; and 82 percent of the arrested D.C. residents who were processed by the D.C. Bail Agency were not in the directory. The Polk Directory also discriminates decisively against the young. (*United States v. LaVance Green,* 72-1130 (D.D.C., 1972); *United States v. Randolph Greene,* 72-1272 (D.D.C., 1972).)

is seriously biased in favor of men, the middle aged, and the middle class. A few jurisdictions have experimented with the customer lists of gas and electric companies, but these lists are also seriously biased in favor of men and the more affluent.

The drivers' license list overcomes most of these faults in a majority of areas. In most parts of the United States, a very high percentage of adults have drivers' licenses; generally, more people have drivers' licenses than are registered to vote. Young people particularly obtain drivers' licenses in much larger proportions than they register to vote. Poor people and nonwhites also tend to obtain drivers' licenses somewhat more frequently than they register to vote. In Michigan, nine out of every ten people of driving age are licensed to drive.[57] In California, the State Department of Motor Vehicles has an automatic file containing (as of April 1973) about 12.4 million names—compared to only 8.7 million people who were registered to vote in the state for the November 1970 election. Even after subtracting the approximately 400,000 who are sixteen and seventeen,[58] the list of drivers approaches the entire over-18 population in the state (as of the 1970 census) of 13.3 million. Because of these arguments, the California Legislature in 1975 specifically authorized the courts of California to start using the drivers' license lists as a supplemental source of jurors,[59] and many counties have begun to take advantage of this opportunity.

The exclusive use of the list of drivers' licenses would undoubtedly discriminate against certain persons—particularly the elderly, who tend to drive less frequently than the young; the poor, especially in urban areas; and to a lesser extent women, who hold only 43.2 percent of America's drivers' licenses.[60] But—as the discussion below of the experiences in Colorado and North Dakota indicates—the drivers' license list can be a valuable supplemental source of names. Since the elderly and women are underrepresented primarily because of excuses, increasing their numbers on the wheel is generally not one of the goals of supplementation.

Other sources have also been suggested and used. Attorneys have from time to time proposed a wide variety of supplemental lists—including lists of welfare recipients, lists of selective-service registrants, and tribal rolls. These lists should be seriously considered when particular population groups are missing from jury panels in parts of the country where drivers' lists may not be so complete. In Alaska, lists of persons with hunting and fishing licenses are used as a source for jurors, in addition to lists of voters and tax rolls. In Washoe County, Nevada (containing Reno), the list of registered voters is taken off a computer tape, and then a small number of names are taken from the city directory, the tax list of homeowners, and lists of union members, and compared with the list of voters. This comparison is done by hand by the clerical workers in the county courthouse and is largely symbolic but it nonetheless ensures that voters are not the only ones subject to jury duty.

The most significant efforts at supplementation have been undertaken in those states that have adopted the Uniform Jury Selection and Service Act: Colorado, Idaho, and North Dakota. Their experiences point up some of the problems and achievements of combining various lists.

In Colorado, the voter registration list was supplemented in 1972 by the city directories compiled by the Polk Company in the large cities and by the Johnson Company in smaller towns, but this source alone was not considered adequate because of the decidedly middle-class nature of the directories. Thus, in 1973, the list of the holders of drivers' licenses and the motor vehicle registration list were also used. Because the motor vehicle list was found to add only a few names, it was dropped for 1974. The three remaining lists—voter registration, city directories, and drivers' licenses—are fed into a computer programmed to sort out duplicates and produce a master list.

The process of sorting out duplicates is still somewhat imperfect because names appear in different ways on different lists. For instance, Robert F. Doe may be listed as R.F. Doe in the city directory, Robert Doe on his voter registration affidavit, and Bob Doe on his driver's license. The computer checks for duplicates by scanning the last name and title (i.e., Jr., Sr., etc.), the first four letters of the first name, and the first four digits of the house number, but not the street name. If a perfect match is found, the second name is dropped from the master list; otherwise, it is retained. The Colorado Judicial Department estimates that about 10 percent of the names on its master lists are still duplicates even after the computer's scanning efforts are completed. A few genuinely different people are, in addition, eliminated because of coincidental similarity in names and addresses.

A 10 percent duplication figure seems acceptable when one notes the impressive number of names added by the two supplemental lists. After the 1974 master list was developed, for instance, most Colorado counties had almost twice as many names for potential jurors as they had from the voters' list alone. In Denver County, for instance, 280,836 persons had registered to vote, but 307,202 persons held drivers' licenses and 219,427 names were listed in the City Directory. After the three lists were combined, and 249,447 duplicates (30.9 percent) were eliminated, the master list contained 558,018 names, almost exactly double the number of voters.[61]

In Idaho, the procedure of adding names has been more difficult and less successful than in Colorado. Idaho's Supreme Court decided in 1972 that the list of registered voters should be supplemented with names from public utilities and drivers' licenses lists, but because the Master Drivers' License file was not automated until 1975, Idaho counties were obliged to proceed for several years with only the list of the electric company's customers. This one additional list produced an enormous number of duplicates and only a few new names.[62] The task of sorting out the duplicates has been arduous, since as of 1973 only one county (Kootenai) had a computerized operation. In Ada County (containing Boise), duplicates were not sorted out until names were selected from the two lists.[63] Thus, a person on both lists had twice the chance of being selected as a juror as a person on only one of the lists, defeating the goal of eliminating the discrimination caused by the use of any one list.

District Judge Alfred C. Hagan of Boise, who was one of the drafters of the Uniform Act and who has been instrumental in implementing the act in Idaho, has been rather unhappy about the way the supplementation process has been undertaken and would prefer a more flexible approach, which would require each judicial district "to use those lists indigenous to the population of that particular district." For instance, he suggests that in Bannock County (Pocatello), which contains an Indian reservation, tribal rolls should be used, and in Canyon County, containing a large migrant worker population, lists of those migrant workers should be obtained from their employers.[64]

In North Dakota, where most counties do not have voter registration, the list of actual voters is supplemented with that of drivers' license holders, with good results in terms of adding new names. In three of the larger counties, where duplicates were eliminated by hand (an arduous process), the wheel was increased by 80 percent in two cases and 100 percent in another. The system has been particularly impressive in discovering young jurors, who tend to be underrepresented on voter registration lists but overrepresented on drivers' license lists. (See pp. 345-46.)

**Revolving the Wheel.**   Whether prospective jurors come from only the voter registration list or from other sources as well, the method in which the jury wheel is compiled and refilled can dramatically affect the ultimate demographic make-up of a court's jurors. In the federal system, the master wheel is compiled by taking names from the voter registration list at given numerical intervals. Many of the more populated districts enlist a computer to perform this task, and, if so, the possibility of human bias in the preparation of the master wheel is eliminated. In some districts, however, clerks still wade through the voter lists by hand, and here the temptation to examine the list when selecting names remains. Three political scientists from the Massachusetts Institute of Technology examined the voter lists used by the federal court for the District of Massachusetts between 1968 and 1972 and discovered that although the requisite "interval number" for selecting names was 498, the intervals between names selected in fact fluctuated from 469 to 499. In addition, the lists of voters from some Massachusetts towns had fewer than 498 names on them, and in those situations, the clerks usually selected the last name on the list.[66]

In all federal courts, the statutory requirement that the master wheel be filled only every four years[67] accentuates the weakness of the voter registration lists (which already overrepresent the older and more stable members of the community) by discriminating against the young and those who move frequently. By the fourth year of the wheel's existence, no one under 22 will be on it, and a high percentage of those over 22 but under 30 or 35 who are in the wheel will have moved. This difficulty may be aggravated still further if obtaining the voting lists involves any particular difficulty. In the federal court for the District of New Mexico, for instance, it takes the clerk's office a year to round up the voting lists from throughout the state, meaning that these lists are at least a year old before they go into the federal master wheel.[68] During the final year of that wheel's operation, no persons under 23 will be called for jury duty.

The Uniform Jury Selection Act provides for refilling of the master jury wheel every two years—an improvement over the federal system but still tending to underrepresent the young. A "Model Jury Selection and Service Act" proposed in March 1973 by the National Conference of Metropolitan Courts, an assembly of big-city trial judges—which followed the lead of the Uniform Act in requiring that some supplementary lists be used in addition to the list of voters— insisted that a new list of voters be obtained at least once a year to avoid the "decay" in the voter lists which "is great in areas with mobile populations."[69] This seems the best means to minimize discrimination against certain groups.

\* \* \* \* \*

Many courts have made definite progress toward obtaining juries that represent a fairer cross-section of the community, but this progress is not yet complete. Some states still use the key-man system, or variations on it, to select their jurors. Most use voter registration lists as the basis for their jury wheels. Although exclusive use of voter lists has administrative advantages that make many courts reluctant to supplement them, the disparities between the representation of some groups in the population and on voter lists, and the negative effect of making jury duty a "penalty" for voting, make supplementation essential. The Federal Jury Act and the State Uniform Jury Selection Act both recommend use of supplemental lists where necessary, although the latter is more firmly committed to this procedure. The success of states that have undertaken serious efforts at increasing the base of prospective jurors argues strongly for a policy of supplementation. As more courts gain experience with supplementation, the trial-and-error nature of experiments such as Colorado's will no longer be necessary, although each jurisdiction will have to discover its best combination of lists. Consideration should be given to using government sources such as the Census and Social Security lists for jury duty, as these lists would probably prove to be the most representative juries of all.

The ideal of a representative jury, a right of all defendants, should not be forgotten in satisfaction over the progress achieved by abandoning the "blue ribbon" juries of the "key-man" selection system. And assembling a list of possible jurors is just the beginning of the selection process. The major stages to come—excuses, *voir dire*, and peremptory challenges—can undo much of the gains achieved through better master lists.

## NOTES

1. 28 *U.S.C.* sections 1861-69.

2. 28 *U.S.C.* sec. 1861 (emphasis added).

3. 28 *U.S.C.* sec. 1862.

4. 28 *U.S.C.* sec. 1863 (b) (2).

5. 28 *U.S.C.* 1863 (b) (4), as amended by Public Law No. 92-269, Section 3 (c) (April 6, 1972).

6. Letter from the Clerk of the U.S. District Court, Western District of Texas, printed in Subcommittee on Improvements in Judiciary Machinery of the Senate Judiciary Committee, *Hearings, Federal Jury Service*, 90th Cong., 1st Sess., March 21-July 20, 1967, pp. 415-16.

7. See, e.g., Charles A. Lindquist, "An Analysis of Jury Selection Procedure in the United States District Courts," *Temple Law Quarterly* 41 (1967): 32; Edwin S. Mills, "A Statistical Study of Occupations of Jurors in a United States District Court," *Maryland Law Review* 22 (1962): 205; Edwin S. Mills, "A Statistical Profile of Jurors in a United States District Court," *Law and the Social Order* (1969): 329.

8. *Mass. Gen. Laws Ann.*, ch 234, sec. 4 (Supp. 1972).

9. *Code of Alabama*, Title 30, sec. 24.

10. Note particularly *Norris v. Alabama*, 294 U.S. 587 (1935); *Swain v. Alabama*, 330 U.S. 202 (1965); *Bokulich v. Jury Commission*, 394 U.S. 97 (1969); *Carter v. Jury Commission*, 396 U.S. 320 (1970); *Black v. Curb*, 464 F.2d 165 (5th Cir. 1972); *Preston v. Mandeville*, 428 F.2d 1392 (5th Cir. 1970) and 479 F.2d 127 (5th Cir. 1973); *Penn v. Eubanks*, 360 F. Supp. 699 (M.D.Ala. 1973).

11. See, e.g., *Pierre v. Louisiana*, 306 U.S. 354 (1939); *Patton v. Mississippi*, 332 U.S. 463 (1947); *Avery v. Georgia*, 345 U.S. 559 (1953); *Reece v. Georgia*, 350 U.S. 85 (1955); *Eubanks v. Louisiana*, 356 U.S. 584 (1958); *Arnold v. North Carolina*, 376 U.S. 773 (1964); *Whitus v. Georgia*, 385 U.S. 545 (1967); *Jones v. Georgia*, 389 U.S. 24 (1967); *Sims v. Georgia*, 389 U.S. 404 (1967); *Turner v. Fouche*, 396 U.S. 346 (1970); *Alexander v. Louisiana*, 406 U.S. 625 (1972); *Taylor v. Louisiana*, 419 U.S. 522 (1975).

12. *S.C. Code*, sec. 38-52.

13. Cal. Const., Art. 1, sec. 8.

14. For more complete discussions of grand juries, see Van Dyke, Wolinsky, Broder, Elliott, and Reilly "Quadra v. Superior Court of San Francisco: A Challenge to the Composition of the San Francisco Grand Jury," *Hastings Law Journal* 27 (1976): 565-636; and Van Dyke, "Grand Juries: Representative or Elite?" *Hastings Law Journal* 28 (1976): 37.

15. Interview with A. Erickson, Denver County Jury Commissioner, July 3, 1972.

16. *Arkansas Statutes*, 39-101 and 102.

17. Putnam and Wilson, "The Arkansas Jury Wheel Act of 1969," *Arkansas Law Review* 24 (1970): 50; and see Light, "Does Arkansas Need the Jury Wheel?" *Arkansas Lawyer* (June 1967): 6.

18. U.S. Bureau of the Census, *Current Population Reports*, Series P-20, No. 253, "Voting and Registration in the Election of November 1972," (Washington, D.C.: Government Printing Office, 1973).

19. *State v. Campbell et al.*, Nos. 29, 155-56 (Shawnee County, Kansas, District Court, October 11, 1974), *reversed* 217 Kan. 756, 539 P.2d 329 (1975).

20. "Operation of the Jury System," 42 F.R.D. 353, 362 (1967).

21. *Hearings, Federal Jury Service*, p. 253.

22. Jury Selection and Service Act of 1968, *U.S. Code Congressional and Administrative News* (House Report No. 1076) (1968), pp. 1792, 1796.

23. "Report of Committee on Jury Selection" (Jan. 29, 1965), prepared by the Milwaukee Circuit Judges Max Raskin and Herbert J. Steffes and County Judge William R. Moser (unpublished).

24. Sen. Gale McGee, "Postcard Voter Registration," *Virginia Law Weekly (Dicta)* 26 (1973): 1.

25. *New York Times*, Nov. 4, 1973, p. 36 (city ed.).

26. Clayton Fritchey, "Blaming the Pols for the (Low) Ballot Count," *Washington Post*, Dec. 16, 1972, sec. A, p. 19.

27. McGee, "Postcard Voter Registration."

28. *United States v. Whitley*, 491 F.2d 1248, 1249-50 (8th Cir. 1974).

29. *New York Times*, May 4, 1975, p. 19; and July 29, 1975 (both city editions).

30. 93rd Cong., S. 352., H.R. 8053.

31. *New York Times*, March 16, 1972, p. 1 (city ed.).

32. Senator Sam J. Ervin, quoted in *New York Times*, May 11, 1973, p. 63 (city ed.).

33. *United States v. Burkett*, 342 F. Supp. 1264, 1265 (D.Mass. 1972).

34. *Taylor v. Louisiana*, 419 U.S. 522, 527 (1975).

35. 28 *U.S.C.* sec. 1863 (b) (2).

36. 28 *U.S.C.* sec. 1867 (a) (emphasis added).

37. "Report of the District Court Panel on Jury Selection in the District of Massachusetts," 58 F.R.D. 501, 505-506 (1973).

38. 385 F. Supp. 1392 (N.D.Miss. 1974).

39. *Congressional Record* 114 (90th Cong., 2nd Sess.): 3998 (emphasis added).

40. *Ibid.*, p. 3990 (emphasis added).

41. This term, "rate of error," is used in the Appendixes of this volume and was used by Federal District Judge Charles B. Renfrew in the case of *Quadra v. Superior Court of San Francisco (II)*, 403 F. Supp. 486, 495, n.9 (N.D.Cal. 1975).

42. Examples explaining both the comparative and absolute methods are given in Gewin, "An Analysis of Jury Selection Decisions . . . ," 506 F.2d 805, 818.

43. See, e.g., *United States v. Jenkins*, 496 F.2d 57 (2d Cir. 1974), and *United States v. Goff*, 509 F.2d 825 (5th Cir. 1975).

44. *Sanford v. Hutto*, 394 F. Supp. 1278, 1281-82 (E.D.Ark.), *affirmed*, 523 F.2d 1383 (8th Cir. 1975); see also *Murrah v. Arkansas*, 532 F.2d 105 (8th Cir. 1976), involving similar statistics from Miller County, Arkansas.

45. *Ford v. Hollowell*, 385 F. Supp. 1392, 1398 (N.D.Miss. 1974).

46. *Quadra v. Superior Court of San Francisco* (II), 403 F. Supp. 486, 495-96 (N.D.Cal. 1975).

47. 399 F. Supp. 683 (D.Colo. 1975).

48. *Ibid.*, p. 697.

49. See Gewin, "An Analysis of Jury Selection Decisions . . . ," p. 818.

50. Much of this discussion is taken from McKusick (who was the chairman of the committee that drew up the Uniform Act) and Boxer, "Uniform Jury Selection and Service Act," *Harvard Journal of Legislation* 8 (1971): 280.

51. *Report of the President's Commission on Registration and Voting Participation* (Washington: Government Printing Office, 1963), p. 38; "Juries: The Ordeal of Serving," *Time*, Feb. 7, 1969, p. 35; Senator Edward M. Kennedy, "Use of Voter Registration Lists for Jury Selection," U.S. Senate, 94th Cong., 1st Sess., April 15, 1975 (*Congressional Record*, p. S5985).

52. *Honolulu Advertiser*, Sept. 17, 1976, p. C-7.

53. See, e.g., Kairys, "Juror Selection: The Law, a Mathematical Method of Analysis, and a Case Study," *American Criminal Law Review* 10 (1972): 771.

54. Mass. House Bill No. 5889, sec. 12 (1974).

55. Letter from the Hon. Frederick Woleslagel, Twentieth Judicial District,

Lyons, Kansas, Feb. 28, 1972. See *State v. Campbell*, 217 Kan. 756, 539 P.2d 329 (1975).

56. See, e.g., *Wright v. Smith*, 474 F.2d 349 (5th Cir. 1973); *Donlavey v. Smith*, 426 F.2d 800 (5th Cir. 1970); *Roach v. Maudlin*, 391 F.2d 907 (5th Cir. 1968), cert. *denied*, 393 U.S. 1095 (1969); *Acuff v. State*, 283 P.2d 856 (Okla. Cr. 1955); *Porter v. District Court of Oklahoma County*, 462 P.2d 338 (Ct. Crim. App. 1969); *Leggroan v. Smith*, 498 F.2d 168 (10th Cir. 1974).

57. *New York Times*, March 28, 1973, p. 12 (city ed.).

58. Robert J. Cozens, *Projected Motor Vehicle Registration and Drivers Licenses Outstanding, 1970-90*, Report No. 48 (Sacramento: Department of Motor Vehicles, October 1974), p. 16.

59. California Code of Civil Procedure, sec. 204e, as amended by 1975 Statutes, c. 657, sec. 3.

60. *New York Times*, July 15, 1973, p. 54.

61. From interviews and correspondence with Rayma Cox and Ed Zimny of the Colorado State Judicial Department, Denver, in 1974 and 1975.

62. Note, "Voter Registration Lists: Do They Yield a Jury Representative of the Community?" *U. of Michigan Journal of Law Reform* 5 (1972): 400.

63. Letter from Alfred C. Hagan, Ada County District Judge, April 9, 1973.

64. *Ibid.*

65. *New York Daily News*, June 9, 1976.

66. Hayward R. Alker Jr., Carl Hosticka, and Michael Mitchell, "The Jury Selection Process in Eastern Massachusetts" (1973), pp. 17-18 (unpublished).

67. See note 5.

68. Interview with L.G. Kanaly, Clerk, District of New Mexico, Albuquerque, June 3, 1974.

69. National Conference of Metropolitan Courts, *Final Report on the Jury Administration Project* (Los Angeles: The author, March 1973), p. 54.

## Chapter Five

## The Second Stage: Excuses

The second stage of selection—excuses—presents its own share of obstacles to impaneling a representative jury.

Although jury service is supposed to be a right and privilege of citizenship, most people consider it a nuisance. Being a juror is time-consuming and inconvenient, and it is frequently a financial hardship as well. In some jurisdictions, jurors may be required to serve for several months, continuously. Getting to the courthouse every day may be a problem. Those who care for children or the old or infirm must find someone to do that task, possibly at considerable cost. Those with heavy responsibilities in their work believe they cannot be absent for a few weeks or longer; those in insecure positions may fear loss of their jobs. Many in fact will lose income.

About 60 percent of all people whose names are pulled from the master wheel and who receive a questionnaire seeking to determine their qualifications for jury service return the document requesting to be excused. The excuse stage actually involves three separate procedures in many courts, each with its own criteria: disqualifications, automatic exemptions, and excuses (which are generally discretionary and determined by personal hardship). Excuses may be granted, furthermore, at three different points in many courts: first, when persons selected from the "master wheel" are sent questionnaires; second, if they pass the first hurdle and are put onto the "qualified wheel," when they are sent a summons for jury duty; and third, when they come to the courthouse on the day they are called for jury service. Some courts use their master list as the qualified wheel, skipping the first stage, and reducing the opportunity for prospective jurors to claim an excuse. The courts' response to requests for excuses plays a major role in determining the makeup of juries. The standards by which courts evaluate potential jurors, although varying greatly among jurisdictions, generally tend to create disparities among groups, even where the master wheel fairly represents the population.

Most courts accommodate those who do not want to serve. The courts have generally found it easier, administratively and financially, to excuse unwilling people from service on juries than to try to ensure that all qualified jurors are able to serve. The fact that certain types of people tend to be excused at a higher rate than others means that the goal of representative juries is frequently impeded. Women, blue-collar workers, the aged, and the young are those most often assumed by courts to be inconvenienced by jury service. But the real problems of serving are rarely dealt with in a way that will increase participation by a broader range of people.

**Money.** Economics play a large role in the maneuvering about who ends up sitting in a jury room and who manages to avoid it. Courts are generally underfunded and jurors are underpaid. In what seems to be a vicious cycle, because jurors are paid so little, they are not used efficiently, and jury service becomes that much more underpaid for its inconvenience and apparent uselessness.

Federal jurors receive $25 a day or $3.13 an hour, only slightly more than the 1976 minimum wage of $2.30 an hour. Extended over an average working year of 250 days, the $25 payment would provide a worker with $6,250, which is just barely above the poverty line. Of the state court systems, about 40 percent still pay their jurors less than $10 a day, and included among these are some of the richest and most populous states, such as California, New Jersey, Ohio, Pennsylvania, and Texas. Just twelve states pay over $12 per day, and only five—Alaska, Hawaii, Maine, North Dakota, and South Dakota, an improbable group—pay $20 per day. Delaware raised its juror pay to $20 in 1970 but reduced it again to $15 the following year.

Few persons making more than the minimum wage can afford a sudden and involuntary cut in pay for a period of weeks or more. Only those earning less than they would be paid as jurors and those whose economic prosperity enables them to absorb the "cost" of jury duty would not suffer financially. For those who are employed, the question whether their salary will be continued during jury duty is of paramount importance. Current practices form a patchwork, but two generalizations can be made: (1) the larger the employer, the more likely it is to continue paying employees during jury duty; and (2) white-collar workers are more likely to be paid than blue-collar workers. A nationwide survey of employers conducted in 1961 by the National Industrial Conference Board found that 91 percent of those with 5,000 or more employees were paying their employees during jury service, but fewer than 70 percent of those with less than 1,000 employees continue payments during jury service. Many manufacturing companies pay white-collar but not blue-collar employees, and a substantial number of companies allow their white-collar employees to keep their juror fees plus their regular salary, while requiring blue-collar employees to turn over their jurors' fees to the company.[1] A 1967 California study of 1,812 union agreements discovered that only 539 agreements (29.7 percent), covering only 33.5 percent of 1.5 million workers, included a salary-continuation clause; and that workers in manufacturing industries were more likely to be compensated than workers in nonmanufacturing industries (61.4 to 19 percent, respectively).[2] This situation is gradually improving, and a 1973 study by the U.S. Labor Department found that 847 out of 1,339 collective bargaining agreements examined (covering 4.2 out of 6.7 million workers) did have some kind of a provision to help compensate workers while on jury duty.[3]

Those whose salaries will be continued tend to serve on juries, while those who will not be paid request—and are usually granted— excuses. In Shelby County (Memphis), Tennessee, juries tend to include a disproportionately high number of persons employed by the large companies that do continue salaries. A survey of jurors who served during September and October 1972 by James Cole, a reporter for the *Memphis Commercial Appeal*, discovered that 133 of the 480 persons (or 27.7 percent) who finally "qualified" for jury duty worked for only seven large organizations.[a] International Harvester, which employs fewer than 0.5 percent of the county's population (3,200 workers), supplied 8.8 percent of the jurors, an astounding average of one person per jury.[4]

In order to equalize the economic burden of jury duty, two

| | |
|---|---|
| [a]International Harvester | 42 |
| Defense Depot Memphis | 20 |
| United States Post Office | 19 |
| Memphis Light, Gas & Water Division | 17 |
| Firestone Tire & Rubber Company | 16 |
| Kimberly-Clark Corporation | 11 |
| South-Central Bell | 8 |
| | 133 |

states—Hawaii and Alabama—have passed statutes requiring employers to continue an employee's salary during jury service. The Hawaiian law, which required every employer with more than 25 workers to continue the salary of any employee who served on a jury or participated on any public board,[5] was declared unconstitutional in 1970 by the Hawaii Supreme Court as a violation of the equal protection and the taking clauses of both the United States and Hawaiian Constitutions.[6] The Alabama statute, which requires the employer to pay an employee called for jury duty the worker's normal salary less the $6 per day received for jury duty,[7] was also attacked on constitutional grounds in a case that went to the United States Supreme Court. The Court decided in 1973 that the U.S. Constitution does not bar such a requirement, which is simply an economic decision and thus up to the legislature to make.[8] Because the Hawaiian decision rested on the Hawaiian Constitution as well as the federal Constitution, the U.S. Supreme Court cannot review that decision, but its 1973 decision may at least have persuasive value on other states that might consider such a statute.

These statutes simply make mandatory a practice already common among large businesses. They leave out, however, many persons usually left off juries—the hourly-wage and daily-wage earners, the underemployed, and the unemployed. Those whose livelihood depends largely on commissions are also not adequately compensated by simple salary-continuation plans. Thus, although such laws are helpful in equalizing the burden of service to prospective jurors, they must be combined with a higher daily compensation.

In 1974, Congress raised the fee paid to jurors in federal court from $20 to $25,[9] but that is still totally inadequate to compensate jurors for the time demands imposed upon them and to encourage the courts to use jurors' time wisely. A fee of $40 was proposed by the Chief Judge of the Suffolk County (Boston) Superior Court in 1974.[10] With the continuation of inflation since then, the proper figure now is probably $50 a day, which is equivalent to an annual salary of $12,500, still below the national family average, but a reasonable wage (and one that would encourage the courts to use their jurors' time more efficiently).

**Time.**  As important as the monetary consequences of jury duty for many is the amount of time involved. These may of course be related; for those who do not receive salary continuation, or whose livelihood depends on commissions or part-time work, the length of service is especially important. Many of the contract agreements that do continue a worker's salary during jury duty impose a maximum time limit, frequently as low as two weeks. Even aside from monetary considerations, the prospects of a long period of service may discourage most people from willingly serving as jurors. (For compensation and length of service in federal and state courts, see Table 5-1.)

Jurors in many federal courts are on call for 4 months and report for duty on 30 separate court days. Some courts (the Superior Court in San Francisco, California, for instance) keep jurors "on call" for a year, and a month or more of actual service is not at all uncommon. An on-call system is particularly disruptive because the calls are not predictable, and prospective jurors cannot arrange their lives with certainty. The courts that require a month or more of jury service do so on grounds of administrative convenience, arguing that the first day of service is frequently taken up with procedural matters and that once a juror is selected, qualified, summoned, and oriented, the court wants to use the juror for an extended period.

In fact, a great deal of the prospective jurors' time is spent waiting. Perhaps the low compensation most courts provide jurors fosters this lack of efficiency, for the courts apparently feel they are losing relatively little in wasting jurors' time. Most jury commissioners summon many more jurors than they need, which in addition to wasting money also discourages many from making the necessary sacrifices to report for jury duty. Many never actually sit on a jury. In the federal system, which has perhaps the best-trained court administrators in the country, 43.5 percent of the persons called for jury services on an average day between July 1, 1972, and June 30, 1973, never sat on a jury that day; 28.4 percent of them were not even sent into a courtroom and hence served no purpose. The annual dollar cost of this excess was $6.2 million (out of the total annual trial jury expenditure of $14.2 million), and the cost of the jurors not even sent into a courtroom was $4 million.[11] The monetary loss nationwide caused by inefficient use of jurors is probably about $50 million[12]—money that could be saved by more effective jury management and pumped back into the system to produce more representative jury panels.

Inefficient use of jurors fosters lack of respect for the jury system. Chief Justice Warren Burger has stated that the "most severe criticism of the courts in general and the jury system in particular has come in recent years from laymen who have served on juries."[13] If citizens are to welcome, rather than resent, the call to jury duty, their time must be put to good use, and their sacrifice must be respected by the courts. The Federal Judicial Center, in a publication on juror utilization, noted that most jurors complain about waiting

**Table 5-1. Compensation and Length of Service for Jurors (State and Federal Courts)**

| Court | Fee Paid to Juror, Per Day | Length of Required Service |
|---|---|---|
| All Federal Courts | $25 | On-call up to 4 months; cannot be forced to serve more than 30 court days unless a trial is in progress |
| Alabama | $6 | 1 week |
| Alaska | $21 | 3 months |
| Arizona | $12 for Superior Court; $4 for Justice Court or Inquest | 5-20 days; on-call for 60-120 days |
| Arkansas | $7.50; $5 if not selected to serve on a trial | 24 days of actual service or on-call for 6 months, whichever is shorter |
| California | $3 to $10, varies by county; $5 in San Francisco (including mileage); $5 in Los Angeles | 4-20 court days; on-call for 3 months to a year. San Francisco— 20 court days, Los Angeles—30 calendar days |
| Colorado | $6 if selected to serve on a trial, $3 if not | 2-4 weeks |
| Connecticut | $10 | 4 weeks; on-call for one year |
| Delaware | $15 | 5-6 weeks |
| District of Columbia | $25 | Subject to call over a 2 month period. Average 10-15 days of service. 1 month in the Superior Court |
| Florida | $10; $25 for statewide grand juries | 1 week |
| Georgia | $5-$25 ($15 in Fulton County [Atlanta]) | Maximum of 4 weeks (4 days in Fulton County [Atlanta]) |
| Hawaii | $20 | 30 calendar days |
| Idaho | $10; $5 for half day | 10 court days or 60 calendar days, whichever comes first. |
| Illinois | $4-$10 ($10 in Cook County) | 2 weeks |
| Indiana | $7.50; $5 in city courts; $20 in Lake County only | On-call for 3 months (usually less than 2 weeks of actual service) |
| Iowa | $5 | Minimum of 2 trials; maximum of 2 months in counties with more than 50,000 people, 3 months in less populated counties |
| Kansas | $10 | 2 weeks |
| Kentucky | $5 | 1 month |
| Louisiana | $8 | 1 week |
| Maine | $20 | 15 court days |
| Maryland | $5-$15. Prince George's County and City of Baltimore pay $10; Montgomery County pays $15 | Generally 2-4 weeks; in Prince George's County: 5 weeks of service over a 6 month period |

**Table 5-1.** (cont.)

| Court | Fee Paid to Juror, Per Day | Length of Required Service |
|---|---|---|
| Massachusetts | $14-$22, depending on the type of case | Varies from county to county. 20 days in Suffolk County (Boston). |
| Michigan | $15; $7.50 for half day | 1 term of court (3 months); 1 day or 1 trial in Wayne County (Detroit) |
| Minnesota | $10; $6 in some counties | 30 calendar days; 10 court days in Hennepin County (Minneapolis). |
| Mississippi | $8 | 1 week |
| Missouri | $12 - City of St. Louis; $6 elsewhere | 2 weeks in counties of fewer than 200,000; 1 week in more populous counties |
| Montana | $12 | 90 days to one year |
| Nebraska | $10 | 2 weeks |
| Nevada | $15 for actual service, $9 for reporting to duty | Reno: 3-8 court days; on call for 6 months |
| New Hampshire | $15 | Terms of court are 2½-3½ months. No one is obliged to serve more than 30 actual days |
| New Jersey | $5 | 1 session (varies by county); 10 days in Essex County (Newark). |
| New Mexico | $1.60 per hour | 30 calendar days (average of 12 appearances) |
| New York | $12 | 2 weeks to one year |
| North Carolina | $8 | 1 week |
| North Dakota | $20 ($8 in lower courts) | 10 days |
| Ohio | Set by County Bd. not to exceed $10; $5 in Cuyahoga County (Cleveland) | 2-3 weeks |
| Oklahoma | $7.50 | 3 weeks, subject to a 6 day extension |
| Oregon | $10 | 4 weeks |
| Pennsylvania | $9 | 2-3 weeks |
| Rhode Island | $15 | 2 weeks |
| South Carolina | $2-$10 | 1 week |
| South Dakota | $20 | One term of court (varies by county) |
| Tennessee | $10 | Usually 2-4 weeks (varies by county) |
| Texas | $4-$10 (usually $5) | 1-2 days, one trial per juror |
| Utah | $8 | Once a week for 3 months |
| Vermont | $15 | 90 calendar days |
| Virginia | $12 | An average of 7-10 days, on-call for 1-2 months |

**Table 5-1.**  (cont.)

| Court | Fee Paid to Juror, Per Day | Length of Required Service |
|---|---|---|
| Washington | $10 | 4 weeks |
| West Virginia | $5-$8 | Varies by county |
| Wisconsin | $4-$16 ($12 in Milwaukee) | 1-2 months |
| Wyoming | $12; $6 for half day | On-call for 6 months to 1 year |

time.[14]  Presently, only the judge's time is valued in most courts, and a surplus of jurors is called to fulfill every possible need. The Federal Judicial Center recommended that judge costs be balanced with juror costs, which are now ignored, and that courts should call a smaller number of jurors after calculating the acceptable risk that there might be too few jurors for the day's schedule.

The statutory length of jury service should also be reduced. Requirements for service of more than two weeks seem unnecessary, and a one-week obligation would be best because only a few people could then honestly complain about economic hardships. Only a very few trials last more than a week, making a short term possible for most jurors. In the federal courts in 1972, only 22.8 percent of all jury trials lasted more than three days, and only 2.9 percent exceeded nine days.[b,15]

The Uniform Jury Selection and Service Act limits jury service to ten court days, and the Model Act prepared more recently by the National Conference of Metropolitan Courts recommends that service be limited still further, to five days, in order to impanel the most representative jury possible.[16]  The Texas Legislature passed a law in the early 1970s stating that a juror's tour was over whenever that juror had sat on one trial to a verdict or had been challenged peremptorily or for cause during the selection process, and as a result, the average juror now serves for only one or two days. The proposed jury bill for Suffolk County (Boston), Massachusetts, would limit jury service to five days, unless a trial were in progress.[17]  Such limitations reduce the financial, employment, and personal inconvenience for all potential jurors and would almost certainly produce more representative jury panels. Jury service should be

bAnother reason for limiting the time of service is if persons serve as jurors for a number of weeks, they become "professional" jurors, applying the instructions given in one case to the facts of another, comparing arguments with each other, and losing the fresh approach that a juror has in her or his first trial. See Broeder, "Previous Jury Trial Service Affecting Juror Behavior," *Insurance Law Journal* (1965): 13.

considered in fact—as well as in theory—an obligation of citizenship, but it should not be an onerous burden.

Efforts that make it easier to serve as a juror are unfortunately still the exception rather than the rule. Attempts to streamline court procedures, to improve juror pay and treatment, and to deal rationally with requests for excuses are rare. The courts' consideration of the inconvenience of jury duty should be balanced by an awareness of the importance of serving on a jury, for the defendant and for society as a whole. But most courts pursue the path of least resistance, many permitting those who protest any kind of inconvenience to be excused, and others grant excuses readily to certain categories of people, while subjecting others to stricter tests of hardship—a situation that often makes for less representative juries.

**Excuses.** Whenever an excuse is offered to a particular group of persons, most in the eligible group will take advantage of the offer. Jury service involves a major time commitment and offers practically no financial rewards, so when an excuse is offered it is fair to say that the person offered the excuse is "induced" to take it. Generally, only those who are obliged to serve will actually do so.

**Economic Hardship.** The low wage paid to most jurors and the possibility of an extended period of service make excuses for economic hardship very common. These excuses affect not only the socioeconomic composition of juries but often the facial makeup as well since a large number of nonwhites are also in lower socioeconomic strata. Most jury commissioners and judges will automatically excuse laborers and sole proprietors of business who claim that jury service will cause them to lose their daily wage or to close up their business for a period of time. As noted in Chapter Three, in the same Supreme Court case—*Thiel v. Southern Pacific Co.* (1946)—where explicit exclusion of hourly workers was prohibited, the principle was expressed that "a federal judge would be justified in excusing a daily wage earner for whom jury service would entail an undue financial hardship."[18] This is still the policy of most federal and state courts, as the following examples suggest:

1. In Honolulu, 10.7 percent of all persons who received jury questionnaires in 1974 were granted a discretionary excuse because they were "hourly employees," working on a commission, were self-employed, or would suffer some other job-related hardship (this figure is in addition to all persons who are statutorily excused).[19]

2. J. William Devereaux, the jury commissioner in Denver, Colorado, has stated flatly that he excuses anyone who is not being compensated by his or her employer during jury service.[20]
3. During the selection of jurors for Angela Davis's 1972 murder trial in San Jose, California, Judge Richard Arnason automatically excused all those who would not continue to draw their salaries during the trial, and the California Supreme Court specifically approved this practice as recently as March 28, 1973.[21]
4. Some judges in Maryland ask for volunteers among prospective jurors when a trial is likely to extend longer than two weeks, and a Maryland appellate court upheld that practice in 1973 even though it clearly eliminates many laborers.[22]

Such practices obviously affect the representativeness of the resulting juries, as described by H.M. Frediani, Jury Commissioner in Riverside County, California:

> Far too many citizens in lower income brackets who are summoned from the voters list, find it an economic impossibility to serve. Young adults starting in the working world, and other adults in low income situations, who are not compensated by their employer while serving on jury duty, cannot afford to give up their salary or commission to serve. This becomes even more critical when they have the responsibility for the support of others. *Unfortunately, this exclusion hits rather heavily at the minority groups, especially Black and Mexican-American citizens, due to their economic situation.*[23]

A similar picture was drawn by W. Otis Higgs, Jr., the only black judge in Shelby County, Tennessee:

> I've had occasion to qualify venires. To begin with, there are as many blacks as there are whites. Then you get the legitimate excuse that "Judge I can't live on eight dollars a day." Most of these people are black.
> The salary ought to be raised. Perhaps the answer is a legal requirement for all employers to compensate for jury duty. But there has to be some scheme to allow poor people to serve.[24]

The specific effect of such exclusion has been documented in a number of studies:

1. Because of the lengthy time commitment on many grand juries and their elite tradition, excuses for economic hardship are particularly common. Sacramento County, California, selects some of its grand jurors from the same voter registration list that serves as a source for jurors, but the jury commissioner meets with

every prospective grand juror and tells him or her about the extensive time commitment involved and the relatively low payment provided ($10 per day). Although 39.8 percent of the county's employees hold blue-collar jobs, and 32.3 percent of those sitting on trial juries are blue-collar workers, only 12.4 percent of those who choose to put themselves in the grand jury pool are blue-collar employees.[2 5]

2. Prior to the 1968 murder trial of Huey P. Newton in Alameda County (Oakland), California, the defense team examined the granting of excuses in the county and discovered that 44.5 percent of all persons receiving questionnaires during the period studied were found qualified countywide, but in the heavily black section of West Oakland, only 30.1 percent of recipients passed into the qualified wheel after excuses.[2 6]

3. Law students at Arizona State University examined the flow of prospective jurors through the Maricopa County (Phoenix) courts in the spring of 1972. According to the census data, 57 percent of the employed population in the county work on blue-collar jobs. Of the 744 employed persons who received summonses to be jurors, only 50.5 percent had blue-collar jobs, and of those who actually served as jurors only 45.5 percent had blue-collar jobs.[2 7]

4. Finally, the Los Angeles Public Defender's Office made a study in the early 1970s of the excusing process in Los Angeles County and discovered that persons living in low-income areas request economic hardship excuses at a rate almost twice as high as persons who live in middle-class areas (22 percent as compared to 12 percent).[2 8]

These disproportions that result from excuses for economic hardship are antithetical to our concept of a representative jury. Increased compensation and a reduced period of service would eliminate the need for such excuses.

**Women.** In a great many jurisdictions, excuses to women outnumber all others except those for poor health. Virtually all the state and federal courts grant excuses liberally to women (in their role as mothers). Forty-six of the 94 federal districts grant an excuse to mothers of children under the age of ten, two districts excuse mothers of children under seven, one sets the age at 5, seven at 12, one at 13, three at 14, one at 15, and six at 16.[2 9] Most of the other districts have a vague provision that permits the clerks to exercise their own discretion. The only consistency among federal courts is that almost all the districts that permit this type of excuse grant it only for women, thus discriminating against those men who bear primary or equal responsibility in the raising of their children.

The statutes of five state courts (Alabama, Georgia, Massachusetts, Missouri, and Tennessee) permit women to be excused from jury duty automatically, and in each of these states, juries are heavily dominated by men (see Chapter Two, p. 40). New York State's automatic excuse for women was removed from its statutes in 1974, and Louisiana's practice of summoning only those women who volunteer for jury duty was struck down by the U.S. Supreme Court in 1975 as being discriminatory.[30] In Tennessee, bills to remove the automatic excuse are regularly introduced into the legislature, but they rarely move beyond the initial hopper. The Shelby County Jury Commissioner, Robert Horne, has said that he is in favor of changing the Tennessee statute ("I think women are just as aware of what's going on as men, with the news media like it is today"),[31] but his practice has nonetheless been to summon only one woman for every fifteen men[32] on the ground that those summoned will simply ask for an excuse if called, thus increasing his administrative work. In addition, women jurors summoned for a complicated trial requiring sequestration are excused for cause by the court in Shelby County because the court is unwilling to pay the extra expense of sequestering a female juror in a hotel and paying a female sheriff overtime to supervise her activities (sequestered male jurors are placed in a dormitory facility in the Shelby County jail).[33]

As would be expected, those jurisdictions that permit an excuse for those who care for young children or the aged and infirm experience a sharp drop-off in the number of women jurors. The surveys taken by the federal courts themselves (see Appendix I, p. 350) show that this underrepresentation-through-excuses is a nationwide phenomenon. In 83 percent of the surveys taken by the federal district courts themselves, the percentage of women on their juries was smaller than the percentage of women on the master wheels from which jurors are originally drawn, and frequently the reduction was dramatic (see Appendix K, p. 392).[c] In the Northern District of California, for example, over half the women between the ages 25 and 44 who receive questionnaires are excused because they have children. Virtually no men are excused for this reason.[34] In the Northern District of Florida, according to a survey by sociologist Jay Schulman, the questionnaires of 246 women who had been excused in 1973 for the care of children revealed that 121 of the 246 women (49.2 percent) were either employed or actively seeking employ-

---

[c]See Chapter Two for a more complete discussion of the underrepresentation of women on juries (pp. 39-42).

ment.[35] These women thus had some method for caring for their children other than personal supervision, but were nevertheless excused from jury duty.

Because most people who are offered an automatic excuse will take it, the policy of offering such excuses to women with children almost ensures an underrepresentation of this group on juries. If courts paid a daily fee high enough to cover child care and reduced the time of jury duty to a manageable limit in areas where it now exceeds a week, more mothers would be likely to serve. It should be noted that most of the 13 states that automatically excuse mothers with children permit such an excuse if children are from 10 to 16 years old. Although it might be reasonable to allow parents of infants or preschoolers to be at home with their children, it is certainly unnecessary to consider those with children over the age of 6 as indispensable at home during the day (again, given adequate child care possibilities).

**The Aged and the Young.** Automatic excuses for the aged are given in 28 states plus the District of Columbia, and even in those states that do not authorize an excuse by statute, the elderly can frequently obtain one very easily. California, for instance, authorizes no excuse for the aged. Yet any person in Sacramento County over 65 who requests an excuse obtains one, whether or not a letter from the doctor accompanies the request; persons under 65 seeking a medical excuse must have a doctor's letter.[36] Colorado similarly grants no excuse for the aged by statute, but in Denver, such excuses are granted automatically to anyone over 65 who requests one.[37] The state of Washington grants excuses by statute to persons over 60, and a specific request does not appear to be required. Former Supreme Court Justice William O. Douglas, a resident of Goose Prairie, Washington, received a jury questionnaire when he was still on the Court in 1973, dutifully filled it out without requesting an excuse, and was automatically excused because he was 74.[38]

All of the 94 federal districts, except the Southern District of Mississippi, the Southern District of Iowa, and the Eastern District of Kentucky, have some provision regarding an excuse or exemption for the aged, but the provisions vary widely. Fifteen districts, most of them in the Fifth Circuit (which stretches from Texas to Florida), forbid persons over 70 from becoming jurors; sixty-five other districts allow the over-70 to serve, if they want to, but do not require them to become jurors; seven districts set the age for automatic excuses at 65; and three districts, all in the mid-Atlantic districts of the Fourth Circuit, will only permit persons over 75 to have an automatic excuse.[39]

The young are also excused in large numbers for a variety of reasons—they are attending school, have young children at home, are in an economically precarious position and will not receive any salary while on jury duty, are in the military, or have moved. Most jury commissioners are particularly receptive to excusing students.[40] Some try to postpone the student's service to another time of year, but too often the student becomes lost in the administrative shuffle or ignored because fewer trials occur in summer. A number of courts—particularly those with a heavy concentration of students (such as the municipal court in Berkeley, California, and the Federal District Court for the Northern District of California)—do give an automatic excuse to students. The federal statute does not authorize the granting of excuses to students, but 17 of the 94 districts (most of them in the Midwest) nonetheless do so. Five other districts (all in the mid-South) grant excuses only to medical students, and one district (the Southern District of New York) grants excuses only to law students.[41] In 1972, the U.S. Circuit Court of Appeals for the Ninth Circuit dismissed a challenge to the granting of excuses to students, saying that the actions of the district courts with regard to the granting of excuses will be virtually unreviewable.[42]

If jury duty were limited to one week, and a system was established for rescheduling students during vacation periods, the underrepresentation of young people on jury panels could be reduced. As for the elderly, those who are physically unable to serve should be excused, but no one should be excluded merely because they are a certain age. Even many who are ill at the time they are called may be well enough to serve later and should be recalled if their illness is such that they will probably be able to serve at another date.

**Transportation.** Some people are excluded from juries because they live more than a certain distance from the court. The Federal Jury Selection Act authorizes each district to set maximum distances (in either miles or hours) beyond which jurors need not travel. As might be expected, given the vast difference in geography from district to district, not to mention varying attitudes about excuses, the rules vary greatly. The mileage figures range from 25 miles (in the federal court for the Eastern District of New York) to 250 miles (for grand jurors in South Dakota). The federal court in Hawaii does not require residents of islands other than Oahu to travel to the courthouse in Honolulu for jury duty. Thirty of the 93 federal districts do not set a maximum mileage despite the instruction in the statute; these include some huge districts, such as three of the four districts in Texas, the three districts in Florida, and the District of Maine. The local clerical officials in those areas excuse persons for travel difficulties unguided by specific rules.[43]

State courts, of course, also excuse some people because they live too far from the courthouse. The Superior Court of San Bernardino County, California, the largest county geographically in the continental United States—with 20,117 square miles encompassing most of the desolate Mojave Desert—excuses any prospective juror who lives more than 25 miles from the county courthouse. This rule eliminates 17.1 percent of the population and all of the people who live in the desert oases (some parts of the county are 300 miles from the courthouse). The California Court of Appeals for the Fourth District dismissed a challenge to this mileage limitation, saying: "While experience tells us attitudes may differ along lines of education, sex, age, race and social and economic class, we are not aware they normally differ along lines respecting place of residence within a county."[44]

If mileage limits do not discriminate against any particular group, they should be viewed as matters of administrative discretion and should raise no grave problem. Persons living in rural areas do, however, have different perspectives and perceptions than persons who live in the cities and suburbs, and in that case, representativeness *is* affected. In some locations, the problem may be more serious than simply a rural-urban split. The Alaska Supreme Court struck down in 1971 a state law granting an automatic exemption to anyone living more than 15 miles from the courthouse on the ground that virtually all the native Alaskans (Aleuts) were thereby eliminated from jury service.[45] (The federal district court in Alaska has set 50 miles as the limit beyond which residents will be given an excuse upon request.) Similar situations occur in other parts of the country. The travel exemption, for instance, for the U.S. District Court for the Southern District of California in San Diego is 40 miles, which eliminates most of the residents of Imperial County, which has a higher percentage of Chicanos than does San Diego County.

Some jurisdictions do succeed in including people from outlying areas on their juries. Inyo County, California, which contains 10,130 square miles (including Death Valley), provides lodging expenses for people who live more than 75 miles from the courthouse rather than automatically excusing them from jury service. And Placer County, California, has a major population center (Lake Tahoe) 88 miles from its courthouse in Auburn but will not grant an excuse simply because of the distance involved. Although accommodating those who live at significant distances from the court will probably be a low-priority issue, even for those concerned with representative juries, the experience of areas that have managed to encourage jury service by those living in outlying areas—through positive incentives like Inyo County's lodging fees or negative ones like Placer County's unwillingness to grant automatic excuses—should be studied.

**Illness.** Some excuses are unavoidable and necessary, for persons who have recently served as jurors, for example, or who are ill. In fact, in most of the courts surveyed, poor health was a leading cause for excuses. Most jury commissioners require a letter from a doctor before they will grant a health excuse, but none has developed guidelines concerning what type of illness or incapacity will justify a permanent excuse. The lack of clear guidelines is illustrated in the wide fluctuation of excuses in Honolulu County for "physical defects," the general health category used in that court: in 1968, 1,498 persons (5 percent of those sent questionnaires) were excused for this reason; in 1969, 584 (1.8 percent); in 1970, 1,210 (3.9 percent); in 1971, 1,163 (3.6 percent); in 1972, 42 (0.1 percent); in 1973, 1,211 (3.8 percent), and in 1974, 1,583 (5.9 percent).[46] Assuming a relatively constant number of sick people, it is difficult to imagine strict standards producing such results.

In most cases, a letter from a doctor, no matter what it says, will lead to a person's being permanently struck from the jury rolls. Only a few jury commissioners grant temporary excuses and then call the person again when he or she recovers, because it is so much easier administratively to summon some other name off the master wheel than to bother keeping track of those who are excused for illness. It is impossible to know whether permanent removal of these names results in less representative juries, although it is likely that a large number of the sick are also elderly and that the proportion of the elderly is thus reduced.

**Rationalizing the Excusing Process.** Few courts give much thought to the validity of excuses or their effects on the juries ultimately impaneled. Yet it is in the excusing process that the greatest amount of court discretion concerning jury service comes into play. The clerical officials who examine the daily stack of returned questionnaires requesting excuses must either grant automatically all of the requests; consider each request on an ad hoc basis, without any guidelines; or review them according to some formula developed by their office or their judges. Statutes provide guidelines but leave wide room for variation.

The Federal Jury Selection and Service Act instructs each federal district court to prepare a list of occupational classes whose members should be excused because their service would "entail undue hardship or extreme inconvenience," as long as no particular discrimination would result thereby.[47] The Senate and House reports on the bill provide little guidance to the district courts in their efforts to determine what groups should be excused, saying only:

> Such groups might include among others, doctors, ministers, sole proprietors of businesses, and mothers of young children. Members of excused groups could serve if they desired to do so, but a request for an excuse must be granted. For example, a mother with young children might prefer to hire a babysitter in order to be free for jury duty, but if she chooses not to hire one her request for an excuse must be granted.[48]

The plans for the 94 district courts differ dramatically in their listings of occupational excuses. Three districts—South Carolina, western North Carolina, and western Virginia—grant no occupational excuses whatsoever. The other districts all have elaborate lists that invariably include doctors, lawyers, and nurses, and frequently clergy (83 percent of the districts), school teachers (65 percent), and sole proprietors of businesses (42 percent). But except for these more-or-less agreed-upon occupations, the various plans have no semblance of uniformity. Eight districts grant excuses to "licensed practitioners of the healing arts and professions, who are actively engaged therein"; twenty-two districts excuse pharmacists; ten districts excuse veterinarians; one district excuses embalmers, six excuse morticians, four excuse funeral directors, and one excuses employees of funeral parlors. Among other occupations automatically excused by at least one federal district are farmers, commercial airline pilots, telegraph and telephone operators, carriers of the U.S. mail, and full-time salespersons working for commissions.[49] Most states also have their own unique set of occupational excuses, as Appendix C shows (p. 271).

Individuals who are not members of designated groups may also be excused, but in their cases, the personal discretion of the jury commissioner, judge, or court clerk can be expected to play a bigger role in determining whether they will be excused. Theoretically at least, they will have to prove that jury service will entail a hardship.

It is difficult to determine from statistics which courts grant excuses on an ad hoc basis and which ones use more standard guides to determine whether an individual should serve. One thing that is clear from surveys of the first two stages of excusing (questionnaires and summonses, which are discussed in Appendix K, p. 383) is that courts vary widely in the proportion of prospective jurors that they excuse.

Even within jurisdictions, there can be widely varying standards and practices. A memorandum written by John O'Hagan, shortly after he was named jury commissioner for the Fremont, California, Municipal Court in August 1972, to his colleagues in Alameda County (California) describes the erratic nature of granting excuses that then existed:

> There is a vast disparity in the interpretation of section 200 C.C.P [which at that time listed the statutory excuses and exemptions in California] as far as exemptions go. Berkeley [Municipal Court] excuses full-time students, no-one else does. This court [Fremont Municipal] excuses people who don't drive, no-one else does. The Superior Court [in Oakland] excuses all city and county employees; the municipal courts don't; and the Superior Court excuses jurors for ten years after serving, the Municipal Courts excuse them for only one year. In short, the present system is one replete with all of the failings so often applied to bureaucracies as indications of their ineptness. It has duplicity, confusion, wastefulness, inefficiency, and lack of central accountability built into it.

The states that have adopted the Uniform Jury Selection and Service Act (Colorado, Idaho, and North Dakota) plus eight states that have recently enacted reforms in their jury selection schemes (Arizona, California, Kansas, Kentucky, Maryland, New Mexico, Texas, and West Virginia) have eliminated most automatic excuses from their statutes and now require a particular showing of hardship before excusing anyone. The Uniform Act stipulates that the only excuses that will be granted are those required by "undue hardship, extreme inconvenience, or public necessity," and that when such excuses *are* granted, they should be limited in time "for a period the court deems necessary, at the conclusion of which the person shall reappear for jury service in accordance with the court's decision."[50] The proposed 1974 Suffolk County (Boston), Massachusetts, jury bill similarly would give each juror the right to select the week that would be most convenient at any time within eight months after the juror was summoned.[51]

The official "comment" to the Uniform Act sets the stage for the controversy over excuses and exemptions:

> The Uniform Act proceeds on the principle that jurors should be selected by random methods from the widest possible list of citizens. The corollary is that actual service on the jury should be shared as widely as possible and in particular that professional and business groups be excused only in cases of demonstrated need. The so-called "blue-ribbon jury" is outlawed by the Uniform Act. At the same time, business and professional groups within the community should not be permitted to avoid jury service. *It is also*

*believed that citizens in general will be more willing to perform jury service if it is known throughout the community that jury service is universal, barring only particular hardship in specific cases.*[52]

This approach recognizes that juries will not be representative unless representative source lists are used *and* unless as many people as possible from those lists are actually brought onto the jury panels. The rationale for excluding members of some professions—doctors and teachers, for example—on the ground that their services cannot be spared by the community can be answered by efforts to make jury duty less inconvenient and time-consuming and by rescheduling jury service where possible.

The philosophy expressed in the Uniform Jury Selection Act is not shared by most courts, state or federal (and it has not even been followed rigorously in the states that have adopted the act). Most jury commissioners do not question a request for excuse, no matter what the juror's occupation, because they know they can fill the jury boxes with individuals who will not resist the call. It is simply easier to summon large numbers of jurors than to pursue rigorously a smaller number. In fact, one study on court efficiency, prepared by the Institute of Judicial Administration in 1971, proposed that clerks should be more lenient in granting excuses in order to reduce the time required to impanel a jury once the trial is ready to begin (see Appendix K, p. 391).

The practice of excusing everyone who asks to be excused has an enormous number of adherents. George Hart, until recently the Chief Judge of the U.S. District Court for the District of Columbia, says that he excuses virtually everyone who requests an excuse "because I don't think a person who wants to be excused will make a good juror, and it would not be fair to the court, to the litigants, or to the public to make him serve. I remember in Virginia a juror who didn't want to serve was forced to and he hung every case he sat on."[53] Federal District Judge David Middlebrooks of the Northern District of Florida similarly believes that people who request even temporary postponements will make poor jurors, and he excuses them permanently from jury service.[54] The same pattern prevails in state courts. Many court officials in all parts of the country told me candidly that they followed the rule that, as the jury commissioner of Marin County, California, put it, "A person who resents jury service, even if he has no legal excuse, won't do you any good in the long run."[55]

But the objective of a jury fairly representing a cross-section of the community will be sacrificed when only the eager actually serve as jurors. The more discretion permitted those who process question-naires and grant excuses, the greater the opportunities for bias. The implications of granting excuses to all who request them are serious because those who remain after all requests for excuses are granted are in essence volunteers. They are not "randomly selected" and very possibly not representative. Very few people welcome the call to jury service. Many people, of course, do feel a duty to serve despite the inconvenience, but generally the inconvenience of serving outweighs their sense of duty. Easy excuses remove these persons from the jury panel. Where excuses are granted automatically, or almost automati-cally—as for women with children and the elderly—the proportion of that segment of the population on the jury panel is almost inevitably reduced.

The only way to prevent clerks and judges from altering the representative qualities of a jury wheel through the wholesale excusing of all who request excuses is to insist upon written guidelines to govern the granting of excuses. The National Confer-ence of Metropolitan Courts, a body of judges from the nation's biggest cities, recommended such written guidelines in their March 1973 report on jury selection:

> During those stages of the selection process where large lists of names are reduced to smaller lists, *prescribed methods should be used that are unambiguous*. If a decision of a discretionary nature must be made in regard to a juror's ability to serve on a jury, such decision should be made by the jury commissioner *pursuant to authority prescribed by statute or by written rule of court*, and said statute or court rule should provide that any such determination not satisfactory to the prospective juror shall be heard on appeal by a judge of the court.[56]

The judges and the legislators must prepare guidelines governing excuses for use by the clerks and secretaries who perform the day-to-day work of processing requests for excuses.

**Exemptions.** In addition to those excused for cause (whether automatically or through showing of hardship), a significant number of people in many jurisdictions are "exempted" from jury duty because of their occupations. The usual explanations for such exemptions fall into the following categories: (1) persons in some occupations perform such vital functions for society that it would be wasteful to use their time as jurors (elected officials, clergy, doctors, police officers, members of the military); (2) some persons should be excluded from jury service because they might exert an unusual amount of influence on the other jurors (lawyers and police officers);

and (3) some persons should be excluded because they have an occupational prejudice on the question of guilt or innocence (clergy and police officers). Although difficult policy questions are involved in deciding whether these assertions are true, the elimination of any occupational group diminishes the representativeness of the jury, and hence the burden should be those who would argue in favor of excluding any group. The federal act, which is typical, lists as exempt from jury service (and hence ineligible to serve even if they desire to) those persons who are (1) on active duty in the military forces; (2) firemen or policemen; and (3) "public officers" in the federal or any local government.[57] Most states do not draw a sharp distinction between "exemptions" and "excuses" and will "excuse" automatically these or similar groups (see Appendix C, p. 271).

The Uniform Jury Selection and Service Act eliminates all exemptions on the ground that "[e]xemption of particular classes by statute is believed inadvisable. . . . The individual should not be given an automatic exemption merely because he comes within a particular class, but rather should be required to make out a case of hardship to the court."[58] The California Court Administrators-Jury Commissioners Association, a collection of county officials from throughout California, concluded unanimously at their 1973 meeting that all statutory exemptions from jury service should be abolished because "the administration of justice in California requires that juries be constituted from the broadest possible spectrum of the citizens of this State," and because "the statutory exemptions from jury service for certain privileged occupational and professional classes tends to defeat the time-honored principle that the duties and obligations of citizenship should be equally shared."[59] The California legislature subsequently agreed and eliminated all occupational excuses in 1975.[60]

**Disqualifications.** Even before consideration of exemptions and excuses, some individuals are eliminated from jury panels because they do not meet certain qualifications or because they did not receive or return their questionnaires. The federal act disqualifies those who are not citizens old enough to vote; those who have not resided in the judicial district for one year; those unable to read, write, and understand English "with a proficiency sufficient to fill out satisfactorily the juror qualification form"; those with a mental or physical infirmity that would render them unable to perform as a juror; and persons under felony indictment or who have been convicted of a felony. State laws list similar disqualifications. Although arguments can be made to justify these qualifications, some bear closer examination.

The requirement of literacy does not seem entirely logical because the testimony jurors are asked to evaluate is almost exclusively oral and because many courts will not allow jurors to take notes for fear that those who take notes well may dominate the jury deliberations. The drafters of the Uniform Jury Selection and Service Act tried to reduce the impact of this requirement somewhat by requiring that jurors be required only to "read, speak, and understand" English, thus eliminating the requirement of writing.[61] It should be noted that the literacy requirements for voters of most states were enacted in direct response to an unwanted group, such as European immigrants in New England,[62] Chinese in California,[63] natives in Alaska,[64] and blacks in the South.[65] In order to counter the abuses of such requirements, Congress in 1970 voted to end literacy tests as a requirement for voting,[66] and the 1975 amendments now require bilingual ballots and education. Although the necessity of understanding the proceedings cannot be disputed, the requirement that jurors write and perhaps even read English should probably be considered in the light of the known effect of such requirements on the franchise.[d]

The exclusion of aliens, which most of us take for granted, should also be looked at in its legal and historical perspective. The Supreme Court has ruled that depriving aliens of rights that are granted to citizens creates a "suspect category" that will be examined with "strict scrutiny" and struck down unless that state can demonstrate a "compelling interest" that would justify the discrimination against aliens.[67] This method of analysis has, for instance, led the Court to declare unconstitutional statutes that barred aliens from becoming attorneys[68] and from holding government jobs.[69] For reasons never fully articulated, however, the Court has said that this line of decisions does not apply to the question of whether aliens can vote or hold elected office.[70] One federal court has said that it is

---

[d]The requirement that jurors speak *English* seems particularly outrageous as applied to the federal district court in Puerto Rico, because only a minority of Puerto Ricans speak English, a minority composed of the more affluent.

The United States is increasingly becoming a multicultural nation, and the U.S. Senate passed in 1975 legislation that would require each federal district containing either 5 percent of its population or 50,000 persons (whichever is less) who do not speak and understand English easily to have a foreign-language translator available (S. 1724, introduced May 7, 1973; passed by the Senate July 14, 1975. *New York Times*, July 16, 1975, p. 5). Such districts would (if the legislation also passes the House and is signed into law) have equipment for simultaneous translations of all trials, and jurors as well as litigants could hear the proceeding in a language other than English. Although such translating devices may seem more familiar in the United Nations than in our local courts, simultaneous translation is the only way to avoid discriminating against significant population groups.

constitutional to bar aliens from our juries because we cannot be sure of their loyalty to our form of government, our history, and our traditions.[71] It seems odd to allow aliens to serve as attorneys, who are "officers of the court," but not allow them to serve as jurors. At earlier periods in our history, aliens did serve on juries, without apparent ill effects. Juries consisting of half citizens and half aliens for trials in which the defendant was an alien were rather common in the nineteenth century, in fact.[72] In Miami, Florida, some 30 percent of the population are resident aliens, mostly Cubans,[73] so this exclusion can eliminate substantial sectors of the community.

As to the two remaining exclusions, the disqualification of felons from juries is consistent with their exclusion from the voting rolls in most states, but the justice of continuing to punish former convicts after they have served their sentences is highly questionable. The retention of residency requirements, by contrast, conflicts with the practice in many government functions (including voting), where they have been declared illegal.[e]

**Questionnaires.** Many people do not become jurors because they do not receive or return their questionnaires. Most jury commissioners who process returned questionnaires do nothing about the people who do not respond at all. The clerks in most courthouses do not even send out a second notice to these people, thus losing from 15 to 30 percent of their potential jurors.[74] The failure to fill out a jury questionnaire is a crime almost everywhere,[75] but prosecutions for the commission of this "crime" are virtually unheard of. It is easier for the clerk's office to mail questionnaires to a new set of names than to keep track of follow-ups. The poor, the undereducated, and the mobile are the most likely to be missed in this process.[76]

Those clerks who have experimented with follow-up letters have discovered that many of those who do not answer the first time will eventually respond. In the City and County of Honolulu, the practice until 1972 had been to ignore those who did not respond, and from 1968 to 1971, the rate of completed questionnaires was between 74.5 percent and 88.3 percent. In 1972, the initial mailing to prospective jurors brought a higher-than-average response of 91.1 percent and a second mailing brought the total response rate to 96.6 percent—about as high as can ever be expected.[77] The clerk in Bannock County (Pocatello), Idaho, sends a second notice by certified mail to those who do not respond at first, telling the prospective jurors of the possibility of prosecution. Of the 950

---

[e]See Chapter Three, pp. 72-76.

people who received questionnaires in 1971, only two did not respond in any way after the second notice, and the figures the following year were almost identical.[78] These testimonials of diligence are, however, the exception rather than the rule, and most counties simply forget about those who do not respond.

\* \* \* \* \*

The second stage of jury selection includes almost limitless opportunities to reduce the representativeness of the jury pool. From the time questionnaires are returned to the day final excuses are granted, when jurors enter the courthouse, the pool of jurors is steadily reduced. Some reduction is necessary, as certain people are unable to serve under almost any circumstances. The way in which some people are eliminated from the list of qualified jurors, however, is not oriented in most courts toward ensuring that a cross-section of the community—if one exists in the master wheel—remains after all excuses have been granted.

Courts generally have been lax in permitting excuses rather than aggressive in encouraging those who are called to serve on juries. The Uniform Jury Selection Act, and other recent state statutory reforms, recognize that only through strict granting of excuses can the community be represented on juries, but much remains to be done. Improved compensation, more widespread salary continuation, reduction of the period of service, and more efficient use of jurors are administrative steps that should be planned in all courts. At the same time, the tendency to grant automatically all excuses asked for, or excuse all those in a certain category, should be reexamined and resisted. An improved jury system would include, on the one hand, government incentives to service (better pay, less time, more efficient procedures, assistance with transportation where feasible) and, on the other, greater willingness on the part of those called to fulfill their obligation to serve on a jury. As long as excuses are easy to obtain and the inconveniences very real, it is unrealistic to expect an improved attitude on the part of the public toward jury duty.

## NOTES

1. National Industrial Conference Board, "Time Off With Pay: A Research Report from the Conference Board," *Studies in Personnel Policy*, No. 196 (1961), p. 18.

2. California Department of Industrial Research, Division of Labor Statistics and Research, *California Industrial Relations Reports*, No. 30 (1967).

3. A July 1, 1973, report of the U.S. Labor Department, quoted in William

R. Pabst, Jr. and G. Thomas Munsterman, "The Economic Hardship of Jury Duty," *Judicature* 58 (1975): 498.

4. James Cole, "Justice Is a Man Wearing a Hard Hat," *Memphis Commercial Appeal*, Dec. 24, 1972.

5. *Hawaii Rev. Stat.*, sec. 388-32.

6. *Hasegawa v. Maui Pineapple Co.*, 52 Haw. 327, 475 P.2d 679 (1970).

7. *Ala. Code*, Tit. 30, sec. 7(1).

8. *Dean v. Gadsden Times Publishing Corp.*, 412 U.S. 543 (1973).

9. S. 3265.

10. Section 35 of a bill prepared March 5, 1974; interview with Joseph Romanow, assistant to the Suffolk County Chief Judge, June 10, 1974. This bill was not enacted.

11. Administrative Office of the U.S. Courts, *1973 Juror Utilization in United States Courts* (Washington: Government Printing Office, 1974) pp. 4, 116.

12. See Pabst and Munsterman, "Economic Hardship of Jury Duty," p. 496.

13. *U.S. News and World Report*, Dec. 14, 1970, p. 40, quoted in Federal Judicial Center, *Guidelines for Improving Juror Utilization in U.S. District Courts* (Washington: Government Printing Office, Oct. 1972), p. 3.

14. *Ibid.*

15. Administrative Office of the United States Courts, *1972 Annual Report of the Director* (Washington: Government Printing Office, 1972), p. II-73.

16. National Conference of Metropolitan Courts, *Final Report on the Jury Administration Project* (Los Angeles: The author, March 1973), p. 69.

17. House Bill No. 5889, sec. 31 (1974).

18. 328 U.S. 217 at 224 (1946).

19. From official court statistics, provided by Patrick J. O'Sullivan, Jr., chief clerk of the First Circuit Court, Honolulu, Hawaii, November 14, 1974.

20. Interview, June 24, 1974.

21. *People v. Milan*, 9 Cal.3d 189, 195-96, 507 P.2d 956, 962-63, 107 Cal. Rptr. 68, 74-75 (1973).

22. *Gordon v. Contractors Transport Corp.*, 18 Md. App. 284, 306 A.2d 573, 575 (1973).

23. Letter sent to this author, December 1971 (emphasis added).

24. Cole, "Justice Is a Man Wearing a Hard Hat."

25. From data made available by Sacramento Jury Commissioner Richard Didion, in 1972.

26. Ann Fagan Ginger, ed., *Minimizing Racism in Jury Trials* (Berkeley: National Lawyers Guild 1969), pp. 207-208.

27. Note, "Juries and Jurors in Maricopa County," *Law and the Social Order* (1973): 188.

28. *People v. Jones*, 25 Cal.App.3d 776, 781-82, 102 Cal. Rptr. 277, 280-81 (1972).

29. From the brief of the Center for Constitutional Rights, filed in the U.S. Supreme Court for the case of *Edwards v. Healy*, No. 73-759, May 7, 1974.

30. *Taylor v. Louisiana*, 419 U.S. 522 (1975).

31. Cole, "Justice Is a Man Wearing a Hard Hat."

32. This author's examination of the May 1972 list of jurors summoned.

33. Cole, "Justice Is a Man Wearing a Hard Hat."

34. From a survey of all juror questionnaires prepared for the case *United States v. Martin*, No. CR-70, 532 SAW, (N.D.Cal 1971).

35. Affidavit in *United States v. Briggs*, GCR-1353 (N.D.Fla. May 6, 1973).

36. Interview with Richard Didion, Sacramento County Jury Commissioner, May 9, 1973.

37. Interview with J. William Devereaux, Jury Commissioner in Denver County, June 24, 1974.

38. *New York Times*, July 3, 1973.

39. These data have been assembled in part by reference to an unpublished paper written in 1968 by Ronald M. Etters for the General Counsel of the Administrative Office of the United States Courts, entitled "A Critique of the Excuse Structure of the District Plans for Random Jury Selection," and has been supplemented by this author's inspection of the district plans whenever possible.

40. Interview with Unwar J. Samaha, Rockingham County, N.H., June 10, 1974. Many other jury commissioners expressed the same sentiment in interviews.

41. See footnote 39, above.

42. *United States v. Ross*, 468 F.2d 1213, 1219 (9th Cir. 1972), *cert. denied* 410 U.S. 939 (1973).

43. See footnote 39, above.

44. *People v. McDowell* 27 Cal.App.3d 864, 104 Cal. Rptr. 181, 188 (1972); other cases rejecting challenges attacking transportation excuses include *United States v. Valentine*, 472 F.2d 164 (9th Cir. 1973), and *United States v. Fernandez*, 480 F.2d 726 (2nd Cir. 1973).

45. *Alvarado v. Alaska*, 486 P.2d 891 (Alaska 1971).

46. Figures provided by Patrick J. O'Sullivan, Chief Clerk, First Circuit Court, Honolulu, Hawaii, November 14, 1974.

47. 28 *U.S.C.*, sec. 1863(b)(5).

48. Senate Report 891, 90th Cong., 1st sess. (1967), pp. 28-29; House Report 1076, 90th Cong., 2d Sess. (1968), p. 11.

49. See footnote 39, above.

50. Section 11(b) (see Appendix M, pp. 418-20).

51. House Bill No. 5889, sec. 29 (1974).

52. Comment to Section 11(b), (see Appendix M, pp. 419-20) (emphasis added).

53. Interview, June 17, 1974.

54. Jay Schulman, "A Systematic Approach to Successful Jury Selection," *Guild Notes*, Dec. 1973, p. 13.

55. Interview with George Gnoss, Dec. 1, 1971.

56. National Conference of Metropolitan Courts, *Final Report on the Jury Administration Project*, p. 29 (emphasis added).

57. 28 *U.S.C.*, sec. 1863(b)(6).

58. Comment to sec. 10 of the Uniform Jury Selection and Service Act (1971) (see Appendix M, p. 418).

59. Passed unanimously May 11, 1973, Lake Arrowhead, Cal.

60. *Cal. Code of Civil Procedure*, sec. 200, as amended 1975.

61. Section 8(b)(2) (see Appendix M, p. 417). This limited provision was also adopted by the National Conference of Metropolitan Courts in their Model Act, sec.8(b)(2). See their *Final Report on the Jury Administration Project*, pp. 41, 55-57.

The Arkansas Supreme Court ruled in 1974 that an illiterate person was not necessarily unqualified to serve as a juror in a case in which the plaintiff sought damages for lost earnings, because the juror's illiteracy did not necessarily mean that the juror could not do the required mathematical calculations. *Arkansas Louisiana Gas Co. v. Morgan*, 506 S.W.2d 560, 561-62 (Ark. 1974).

62. See *Katzenbach v. Morgan*, 384 U.S. 641, 654 (1966); Kirk H. Porter, *A History of Suffrage in the United States* (Chicago, University of Chicago Press, 1918), pp. 112-19; Liebowitz, "English Literacy: Legal Basis for Discrimination," *Notre Dame Lawyer* 45 (1969): 34 n.194.

63. See *Castro v. State of California* 9 Cal.App.3d 675, 88 Cal. Rptr. 500 (1970); Porter, *A History of Suffrage in the United States*, pp. 126-27.

64. See Liebowitz, "English Literacy," pp. 36-37 n.200.

65. See *Louisiana v. United States*, 380 U.S. 145 (1965); *United States v. Mississippi*, 380 U.S. 128 (1965); Lewinson, *Race, Class & Party*, (New York: Universal Library, 1965), pp. 79-97.

66. 1970 Voting Rights Act, 38 U.S.L.W. 99, Title II.

67. See, e.g., *Graham v. Richardson*, 403 U.S. 365 (1971); *Examining Board of Engineers, Architects and Surveyors, etc. v. Flores de Otero*, 96 S.Ct. 2264 (1976).

68. *In re Griffiths*, 413 U.S. 717 (1973).

69. *Sugarman v. Dougall*, 413 U.S. 634 (1973); *Hampton v. Mow Sun Wong*, 96 S.Ct. 1895 (1976).

70. *Sugarman v. Dougall*, 413 U.S. at 648-49. And see *People v. Rodriguez*, 35 Cal.App.3d 900, 111 Cal. Rptr. 238 (1973), and *Padilla v. Allison*, 38 Cal.App.3d 784, 113 Cal. Rptr. 582 (1974).

71. *Perkins v. Smith*, 370 F. Supp. 134 (D.Md. 1974) (3-judge court).

72. See discussion in Chapter One, p. 11.

73. See, e.g., *United States v. Gordon-Nikkar*, 518 F.2d 972, 975 (5th Cir. 1975).

74. See, e.g., *People v. Murphy*, 35 Cal.App.3d 905, 111 Cal. Rptr. 295, 302 (1973).

75. See, e.g. Kansas Stat. 43-165 (1971); N.H. Stat. 500-A:12; *United States v. Hillyard*, 52 F. Supp. 612 (E.D.Wash. 1943).

76. See, e.g., *People v. Jones*, 25 Cal.App.3d 776, 102 Cal. Rptr. 277, 281 (1972).

77. These are all official statistics prepared by the chief clerk of the First Circuit Court in Honolulu, Patrick J. O'Sullivan, Jr., in May of 1972.

78. Statements by Tim Erikson, Jury Commissioner for Bannock County, June 1972 and June 1973.

※ *Chapter Six*

## The Third Stage:
## Challenges

The third stage of jury selection, during which prospective jurors are questioned and challenged for bias, can turn out to be a battle of wits and maneuvering more dramatic than the trial itself. Many attorneys believe that trials are frequently won or lost during this process. Especially when the stakes are high—as in highly publicized cases such as the trials of John Mitchell and Maurice Stans, Angela Davis, and Joan Little—considerable amounts of time and money have been spent by both sides to shape the jury to their needs. A jury so "shaped" is likely to be quite different from the jury wheel in its demographic characteristics.

The purpose of challenges is to eliminate jurors who may be biased about the defendant, the prosecution, or the case, and who thus might threaten the jury's impartiality. Challenges can theoretically serve to even out the disproportions when the process of selecting jurors has distorted the demographic profile of the community, as is often the case.[a] They may, however, make the jury still less representative, even to the point of removing all members of a certain race or social group from the jury. And if the jury panel sent into the courtroom *is* representative and thus fairly reflects the community's biases, challenging certain jurors because of their prejudices may alter the cross-section of views represented.

Prospective jurors can be challenged in two ways: *challenges for cause*, on a "narrowly specified, provable and legally cognizable basis of partiality," and *peremptory challenges*, which are made without giving any reason, "without inquiry and without being subject to the

[a]See Chapters Four and Five, above.

court's control."[1] These challenges are exercised during a procedure known as *voir dire*, an ancient term variously translated as "to speak the truth" or "to see what is said." An unlimited number of jurors can be challenged for cause by the defense and prosecution, but the judge must agree that the juror is indeed prejudiced before he or she can be removed. The court's acceptance of challenges for cause will probably depend upon a finding of specific bias—as in the potential juror's relationship to the defense, prosecution, or witnesses—or nonspecific bias—as against race, religion, etc.—that plays a part in the case. Although an unlimited number of jurors may be challenged for cause, a typical number in an average trial would be only one, two, or three to assemble a jury of twelve. For a normal felony trial, from 24 to 48 jurors are normally sent to be questioned, the number varying widely from one state to another depending primarily on the number of peremptory challenges available to each side. Only a limited number of jurors, as specified by statute in each jurisdiction according to the seriousness of the crime (and sometimes differing as between defense and prosecution), may be challenged peremptorily.

Challenges are essentially a negative kind of selection, because attorneys try to eliminate those jurors they believe unsympathetic to their cause or sympathetic to the other side, but the attorney generally cannot choose their replacements. The ability of either side to impanel the kind of jury it wants is generally limited by two factors: (1) success in proving a juror's bias to the judge's satisfaction, in a challenge for cause, and (2) the number of peremptory challenges they have and how they are exercised. Challenges for cause have the virtue of being unlimited, and peremptories have the advantage of not needing to be defended.

Questioning can be expected to take different forms depending upon the area being investigated. For example, an attorney in a personal-injury case resulting from an automobile accident will probably ask prospective jurors about their profession (to discover, among other things, those in the insurance or auto business, who may have a personal interest in the issue) and whether they have been in an accident or had a close friend or relative suffer an injury (which would presumably make them sympathetic to the injured party and possibly antagonistic to the driver). When the problem is that of pretrial publicity—in a sensational murder case, for example—careful questioning of the prospective jurors can help to separate those who have preconceived ideas about the case from those who have maintained an open mind.

When the problem is that of racial, ethnic, or other prejudice, the feelings may be so deeply ingrained in the prospective juror that much more probing questioning is often employed.[2] The juror may be encouraged to talk about some personal experience to determine his or her true feelings about those of the defendant's race. The reason such specific questions must be posed, according to many attorneys, is that most people will say no when asked generally if they are prejudiced against the defendant because he or she is black, or prejudiced against blacks (or whatever group is relevant to the case) in general. For example, during the questioning of prospective jurors for the 1971 murder trial of Black Panthers Bobby Seale and Ericka Huggins in New Haven, defense attorney Catherine Roraback asked a juror who had said repeatedly that she could be fair, "Is there anything about your attitude or experiences we haven't covered in all these questions that would make you unable to listen to the evidence in this case and reach an unbiased verdict?" The prospective juror looked directly at the defendant for the first time and burst out, "She's guilty!" A startled Judge Harold M. Mulvey asked, "What did you say?" and the woman in the jury box repeated, "She's guilty." The judge promptly excused her for cause.[3]

The success of sophisticated challenge efforts such as these are dependent upon the judge's acceptance of detailed questioning and upon a generous number of peremptory challenges. In most courts in the past, and in many today, wide-ranging challenges have not been considered legitimate. Considerable debate continues over the grounds for challenges as well as the methods.

**The Scope of Voir Dire.** Challenges for cause are of ancient origin but have taken new forms in the United States. In the early English jury, jurors could be challenged only for *specific* bias, such as blood, marriage, or economic relationship to a litigant. A *nonspecific* bias, such as ill-feeling toward a litigant's class or religion, could not be the basis for a challenge for cause, and no questioning on such matters was allowed. The earliest jurors were expected to be familiar with the dispute, and because they were selected from the propertied class, they were expected to favor the Crown in criminal cases.[4] When a prospective juror was charged with specific bias, the justice appointed two impartial "triers," who might be coroners, attorneys, or unchallenged members of the jury; these triers decided whether the challenged juror should be removed, based on evidence offered by the challenging party and any rebuttal presented.[5]

This limited challenging procedure was the practice in the colonies at the time of the American Revolution, when, because of the controversial trials that became a focal point for political disputes, the revolutionaries demanded the right to question jurors about their prejudices. Patrick Henry declared that he would prefer to be tried by a judge alone than by a jury selected without the right to question and challenge.[6] The Select Committee of the House of Representatives that was empowered to draft the Bill of Rights specifically mentioned "the right of challenge" in its first draft of what became the Sixth Amendment, for this was one of the rights considered by many to be inadequately guaranteed in the Constitution of 1787. (This language was later excluded because the words "an impartial jury" in the Sixth Amendment, when considered in conjunction with the Ninth Amendment's reservation of unmentioned rights to the states and the people, was thought to be sufficiently precise to protect the right to question and challenge jurors.[7])

The right to question jurors for bias that was not based on personal knowledge or a personal relationship was firmly established in 1807 by Chief Justice John Marshall (sitting as a trial judge) in the trial of Aaron Burr for treason.[8] Burr had been vice-president under Thomas Jefferson from 1801 to 1805, but they were political enemies throughout this period, and their enmity grew when Burr killed Alexander Hamilton in a duel in 1804. Shortly thereafter, Burr apparently assembled a small army in Kentucky, and Jefferson brought treason charges against him. The media of the day described the feud between Jefferson and Burr in detail, the citizenry chose sides, and the difficulties in selecting an impartial jury increased. John Marshall was no friend of Jefferson's, and he made a number of rulings during the trial that have stood the test of time but may initially have been made at least in part for partisan reasons.

The government attorneys in the Burr case argued that jurors should not be disqualified simply because they had some preconceived notions about the dispute. Marshall rejected this argument and ruled that such prejudice was ground for a challenge for cause, and that the jurors should therefore be questioned to determine their feelings on the evidence. Marshall compared the situation to that of a juror who is distantly related to a litigant:

> The relationship may be remote; the person may never have seen the party; he may declare that he feels no prejudice in the case; and yet the law cautiously incapacitates him from serving on the jury because it suspects prejudice, because in general persons in a similar situation would feel prejudice.[9]

A person who has preconceived ideas about the matter, Marshall argued, just as a person who has some relationship with a litigant, cannot be expected to be an impartial judge:

> He will listen with more favor to that testimony which confirms, than to
> that which would change his opinion; it is not to be expected that he will
> weigh evidence or argument as fairly as a man whose judgment is not made
> up in the case.[10]

Because of the persuasiveness of this decision, virtually all the
state courts authorized the questioning of jurors in areas of nonspecific bias,[11] a sharp departure from the practice in England and
Canada, which to this day do not permit such questioning.[12] Today,
the kind of prejudice involved in the Burr trial comes into play in
widely publicized cases, both political and criminal. Prospective
jurors in such cases are questioned about their opinions on the facts,
the defendant, and expected witnesses to determine whether they
have made up their minds about the verdict.

The situations that authorize a challenge of a prospective juror
"for cause" are established by statute. California is typical of most
states[13] in permitting a prospective juror to be challenged for cause
(1) if the juror is related to a party to the litigation; (2) if the juror
has a unique interest in the subject matter;[14] (3) if the juror has
served in a related case or on the grand jury that indicted the
accused; or most importantly (4) if the juror has "a state of mind"
that will prevent her or him from acting with entire impartiality and
without prejudice to the substantial rights of either party.[15] The
difficult question is how to define that important "state of mind."

It is impossible to expect jurors to come into court with no
preconceptions at all on the issues to be tried, and if we were to
insist on such a rule, all alert citizens would be excluded from jury
duty. As John Marshall said at the Burr trial:

> It would seem to the court that to say that any man who had formed an
> opinion on any fact conducive to the final decision of the case would
> therefore be considered as disqualified from serving on the jury, would
> exclude intelligent and observing men, whose minds were really in a
> situation to decide upon the whole case according to the testimony, and
> would perhaps be applying the letter of the rule requiring an impartial jury
> with a strictness which is not necessary for the preservation of the rule
> itself.[16]

In a more recent context, Judge John Sirica asked the panel of
prospective jurors summoned to consider the first Watergate indictments in January 1973 whether they had heard of the case, fully
expecting the entire panel to respond affirmatively. When a handful
indicated they had not heard of the scandal, he expressed astonish-

ment and indicated that those persons ought perhaps to be the least qualified to sit on the jury.[17] The *voir dire* must strike a balance to separate those few whose inflamed passions make it impossible to be impartial from the rest who can conscientiously concentrate on the evidence presented at trial, even though they are somewhat familiar with certain aspects of the case.[18]

In recent years, questioning for nonspecific bias has been expanding. Prejudice against a particular race, religion, ethnic or other group, where it may be applicable to the case, has been increasingly accepted by the courts as an appropriate area for questioning. Following the logic John Marshall used in the Burr trial, it has been felt that a person who is prejudiced against people of the defendant's race can be expected to have formed an opinion about the accused's guilt or innocence and to "listen with more favor to that testimony which confirms, than to that which would change his opinion."[19]

Race prejudice is the most obvious and prevalent bias in America, and questioning along these lines has been almost universally accepted in recent years.[20] Courts have also sanctioned questioning for prejudice against many other groups. In 1943, the U.S. Court of Appeals for the Seventh Circuit ruled that an accused Jehovah's Witness could ask prospective jurors whether they might be prejudiced against Jehovah's Witnesses, even though religion was not an issue at the trial.[21] The Supreme Court ruled during the early Cold War days in a case involving contempt of the House Un-American Activities Committee that prospective jurors who were government employees had to be asked about the possible influence of a "Loyalty Order" on their ability to remain impartial.[22] Because the Loyalty Order—which said that special vigilance should be exercised to prevent disloyal persons from entering the federal government— might render government employees reluctant to acquit an accused Communist (for fear that they might then be suspect as disloyal themselves), inquiry about possible prejudice against left-of-center defendants was required to ensure the possibility of a fair trial. In 1960, the United States Court of Appeals for the Seventh Circuit ruled that a defendant accused of evading wagering taxes could ask prospective jurors whether they held religious scruples against gambling.[23] In 1972, on reviewing the 1969-70 Chicago Conspiracy Trial, the same court held that this right to inquire extended to any other significant possible prejudice, such as prejudice against antiwar activists and against the youth culture.[24] The rationale for these decisions was simply: "We do not believe that the court could safely assume without inquiry, that the veniremen had no serious prejudice on this subject, or could recognize such prejudices and lay them aside."[25]

The trial judge has, however, broad discretion to decide what questions should be asked of prospective jurors to discover prejudices relevant to the facts at issue, and appellate courts will only rarely reverse a trial judge's decision. In 1973, the Supreme Court examined the case of Gene Ham, a young, bearded black who had been active in civil rights in South Carolina and was convicted of possessing marijuana and sentenced to 18 months' imprisonment.[26] Prior to the trial, the judge had asked the prospective jurors whether they were conscious of any bias for or against him and whether they could be fair and impartial. The judge refused, however, to ask whether the jurors were prejudiced against blacks, whether they would be influenced by the term "black," whether they could disregard the defendant's beard, and whether they had been influenced by local publicity involving the drug problem. In an opinion written by Justice William Rehnquist, the Court ruled that the trial judge had erred by not posing the racial prejudice question, but that the Constitution does not require that questions about beards be asked. Justice Rehnquist said that he was unable to "constitutionally distinguish possible prejudice against beards from a host of other possible similar prejudices," and therefore would not require that any questions about beards be asked.[27] In two later cases, decided in 1974 and 1976, the Court ruled that *Ham* required questioning about racial prejudice only "in *certain* situations" and that a trial judge has almost unreviewable discretion over what other questions are appropriate.[28]

**Peremptory Challenges.** Unlike challenges for cause, peremptory challenges do not have to be defended by an attorney or approved by a judge. After all prospective jurors who have displayed any overt bias are challenged for cause, each litigant is permitted a certain number of peremptory challenges, which can be used to remove those jurors who are believed for some reason or another to favor the other side. The function of the peremptory challenge, as Justice Byron R. White wrote in *Swain v. Alabama* (1965), is

> to eliminate the extremes of partiality on both sides, [and] to assure the parties that the jurors before whom they try the case will decide on the basis of the evidence placed before them, and not otherwise.[29]

The questioning of jurors during the *voir dire* sets the stage for peremptory challenges as well as challenges for cause—in most courts. The United States Supreme Court stated specifically in 1965 that questioning to form the basis for a peremptory challenge is appropriate: "The voir dire in American trials tends to be extensive and probing, operating as a predicate for the exercise of peremptories. . . ."[30] (The opposite rule is in force in California state courts, however, where the California Supreme Court restricts questioning to areas relevant to the challenge for cause and prohibits questioning of a juror "solely for the purpose of laying the foundation for the exercise of a peremptory challenge."[31] The argument in favor of the California rule—that the grounds for challenges for cause are broad enough to permit questioning preparatory to the intelligent exercise of peremptory challenges—reduces the significance of peremptories and turns them into mere extensions of the challenges for cause.)

Peremptory challenges may be used when an attorney suspects a prospective juror of being biased but cannot prove it to the judge according to the guidelines set down for challenges for cause. Many judges, when faced with a juror's statement that he or she is not prejudiced against an individual or group involved in the case, will accept that statement at face value (as perhaps the judge must, if he or she is not to make judgments on the juror's personal integrity). The attorney may still suspect prejudice but be unable to prove it. In such a case, the prospective juror can be challenged peremptorily. Similarly, jurors who belong to certain professions not directly connected with the case at issue (and thus not challengeable for cause) may be challenged peremptorily, as may those of a particular age, race, or religion that the attorney suspects—but cannot prove—will dispose the juror unfavorably toward the client. The prospective juror's personality, which the attorneys can gauge through the voir dire, may also suggest that a peremptory challenge would be in order. So might a juror's dress or bearing—or any factor whatsoever, for peremptories are truly arbitrary and can be made purely on the attorney's intuition.

Attorneys usually must exercise some restraint in exercising peremptory challenges and will only eliminate those persons who appear "worse" than average. Under the usual system, a juror challenged peremptorily is replaced in the jury box by someone selected randomly from among the remaining prospective jurors, and the new juror may be someone worse (from the perspective of the litigant exercising the challenge) than the person just challenged. The new juror may also be challenged, if any challenges are left.

A second system of exercising peremptory challenges, the "struck-jury" system, permits peremptories to be employed in a more sophisticated manner and gives both sides more opportunity to manipulate the jury. Under this system, the attorneys and the judge question the prospective jurors and make their challenges for cause until a number of "qualified" jurors are assembled equal to the size of the jury (usually 12) plus the number of peremptory challenges available to the two sides. Each side then uses its "peremptory strikes" to whittle the venire down to its final size. There are many variations on the struck-jury system. One was used in the 1972 Harrisburg Seven trial, where the 46 qualified jurors remaining after challenges for cause were reduced to 12 in the following way: the defense had a combined total of 28 peremptory strikes, and the prosecution had 6; they exercised their strikes in an alternating pattern until 12 jurors remained. In civil cases in Virginia, 13 qualified jurors are found, and a list with the 13 names is passed between the attorneys, who each cross off three, leaving a jury of 7. In New Jersey's unique struck-jury system, which it uses when "the nature and importance of the matter in controversy render it reasonable and proper,"[32] the clerk prepares a list of 36 or 48 or more jurors, according to the judge's instructions, and then the judge on his own motion or that of a party strikes off names of those "unfit or not well qualified for service as struck jurors."[33] When half the list is eliminated, jurors are summoned into court, and the normal *voir dire* begins, with each party exercising peremptories as usual (although in civil cases the number of peremptories drops from six to three.[34] Although the "struck jury" system gives attorneys great power to change the jury profile, it has consistently been upheld as sufficiently "impartial" to satisfy the Constitution.[35]

Peremptories have been subject to abuse from the time juries were first introduced in England, and the history of peremptories is worth retelling because it reminds us that the exercise of peremptories—particularly by the prosecution—has not always been permitted, but has instead been a subject of constant debate. The earliest juries were effectively hand-picked by the crown or its allies, and if someone unacceptable should by chance appear on the jury list, the crown could remove him because it claimed an unlimited number of peremptory challenges. In 1305, the English Parliament decided that this type of jury—which was not impartial but rather biased toward the prosecution[36]—was obnoxious to their idea of justice.

In that year, a statute was passed that limited the crown to challenges for "cause certain" and eliminated completely the right of the king's attorneys to exercise peremptory challenges.[37] Criminal defendants were, however, still allowed to challenge jurors peremptorily. Sir William Blackstone, an influential legal commentator of the eighteenth century, saw the peremptory challenge clearly as the defendant's right—"a provision full of that tenderness and humanity to prisoners for which our English laws are justly famous."[38] Defendants were originally granted thirty-five peremptory challenges, but the number was reduced in 1530 to twenty in all cases except high treason[3 9] and is now set in England at seven.[4 0]

The prosecution in England still has no statutory right to exercise peremptory challenges, but the crown's attorneys are nonetheless able to remove jurors they do not like without showing "cause" because the English judges created the doctrine of "standing jurors aside." Although the 1305 law clearly states that the crown can remove jurors only for "cause certain,"[b] the English judges have assumed that cause existed whenever the crown wants to challenge a juror. The system works as follows: When panels of jurors are examined, the defendant presents challenges for cause (which the judge promptly rules upon) and exercises peremptory challenges. The crown also raises certain challenges for "cause" but does not offer any explanation, and the judge then directs the jurors so challenged to "stand aside." If a panel of twelve unchallenged jurors can be assembled, the jurors whom the crown had asked to "stand aside" are permanently dismissed, even though the prosecution has never explained why the potential juror cannot be impartial. On the rare occasions that the entire jury panel fails to produce twelve unchallenged jurors (rare because large numbers of jurors are summoned), the judge then asks the prosecutor why the jurors who are "standing aside" are incapable of rendering an impartial verdict. This question has been asked so infrequently that when on July 16, 1699, a prosecutor was asked to "show cause" for the persons who were "standing aside," he replied: "I do not know in all my practice of this nature, that it was ever put upon the King to show cause and I believe some of the King's counsel would say they have not known it done."[4 1] Court practice thus allowed the crown to continue a procedure that Parliament had explicitly eliminated. The practice of standing jurors aside was challenged numerous times on behalf of defendants, but never successfully.[4 2]

In the early colonial and state courts in North America, the 1305 statute providing for peremptory challenges by defendants was accepted as a part of the received common law.[4 3] The prosecution's practice of "standing jurors aside" was, however, more controversial, and substantial popular protest was raised against it. The two most populous states, New York[4 4] and Virginia[4 5] both denied the prosecution any peremptory challenges for most of the nineteenth

---

[b]The text reads: "He that challenges a juror or jurors for the King shall shew his cause . . . but if they that sue for the King will challenge any of those jurors, *they shall assign of their challenge a Cause Certain, and that the truth of the same challenge shall be enquired of according to the custom of the court. . . .*" (33 Edw. I, Stat. 4 [1305], [emphasis added].)

century.[46] Some states continued to authorize "standing aside,"[47] and some gradually began allowing the prosecution to challenge peremptorily, but most of the states that gave the government peremptory strikes limited the number severely. Delaware, for instance, gave the defendant six peremptory challenges and allowed the government to exercise three, but for each challenge the state actually used, the defendant was given a compensating extra peremptory strike.[48] In Alabama, the prosecutors were given only four peremptory challenges, while the defendant had sixteen challenges in capital cases and twelve in noncapital cases.[49] In two states, Kentucky and Maryland, efforts in the middle of the nineteenth century to give the government the right to strike peremptorily were decisively beaten back at constitutional conventions.[50]

The U.S. Congress passed a statute in 1790 giving defendants in federal courts 35 peremptory challenges in cases of treason and 20 in other capital cases but made no mention of the right of the state to exercise peremptories.[51] The federal courts were thus soon faced with the question whether the right to "stand aside" existed. One supporter of "standing aside" and the exercise of peremptories by the government wrote in 1817 that although the prosecutor might be sure that allowing a certain individual to serve as a juror would "altogether defeat the ends of public justice," he might be unable to prove it,[52] and that "standing aside" was quicker than proving bias. And as for peremptories for the prosecution, this commentator argued that in America the government did not have to be feared:

> There cannot exist the same cause of jealousy, in regard to challenge on the part of the prosecution *here* that might be well founded in *England*, where the influence of the crown, especially in former times, was exerted to convict those who were obnoxious to the king. *Here*, the accused has nothing to fear from those in power. The sole object of prosecutions . . . is to maintain the public peace and safety, by enforcing laws of unexampled mildness.[53]

Ten years later, in 1827, the very influential Supreme Court Justice Joseph Story asserted that the "standing aside" procedure had always been part of the common law and was still the law.[54] Although this remark was not directly relevant to the case before the Court and hence not a binding holding, it was nevertheless followed by most federal judges because of Story's prestige. One federal judge did protest, however, in a dissenting opinion, that the prosecution was being given an unfair advantage:

The whole theory of criminal jurisprudence looks to placing the advantage, if one accompanies the case, on the side of the accused; and I think that, after the efforts almost universally put forth in the United States to strengthen and extend such privilege, particularly to a person on trial for his life, we are taking a long step backwards in setting up the practices of the English assizes, originating in an age of colder sympathy for human life than pervades our era and the jurisprudence of the United States.[55]

Through the nineteenth century, peremptories for the prosecution gradually became the rule rather than the exception. The Supreme Court ruled in 1856 that federal courts were not required to permit "standing aside" and should follow the lead of the courts of the state in which they sat,[56] but by this time states had begun authorizing peremptory challenges by the prosecution, and so the "standing aside" procedure became unnecessary.[57] The mistrust of government typical of the Revolutionary era had given way to increasing acceptance of state power. An 1887 Supreme Court decision, upholding a Missouri statute that gave the prosecution 15 peremptory challenges in capital cases tried in cities of over a hundred thousand (i.e., Kansas City and St. Louis) but only 8 challenges in other areas (the defense had 20 in either case),[58] attempted to justify the government's need to challenge jurors peremptorily:

> In our large cities there is such a mixed population; there is such a tendency of the criminal classes to resort to them, and such an unfortunate disposition on the part of business men to escape from jury duty, that it requires special care on the part of the government to secure there competent and impartial jurors.[59]

The government, in this view expressed by Justice Stephen Field, had a legitimate interest in trying to keep certain elements off juries.

By the beginning of the twentieth century, the government's right to exercise peremptory challenges was firmly established. So was its ability, especially where the struck-jury system was employed to use this power to eliminate entire races or classes of people from jury venires. For almost a century after the Civil War, blacks rarely appeared on jury lists at all in the South, and when—after years of litigation—they were finally included on the qualified list, the prosecution frequently used its peremptory challenges to exclude them from the jury box.[60] It was this pattern of challenges that led to a major attack on peremptories in 1965.

The case was *Swain v. Alabama* (1965),[61] and the Supreme Court ruling put only theoretical limits on the government's power.[c] In

---

[c]For a discussion of other aspects of this case, see Chapter Three, pp. 56-58.

*Swain*, a young black convicted and sentenced to death for raping a young white woman complained that, although an average of six or seven blacks appeared on the trial jury lists for criminal cases, not one black person had served on a jury since 1950. Eight black men were on the panel that was called for Swain's trial, but none served; two had been excused and the prosecutor peremptorily challenged the other six. Despite these figures, the Supreme Court, in an opinion written by Justice Byron R. White, held that the defendant had not proved that the prosecution systematically and deliberately used its challenges to deny black persons the right to participate in the jury system, and thus affirmed Swain's death sentence.

Justice White did say that a prosecutor's systematic exclusion of a race from jury panels by the continued use of peremptory challenges, time after time, whatever the circumstances, the crime, or the defendant, would be a violation of the Fourteenth Amendment, but he put the burden squarely on the accused to prove such systematic exclusion.[62] Justice White argued that peremptory challenges play a major role in ensuring that the impaneled jury is unbiased, noting that they are to be used against real or imagined partiality that is difficult to designate or demonstrate and may be exercised on grounds normally thought irrelevant to official action or legal proceedings, such as race or religion.[63] In their dissent to *Swain*, Justices Goldberg, Douglas, and Warren applied standards of earlier jury discrimination cases and concluded that the state should be required to rebut the prima facie showing of total exclusion by showing that reasons other than racial discrimination were responsible for the total exclusion of blacks from jury panels since 1950 and that peremptory challenges were not being used as a form of state discrimination.[64] They complained that Justice White gave too much importance to the state's use of peremptory challenges, which had, after all, been recognized chiefly as a device to protect defendants. The majority had confused its priorities, for the peremptory challenge is not a constitutional requirement, but trial by an impartial jury is. The dissenters charged that Justice White's opinion was in effect a holding that "[t]here is nothing in the Constitution of the United States which requires the State to grant trial by an impartial jury so long as the inviolability of the peremptory challenge is secured."[65]

The majority opinion in *Swain* has set the tone for subsequent cases, and although the prosecution has frequently used its peremptories to remove all members of a particular ethnic group, no litigant has ever been successful in challenging this practice on appeal.

**Challenges and Representativeness.** The prosecution's removal of all blacks from the jury panel through peremptories, as occurred in *Swain*, indicates in the extreme the effect of challenges on representativeness (this was not, however, an isolated instance of such exclusion). The two-step challenge procedure inevitably means a steady reduction in the jury pool until the requisite number—usually twelve—is chosen for a jury. This reduction, although aimed at eliminating bias and impaneling an impartial jury, may in fact—by excluding certain types of people from the jury panel—increase the jury's bias. Both sides attempt to use challenges to eliminate the kinds of jurors they do not want and frequently will look to people of certain races, ages, or occupations as those most likely to be unfavorable to their side. In general, the defense and the prosecution are looking for opposite things in jurors and will use challenges to try to gain an advantage. Because peremptory challenges do not have to be approved by the judge, they tend to exert the strongest effect on jury representativeness.

The prosecution is frequently looking for a juror who is middle-aged, middle-class, and white, on the assumption that this type of juror identifies with the government rather than the defendant and will thus be more likely to convict. An unusual insight into the aims of one prosecutor's office was provided by the weekly *Texas Observer* in the spring of 1973, when it obtained and reprinted parts of a book prepared in the Dallas County District Attorney's Office to help train prosecuting attorneys in Texas. The chapter in *Prosecution Course* on "Jury Selection in a Criminal Case" was written by an assistant district attorney in Dallas named Jon Sparling, who had become locally famous for persuading a jury to impose a 1,000-year sentence on a convicted felon, and the advice seems to reflect his intense prosecutional zeal:

> . . . Who you select for the jury is, at best, a calculated risk. Instincts about veniremen may be developed by experience, but even the young prosecutor may improve the odds by the use of certain guidelines—if you know what to look for. . . .
>
> III. What to look for in a juror.
>
>   A. Attitudes
>     1. You are not looking for a fair juror, but rather a strong, biased and sometimes hypocritical individual who believes that Defendants are different from them in kind, rather than degree.
>     2. You are not looking for any member of a minority group which may subject him to oppression—they almost always empathize with the accused.

3. You are not looking for the free thinkers and flower children.
B. Observation is worthwhile.
   1. Look at the panel out in the hall before they are seated. You can often spot the showoffs and the liberals by how and to whom they are talking.
   2. Observe the veniremen as they walk into the courtroom.
      a. You can tell almost as much about a man by how he walks, as how he talks.
      b. Look for physical afflictions. These people usually sympathize with the accused.
   3. Dress
      a. Conservatively, well dressed people are generally stable and good for the State.
      b. In many counties, the jury summons states that the appropriate dress is coat and tie. One who does not wear a coat and tie is often a non-conformist and therefore a bad State's juror.
   4. Women
      a. I don't like women jurors because I don't trust them.
      b. They do, however, make the best jurors in cases involving crimes against children.
      c. It is possible that their "women's intuition" can help you if you can't win your case with the facts.
      d. Young women too often sympathize with the Defendant; old women wearing too much make-up are usually unstable, and therefore are bad State's jurors.[66]

This may seem an extreme example of the prosecution's view of jurors, but if expressed more subtly, it is probably not out of line with what we might intuitively expect the government to be looking for.

Trial lawyers have for centuries attempted to categorize people in their eternal quest for "the right juror." The traditional trial-lawyer lore dictates, for instance, that in complicated cases the young should be preferred over the old and men over women. When a child is either the victim or the plaintiff, women jurors are considered desirable, but when women are parties, female jurors should be avoided because they are hard on their own sex. The Irish, Italians, Jews, French, blacks, Chicanos and those of Balkan heritage are said to sympathize with plaintiffs in civil suits and defendants in criminal actions. The English, Scandinavians, and Germans allegedly have the opposite perspective.[67] (Many of these generalizations are inconsistent with the studies on jury behavior discussed in Chapter Two.)

Lawyers who regularly try personal injury cases have another set of stereotypes about who should be picked as jurors and who should be avoided.[68] One attorney who represents plaintiffs says that he tries to impanel older jurors, persons who are in low-income categories, persons who are the same sex as the plaintiff, and in general people who like other people.[69] Another plaintiff's attorney says that he usually challenges retired military officers, accountants, engineers, and postal employees, because these persons tend not to give large monetary awards.[70]

Attorneys for both sides are eager to remove those who are believed to hold extreme views. Richard Christie, who with Jay Schulman assisted the defense in trials such as the Harrisburg Seven and Joan Little cases by conducting voir dire using sociological and psychological tests, stated: "Essentially what we are trying to do in these cases is to get rid of the kooks, the very overrigid, irrationally law-and-order people. We are looking for fair-mind jurors willing to listen to the evidence."[71] An assistant district attorney in Albuquerque, New Mexico, similarly said that he considered voir dire to be necessary to remove the "nuts" from the jury, who might create a hung jury by holding out for acquittal in the face of eleven other jurors who might want to convict. "We have to question them." he said, "to get the flakey weirdos off the jury."[72] A "kook" or "weirdo" in one attorney's view, however, may be an ideal juror in the opinion of the other side. In many—perhaps most—cases, the challenges of the two sides tend to cancel each other out. They remove—as representatives of both the defense and prosecution declare—those who appear to hold strong opinions. The result is often to leave the least offensive jurors who, if the attorneys have been successful, probably also have the least distinctive points of view on issues. This practice necessarily means that the resulting jury will be less representative than the panel that is first sent into the courtroom, because anyone who is idiosyncratic or strange in any observable way will be challenged by one side or the other.

All too frequently, challenges can result in the radical reduction or total elimination of a particular segment of the population, as did the prosecution's challenges in the *Swain* case. Although the power to control the outcome was especially great in that case because of the struck-jury system, if a large number of peremptory challenges are given they may go far to reduce the representation of a particular group. If, for example, each side has twenty peremptory challenges and there are ten blacks in a venire of sixty, it will generally be possible for the prosecution to eliminate, gradually, all of the black jurors.

The effect of peremptory challenges on representation of certain groups has been documented in a number of prominent cases (the groups challenged fit the pattern of those conventionally believed to be pro-defense or pro-prosecution):

- The prosecution in the 1975 murder trial of Joan Little used eight of its nine peremptory challenges to eliminate blacks from the jury.[73]
- In the 1968 murder trial of Black Panther Huey P. Newton, the prosecution used three of its fifteen peremptories against blacks, to eliminate all but one black from the resulting jury panel; when four alternates were picked, the prosecution used five of its six peremptories against blacks to eliminate all the black people on the venire. (Sociologist Robert Blauner, who observed the jury selection, wrote later that all the prosecutor's peremptory challenges "could be divided neatly into three main categories: blacks, Berkeley residents, and anti-capital-punishment people."[74])
- During the selection of jurors prior to the 1972 murder trial of Angela Davis in Santa Clara County, California, the prosecution challenged peremptorily the only black who was on the venire, and when alternates were picked, the prosecution challenged a Native-American, the only other nonwhite to reach the jury box.[75]
- The prosecution in the 1972 Harrisburg Seven case challenged two blacks and four whites who expressed antiwar or liberal views. The defense used its 28 challenges to eliminate the most prosperous and most "establishment" prospective jurors.[76]
- The defense in the 1974 John Mitchell-Maurice Stans conspiracy trial used its 20 peremptories to eliminate all persons with a college education from the twelve-person jury (although one college-educated person selected as an alternate did subsequently join the jury when a vacancy appeared).[77]

The exclusion of whole groups of prospective jurors is not, of course, limited to prominent trials such as these:

- In the 53 criminal trials conducted during the years 1972 and 1973 in the U.S. District Court for the Eastern District of Louisiana, the federal prosecutor used 68.9 percent of all its challenges against black prospective jurors, although blacks constituted only about one-fourth of the persons on the jury venire.[78]
- A reporter for the St. Louis *Post-Dispatch* observed the voir dire of 31 trials with black defendants in St. Louis County in the years 1971 to 1973 and found that of the 77 blacks who were qualified to serve as jurors for these trials and who were not challenged for cause, 57 of them (74 percent) were challenged peremptorily by the prosecution and another 5 (3.9 percent) were struck by the defense.[79] Thus, although black people appeared on the jury

venire in roughly their proper proportion of the county's population, by the time the challenging process was completed their ranks were dramatically depleted. The reporter noted that the prosecutors reduced their number of black strikes somewhat when they discovered that he was observing trials to record this data.[80]

- Similarly, in the federal court for the Western Division of the Western District of Missouri, 70 black jurors appeared for service in the fifteen trials held in 1974 involving black defendants, and 57 of them (81.4 percent) were peremptorily challenged by the prosecution. One black was challenged by the defense, so 12 blacks remained, constituting only 6.7 percent of the actual jurors, compared to their proportion in the adult population of 11.2 percent, an underrepresentation of 40.2 percent.[81]

- Seventeen black jurors were questioned to be jurors in the thirteen trials involving black defendants in Spartanburg County, South Carolina in 1970 and 1971, but 14 were challenged peremptorily by the prosecution and 1 by the defense. Blacks thus constituted 21.1 percent of the County's population and 10.6 percent of the jury venire, but only 2.6 percent of the sitting jurors.[82]

A whole series of cases in which all or almost all blacks have been eliminated from jury panels in recent years can be cited from Arkansas,[83] Georgia,[84] Louisiana,[85] Maryland,[86] Mississippi,[87] Missouri,[88] North Carolina,[89] Tennessee,[90] and Texas.[91] Nor is the problem unique to the South: the prosecution has sought to eliminate all blacks from juries in California,[92] Illinois,[93] Massachusetts,[94] Michigan,[95] New Jersey,[96] Pennsylvania,[97] and in the federal courts.[98]

An example of the virtual impossibility of proving "systematic exclusion" to meet the *Swain* test is found in *Ridley v. State* (Texas, 1972)[99] where the Harris County (Houston) prosecution peremptorily challenged seven black prospective jurors. After the jury convicted the defendant (of robbery by assault), the defendant moved for a new trial and attempted to show that the Harris County prosecutor invariably tried to remove blacks from the jury panel whenever the defendant was black and the victim was white. Several active criminal lawyers were put on the stand and they all testified that the prosecutor always challenged blacks in such a situation. One defense lawyer said that in ten out of the eleven cases he had tried during the previous year, the prosecution had exercised all ten of its peremptories to exclude blacks. Erwin Ernst, an assistant district attorney in Harris County for fifteen years, was then put on the stand, and he admitted that using peremptories to eliminate blacks when the defendant was black and the victim white was "a matter of common sense."[100] The Texas Court of Criminal Appeals nonetheless affirmed the conviction, concluding that "where the accused is black and the victim white it is not unreasonable that race becomes a trial-related consideration."[101] This Texas court thus seems to have said that even if "systematic exclusion" is shown, the prosecutor's action will be permitted because it is reasonable to exclude blacks systematically.

All of these maneuvers have the effect of altering the representative qualities of the jury, and of altering the verdict in many cases. Imagine the anger of a black defendant who sees the only black on his jury panel removed without explanation by the prosecution; or, worse yet, who sees half a dozen or more blacks peremptorily challenged. How can this defendant respect the verdict of the resulting all-white jury?

Hard data over a period of time is difficult to assemble, but the Bernalillo County Court in Albuquerque, New Mexico, is one court that maintains a record of what happens to the jurors who are sent into each courtroom, along with demographic information about each juror. This data, assembled between 1972 and 1974 and presented in Table 6-1, demonstrates how the competing sides use their peremptory challenges. These figures are not typical of all other parts of the nation because the number of challenges is small and the defense has more than the prosecution. New Mexico gives the defense 5 peremptories in the usual criminal trial and allows the prosecution only 3. Most states give equal numbers of peremptories to each side (see Appendix D, p. 281). The prosecution in New Mexico is thus less able to alter the demographic make-up of the jury than is the defense. The statistics indicate that the prosecution uses its peremptory challenges to reduce the numbers of young and nonwhite jurors, while the defense tries to remove the older and more established jurors. To some extent the challenges cancel each other out, but some disproportions do result.

It is hard to extrapolate this data from New Mexico into a more urban court system where both sides have many more challenges, but it is interesting that most of the states that allow a large number of peremptories are heavily populated urban states with heterogeneous populations, including California (13 peremptories for each side, even for misdemeanors), Illinois (10 peremptories for each side for felonies), Indiana (10), Louisiana (12), Maryland (10 for the prosecution, 20 for the defense); New Jersey (10) (see Appendix D for a full list of all the states).

Because of the diverse populations in these states, it is perhaps believed, more peremptories are needed to produce the desired

**Table 6-1.   The Effect of Challenges on Representativeness**

Bernalillo County (Albuquerque) New Mexico (1972, 1973, and 1974)

| | All Persons Questioned As Prospective Jurors | Excused for Cause | | Challenged Peremptorily | | | | Persons Who Actually Became Jurors | |
| --- | --- | --- | --- | --- | --- | --- | --- | --- | --- |
| | | | | By the Prosecution | | By the Defense | | | |
| | # | # | % of prospective jurors in category | # | % of prospective jurors in category | # | % of prospective jurors in category | # | % of prospective jurors in category |
| Totals | 2185 | 114 | 5.2 | 162 | 7.4 | 497 | 22.7 | 1412 | 64.6 |
| *Race* | | | | | | | | | |
| Anglo-European | 1515 | 77 | 5.1 | 94 | 6.2 | 405 | 26.7 | 939 | 62.0 |
| Hispanic | 426 | 25 | 5.9 | 53 | 12.4 | 47 | 11.0 | 301 | 70.7 |
| Black | 20 | 0 | 0 | 5 | 25.0 | 2 | 10.0 | 13 | 65.0 |
| Native-American | 18 | 0 | 0 | 2 | 11.1 | 1 | 5.6 | 15 | 83.3 |
| No Response | 206 | 12 | 5.8 | 8 | 3.9 | 42 | 20.4 | 144 | 69.9 |
| *Sex* | | | | | | | | | |
| Male | 949 | 53 | 5.6 | 86 | 9.1 | 255 | 26.9 | 555 | 58.5 |
| Female | 1221 | 60 | 4.9 | 75 | 6.1 | 237 | 19.4 | 849 | 69.5 |
| Unknown | 15 | 1 | 6.7 | 1 | 6.7 | 5 | 33.3 | 8 | 53.3 |
| *Age* | | | | | | | | | |
| 18-20 | 96 | 6 | 6.3 | 21 | 21.9 | 3 | 3.1 | 66 | 68.8 |
| 21-24 | 147 | 9 | 6.1 | 22 | 15.0 | 7 | 4.8 | 109 | 74.1 |
| 25-29 | 263 | 18 | 6.8 | 33 | 12.5 | 37 | 14.1 | 175 | 66.5 |
| 30-34 | 235 | 15 | 6.4 | 22 | 9.4 | 42 | 17.9 | 156 | 66.4 |
| 35-39 | 216 | 11 | 5.1 | 14 | 6.5 | 49 | 22.7 | 142 | 65.7 |
| 40-44 | 241 | 11 | 4.6 | 4 | 1.7 | 66 | 27.4 | 160 | 66.4 |
| 45-49 | 252 | 13 | 5.2 | 13 | 5.2 | 69 | 27.4 | 157 | 62.3 |

| | | | | | | | | |
|---|---|---|---|---|---|---|---|---|
| 50-54 | 242 | 8 | 3.3 | 10 | 4.1 | 70 | 28.9 | 154 | 63.6 |
| 55-59 | 189 | 9 | 4.8 | 3 | 1.6 | 57 | 30.2 | 120 | 63.5 |
| 60-64 | 99 | 5 | 5.1 | 3 | 3.0 | 41 | 41.4 | 50 | 50.5 |
| 65-69 | 40 | 1 | 2.5 | 4 | 10.0 | 19 | 47.5 | 16 | 40.0 |
| 70 and over | 15 | 0 | 0 | 0 | 0 | 7 | 46.7 | 8 | 53.3 |
| No Response | 150 | 8 | 5.3 | 13 | 8.7 | 30 | 20.0 | 99 | 66.0 |

**Hispanic Defendants**

*Race of Juror*

| | | | | | | | | |
|---|---|---|---|---|---|---|---|---|
| Anglo-European | 842 | 36 | 4.3 | 39 | 4.6 | 228 | 27.1 | 539 | 64.0 |
| Hispanic | 237 | 12 | 5.1 | 31 | 13.1 | 23 | 9.7 | 171 | 72.2 |
| Black | 10 | 0 | 0 | 1 | 10.0 | 2 | 20.0 | 7 | 70.0 |
| Native-American | 7 | 0 | 0 | 0 | 0 | 0 | 0 | 7 | 100.0 |
| No Response | 116 | 5 | 4.3 | 4 | 3.4 | 17 | 14.7 | 90 | 77.6 |
| Totals | 1212 | 53 | 4.4 | 75 | 6.2 | 270 | 22.3 | 814 | 67.2 |

**Other Defendants**

*Race of Juror*

| | | | | | | | | |
|---|---|---|---|---|---|---|---|---|
| Anglo-European | 662 | 42 | 6.3 | 54 | 8.2 | 172 | 26.0 | 394 | 59.5 |
| Hispanic | 205 | 15 | 7.3 | 23 | 11.2 | 30 | 14.6 | 137 | 66.8 |
| Black | 9 | 0 | 0 | 3 | 33.3 | 0 | 0 | 6 | 66.7 |
| Native-American | 11 | 0 | 0 | 2 | 18.2 | 1 | 9.1 | 8 | 72.7 |
| No Response | 86 | 4 | 4.7 | 5 | 5.8 | 24 | 27.9 | 53 | 61.6 |
| Totals | 973 | 61 | | 87 | | 227 | | 598 | |

homogeneous jury. But what such large numbers of peremptories do is give the attorneys vast power to mold jury composition; this procedure is insulting to potential jurors. Can there really be 13 people on each panel in California that each attorney would view as insufficiently fair? Most potential jurors in such a system realize they will be challenged, and this has a demoralizing effect on jurors, and discourages people from making the time sacrifices required of jury duty. It also distorts the population mix on the jury wheel.

## REASSESSING THE SYSTEM

The potential of challenges to distort the demographic profile of juries should be examined as part of any serious effort to make juries more representative of the community. No juror can truly be "unbiased"—because no one is totally without viewpoints formed by their personal experiences—and the reason for wanting a jury representing a fair cross-section of the community is to attempt to balance those views. If a jury panel is truly representative, why single out some people for their biases and once again unbalance the jury?

**The Voir Dire.** In some cases, for example if a juror is related to a defendant or acquainted with an attorney, personal feelings may indeed color the juror's impartiality. The acknowledgment of such bias—which is not one fundamentally of viewpoint but of emotion—has ancient historical roots. It is not reasonable to expect someone with a personal interest to be impartial, and thus challenges for this reason should remain as part of the effort to impanel an impartial jury.

What then of the reasoning of Chief Justice John Marshall, who extended the right of questioning to include nonspecific biases, those biases not resulting from personal relationships but appearing to have similar impact on a juror's impartiality? What about questioning to discover racial prejudice, or political prejudice, or influence on a juror by journalistic accounts of the events to be considered at trial? Some recent studies have shown that most jurors—if carefully instructed by a judge—can put aside what they have read and heard and limit their decision to the evidence presented in court.[102] Marshall explained that it was unnecessary and undesirable to equate familiarity with the case—and even having some opinions on it—with bias, and in many well-publicized trials, it has been possible to assemble an impartial jury.[d] Jurors should also be able to set aside

---

dFor a discussion of juries in highly publicized cases, see Chapter Seven below, pp. 177-91.

their racial and political prejudices, if the judge is sensitive enough to these prejudices to give a careful and convincing instruction on these subjects. The Supreme Court has recently limited the grounds of required questioning for race or ethnic prejudice to cases where race issues are a part of the case and where the court finds a "significant likelihood" that prejudice will affect the trial.[103]

But some questioning of jurors and a few challenges are still necessary to protect litigants from an erratic or unusual panel. The vast majority of people can be fair in any trial, but a few may be unable to be completely open to a fair examination of the evidence in certain difficult situations, and the litigants should be able to protect themselves against such unusual jurors. Numerous cases show us that racial and political prejudice have not always been neutralized and have frequently influenced the verdicts of juries.

The widespread use of nonrepresentative master lists is another consideration that justifies some questioning and a few challenges of prospective jurors. So long as juries are not selected by a truly random method (and most now are not), the voir dire remains a useful tool for attorneys to discover prejudice and form the basis for challenges for cause and peremptory challenges. If a jury panel underrepresents blacks and the young, for example, as most today do, attorneys can use questioning for bias against these groups to try to rectify the disparities. With the present lists in use, the abandonment of the voir dire would mean that the jury would be less a voice of the people and more an extension of government. If more blacks and young adults were on juries, their presence would frequently blunt the prejudices against these groups.

Even in cases where selection is genuinely random, the luck of the draw may mean that twelve persons summoned into a jury box do not in fact represent the larger pool. Only through proportionate representation, a kind of quota system which is not constitutionally permissible or practical, could each jury be designed to reflect the community. Thus, even if the list of jurors is complete and excuses have not distorted the panel's composition, the twelve might be heavily weighted in one direction or another.[e] Some questioning and challenging is thus required, because of the important need for each individual jury to be "impartial." This questioning must intrude into areas of "nonspecific" bias when the facts of the case indicate that prejudice may play a role. The number of peremptory challenges should be substantially lowered (as will be explained below), particu-

---

eSuch skewing is much more probable with a smaller jury and is an important argument against using a jury of less than twelve, as is discussed in Chapter Eight, pp. 193-218.

larly those of the prosecution, so that the attorneys cannot manipulate the jury composition to the extent they do today. But even after we start using more complete lists, some questioning and limited challenging must be permitted.

The use of wide-ranging voir dire to discover nonspecific bias needs to be carefully evaluated, however. Recent Supreme Court decisions limiting appellate review of voir dire[104] point in the direction of more restricted questioning, and the sophisticated challenge procedures used in some highly publicized cases cast doubt about the appropriateness of extensive probing of jurors. The heavy reliance of attorneys in many cases on challenges to produce a "sympathetic" jury must be analyzed for its effect on the jury's impartiality.

The argument against permitting questioning for nonspecific bias proceeds along the following lines: Our goal is to achieve an impartial jury, but in reality it is impossible to find twelve impartial people because everyone is partial in the sense that we have all been influenced by our experiences, which mold the manner in which we perceive events. The best way to ensure impartiality, therefore, is to ensure representativeness, which will guarantee that the different viewpoints in our community can all be applied to the factual situation at issue in the trial.

Challenges can turn a representative jury into a nonrepresentative jury and thus should be looked upon with suspicion. Particularly when each side has a large number of peremptory challenges—and California (as of January 1, 1976) raised each side's number of permissible peremptory challenges to 13[105]—the jury that survives these challenges will only have a vague resemblance to the cross-section of the community that was assembled in the panel room.

"Impartiality" cannot exist in a vacuum, and we do not have the tools to discover who is and who is not impartial, even if we knew exactly what we are looking for, which we do not.

The jury is fundamentally a human institution, relying on the personal wisdom and judgment of ordinary individuals, rejecting the concept of "expert" wisdom. The impartial jury must be a balance between the diverse views and experiences in our society; only then will it have the respect of the community for its integrity. The jury cannot be anything more objective—a computer, for example, which would weigh the evidence according to mathematical formulas. Extended questioning of jurors about their personal opinions contradicts the principle on which the jury system is based—that a random selection of twelve persons will be as qualified as any other to decide the fate of a defendant or resolve a civil dispute. Nor does questioning necessarily uncover the biases that might truly affect a verdict. The individuals being interrogated are likely to answer questions according to whether they want to serve or not, and may not admit to certain prejudices, especially race and religious prejudices.[106] Sophisticated questioning can help uncover some prejudices, but even when it does, it cannot predict how jurors will respond during a trial. The difficulty of evaluating jurors' attitudes and predicting their behavior is a real—and fortunate—one, for if we could gauge behavior in advance, we would not need a jury.

The process of winnowing out potential jurors has a serious demoralizing effect on everyone who receives a jury summons. When the summoned citizen knows that the odds are at least two-to-one against actually sitting on a jury after reporting to a courtroom, the citizen is encouraged to seek to be excused rather than wasting time sitting around. If, on the other hand, the summoned juror felt that the time spent was going to be used wisely by the judicial system and that she or he would probably sit as a juror whenever summoned to the courthouse, the willingness to accept the obligation and serve would unquestionably increase, as would representativeness.[f]

The method of questioning and length of time spent on the voir dire discourage potential jurors from serving and can cause resentment in those who do. Some jurors take offense at being asked highly personal questions aimed at discovering prejudices that attorneys believe cannot be discovered merely by direct questioning. The assumptions behind such questions—that jurors may not tell the truth when asked straightforward questions about bias and that jurors cannot put aside their prejudices—are considered by many to be insulting. Such questioning may uncover some prejudices, but the attorneys' possible success in rooting out jurors too biased to judge a case fairly has to be evaluated against their effect in alienating essentially fair-minded jurors. It denies the fact that everyone brings some biases into the jury room, but that the jury system, by its very nature, is designed to balance and, it is hoped, overcome those biases.

The problem—articulated by Chief Justice Marshall over 150 years ago—remains how to determine when bias can realistically be expected to affect a verdict and thus should be rooted out. Where should we draw the line between necessary and improper questioning, between a sincere effort to obtain an impartial jury and one subject to the charge of jury-tampering? Because each case is different, the grounds of acceptable questioning will not be the same in any two given cases, and firm guidelines are not possible. But the

---

[f]Shortening jury service to a week and raising payments should also increase willingness to serve. See Chapter Five, pp. 112-19.

goal of a representative jury must be kept in mind and, as a result, questioning and challenges should be kept to a minimum. An awareness that strong prejudice does exist should be balanced by a belief in the capacity of most jurors, especially in a jury that includes a broad cross-section of the population and thus is less likely to be dominated by the biases of one group, to overcome their biases and judge the evidence as fairly as humanly possible. Questioning for specific bias must continue, but questioning for nonspecific bias does not normally have to be extensive.

A debate is already under way about the conduct of the voir dire, resulting in part from a concern about perceived abuses in many trials and in part from a desire to make jury selection more efficient. The main question is who should conduct the voir dire: the judge, the attorneys, or both? Present practice varies greatly among jurisdictions. Federal judges have been given exclusive control over voir dire since 1944.[107] A 1970 study of 219 federal judges showed that 53.4 percent questioned jurors by themselves, 31.1 percent allowed attorneys to ask some supplemental questions, 13.2 percent allowed attorneys to ask all the questions, and 2.3 percent authorized the questioning of jurors by a clerk or the attorneys outside the judge's presence.[108] Judges now have exclusive control over the questioning in eleven states as well.[g]

The main reasons advanced for having attorneys conduct the voir dire are that it permits them to discover any personality conflicts between jurors and either the attorney or the client that might lead the attorney to challenge the juror, that it permits attorneys to establish rapport with jurors, that only attorneys can knowledgeably question jurors to lay the groundwork for challenges, and that questioning by attorneys is essential to preserve the adversary system of justice. Proponents of attorney-conducted voir dire maintain that personal contact and selection of questions relevant to the particular trial are necessary for informed challenges, that only the attorney knows what prejudices are important to explore, and that judges may ask questions that are too general or may question jurors together—a procedure that often fails to elicit candid responses. Some argue that if attorneys are not allowed to question jurors the jury will in effect be selected by a representative of the government—the judge—and that this procedure would defeat the purpose of the jury, namely, to protect the citizen from governmental oppression.[109]

Proponents of judge-conducted voir dire argue, on the other hand, that lawyer-conducted questioning takes excessive amounts of

gSee Appendix D, p. 281.

time[h] and that lawyers "abuse" their "privilege" by asking inappropriate questions and indoctrinating the jurors.[110] Attorneys frequently attempt to explain elements of their case in a sympathetic manner to the prospective jurors or to influence the jurors on questions of law while they are trying to establish "rapport," and it is this subtle indoctrination that has offended many judges and commentators, who argue that such adversary arguments have no place in the jury-selection phase and should wait until the trial actually begins.[111] Some judges state that a litigant has no right to a favorable jury, but only to an impartial jury, and that any questioning that tends to "indoctrinate" the jurors or to obtain a jury sympathetic to one side or the other is improper.[112] Only if the judge is at the questioning helm, according to this view, can we be sure that no abusive, embarrassing, or improper questions will be asked of jurors because the judge's experience and neutrality make the judge better qualified to identify bias without alienating one side or another.

A compromise proposed by the American Bar Association and in use in many courts appears to be the best solution to the question of who should conduct the voir dire. According to this compromise, the judge conducts the initial questioning and then permits supplemental questioning by lawyers, which can be controlled by the judge if it becomes improper.[113] (This procedure was agreed upon on the theory that more time could be saved by it than by a procedure originally outlined in the ABA's 1968 *Standards Relating to Trial by*

---

[h]A study of voir dire times by the author, printed in the *Hastings Constitutional Law Quarterly* 3 (1975): 84-88, suggests that the time differences between voir dire conducted by attorneys and by a judge are actually not dramatic. Times ranged from less than 30 minutes to 2 hours and did not fall into any clearly discernible pattern. Although it is not insignificant that 15 minutes or a half hour might be saved in each trial, the differences are not large enough to lead to a restructuring of our conduct of voir dire if other factors that relate to the due process rights of litigants are involved. Furthermore, the evidence does not indicate conclusively that any of the systems is necessarily less time-consuming than the others. Surveys by the California Judicial Council in the early 1970s produced the seemingly incongruous conclusion that judge-conducted voir dire in civil cases actually takes 2 minutes longer than attorney-conducted voir dire when the time for the pre- and post-examination conferences is included—as it must be if the real concern is time.

Variables other than how the questioning is conducted are probably more important. A careful judge can guide attorney questioning in the normal case so that it proceeds expeditiously and without "abuses." A careless or indifferent judge might abuse the prospective jurors as much as a sloppy attorney, or worse still, conduct only perfunctory questioning. The important considerations are thus not who asks the questions but what kinds of questions are asked and how the attorneys and the judge relate to each other.

*Jury*, which stated that after the judge conducts the initial questioning, opposing counsel would submit additional questions which the judge would ask as he or she deemed appropriate.[114]) To vest the trial judge with absolute control over the voir dire would challenge the very foundation of the adversary system, where the judge moderates a confrontation but does not play an active role in it, and reduce the possibility of exposing bias in controversial cases, where the attorneys may have a unique understanding of the issues. To give lawyers uncontrolled discretion over the conduct of the questioning, on the other hand, can waste valuable time and result in questioning that is not necessary or appropriate. Each side should play a role in the voir dire, and each should be flexible enough to keep the objective of the process in mind: obtaining an impartial jury.

**Peremptory Challenges.** The most important structural change that needs to be considered at this stage of jury selection is the number of peremptory challenges granted to the two sides, particularly to the prosecution. Peremptories have come to be looked upon as a permanent and inevitable part of our system. They have indeed been a part of our criminal trials for centuries, but—as its history recounted earlier makes clear—the right of the prosecution to exercise these challenges has not always been accepted. Even those early courts that were least critical of the practice of allowing the prosecution to stand jurors aside felt that the practice should end if the prosecutor abused it.[115] The practice *is* being abused—the prosecution frequently uses its peremptories to eliminate entire ethnic groups—and it is time to consider some remedial measures. Three such measures follow.

1. As a minimum first step, courts should stop treating prosecutorial use of peremptory challenges as a sacred right. Most courts, particularly after *Swain v. Alabama* (1965),[116] have accepted the principle that we cannot inquire into the motives of any peremptory challenge exercised by the prosecutor. Yet if we suspect that these challenges are endangering the right to trial by an impartial jury, as by removing all blacks from the jury venire, we must inquire into the practice. The Supreme Court in *Swain* ruled that the prosecution's exercise of peremptories is not open to challenge unless the accused can demonstrate that the prosecutor has systematically excluded persons from jury service on the basis of race over a long period of time. The burden of proof is placed on the shoulders of the accused and can be sustained only if the accused has had an associate sitting in courtrooms throughout the area over a long period of time, which is highly unlikely.

A more equitable rule would be one that would allow the accused to establish a prima facie case of improper exclusion by citing as an example to the court the specific practices in the case at hand. If the prosecution has used most of its peremptory challenges against members of one race or has eliminated most members of a certain race from the jury venire, then the burden of proof should shift to the prosecutor to explain why this phenomenon occurred. If the prosecutor can bring in statistics showing that this racial exclusion is an isolated occurrence, then the trial should begin. If not, then the impaneled jury should be dismissed, the prosecutor admonished or punished for the improper action, and jury selection should begin anew. The manner in which the prosecution exercises peremptory challenges is information peculiarly within the knowledge of the state's attorneys themselves and is almost always beyond the grasp of the accused. It is appropriate, therefore, that when racism or other discrimination is suspected, the state should be obliged to explain itself.[117]

2. A second alternative is to take away all peremptory challenges from the prosecution. It is the duty of the prosecutor, as an officer of the state, to see that the accused is tried by a fair, impartial, and representative jury; it is not the role of the prosecutor to attempt to impanel a jury composed of those most likely to convict. In fact, the presumption of innocence requires that all jurors at the outset of the trial believe the defendant to be innocent. People who are unfit to be jurors can be challenged for cause, but the prosecutor should not be given enough unexplained challenges to eliminate whole groups of persons whose race, ethnic group, or opinions are not pleasing to the prosecutor's office. If the jury is to represent the conscience of the community in all its diversity, then no shade of opinion should be excluded. Otherwise, the defendant is not being judged simply by his community but rather by those members of his community who are approved—to the extent possible depending upon the number and method of peremptory strikes—by the government's representative in court.

It would clearly not be revolutionary to deprive the prosecution of its right to challenge without explanation. The two most populous states in the first century of this country's existence operated under such a system. New York, which had abolished the standing aside privilege by statute in 1786, did not accord the state peremptory challenge rights until 1881.[118] The state of Virginia, which never recognized the practice of standing aside, did not allow the prosecution peremptory challenges until 1919.[119]

3. It may be appropriate to eliminate peremptory challenges by

both sides—prosecution and defense. This idea is offered cautiously because good reasons exist for giving the defense peremptories. Attorneys representing nonwhite defendants argue, for instance, that they must have an adequate number of peremptory challenges if they are to have any hope of impaneling an unbiased jury. Challenges for cause are inadequate to eliminate biased persons because for such a challenge to succeed the judge must be convinced of its validity. A black defendant may be thoroughly convinced of the racism of a potential juror because of the defendant's experience with the numerous subtle manifestations of racism, but the defendant's attorney may nonetheless be unable to convince a white judge of the presence of that bias. A major source of the problem is the natural reluctance of people to admit to harboring racist attitudes, or to admit these feelings even to themselves. As sociologist Robert Blauner observed after viewing the voir dire in a racially sensitive case: "[I]t is interesting that people were more honest about case bias than about race bias; the former is still socially acceptable, the latter no longer is."[120] The tendency, at least initially, always to give the "right" (i.e., socially acceptable) answers to questions probing for racist attitudes is added to the often solicitous attitude of the judge and prosecution toward the potential juror. They do not wish to see the juror embarrassed or personally challenged because the juror is, after all, a citizen performing a civic duty at, no doubt, some personal inconvenience. In such situations, criminal defense attorneys argue, the defendant's only recourse is the use of a peremptory challenge.

Nonetheless, if we are committed to a completely representative jury, it is anomalous to allow either side to eliminate a juror thought to be unfriendly to its position. The use of peremptory challenges inevitably makes the jury more homogeneous than the population at large—because each side is eliminating the persons who are suspected of holding extreme positions on the other side—and to that extent the jury becomes less representative. Many states grant far too many peremptory challenges. As the chart in Appendix D, (p. 281) indicates, eleven states grant ten or more peremptories to both sides in all felony trials, and most of the nation's urban centers are included in this group. New Mexico's system of giving the defense five peremptories and the prosecution only three seems more than adequate to protect the litigants against the rare irresponsible juror and yet does not allow the attorneys to alter the basic random character of the jury.

A bill that would have eliminated all peremptory challenges in both civil and criminal trials[121] was introduced in 1974 in the

Massachusetts House of Representatives by David Mofenson at the urging of the Chief Judge of the Suffolk County (Boston) Superior Court. This bill was tentatively supported by the Massachusetts Bar Association on the condition that lawyers could conduct the questioning of the jurors—which is now done in Massachusetts by judges.[122] This section of the bill did not pass in 1974, but its consideration indicates that this is an idea whose time may be coming. Carl Imlay, general counsel to the Administrative Office of the United States Courts, has also suggested abolishing peremptories because they reduce the representativeness of our juries.[123] The English have already abolished the use of peremptories in the few civil trials that use juries, and English barristers rarely exercise them in criminal jury cases.[124]

The appropriate compromise is probably to allow a few peremptories to be exercised, perhaps three to five, with the defense given more than the prosecution, but not so many that either side can dramatically change the jury's demographic composition. And more work needs to be done to ensure that the lists with which we begin the selection process are completely representative and that fewer persons are given excuses from jury service. If our jury panels reflect more closely the population at large, then the need for extensive questioning and prolonged challenging will be greatly reduced.

## NOTES

1. *Swain v. Alabama*, 380 U.S. 202, 220 (1965).

2. See generally Ann Fagan Ginger, *Jury Selection in Criminal Trials* (Tiburon, Calif.: Lawpress, 1975).

3. Ginger, "What Can Be Done to Minimize Racism in Jury Trials," *Journal of Public Law* 20 (1971): 437-38.

4. See, e.g., Gutman, "The Attorney-Conducted Voir Dire of Jurors: A Constitutional Right," *Brooklyn Law Review* 39 (1972): 292.

5. Moore, "Voir Dire Examination of Jurors: I. The English Practice," *Georgetown Law Journal* 16 (1928): 443; J. Profatt, *A Treatise on Trial by Jury* (San Francisco, 1877), p. 247.

6. Gutman, "Attorney-Conducted Voir Dire," pp. 296-97.

7. *Ibid.*, pp. 297-99.

8. *United States v. Burr*, 25 F. Cas. 49 (No. 14,692g) (D.Va. 1807).

9. *Ibid.* p. 50.

10. *Ibid.*

11. Gutman, "Attorney-Conducted Voir Dire," pp. 307-308 n.54.

12. See Moore, "Voir Dire Examination," p. 453; Maxwell, "The Case of the Rebellious Juror," *Denver Law Journal* 47 (1970): 468; Note, "Judge-Conducted Voir Dire as a Time-Saving Trial Technique," *Rutgers-Camden Law Journal* 2 (1970): 161; Sir Patrick Devlin, *Trial by Jury* (London: Stevens & Sons, 1956), pp. 27-37.

13. See, e.g., American Law Institute Code of Criminal Procedure, sec. 277, reprinted in American Bar Association Project on Standards for Criminal Justice, *Standards Relating to Trial by Jury* (New York: Institute of Judicial Administration, 1968), pp. 68-69.

14. See, e.g., *United States v. Poole*, 450 F.2d 1082 (3d Cir. 1971), where the court held it to be reversible error to refuse to ask the prospective jurors, "Have you or any member of your family ever been the victim of a robbery or other crime?" in a bank robbery trial.

15. California Penal Code, sec. 1073. See also sections 1072 and 1074 of the Penal Code, and sec. 602 of the California Code of Civil Procedure.

16. *United States v. Burr*, 25 F. Cas. at 51.

17. The United States Supreme Court reaffirmed the approach taken by Chief Justice John Marshall and District Judge John Sirica in the recent case of *Murphy v. Florida*, 421 U.S. 794 (1975). Justice Thurgood Marshall's opinion for the majority stated that "[q]ualified jurors need not . . . be totally ignorant of the facts and issues involved" (*ibid.*, at 799-800) and that the governing standard was whether the prospective juror exhibited "a partiality that could not be laid aside." (*Ibid.*, at 800.)

18. See, e.g., *Irvin v. Dowd*, 366 U.S. 717, 722-23 (1961); *Silverthorne v. United States*, 400 F.2d 627 (9th Cir. 1968).

19. *United States v. Burr*, 25 F. Cas. at 50.

20. *Ham v. South Carolina*, 409 U.S. 524 (1973); but see *Ristaino v. Ross*, 96 S.Ct. 1017 (1976).

21. *United States v. Daily*, 139 F.2d 7 (7th Cir. 1943).

22. *Morford v. United States*, 339 U.S. 248 (1950).

23. *United States v. Clancey*, 276 F.2d 617, 632 (7th Cir. 1960), *reversed on other grounds*, 365 U.S. 312 (1961).

24. *United States v. Dellinger*, 472 F.2d 340 (7th Cir. 1972).

25. *Ibid.*, at 368.

26. *Ham v. South Carolina*, 409 U.S. 524 (1973).

27. *Ibid.*, at 528.

28. *Hamling v. United States*, 418 U.S. 87, 140 (1974) (emphasis added); *Ristaino v. Ross*, 96 S.Ct. 1017 (1976).

29. *Swain v. Alabama*, 380 U.S. 202, 219 (1965).

30. *Swain v. Alabama*, 380 U.S. 202, 218-19 (1965); but see *Ham v. South Carolina*, 409 U.S. 524 (1973).

31. *People v. Ferlin*, 203 Cal. 587, 598, 265 Pac. 230, 235 (1928) *quoted with approval* in *People v. Rigney*, 55 Cal. 2d 236, 244, 359 P.2d 23, 27, 10 Cal. Rptr. 625, 629 (1961), and *People v. Crowe*, 8 Cal. 3d 815, 830, 506 P.2d 193, 203, 106 Cal. Rptr. 369, 379 (1973).

32. New Jersey Stat. Ann. 2A: 75-1.

33. New Jersey Stat. Ann. 2A: 75-3.

34. New Jersey Stat. Ann. 2A: 78-7.

35. See, e.g., *Pointer v. United States*, 151 U.S. 396 (1894); *Brown v. State*, 62 N.J.L. 666, 42 Atl. 811 (1899), affd. 175 U.S. 172; *Swain v. Alabama*, 380 U.S. 202, 218 (1965); *Amsler v. United States*, 381 F.2d 37, 44 (9th Cir. 1967); *United States v. Peterson*, 475 F.2d 806, 812 (9th Cir. 1973).

36. *United States v. Douglass*, 2 Blatchf. 207, 25 Fed. Cas. 896, 898-99 (S.D.N.Y. 1851).

37. Statute of 33 Edw. I, Stat. 4 (1305).

38. *Blackstone's Commentaries* Vol. 4, p. 353.

39. 22 Henry VIII, c. 14 sec. 6, and 32 Henry VIII, c. 3; *Regina v. Gray*, 11 C. & Fin. 427 (House of Lords, 1843).

40. Halsbury's *Laws of England* (3d ed.; London: Butterworth, 1975), vol. 23, sec. 6, para. 48, p. 26.

41. Merriam, "The Right of Prosecutors to Stand Jurors Aside," *Central Law Journal* 14 (1882): 403, quoting from 13 How. St. Tr. 1108. (Trial of Spencer Cowper, et al, at Hertford Assizes, for the murder of Mrs. Sarah Stout, 11 William III, 1699).

42. See, e.g., Anonymous, I Ventris 309, 86 Eng. Rep. 199; Ford Lord Grey of Werk, 9 State Trials 128 (1682); James O'Coigly, 26 State Trials 1192 (1798).

43. See, e.g., *A Digest of the English Statutes in Force in the State of Georgia* (1826) p. 115; *A Report of All English Statutes Held Applicable to Laws of Maryland by Local Courts of Law or Equity* (1811); *Laws of Kentucky* 1799, Ch. LXXVII, sec. 18, 19; *Laws of New Jersey*, 1800, Juries VI, VII; *Stat. at Large of Virginia*, 1835, Act passed October 1792, Ch. 13, sec. 7, 8.

44. See *People v. Aichinson*, 7 How. Pr. 241 (New York 1852).

45. See *Montague v. Commonwealth*, 10 Grat. 767 (C.A.Va. 1853).

46. New York did not grant the prosecution any peremptory challenges until 1881, and Virginia refused to give the prosecution any peremptories until 1919.

47. Appellate courts in Georgia, Florida, Louisiana, North Carolina, Pennsylvania, and South Carolina approved of the practice in the early nineteenth century.

48. *Laws of Delaware*, 1829, Crimes and Misdemeanors V, sec. 9 (this Act was passed in 1782).

49. *Digest of Laws of Alabama*, 1833, Criminal Law 9, sec. 51.

50. Kentucky Constitutional Convention of 1849, *Debates*, pp. 91-92, 675, 693-94, 1085 (defeated 55-30); *Debates and Proceedings of Maryland Convention* (1851), vol. 1, p. 191 (defeated 42-25).

51. 1 Stats. 119, ch. 30, passed April 30, 1790.

52. Roberts, *A Digest of Select British Statutes Comprising Those Which, According to the Report of the Judges of the Supreme Court, Appear in Force in Pennsylvania* (1817), pp. 229-230.

53. *Ibid.*, pp. 330-31 (emphasis in original).

54. *United States v. Marchant*, 12 Wheat. 480, 483, 6 L. Ed. 700 (1827).

55. *United States v. Douglass*, 25 F. Cas. 896, 900 (S.D.N.Y. 1851) (Betts, J., dissenting).

56. *United States v. Shackelford*, 18 How. 588, 15 L. Ed. 495, 496 (1856).

57. The states authorized government use of peremptories at the times listed: Delaware—1782; Pennsylvania—1813; Tennessee—1821; Georgia—1822; Illinois—1827; North Carolina—1827; Mississippi—1836; Alabama—1837; Arkansas—1837; Louisiana—1837; Indiana—1843; Missouri—1845; California—1851; Kentucky—1854; Connecticut—1858; New Hampshire—1860; Massachusetts—1869; Vermont—1870; New Jersey—1871; Rhode Island—1872; South Carolina—1873;

Florida—1877; New York—1881; Maine—1883; Virginia—1919. Congress gave the prosecutor peremptories in federal courts in 1872.

58. *Hayes v. Missouri*, 120 U.S. 68, 69 (1887).

59. *Ibid.*, at 70-71. This statute is still on the books in Missouri and has recently been upheld in *State v. Granberry*, 284 S.W.2d 295, 299-300 (Mo. 1972).

60. See, e.g., Kuhn, "Jury Discrimination: The Next Phase," *Southern California Law Review* 41 (1968): 235, 283.

61. 380 U.S. 202.

62. *Ibid.*, at 223-24.

63. *Ibid.*, at 220-21.

64. *Ibid.*, at 229-30.

65. *Ibid.*, at 244.

66. *The Texas Observer* 65 (May 11, 1973): 9; see also *Time Magazine*, June 4, 1973, p. 67.

67. See, e.g., Lewis R. Sutin, "The Exercise of Challenges," *Tenth Judicial Circuit Conference*, 44 F.R.D. 286 (1967); Morris J. Bloomstein, *Verdict: The Jury System* (New York: Dodd, Mead & Co., 1968), pp. 64-66; Note, "The Jury Voir Dire: Useless Delay or Valuable Technique," *South Dakota Law Review* 11 (1966): 345-47; Dale W. Broeder, "The University of Chicago Jury Project," *Nebraska Law Review* 38 (1959): 748; Clarence Darrow, "Attorney for the Defense," *Esquire* 80 (Oct. 1973): 224; Laurence Kallen, "Peremptory Challenges Based Upon Juror Background—A Rational Use?" *Trial Lawyers Guide* 13 (1969): 143.

68. See, e.g., Kallen, "Peremptory Challenges. . . ."

69. Interview with San Francisco attorney Joseph Cotchett, August 21, 1972.

70. Interview with San Francisco attorney E. Robert Wallach, August 4, 1972.

71. Edward Tivnan, "Jury by Trial," *New York Times Magazine*, November 16, 1975, p. 64.

72. Interview with Assistant District Attorney Joseph A. Jelso, Albuquerque, New Mexico, June 3, 1974.

73. *New York Times*, July 24, 1975, p. 17 (city ed.).

74. R. Blauner, "The Sociology of Jury Selection," in Ann Fagan Ginger, ed., *Jury Selection in Criminal Trials: New Techniques and Concepts* (Tiburon, Calif.: Lawpress, 1975), p. 450.

75. Notes kept by defense attorney Margaret Burnham, mailed to this author June 19, 1972.

76. Jay Schulman, et al., "Recipe for a Jury," *Psychology Today* 6 (May 1973): 42.

77. *New York Times*, May 5, 1974, pp. 1, 41 (city ed.).

78. *United States v. McDaniels*, 379 F. Supp. 1243 (E.D.La. 1974).

79. Comment, "A Case Study of the Peremptory Challenge: A Subtle Strike at Equal Protection and Due Process," *St. Louis University Law Review* 18 (1974): 674-77.

80. *Ibid.*, p. 676.

81. *United States v. Carter*, 528 F.2d 844, 848 (8th Cir. 1975).

82. *McKinney v. Walker*, 394 F. Supp. 1015 (D.S.C. 1974).

83. *Brown v. State*, 248 Ark. 561, 453 S.W.2d 50 (1970).

84. *Hatton v. Smith*, 228 Ga. 378, 185 S.E.2d 388, 389 (1971); *Hobbs v. State*, 229 Ga. 556, 192 S.E.2d 903 (1972); *Allen v. State*, 231 Ga. 17, 200 S.E.2d 106, 108 (1973), *cert. denied* 94 S.Ct. 919 (1974).

85. *State v. Square*, 257 La. 743, 244 So.2d 200, 230, *penalty vacated and remanded* 408 U.S. 938 (1971) (two black prospective jurors peremptorily challenged); *State v. Richey*, 258 La. 1094, 249 S.2d 143, 152-53 (1971) (two blacks peremptorily challenged); *State v. Amphy*, 259 La. 161, 249 So.2d 560, 564 (1971); *State v. Lee*, 261 La. 310, 259 So.2d 334, 335 (1972); *State v. Shaffer*, 260 La. 605, 257 So.2d 121, 124 (1971); *State v. Lee*, 261 La. 310, 259 So.2d 334, 335 (1972); *State v. Dillard*, 261 La. 701, 260 So.2d 675, 679 (1972); *State v. Smith*, 263 La. 75, 267 So.2d 200, 201 (1972); *State v. McAllister*, 285 So.2d 197 (La. 1973); *State v. Gray*, 285 So.2d 199, 199-200 (La. 1973); *State v. Jack*, 285 So.2d 204, 207 (La. 1973); *State v. Arceneaux*, 302 So.2d 1 (La. 1974); *State v. Anderson*, 315 So.2d 266 (La. 1975); *State v. Curry*, 319 So.2d 917 (La. 1975).

86. *Johnson v. State*, 9 Md. App. 143, 262 A.2d 792 (1970).

87. *Capler v. State*, 237 So.2d 445 (Miss. 1970).

88. *State v. Davison*, 457 S.W.2d 674, 676-77 (Mo. 1970) (prospective jury panel contained 17 blacks and 30 whites; prosecution used all 15 of its peremptories to eliminate blacks); *State v. Bradford*, 462 S.W.2d 664 (Mo. 1971); *State v. Huddleston*, 462 S.W.2d 691, 692 (Mo. 1971) (prosecution peremptorily challenged all four blacks on the jury panel); *State v. Smith*, 465 S.W.2d 482, 485 (Mo. 1971) (prosecution used 13 of its 15 peremptories to eliminate blacks); *Clark v. State*, 465 S.W.2d 557, 558 (Mo. 1971) (prosecution eliminated all the blacks on the jury panel with peremptory strikes); *State v. Brookins*, 468 S.W.2d 42, 46 (Mo. 1971) (again, the prosecution eliminated all blacks with peremptory strikes); *State v. Dinkins*, 508 S.W.2d 1, 8 (Mo. 1974) (prosecution peremptorily challenged only black on panel); *State v. Jacks*, 525 S.W.2d 431 (Mo. App. 1975) (prosecutor challenged all four blacks on venire).

89. *State v. Noell*, 284 N.C. 670, 202 S.E.2d 750, 759 (1974).

90. *Johnson v. State*, 3 Tenn. Cr. 17, 456 S.W.2d 864 (1970), *cert. denied* 400 U.S. 997 (1971).

91. *Hardin v. State*, 475 S.W.2d 254, 255-57 (Tex. Crim. App. 1972); *Ridley v. State*, 475 S.W.2d 769 (Tex. Crim. App. 1972); *Brown v. State*, 476 S.W.2d 699, 700-701 (Tex. Crim. App. 1972); *Reese v. State*, 481 S.W.2d 841, 842 (Tex. Crim. App. 1972) (9 blacks peremptorily challenged); *Hill v. State*, 487 S.W.2d 64, 64-65 (Tex. Crim. App. 1972) (6 blacks peremptorily challenged); and *Noah v. State*, 495 S.W.2d 260, 265 (Tex. Crim. App. 1973).

92. *People v. Boyd*, 16 Cal.App.3d 901, 94 Cal. Rptr. 575 (1971); *In re Wells*, 20 Cal.App.3d 640, 647-48, 98 Cal. Rptr. 1, 5 (1971) (19 blacks peremptorily challenged in this and two related cases); *People v. Allums*, 47 Cal.App.3d 654, 121 Cal. Rptr. 62, 68 (1975); *People v. Gardner*, 52 Cal.App.3d 559, 125 Cal. Rptr. 186 (1975).

93. *People v. Butler*, 46 Ill.2d 162, 263 N.E.2d 89 (1970) (only black member of panel struck).

94. *Commonwealth v. Cook*, 308 N.E.2d 508 (Mass. 1974). *Commonwealth v. Anderson*, 334 N.E.2d 61 (Mass.App. 1975) (when defense counsel complained that prosecution was using its peremptories to exclude all blacks, prosecutor responded that defense counsel "wouldn't give me an Irishman all morning. They have been kicking them off").

95. *People v. Redwine*, 50 Mich.App. 593, 213 N.W.2d 841 (1973).

96. *State v. Smith*, 55 N.J. 476, 262 A.2d 868 (1970).

97. *Commonwealth v. Darden*, 441 Pa. 41, 271 A.2d 257 (1970).

98. *United States v. Pearson*, 448 F.2d 1207, 1216 (5th Cir. 1971) (ten of 12 black prospective jurors in the two trials appealed were peremptorily challenged); *United States v. Cariton*, 456 F.2d 107 (5th Cir. 1972) (all black prospective jurors peremptorily challenged); *United States v. Corbitt*, 368 F. Supp. 881, 886 (E.D.Pa. 1973) (all five black prospective jurors peremptorily challenged); *United States v. Pollard*, 483 F.2d 929 (8th Cir. 1973) (all four black prospective jurors peremptorily challenged); *United States v. Grant*, 471 F.2d 648 (4th Cir. 1973) (five black prospective jurors peremptorily challenged); *Little v. United States*, 490 F.2d 686 (8th Cir. 1974); *United States v. Delay*, 500 F.2d 1360 (8th Cir. 1974); *United States v. Thompson*, 518 F.2d 534 (8th Cir. 1975); *United States v. Neal*, 527 F.2d 63 (8th Cir. 1975) (only black on panel challenged); *United States v. Nelson*, 529 F.2d 40 (8th Cir. 1976).

99. 475 S.W.2d 769 (Tex.Crim.App. 1972).

100. *Ibid.*, at 770.

101. *Ibid.*, at 771.

102. A survey conducted by Marquette University psychology professor Harry Rollings of 438 students' reactions to the publicity surrounding the Patty Hearst case found the students' judgments were not particularly influenced by the news reports. (*New Times*, Feb. 6, 1976.) But a study supervised by Alice M. Padawer-Singer and Allen H. Barton of Columbia University's Bureau of Applied Social Research found that persons exposed to publicity about a case were willing to convict a defendant with a somewhat lower level of evidence than persons without such exposure. (Padawer-Singer and Barton, "The Impact of Pretrial Publicity on Jurors' Verdicts," in *The Jury System in America: A Critical Overview*, ed. Rita James Simon (Beverly Hills: Sage Publications, 1975), pp. 123-39.)

103. *Ristaino v. Ross*, 96 S.Ct. 1017 (1976).

104. *Ham v. South Carolina*, 409 U.S. 524 (1973); *Hamling v. United States*, 418 U.S. 87 (1974); *Ristaino v. Ross*, 96 S.Ct. 1017 (1976).

105. Cal. Penal Code, sec. 1070, as amended; Cal. Civ. Pro., Rule 47, as amended.

106. Broeder, "Voir Dire Examinations: An Empirical Study," *Southern California Law Review* 38 (1965): 505, 510-21.

107. Rule 24(a) of the Federal Rules of Criminal Procedure.

108. *The Jury System in the Federal Courts* (Works of the Committee on the Operation of the Jury System of the Judicial Conference of the United States, 1966-73) (St. Paul: West Publishing Co., 1974), p. 174.

109. Letter by Paul C. Chevigny, staff counsel, New York Civil Liberties Union, in the *New York Times*, May 18, 1972, p. 44.

110. *People v. Crowe*, 8 Cal.3d 815, 825, 506 P.2d 193, 199, 106 Cal. Rptr. 369, 375 (1973).

111. See, e.g., *United States v. Crawford*, 444 F.2d 1404, 1405 (10th Cir. 1971).

112. *Ibid.*, at 824, 828.

113. A.B.A. Project on Standards for Criminal Justice, *Standards Relating to Trial by Jury*, Supplement, sec. 2.4, p. 2.

114. *Ibid.*, at sec. 2.4, p. 63.

115. See, e.g., *State v. Sloan*, 97 N.C. 499, 2 S.E. 666 (1887).

116. 380 U.S. 202.

117. See Kuhn, "Jury Discrimination," pp. 293-303.

118. *Rev. Stat. of New York*, 6th ed., 1029, sec. 9 et seq.; *New York Code of Criminal Procedure*, ch. 442, sec. 370, *Laws of 1881*.

119. *Code of Virginia Annot.*, 1205, sec. 4898 (1924).

120. Blauner, "The Sociology of Jury Selection," p. 463.

121. House Bill No. 2201, sec. 42.

122. Interview with Joseph Romanow, June 10, 1974.

123. Carl H. Imlay, "Federal Jury Reformation: Saving a Democratic Institution," *Loyola-L.A. Law Review* 6 (1973): 269-70.

124. Lloyd E. Moore, *The Jury: Tool of Kings, Palladium of Liberty* (Cincinnati: W.H. Anderson Co., 1973), p. 134.

✳ *Chapter Seven*

# Selecting a Jury in Political Trials

Impaneling an impartial jury in a trial that has received extensive media attention presents problems, especially if it is a political trial, which can be loosely defined as a trial in which political issues, activities, or personalities are central to the case. Because all the participants approach a political trial with combative positions, legal institutions and safeguards are strained and often become vulnerable to manipulation at a time when strength, stability, and impartiality are most needed. The jury, which is given the ultimate decision-making authority in criminal trials "in order to prevent oppression by the Government,"[1] is taxed when the glare of publicity and clash of ideologies combine in a courtroom confrontation. A representative jury is essential in these trials because only a group representing a broad spectrum of viewpoints can resolve the conflicting evidence in a manner that truly reflects the community's consensus and because only the judgment of such a broad-based body will be accepted as legitimate by all the competing factions. Sensational criminal trials present many of the problems of political trials.

## JURY NULLIFICATION[a]

It is usually in political trials that the jury has the opportunity and the motivation to give its own reading not only of the facts but of the law as it is to be applied in the particular situation. The jury's right to render its decision according to its convictions (not merely

---
[a]For a detailed discussion, see Postscript: Jury Nullification, p. 225.

*177*

according to the judge's instructions on the law) was established in the trial of William Penn and William Mead in 1670.[b] The most famous American case of the jury's use of this power, which is frequently called "jury nullification," came in the 1735 trial of John Peter Zenger, who had printed material not authorized by the British mayor of New York and was accused of "seditious libel." Although Zenger had clearly violated the law, the jury refused to convict, following the advice of Zenger's lawyer that they "have the right beyond all dispute to determine both the law and the facts."[2] This right was well established by the end of the eighteenth century. In 1794, for instance, John Jay, Chief Justice of the U.S. Supreme Court, explicitly told a panel of jurors when he was sitting as a trial judge that they had the right "to determine the law as well as the fact in controversy."[3]

But in the nineteenth century, several prominent judges, apparently not accepting the idea that a jury can logically be given the right to mitigate the severity of the law without also having the power to create laws (which clearly is not the jury's role), refused to tell the jury of its power to nullify,[4] and this refusal was approved by the Supreme Court in 1895.[5] The jury in fact still has the power to judge the law and the facts—since acquittals by a jury cannot be appealed on any grounds—but most judges will not inform jurors of this power. Most often, judges will instruct jurors that they have the power only to decide the facts, not the law, and must accept the law as stated by the judge.

The controversy over jury nullification has been renewed in recent years,[6] and in two states (Indiana and Maryland), judges still specifically inform jurors of their authority to nullify the law in appropriate cases.[7] Chief Judge David Bazelon of the U.S. Court of Appeals for the District of Columbia Circuit believes that jurors should be told that part of their job is to pass judgment on the equity of applying the law to the defendant charged in the particular case:

> The [jury nullification] doctrine permits the jury to bring to bear on the criminal process a sense of fairness and particularized justice. The drafters of legal rules cannot anticipate and take account of every case where a defendant's conduct is "unlawful" but not blameworthy, any more than they can draw a bold line to mark the boundary between an accident and negligence. It is the jury—as spokesman for the community's sense of values—that must explore that subtle and elusive boundary. . . . The very essence of the jury's function is its role as spokesman for the community conscience in determining whether or not blame can be imposed.[8]

---

[b]See Chapter One, p. 5.

The Supreme Court has not considered the jury nullification doctrine directly since their 1895 decision, but the Court has in a number of recent cases recognized the jury's role as the community's conscience and has recognized its importance as a law-making body.[9] Perhaps the most telling clue to the Court's view of the jury's role is contained in the following passage from a 1968 opinion written by Justice Potter Stewart:

> [O]ne of the most important functions any jury can perform in making such a selection [between life and death] is to maintain a link between contemporary community values and the penal system—a link without which the determination of punishment could hardly reflect "the evolving standards of decency that mark the progress of a maturing society."[10]

The necessity of impaneling a jury that fairly represents the community in cases where the jury may consider the law as well as the facts cannot be overemphasized.

The parties to political trials clearly realize the importance of jury selection. The methods of selecting juries for these trials have been almost as well publicized as the trials themselves. The prosecution's use of the Federal Bureau of Investigation to investigate prospective jurors and the defense's use of sophisticated psychological and sociological techniques have raised serious questions about the whole process of jury selection, particularly the appropriateness of challenges. Prospective jurors have been so studied, scrutinized, and judged that the juries in some of these trials cannot by any stretch of the imagination be considered a randomly selected cross-section of the community.

This extensive investigation has some justification, to be sure. In well-publicized cases, the government often has advantages that it does not always possess in run-of-the-mill cases. One, of course, is publicity and the feelings it can stir against defendants who hold unpopular views. Two others are picking the location of the trial and sequestering the jury, which can affect the jury in ways that render it more likely to favor the government.

## PUBLICITY

In political trials, both the prosecution and the defense tend to argue in the court of public opinion before the trial even begins. The public first learned about the Harrisburg Seven case when F.B.I. director J. Edgar Hoover, testifying before Congress in November 1970, told his astounded listeners of a plot by members of the "East Coast Conspiracy to Save Lives" to kidnap Henry Kissinger and hold him hostage until the end of the Vietnam War. Hoover's statement made headlines across the country, and Hoover was put under some pressure to deliver evidence. Shortly thereafter, indictments were issued, once again accompanied by massive publicity.[11]

Some government attempts to mold public opinion backfire, and sometimes the defense can compete successfully with the government in the forum of media manipulation. Take the case of the Milwaukee Fourteen. In September 1968, this group, which earned its sobriquet after its arrest, raided a Selective Service office in Milwaukee and burned draft files. They were accused by the state of Wisconsin of burglary, theft, and arson and were convicted after a trial marked by widespread and often hostile media coverage. The defendants themselves issued press releases and encouraged publicity. Subsequent federal charges filed against them were dismissed by the federal district judge after he had questioned 137 prospective jurors and determined that they were so prejudiced that an impartial jury could not be selected (the dismissal was upheld on appeal).[12] Similarly, the 1970 murder charges against Black Panther leaders Bobby Seale and Ericka Huggins in New Haven were subsequently dismissed after one jury was unable to reach a unanimous verdict. The judge ruled that an unbiased jury could not be selected without "superhuman efforts which this Court, the State and these defendants should not be called upon either to make or to endure." Selection of the first trial jury had taken four months and had required the examination of about 1,100 prospective jurors. Then, on the trial's opening day, J. Edgar Hoover had called the Panthers "the most dangerous group in America."[13]

## THE TRIAL SITE

In some political trials, the federal government has used its power to select trial locations in a way that has seemed to increase rather than reduce the prejudice to the accused. In cases of national scope, several trial sites are usually available, and the federal government seems to have tried to choose locations with populations that are most receptive to the government's position.

The trial of Dr. Benjamin Spock, Rev. William Sloan Coffin, and three other antiwar activists in 1968 could have been brought in New York or Washington, D.C., but the government chose Boston—where it expected and obtained a more conservative jury panel and a more conservative judge. The government was also able to obtain a jury venire containing virtually no women to try Doctor Spock, who wrote the most popular book on child care ever published. According to reports, the government somehow persuaded the jury clerk to slip down to the next name whenever he came across a woman.[14] The 1972 trial of the Harrisburg Seven could have been held in Philadelphia, New York, or Rochester—which were all mentioned as locations of draft boards that had been raided—or in Washington, D.C., where the defendants allegedly interfered with heating tunnels and planned to kidnap Henry Kissinger. But the government chose the Middle District of Pennsylvania. Even within this district, the government had a choice of three sites: Lewisburg (a college town and site of the federal prison), Scranton (containing a high proportion of Catholics, Democrats, and militant mine workers), or Harrisburg, the site chosen (with its high proportion of Republicans, a low proportion of Catholics, a high proportion of fundamentalist religious sects and war-related industries).[15] For the Pentagon Papers Trial of Daniel Ellsberg and Anthony Russo in 1973, the government chose Los Angeles—rather than the other possible sites of Boston, New York, or Washington—probably because of Southern California's heavy concentration of defense industries. At one point during the selection of the first jury in July 1972, all 16 prospective jurors picked by lot for preliminary questioning admitted to a personal or family connection, past or present, with the military or a defense industry.[16]

The defense can request a change of venue, but such requests are not necessarily granted. In the Joan Little case, the defense successfully moved to have the trial held in another county after surveying residents of the area in which the stabbing took place and finding that virtually everyone thought the defendant guilty.

## SEQUESTRATION

Sequestration, like selection of a presumably pro-government trial site, also has the potential of affecting the jury's makeup. In plain language, "sequestration" means that the jurors are kept in the custody of the government until they are officially released by the judge, a process that can raise the possibility of prejudice to the defendant and access to the jury by the government. This procedure is used to insulate the jurors from publicity about the trial and information about the defendants that is not admissable into evidence. These objectives are important, but it is also important to realize that when juries are to be sequestered the number of excuses for hardship is increased dramatically, and the representativeness of the resulting jury is affected.

In all cases, jury service is a hardship because of the loss of time and the inadequate pay, but in a protracted trial, this hardship is likely to be substantially more severe, making it that much more difficult to impanel a jury that is representative of the community. Employed persons, particularly those who work at lower-paying or hourly paid jobs, are unlikely to be able to spare the time to serve on a long trial because the compensation for jury duty is so small. When the jury selection for the first Watergate bugging trial began in January 1973, 100 of the 250 persons summoned for jury duty asked to be (and were) summarily excused after Judge John J. Sirica announced that the jury would be sequestered during the trial.[17] The same result occurred when Judge Sirica was impaneling the jury in October 1974 for the major coverup trial.[18]

Once a panel of jurors who can serve for a long trial is assembled, the problem of impartiality remains because the jurors are cut off from the outside world during sequestration except for the contacts that are authorized by the government. For the period of the trial, the government censors the news for the jurors. Jurors may blame the defendant or the prosecutor for their temporary incarceration or resent being locked up while the defendant is allowed to be free.

The government may even try to curry favor with the jurors by indulging their desires. One juror after the 1968 *Spock* case described how the federal government took care of him during sequestration: "We had entertainment—always the best—food always the best, martinis before dinner, the government spared no expense to see that our life was as pleasant as possible. I gained twelve pounds during the trial. We went to the best restaurants and so forth."[19] Another juror was specially escorted by two marshals during the trial to see his son play rugby. The possibility that jurors will feel grateful to the government for such attention may conceivably translate itself into a pro-government bias.

Personality problems that can affect the verdict one way or the other can arise when jurors are sequestered together for a long period of time. When the time for deliberation arrives, the jurors may not be speaking as individuals with different perspectives, coming from different parts of the community, because they may have formed strong relationships with other jurors. Federal District Judge Ray McNichols wrote a report on sequestration for the Committee on the Operation of the Jury System in which he raises this problem:

A more insidious problem may lurk in the background of the practice of isolating 12 to 18 peers, chosen as a representative cross section of their society, from their regular routine and habitat for relatively long periods of time. Nothing suggests to the writer that any definitive study has been made of the psychological impact on an individual or a group of individuals exposed to this experience. Only an educated curiosity forms a basis for posing the problem, and no solution is here proposed. *One wonders*, nevertheless, *what personality or character changes might occur in the panel during a seven months' virtual isolation* [as occurred in the Manson trial] *from normal day to day existence.*[20]

Juries sequestered for shorter periods may form into small factions, and when the deliberations begin, jurors may have teammates who support their arguments. The jury sequestered for the 1974 Mitchell-Stans trial was invited during the trial by juror Andrew Choa to his office for a private screening of a movie, and he—the only affluent member of the jury—provided other small treats during their period of confinement, thus enabling him to assume a dominant role when the discussion began.[21]

Sequestration sometimes does, of course, fulfill its intended purpose of insulating the jurors from improper influences. The defense in the trial of the Harrisburg Seven had originally opposed sequestration but concluded later it helped their side.[22] Post-verdict interviews with seven of the jurors (who substantially acquitted the Seven) revealed that the pressure from friends, relatives, the community, and the media—all of whom assumed the defendants were guilty—might have proved irresistible.

Sequestration is a device used to enable the court to conduct a fair trial without putting limits on the freedom of the press, and because of these competing interests, it is sometimes justified. Its use always raises problems, however, and it should be understood that when a jury is sequestered it is less likely to be representative and that, despite the fact that sequestration is intended to eliminate outside influences on the jury, it may exert its own influences.

## SOCIAL SCIENCE AND JURY SELECTION

To overcome the government's common advantages in highly publicized trials, defense lawyers have been approaching jury selection in a more sophisticated way, drawing upon the knowledge of psychologists and sociologists to help choose the ultimate jury panel. It is in the voir dire that defense lawyers have concentrated a great deal of their attention and energy, in part as a response to the government's use of the F.B.I. to investigate prospective jurors,[23] which was done in the *Spock* and *Harrisburg* cases. Generally, the defendants have no opportunity to obtain this information.[24] The methods used by the defense—and by the prosecution when it employs the F.B.I.—raise serious questions about the integrity of the selection process. A look at the work by the defense teams in the trials of Angela Davis, the Harrisburg Seven, John Mitchell and Maurice Stans, and Joan Little brings into focus the problems of detailed questioning and challenging.[c]

Angela Davis's chief defense attorney, Howard Moore, enlisted the services of a team of black psychologists to help choose a sympathetic jury.[25] During the two-and-a-half weeks that the jury was being selected, the psychologists visited the courtroom each day in teams of two, and during every break and each evening they would meet with defense attorneys to share their impressions. Verbal responses to questions and nonverbal indications of personality and disposition were studied and evaluated. Often the psychologists suggested a line of questions to be pursued by the lawyers. When a jury panel was finally selected, Angela Davis rose and stated to the court: "Although I cannot say that this is a jury of my peers, I can say that, after much discussion, we have reached the conclusion that the men and women sitting on the jury will put forth their best efforts to give me a fair trial."[26] After hearing all the evidence, this jury found her to be not guilty.

The Harrisburg Seven Defense Committee assembled a team of specialists in 1971 to help understand and evaluate the prospective jurors.[27] This team included Jay Schulman and Richard Christie, who helped pioneer the "scientific" method of jury selection in this case and later applied it to other prominent political trials such as the Camden Twenty-eight, Gainesville Eight, the Wounded Knee defendants, and the Joan Little case. In the Harrisburg case, a group of sociologists first conducted a general telephone survey of 1,236 randomly selected registered voters to see if the panel of prospective jurors was in fact representative of the voters in the area. Interviewers requested data on age, sex, education, race, and occupation from the random sample. Partly on the basis of evidence thus obtained, which indicated that the existing panel did not conform to the random-sample statistics, the trial judge ordered a new jury panel selected. The researchers then conducted a series of face-to-face interviews designed to elicit more personal information. Forty-five volunteers were quickly trained to speak to 252 people selected at random from the earlier group of 1,236, and they asked about which newspapers or magazines the interviewees read, which radio and television programs they watched, their knowledge of defendants and the trial, who they considered "the greatest Americans" of the last fifteen years, their trust in government, their children, religious

---

[c]See Chapter Six, pp. 141-45, 160-66.

preferences, hobbies and organizational memberships, their views on antiwar activities and the use of force by police to maintain order, the legitimacy of supporting the government even when one believes that the government is wrong, and whether a person brought to trial is usually guilty.

After the interviewing process was completed, the social scientists assembled the data and concluded that religion was the key factor in the attitudinal scheme of those interviewed. Certain religious affiliations—Episcopalian, Methodist, Presbyterian, and Fundamentalist sects—were found to be strongly opposed to the ideological position of the defendants. Catholics, Brethren, and Lutherans were deemed favorable. Another startling conclusion was that, although education and contact with metropolitan news media is usually equated with liberalism, quite the opposite was the case in the Middle District of Pennsylvania. The liberals among the well-educated apparently leave the Harrisburg area, and those college-educated persons who stay become business and civic leaders and are usually conservative Republicans. The data, in fact, revealed that most people in the Harrisburg area are quite conservative.[d] And the researchers felt that at least four out of every five persons who would qualify as jurors would be opposed to the defendants. The judge's decision to allow counsel to conduct its own voir dire and frame its own questions to the jurors was therefore most beneficial to the defense.

After three weeks, the panel of 465 prospective jurors was narrowed down by excuses and challenges for cause to 46. Federal District Judge R. Dixon Herman used the struck-jury system for peremptory challenges, whereby the defense would exercise its 28 peremptories and the prosecution would use its 6 to pare the 46 down to a jury of 12. The defense strategy was thus to rate these remaining 46 prospective jurors. A scale ranging from 1 (highly favorable juror) to 5 (highly undesirable) was set up, and as much information as possible about each juror was assembled. The two characteristics that seemed especially important to the defense point of view in addition to religion were opposition to authority and a social style that was more "maternalistic"—caring and loving—than "paternalistic"—stern and disciplinary. And at least one juror had to be Catholic in order to inhibit any anti-Catholic sentiments. Using these standards, the defense rated eight of the 46 prospects as #1, five as #2, fifteen as #3, and eighteen as #4 or #5. The prosecutor,

---

[d]Eighty percent trusted the government, compared to the national level of 40 to 50 percent; 87 percent felt that the right to private property is sacred; only 37 percent had heard of Rev. Philip Berrigan, the most well-known of the defendants; 81 percent approved police violence to maintain order; 65 percent thought that government should be supported even when it is wrong.

apparently having made similar judgments about some of the jurors, used his six peremptory challenges against six of the #1's.[e] The defense thus had to decide which five jurors should be chosen from category 3 in addition to the seven it would save from groups 1 and 2.

A major concern was how the members of the jury would relate to each other as a group. How independent would individual jurors be in arriving at their own decisions, and to what extent would they stand firm once they had made up their minds? Responses elicited during the voir dire and information gathered from members of the community furnished some guide in answering these questions, but often the data were conflicting, and hard choices had to be made. The defense felt that a group of women would stick together during the long sequestration, and they hoped that at least one would have a negative reaction to Boyd Douglas, the prosecution's chief witness, who had proposed marriage to several young college students to get information from them. This negative reaction, they thought, might then be passed along to the other women in the subgroup.

The proof of the effectiveness of this mode of jury selection can only be determined after the deliberations are concluded and the verdict is recorded. In this case, it was 10-2 for acquittal on the main charge of conspiracy. Interestingly enough, the only two jurors who voted against acquittal came from the #2 category, not #3.[f] While the jury was deliberating, the defense staff interviewed again 83 people from the original 252 people randomly selected and previously contacted. Of the 61 people who had been following the trial and were willing to express themselves on the guilt or innocence of the defendants, the overwhelming majority thought the defendants were guilty as charged. The jury, on the other hand, voted 10-2 for acquittal on the conspiracy charge. This result tends to confirm the "success" of the defense's methods in selecting a sympathetic jury. Looking for factors that led to the guilty or innocent judgment, the defense found that 37 percent of the interviewed women thought the defendants were guilty on all or most counts, whereas 57 percent of the men made this same judgment. (The jury consisted of nine women, three men.) The most accurate predictors, however, were education and religion; exposure to the media also contributed to an anti-defense attitude.

---

[e]The government used the F.B.I. to check jurors' backgrounds, which meant that they also had detailed information with which to decide whom to challenge.

[f]One of these jurors had not been questioned fully by the defense lawyers because they felt the juror might reveal information to the prosecutor that would encourage him to challenge her. The other had been rated #2 because he gave pro-defense answers, although the social predictors were unfavorable. The defense wondered later if he had told the truth at voir dire.

In the 1974 New York City trial of John Mitchell and Maurice Stans on charges of conspiracy and perjury, the defense, also using social science techniques, had the opportunity to mold the jury in much the same way that the Harrisburg defense shaped their jury. Once again, the judge gave the defense a substantial advantage in the number of peremptory challenges: 20 for the defense and only 8 for the prosecution. Judge Lee Gagliardi (a Nixon appointee) decided on these figures because he felt the substantial pretrial publicity had put the defendants at a disadvantage.[28] Judge Gagliardi made two other decisions that may have helped the defendants. He eliminated for cause many of the better-educated potential jurors because of their possible prejudice,[29] and he excused all persons who indicated that they would suffer a severe hardship by being sequestered for many weeks,[30] thus eliminating the most economically precarious jurors— and many nonwhites—who might differ politically with Stans and Mitchell.

The defendants hired Marty Herbst, a communications consultant, to assist in the jury selection, and he recommended that they seek blue-collar jurors, Roman Catholic if possible, who had not gone to college, earned between $8,000 and $10,000 and read the *New York Daily News* rather than the *New York Times* or *New York Post.* To be avoided were Jews and what Herbst called "limousine liberals." "We wanted," he said later, "people who were home established, to the right, more concerned with inflation than Watergate," and who might somehow associate John Mitchell with John Wayne.[31] At least one person selected to be a juror had never heard of either of the defendants before the trial began.

When the trial ended and the jurors were sent to the jury room for deliberations, they sat for 20 minutes without saying anything. Finally, they asked for copies of the indictment and began taking preliminary votes, which indicated that a majority favored a guilty verdict. But after much discussion, the jury seems to have become dominated by Andrew Choa, an alternate who joined the jury when a vacancy developed and the one juror who did not fit all the criteria layed down by Herbst: He had gone to college (and the Harvard Business School) and was vice-president of the First National City Bank. He not only knew who the defendants were but had in fact contributed to Richard Nixon's presidential campaign. Juror Choa was able to direct the rest of the jury's attention to weaknesses in the prosecution's case and was instrumental in producing the final result: a unanimous verdict for acquittal on all counts. The scenario for acquittal was thus somewhat unpredictable, but certainly some of the defense's tactics paid off.

Social science methods of selection were again used with sophistication in the trial of Joan Little in 1975, where the defense's first step, as in the Harrisburg case, was to survey the county in which the alleged crime took place to gauge public feeling about the case. After finding that most people in the county thought the defendant guilty and, furthermore, that the jury pool substantially underrepresented blacks, women, and young people, they successfully moved for a change of venue. In the new location (Raleigh, in Wake County), the team interviewed almost a thousand residents to obtain their attitudes about police, blacks, rape, and other issues considered important to the trial, and to find out their income, occupation, and other socioeconomic data. After questioning the jury pool in the same way, they found the same profile of responses, meaning that, if their methods were correct, the jury wheel was indeed representative. After charting (with a computer) the correlation between age, education, and other factors with attitudes, they came up with certain standards by which to identify favorable and unfavorable jurors,[32] and discovered that what people read was the most important measure of their views. The jury finally assembled was half black and half white[g] and acquitted the defendant.

Methods such as these may indeed help obtain a jury that acquits a defendant, but possibly at the cost of diminishing respect for the judicial system. Panels that seem to have been manipulated by one side or the other (or both) will not fulfill their purpose of conveying legitimacy to the community. Even people who believe a defendant innocent may wonder at the "justice" being rendered by an apparently hand-picked jury.

Obtaining an impartial jury is admittedly difficult in well-publicized cases, as Chief Justice John Marshall recognized in the trial of Aaron Burr in 1807. The chance that jurors will have formed an opinion on the case is much greater than in other cases. Because of that difficulty, and the importance of impaneling a jury that embodies the community's conscience in such sensitive cases, special care must be taken in jury selection. The question must be asked in these trials, as in the challenge process as a whole, how much and what kind of questioning is really necessary to obtain an impartial jury. There are other steps that can be taken in highly publicized trials that may make extensive questioning and challenges unnecessary and help preserve the random character of the panel.

Judges should be aware of actions that might be taken by the government to increase rather than reduce bias in the jury, and resist them. They should work to ensure that a representative jury is

---

[g]There were originally 7 white and 5 black jurors, but 1 white juror fell ill and was replaced by a black.

impaneled by special attention to actions that can distort the jury's capacity to speak for the community. Exhaustive questioning may in fact be necessary in cases that are nationally publicized. But in most cases, better solutions can be found to reduce the potential bias. One is to change the site of the trial to a location with an ethnic population similar to the area in which the crime allegedly occurred, and with a fair number of persons of the defendant's ethnic background—thus replicating the community's character in a less emotional atmosphere.[33] Another is to make sure that selection procedures are truly random by insisting that the list of prospective jurors is as complete as is humanly possible, resisting all requests for excuses, limiting challenges for cause to cases of clear and unmistakable prejudice, and limiting peremptory challenges to no more than three, or at most five. The body thus empaneled should be truly representative. It will certainly be diverse and may take longer to deliberate, but its verdict—because it will be the expression of a consensus of the community's view—is more likely to be accepted by all factions as impartial and legitimate.

## NOTES

1. *Duncan v. Louisiana*, 391 U.S. 145, 149 (1968).

2. James Alexander, *A Brief Narration of the Case and Trial of John Peter Zenger* (Cambridge, Mass.: Harvard University Press, 1963), p. 78.

3. *Georgia v. Brailsford*, 3 U.S. (3 Dall.) 1, 4 (1794).

4. *United States v. Battiste*, 24 F. Cas. 1042, 1043 (No. 14,545) (C.C.D. Mass. 1835); *United States v. Morris*, 26 F. Cas. 1323, 1331 (No. 15,815) (C.C.D. Mass. 1851).

5. *Sparf and Hansen v. United States*, 156 U.S. 51 (1895).

6. See, e.g., Scheflin, "Jury Nullification: The Right to Say No," *Southern California Law Review* 45 (1972): 168; Sax, "Conscience and Anarchy: The Prosecution of War Resisters," *Yale Review* 57 (June 1968): 481; Howe, "Juries as Judges of Criminal Law," *Harvard Law Review* 52 (1939): 582; Van Dyke, "The Jury as a Political Institution," *Catholic Lawyer* 16, (1970): 224; Simson, "Jury Nullification in the American System: A Skeptical View," *Texas Law Review* 54 (1976): 488; *United States v. Moylan*, 417 F.2d 1002 (4th Cir. 1969); *United States v. Simpson*, 460 F.2d 515 (9th Cir. 1972); *United States v. Dougherty*, 473 F.2d 1113 (D.C. Cir. 1972); *United States v. Dellinger*, 472 F.2d 340, 408 (7th Cir. 1972).

7. *Indiana Constitution*, Art. I, sec. 19; *Pritchard v. State*, 248 Ind. 566, 230 N.E.2d 416, 421 (1967); *Holliday v. State*, 254 Ind. 85, 257 N.E.2d 679 (1970); *Maryland Constitution*, Art. 15, sec. 5; *Wyley v. Warden*, 372 F.2d 742, 743 n.1 (4th Cir. 1967).

8. *United States v. Dougherty*, 473 F.2d 1113, 1142 (D.C. Cir. 1972).

9. *Duncan v. Louisiana* 391 U.S. 145 (1968); *Witherspoon v. Illinois*, 391 U.S. 510 (1968).

10. *Witherspoon v. Illinois*, 391 U.S. at 519 n. 15 (see also p. 244, below).

11. See generally, Jack Nelson and Ronald I. Ostrow, *The FBI and the Berrigans: The Making of a Conspiracy* (New York: Coward, McCann, and Geoghegan, 1972); William O'Rourke, *The Harrisburg 7 and the New Catholic Left* (New York: Crowell, 1972).

12. See Note, "Constitutional Law—Pretrial Publicity—The Milwaukee 14," *Wisconsin Law Review* (1970): 209.

13. See Donald Freed, *Agony in New Haven: The Trial of Bobby Seale, Ericka Huggins and the Black Panther Party* (New York: Simon and Schuster, 1973).

14. Hans Zeisel, "Dr. Spock and the Vanishing Women Jurors," *University of Chicago Law Review* 37 (1969): 1.

15. Carol Tavris, Introduction to Schulman, Shaver, Colman, Emrich, and Christie, "Recipe for a Jury," *Psychology Today* 6 (May 1973): 12.

16. *New York Times*, July 16, 1972, sec. IV, p. 12.

17. *San Francisco Chronicle*, January 9, 1973, p. 8.

18. *New York Times*, October 2, 1974, p. 22 (city ed.).

19. Jessica Mitford, *The Trial of Dr. Spock* (New York: Knopf, 1970), p. 226.

20. Ray McNichols, "Preliminary Report on the Sequestration of Jurors" (mimeographed for circulation among other judges, 1971).

21. *New York Times*, May 5, 1974, p. 41 (city ed.); May 26, 1974, sec. IV, p. 15.

22. Schulman et al., "Recipe for a Jury," pp. 82-83.

23. Mitford, *Trial of Dr. Spock*, pp. 99-100, 217. Use by the prosecutor of information on prospective jurors collected and supplied by the F.B.I. has been upheld on the ground that it does not result in a jury biased against the defendant but rather eliminates bias against the government. *United States v. Falange*, 426 F.2d 930 (2nd Cir. 1970). The argument that such data collection will discourage citizens from serving as jurors has been dismissed as "far-fetched bogies." *United States v. Costello*, 255 F.2d 876, 882 (2nd Cir. 1958). See generally, Okun, "Investigation of Jurors by Counsel: Its Impact on the Decisional Process," *Georgetown Law Journal* 56 (1968): 839; "Editor's Page," *Georgetown Law Journal* 57 (1969): 461-63.

24. Okun, in "Investigation of Jurors by Counsel," p. 854, reports that the scant case law that has addressed itself to the issue concludes that the defense has no right to information obtained by the F.B.I. for the prosecutor. In the trial of Angela Davis, however, the judge granted a defense motion that enabled the defense to share the government's information about prospective jurors. *New York Times*, February 18, 1972, p. 39 (city ed.).

25. See generally, Louie Robinson, "How Psychology Helped Free Angela," *Ebony Magazine*, February 1973, p. 44.

26. *New York Times*, March 15, 1972, p. 39 (city ed.).

27. The information which follows is taken from Schulman et al., "Recipe for a Jury," p. 39.

28. Amitai Etzioni, "Scientific Jury-Stacking Puts Judicial System on Trial," *Boston Globe*, June 23, 1974, p. A-3.

*Chapter Eight*

## Two Steps Back: Juries of Fewer than Twelve and Less than Unanimous Verdicts

The sweeping and constructive reforms introduced into jury selection procedures by the 1968 Jury Selection and Service Act[1] and many similar state statutes to help previously disenfranchised citizens become jurors and thus increase the jury's representativeness have been threatened on two fronts. Just when state and federal juries are becoming more representative, the impact of nonwhites, the young, women, and the poor are being undercut in some courts by reducing the size of the jury and by abandoning the requirement of unanimity. These changes are being promoted as means to obtain efficiency and economy (by reducing the number of jurors) and to cut down the time and difficulty of deliberations (by permitting majority verdicts), but they significantly alter the nature of jury decision-making and cast doubt on the integrity and reliability of jury verdicts.

The Supreme Court ruled in four separate decisions in the early 1970s that the centuries-old traditions of juries of 12 and of unanimous verdicts are not constitutionally required. In 1970, it approved juries of fewer than 12 in state criminal cases[2] and in 1973 in federal civil cases;[3] in 1972, it approved less-than-unanimous verdicts in state criminal cases (and, by implication, state civil cases) but disallowed them for all federal cases.[4] Although not directly related to selection, these changes nonetheless can have a profound effect on the jury's capacity to represent a cross-section of the community.

## JURIES OF FEWER THAN TWELVE

Twelve has been the fixed size of juries in England since the middle of the fourteenth century. Although some of the North American colonies experimented with smaller juries in less important trials, here, too, twelve was the universally accepted number by the eighteenth century. As the New Hampshire Supreme Court wrote in 1860, interpreting its 1783 constitution, "no such thing as a jury of less than *twelve* men, or a jury deciding by less than *twelve* voices, had ever been known, or ever been the subject of discussion in any country of the common law."[5] Although the precise reason for the selection of twelve for the jury is still the subject of controversy among historians, its universality has not been in dispute.

In the 1970 decision of *Williams v. Florida,*[6] the Supreme Court declared that the number twelve was a "historical accident, . . . wholly without significance except to mystics."[7] The court concluded, in an opinion written by Justice Byron R. White, that although the common-law jury was a jury of twelve the history and language of the Sixth Amendment, which provides for trial by an impartial jury in criminal cases, reveals no intention on the part of the writers of the Constitution "to equate the constitutional and common-law characteristics of the jury."[8] Justice White then argued that because *history* is an uncertain guide the constitutional question should be resolved by examining the *function* of the jury, which is to ensure that the common-sense judgment of the community stands between the state accuser and the accused. The use of a jury ensures the participation of the community in the administration of justice and spreads the responsibility for decisions that are made. Justice White felt that as long as certain requirements are met—specifically, that the number of jurors "should probably be large enough to promote group deliberation, free from outside attempts at intimidation, and to provide a fair possibility for obtaining a representative cross section of the community"[9] —then the *function* of the jury will be ensured.

Applying these principles to the six-person jury used in Florida in all but capital cases, Justice White concluded that the smaller size does not impair the function of the jury because he could find "no discernible differences between the results reached by the two-different-sized juries."[10] Furthermore, White wrote, "The reliability of the jury as a fact finder hardly seems likely to be a function of its size."[11,a] Only Justice Thurgood Marshall dissented from the majority's conclusions on jury size.

---

[a]Although this opinion purports to rely upon studies that allegedly prove that few differences would be found in decisions reached by smaller juries (399 U.S.

The Supreme Court examined the question of jury size again in the 1973 case of *Colgrove v. Battin*,[12] which involved a jury of six in a civil case in federal court. Although the case presented the issue in the context of federal rather than state courts and involved civil cases, which are governed by the Seventh Amendment rather than the Sixth (which governs criminal cases), the majority opinion, written by Justice William J. Brennan, Jr., offered no new analysis and simply upheld (by a 5-4 vote) the use of a six-person jury on the authority of *Williams v. Florida*. Justices William O. Douglas and Lewis F. Powell, Jr., dissented on statutory grounds, and Justices Thurgood Marshall and Potter Stewart on constitutional grounds. Justice Marshall's dissenting opinion rested on the reference to "common law" in the Seventh Amendment[b] and the historical fact that a common-law jury was a jury of twelve. He noted that "variations in jury size *do* seem to produce variations in function and result,"[13] and referred to a six-person jury as a "mutation."[14]

Following these two decisions lifting the constitutional bars on smaller juries, a number of states have reduced the size of their juries in civil and misdemeanor cases (see Appendix E, p. 285), but only Arizona (reduced to 8) and Connecticut (reduced to 6) have joined Florida (6) and Utah (8) in lowering the jury size for major felony cases. No state has fewer than 12 jurors for capital cases. Three state supreme courts—California,[15] Rhode Island[16] and Alabama[17]—have interpreted their own state constitutions to require juries of 12. The Alabama court rejected the guidance of the U.S. Supreme Court, applying a *historical* reading to its 1901 constitution[18] and concluding that "[t]o those who framed, amended, debated and passed this organic article, *the number 12 was not merely of mystical significance. It was virtually sacred.*"[19]

No attempts have been made to reduce the size of federal criminal juries, but as of May 1974, 67 of the 94 federal districts had reduced the size of their civil juries,[20] and legislation has been introduced before Congress that would require all districts to reduce the size of their civil juries to six.[21] Many important federal suits have already been decided by only six citizens, including a several-million-dollar defamation suit won in 1974 by Robert Maheu against Howard Hughes in Los Angeles,[22] a $12 million damage suit won by the

---

at 101 n.48), closer examination of the articles cited reveals that the studies relied upon discussed the *time* and *expense* savings that would result from smaller juries but did not present any real evidence about the quality or reliability of decisions. (Hans Zeisel, ". . . And Then There Were None: The Diminution of the Federal Jury," *University of Chicago Law Review* 38 (1971): 713-15.)

[b]The Amendment reads in part: "In suits at common law . . . the right of trial by jury shall be preserved."

A.C.L.U. in Washington, D.C., in 1975 on behalf of 1,200 antiwar demonstrators who had been unlawfully arrested on the steps of the Capitol in 1971,[2 3] and the 1976 suit in ⌐hicago by the families of slain Black Panthers Fred Hampton and Mark Clark seeking $47.7 million from the 31 government officials involved in the 1969 raid that led to their deaths.[2 4]

The question whether the jury's function is indeed preserved in a jury of six or eight, as Justice White asserted in *Williams*, is the subject of some debate. Can a jury of six or eight fairly reflect the community's diversity? Can it render reliable verdicts that will have legitimacy in the community? Careful reasoning and available research suggest that it does not fulfill these functions as well as a jury of twelve.

Smaller juries will inevitably be less representative than larger juries, a fact minimized by Justice White in *Williams v. Florida*:

> As long as arbitrary exclusions of a particular class from the jury rolls are forbidden,... the concern that the cross-section will be significantly diminished if the jury is decreased in size from 12 to six seems an unrealistic one.[2 5]

But in a complex and diverse society, a group of six must be less representative of the community than a group of twelve. Justice Thurgood Marshall, dissenting in *Colgrove v. Battin* (1973), wrote that "[i]t is, of course, intuitively obvious that the smaller the size of the jury, the less likely it is to represent a fair cross-section of community viewpoints."[2 6]

Professor Hans Zeisel of the University of Chicago Law School has offered the following example to demonstrate this phenomenon: Suppose that in a given community, 90 percent of the people share one viewpoint and the remaining 10 percent have a different viewpoint. Suppose further that we draw 100 twelve-member and 100 six-member juries. Using standard statistical methods, it can be predicted that approximately 72 of the twelve-member juries will contain a representative of the 10 percent minority, as compared to only 47 juries composed of six persons.[2 7] This difference is by no means negligible. Some of the New Jersey judges and lawyers who experimented with smaller juries in a 1972 study by the Institute of Judicial Administration commented that the juries of six were "not a balanced cross section of the community."[2 8]

Some federal judges acknowledge the effect of size on representativeness and for this reason disapprove of smaller juries in criminal trials, although they may favor reduction in civil trials. (The effect of

*Williams* and *Colgrove* was to open the way for smaller juries in both kinds of trials.) The Federal Judicial Conference, a body of federal judges, rejected the proposal that federal *criminal* juries be reduced from twelve to six. They reasoned that criminal matters are more "public" than civil suits and thus require more legitimacy if the verdicts are to be accepted, and that criminal juries therefore have a greater need to be representative. Judge Arthur J. Stanley, the head of the federal judiciary's Committee on the Operation of the Jury System, testified before a House subcommittee:

> [T]he issue in a criminal case is essentially a *public one*, relating as it does to an accusation of public wrong, for which a sanction may be imposed. There is more validity to the argument that a panel drawn to judge the facts of a public crime and to render a verdict on behalf of the people of the United States should *represent a broader spectrum of the population.* Every person has a stake in a criminal trial.[29]

Professor Zeisel, testifying later in the same hearings, declared that this argument showed the inadequacy of a six-person jury in *any* case:

> Why, if it makes no difference whether we have 12 or 6-member juries, does your present bill [the bill Judge Stanley was defending] limit the reduction to civil cases? If there is no difference, why not apply the reduction also to criminal cases? . . . [T]he common sense inference is: *Of course, it must make a difference, but civil cases are just less important.*[30]

The difference between these juries is not only in their makeup but in their results.

**Reliability.**  A number of recent studies indicate that, in addition to reducing the jury's capacity to represent the community, smaller juries reduce the reliability of verdicts and thus the jury's legitimacy. Our understanding of the jury system suggests that reliability is in some ways a function of size—twelve decision-makers being better than one "expert"—and studies of six- and twelve-member juries appear to bear this out. The jury has always been preserved for those somewhat exceptional cases in which a defendant or a litigant needs the wisdom of the community to vindicate a right that would otherwise be lost. A substantial majority of criminal trials end in a conviction, no matter what size jury is used, but the jury is maintained as a safeguard to protect defendants in the unusual case, when the police and prosecutor make a mistake or have not been able to assemble convincing evidence. We have preserved the jury over the centuries to ensure that we are *certain* of guilt before we send someone to jail and to ensure that *reliable* verdicts are reached in civil cases. A change in the size of juries must, therefore, be evaluated within that framework: that is, we must ask whether a reduction in size waters down the safeguards of the jury system.

The evidence that reliability is reduced in smaller juries comes from experiments using probability theory and studies of trials. Since the trial studies include a relatively small number of cases, the evidence they provide can only be considered indicative, not definitive, and experiments are of course no more than that. But the paragraphs that follow bring together the data available at this time to help assess the implications of reducing the size of juries. Because reliability is easier to measure in civil cases—where money can provide some concrete gauge—much of this material refers to civil trials, but the evidence is relevant to criminal cases as well.

On a purely statistical basis, the pooling of individual judgments reduces random error: "Four judgments are better than one for the same nonsocial reasons that four thermometers are better than one."[31] A personal illustration of this principle was provided at a 1972 conference of federal judges of the Fourth Circuit by Bernard Ward, law professor at the University of Texas. Ward told of an experience he had when serving on a twelve-member jury that seemed deadlocked until one juror recalled a precise statement on a crucial point that no other juror had remembered until reminded of the matter.[32] The chance that a fact will be recalled, or an insight offered, is simply greater in a jury of twelve, because more people are participating in the decision-making.

In Professor Zeisel's 1973 congressional testimony, he noted how important the size of one's sample is when taking a public-opinion poll. If the Gallup Poll's usual sample of 1,500 were cut in half to 750, he stated, then the " margin of error" would increase "by some 41 percent," and this "margin of error" increases by a similar amount if the jury is cut in half.[33] The term "margin of error" refers to the level of reliability, and when that margin is increased, verdicts can be expected to fluctuate more widely, and their reliability will be reduced. Professor Zeisel has applied this theory to the context of civil jury verdicts with the following demonstration: Suppose that for a given injury one-sixth of the community's population would award the victim $1,000, another one-sixth would give $2,000, a third one-sixth would award $3,000, and so on, with each one-sixth raising the award by $1,000, to maximum of $6,000—meaning that the community's average award is $3,500. Our goal should be to build a jury system in which the jury will serve as a microcosm for the community from which it is drawn, and in which most juries would give the victim about $3,500. Zeisel calculated the probability of the results if 100 twelve-member and 100 six-member juries were assembled and given the case just discussed.[c] According to his calculations, 68.4 percent of the verdicts of twelve-member juries will fall between $3,000 and $4,000, approximating the community's consensus. If six-member juries are used, however, only 51.4 percent of the verdicts will fall within that desired range. In addition, if six-member juries are used, 15.8 percent of the verdicts will fall below $2,500 or above $4,500, whereas if twelve-member juries are used only 4.2 percent of the verdicts will fall in these outer limits. The conclusion of Zeisel's study is that when twelve persons deliberate together the chances that their verdict will accurately reflect the community's view on the question at hand are significantly higher than if it is a smaller group that is deliberating.[34]

This conclusion is supported by two studies of monetary awards rendered by twelve-member and six-member juries. The *University of Michigan Journal of Law Reform*, which compared the results of 193 civil trials heard by juries of twelve in Wayne County (Detroit) between March 1 and August 31, 1969, to those of 292 civil trials considered by juries of six in the same period of 1971, found that results in terms of who won did not differ significantly (the smaller juries ruled in favor of the plaintiff only slightly more often—53.8 percent compared to 52 percent),[35] and the median of the awards was only somewhat higher in the smaller juries (14.5 percent of the amount sought compared to 11.2 percent for the juries of twelve),[36] but the *range of verdicts* was greater in the small juries, particularly in automobile negligence cases. The "standard deviation" of the verdicts, a statistical term that measures the extent of the dispersion of the data, was 24.2 percent higher for the smaller juries in all cases

---

[c] **Percent Distribution of the Average Evaluation by 100 Randomly Selected Juries.**

| Interval | Twelve-member | Six-member |
|---|---|---|
| $1,000-1,499 | – | 0.1% |
| $1,500-1,999 | 0.1% | 1.4 |
| $2,000-2,499 | 2.0 | 6.4 |
| $2,500-2,999 | 13.7 | 16.4 |
| $3,000-3,499 | 34.2 | 25.7 |
| $3,500-3,999 | 34.2 | 25.7 |
| $4,000-4,499 | 13.7 | 16.4 |
| $4,500-4,999 | 2.0 | 6.4 |
| $5,000-5,499 | 0.1 | 1.4 |
| $5,500-6,000 | – | 0.1 |
| Totals | 100.0% | 100.0% |

and 135 percent higher for the smaller juries in automobile negligence cases.[37] A study by Brown University political scientist Edward N. Beiser and his associate Rene Varrin, of 85 civil jury verdicts in the federal district courts of Maine, Massachusetts, New Hampshire, and Rhode Island between July 1970 and June 1972 also found that juries of six are more erratic in their awards, with their verdicts covering a much wider range than juries of twelve.[38]

One possible reason for the more erratic results produced by smaller juries is that the initial position taken by jurors may be more susceptible to change in a small jury. This theory is offered in a study in the *Case Western Reserve Law Review*—based again on probability theory—which concludes that where the number of potential jurors who are inclined to believe the defendant is guilty at the beginning of the deliberation is less than half of the jury, the six-member panel increases the likelihood of conviction. Conversely, where more than half the jurors are inclined initially to find guilt, the defendant has a greater chance of acquittal in the six-member group.[d,39]

An experiment with mock juries by sociologists Richard H. Nagasawa, Beth Eakin, and Richard L. Schuster of Arizona State University in February 1974 produced data that supported this hypothesis. The facts of one civil case were presented to six 6-member juries and six 12-member juries (all composed of students). Each "juror" was first asked to write down in secret an initial verdict, and the "juries" deliberated until a 5/6 verdict was reached. The results showed that the average awards of the smaller juries increased 46.9 percent, but of the larger juries only 9.5 percent.[40] The verdict of the larger jury is thus more likely to reflect the composite judgment of all the jurors; the verdict of the smaller jury may simply be the view of the most persuasive juror.

**Efficiency and Expense.** The assertion that the twelve-member jury is too costly and consumes too much time for the orderly

d **Probability of Conviction**

The fraction of potential jurors inclined to believe defendant is *guilty* at the beginning of jury deliberation appears above the top line, the probability of conviction below each line.

| Jury of | 0 | 0.1 | 0.2 | 0.3 | 0.4 | 0.5 | 0.6 | 0.7 | 0.8 | 0.9 | 1.0 |
|---|---|---|---|---|---|---|---|---|---|---|---|
| Six | 0 | 1% | 6 | 16 | 32 | 50 | 68 | 84 | 94 | 99 | 100% |
| Jury of Twelve | 0 | 0 | 1% | 8 | 25 | 50 | 75 | 92 | 99 | 99 | 100% |

administration of justice, which is frequently made by those in favor of reducing jury size, is also open to question. Proponents of smaller juries usually assume that the costs of selecting and paying jurors can be cut in half if the size of the jury is reduced by half and that this saving will be dramatic. Chief Justice Warren E. Burger declared in early 1971, for instance, that $4 million could be saved if all federal civil juries consisted of but six jurors.[41] A more careful estimate prepared by the Administrative Office of the United States Courts later that year found that the saving would be only $1.8 million, a figure that is about 1.5 percent of the federal judicial budget and an infinitesimal fraction of the entire U.S. budget.[42] Most federal districts have since adopted the six-member jury for civil trials, but, oddly, the Administrative Office has never published the data that would reveal how much money has actually been saved. The data that has been published shows that all districts, both those using six-member and twelve-member juries, have reduced the cost of jury trials somewhat, mostly through better management techniques.[43] Using the cost-per-jury-trial figures provided by the Administrative Office for both civil and criminal trials and the percentage of civil trials in the various districts, and *assuming that every dollar saved* by the courts using six-member juries *is attributable to that decision alone*, the courts using six-member juries are saving only *20 percent* of the costs of selecting and paying jurors compared to those still using twelve-member juries; the dollar savings is thus substantially below both Chief Justice Burger's $4 million estimate and the Administrative Office's estimate of $1.8 million.[44]

The assumption that a reduction in the size of a jury will result in substantial time-savings is also highly questionable. A typical estimate was the one made in 1962 by the Illinois Judicial Conference that the use of a six-member jury would save 40 percent of the time of the judges and lawyers involved in litigation.[45] It is unclear, however, where this time-saving is to come from. Jury selection, under a system in which the judge conducts the voir dire, speaking generally to the entire panel and only occasionally to individual jurors, is not significantly different if twelve jurors are to be selected or only six. In both instances, the judge must describe the case and ask the jurors general questions about bias. The process of challenge will be shortened a bit with a smaller jury, but hardly more than a few minutes in the normal trial. During the conduct of the trial, the size of the jury will make no difference in the time required. During deliberation, a twelve-person jury might take longer, but while the jury is deliberating, the judge and the attorneys are free to conduct other business. It seems improper in any event to try to save time at the expense of a full and frank discussion of the complex issues to be decided.

The studies that have been made to date comparing the efficiency of six-member juries to that of twelve-member juries all report that time-savings for the smaller juries are minimal at best. In the *University of Michigan Journal of Law Reform*'s study of 193 twelve-member juries and 292 six-member juries, the *median* of the trial times from the two samples was *identical*: 3 days. The *mean* of the trial times was also virtually identical: 3.9 days for the twelve-member juries, and 3.8 days for the juries of six.[46]

In Beiser and Varrin's study of twelve- and six-member juries in New England's federal courts, the data available revealed no dramatic savings of time for the smaller juries. The time required for selecting the jury actually rose from an average 40 minutes for the 40 twelve-member juries examined to an average of 42 minutes for 38 six-member juries. The length of jury deliberation declined, the median dropping from 4.2 hours for the 27 twelve-member juries studied to 2.8 hours for the 25 six-member juries, and the mean dropped from 3.2 hours to 2.5 hours. The total time required for the trial could be obtained for only 11 juries of twelve and 19 juries of six, and the median time for those two groups was identical, 12.1 hours. The mean time, influenced by one unusually long trial in the small sample collected, was 16.4 hours for the juries of twelve and 13.2 for the juries of six.[47] Other studies have produced comparable results.[e]

Studies of group dynamics suggest conflicting answers to the ques-

---

[e] A study by William Pabst of Bird Engineering-Research Associates in Vienna, Virginia, of 69 civil trials held before twelve-member juries in the District of Columbia District Court in early 1971 and 78 civil trials held later that year with only six members discovered that the average voir dire was virtually identical: 52.1 minutes for a jury of twelve and 52 minutes for a jury of six. The average trial time for both the twelve- and six-member juries was exactly 7.80 hours. (William R. Pabst, Jr., "Statistical Studies of the Costs of Six-Man Versus Twelve-Man Juries," *William and Mary Law Review* 14 (1972): 327.) The Institute of Judicial Administration at New York University studied over 800 six-member and twelve-member civil juries in New Jersey in 1972, during a period in which attorneys were encouraged to opt for smaller juries but still had the right to demand a larger one if they wanted to. The cases decided by the smaller jury thus tended to be those that were somewhat less complicated, and it is to this difference that the research team believed disparities might be attributable. They found that 21 minutes were saved during the voir dire (25.5 minutes for juries of six, 46.6 minutes for juries of twelve), and that 36 minutes less time (a reduction of 33 percent) was required to reach a verdict by the smaller jury. The researchers stated specifically that "[s]ix-member deliberations in which damages above $10,000 were awarded tended to last roughly as long as similar twelve-member deliberations." (Institute of Judicial Administration, "Report of Committee to Study Less-than-Unanimous Verdicts," p. 7.) No time-saving was noted regarding the passing of exhibits and the filing in and out of the jury box.

tion whether a small group operates more "efficiently" than a large group—something is gained but something is lost. The studies available, which are somewhat primitive but do provide hints about the behavior of groups, indicate that large groups may be able to deal with complex problems more efficiently than small groups,[48] that a larger group may inhibit participation of all members,[49] that a larger group increases factionalization,[50] and that a small group is more likely to be dominated by a single persuasive leader.[51]

Proponents of smaller juries sometimes argue that large juries produce more hung juries than small juries and that the latter are thus preferable. In jurisdictions using twelve-member juries and requiring a unanimous verdict, juries are unable to reach a unanimous verdict—and thus hang—in 5.6 percent of the cases.[52] A survey of a court that uses six-member juries and requires unanimous verdicts, the Miami, Florida, Circuit Court, revealed that the percentage of hung juries in 1969 and 1970 (out of 290 trials) was only 2.4 percent,[53] a little more than two-fifths the national average. Thus, smaller juries do "hang" less frequently.

Whether one considers this smaller percentage "better," however, depends on one's view of the hung jury. Hans Zeisel, who collected the figures on hung juries, believes strongly that fewer hung juries are not "better" for justice. "The hung jury," he writes, "is treasured because it represents the legal system's respect for the minority viewpoint that is held strongly enough to thwart the will of the majority."[54] It is thus yet another institutional device that recognizes our commitment to the idea that the government must prove its case "beyond a reasonable doubt" before any person can be criminally convicted. Research indicates that juries hang only when some substantial controversy exists over the facts at issue, and thus when the matter has simply not been proved "beyond a reasonable doubt."[55] A twelve-member jury consequently is a better safeguard than a six-member jury. Even a small jury, however, may be preferable to a jury whose verdict does not have to be unanimous.

## LESS THAN UNANIMOUS VERDICTS

The hung jury is the exception that makes the jury system what it is. The hung jury is the affirmation of the importance of each juror in the deliberations. It preserves the jury's independence. A unanimous verdict is the confirmation that guilt has been found "beyond a reasonable doubt." It means that the evidence has been weighed and discussed fully to the satisfaction of each juror. It ensures that the verdict actually expresses the conscience of the community, for all voices in the community, if they are represented on the jury, have an equal voice in its decision.

Although we can only guess if the early participants in juries were more than intuitively aware of these facts—because we do not know the precise origin of the unanimity rule[f]—we do know that the requirement that jury verdicts be unanimous has been with us since the latter half of the fourteenth century. Its importance to the jury system is undisputed, as legal historians Frederick Pollock and Frederic W. Maitland have pointed out:

> [F]rom the moment when our records begin, we seem to see a strong desire for unanimity. In a thousand cases the jury is put before us as speaking with a single voice, while any traces of dissent or of a nescience confessed by some only of the jurors are very rare.[56]

Unanimity has also been the near-universal rule in the North American system of criminal justice. During the seventeenth century, the colonies in the Carolinas, Connecticut, and Pennsylvania[57] flirted with majority verdicts, but in the next century, unanimity once again became the rule.[58] When the House of Representatives was drafting the Bill of Rights during the first session of Congress, they began what is now the Sixth Amendment with the following language:

> The trial of all crimes . . . shall be by an impartial jury of freeholders of the vicinage *with the requisite of unanimity for conviction*, the right of challenge and other accustomed requisites. . . .[59]

---

[f]Among the many theories offered to explain the rise of the unanimity rule are: (1) unanimity developed to protect defendants, who were not otherwise protected because rules of evidence and procedure had not yet been fully conceived; (2) unanimity is a historical accident stemming from the requirement that twelve jurors agree and the practice of adding enough jurors until this agreement was reached—thus when the size of the jury froze at twelve, unanimity just "stuck"; (3) unanimity was developed by judges to relieve themselves from the pressure of the crown to convict; (4) unanimity was instituted to counterbalance the harsh penalties (death, banishment, or grotesque prisons) meted out for violations of law; (5) unanimity was required by the medieval concept of "consent," which was necessary to bind the community; (6) unanimity was developed to protect jurors from being punished for erroneous verdicts: if all the jurors agreed, it became more difficult for judges to punish than it was if a few dissented. (*Apodaca v. Oregon*, 406 U.S. 404, 407 n.2 (1972); Ryan, "Less Than Unanimous Jury Verdicts in Criminal Trials," *J. Crim. L., C., & P.S.* 58 (1967): 211; Sir Patrick Devlin, *Trial by Jury* (London: Stevens & Sons, 1956), p. 48.)

The complex social, religious, and political conditions of England during the Middle Ages make all of these explanations plausible, and all may have contributed to the unanimity requirement.

The Senate later deleted the language about unanimity and challenges as being unnecessary because trial by jury was understood to encompass those ideas. Until 1972, the Supreme Court consistently recognized that unanimity was an essential component of the Sixth Amendment's guarantee to trial by jury in criminal cases.[60]

In that year, the Supreme Court upheld two state laws permitting less than unanimous verdicts. One was a Louisiana statute conforming to the state's 1898 constitution, which permits verdicts of 9-3 in all felony cases except capital cases. The second was an Oregon law passed after that state changed its constitution by popular referendum in 1934 to allow 10-2 verdicts in all but capital cases. The winning argument in favor of this amendment was that the change would "tend to eliminate the evil of the hung jury and the consequent expense of the new trial."[61] No other state has permitted a less-than-unanimous verdict to be used in felony trials.

Louisiana's scheme permitting verdicts of 9-3 in major criminal cases was challenged in *Johnson v. Louisiana* (1972)[62] as violating the due process clause of the Fourteenth Amendment. In the earlier case of *Duncan v. Louisiana* (1968), the Supreme Court had implied that state courts would have to provide juries like those found in federal courts because, according to the Court, the Sixth Amendment right to trial by jury in criminal cases is imposed on the states through the Fourteenth Amendment's due process clause.[63] But the petitioner in *Johnson*, who had been convicted of robbery by a 9-3 vote, was unable to rely on the presumably stricter standards of the Sixth Amendment because his trial had been completed before the *Duncan* decision was handed down. Instead, Johnson's claim was that a less-than-unanimous verdict violated his right to the "due process of law" because it watered down the constitutionally required standard of "proof beyond a reasonable doubt."[64] This high standard had been violated, Johnson argued, if he could be convicted even though three members of the jury voted to acquit; the split vote necessarily indicated, he maintained, that some members of the jury had a reasonable doubt. The jury as a whole could not, therefore, be said to have voted for conviction with no reasonable doubt remaining. The Court disagreed by a 5-4 margin.

If the Court's judgment on six-member juries was questionable, its reasoning on unanimity is profoundly disturbing. Some of the positions taken by the Court seem to contradict the fundamental principles of the jury system. The arguments bear some explanation.

Justice Byron White, writing for the majority, found two distinct due process arguments in *Johnson*: first, that the existence of dissenting jurors means that the majority cannot conscientiously vote for guilt beyond a reasonable doubt, and second, that the existence of dissenting jurors necessarily means reasonable doubts exist. Justice White correctly shows that the *first* argument is invalid, since it is possible for some jurors to believe the defendant guilty beyond a reasonable doubt yet know that others disagree with them. As long as the dissenting viewpoint is explained, understood, and evaluated, the majority of jurors could simply reject it as being without merit or as raising irrelevant concerns. But with no requirement for unanimity, the majority may not in fact listen to the dissenters. Indeed, under the less-than-unanimous-verdict system, the initial vote could well constitute the total deliberation of the jury if the majority is large enough to produce a verdict. It is to avoid just such an occurrence that an English law passed in 1967, permitting a trial judge to accept a 10-2 verdict, gives the judge this option only after the jury has deliberated for at least two hours.[65] (Even the English system, of course, does not guarantee or require that the majority will listen to the minority during that two-hour period, but the judge initially urges the jurors to deliberate until they reach a unanimous decision,[66] and they are thus confronted with the desirability of deliberating to reach a verdict before the two-hour period ends.) The Supreme Court in *Johnson* did not substantiate its assertion that deliberation will continue in a nonunanimous system. Justice White simply said that "we can find no basis for holding" that the majority nine were not convinced that the defendant was guilty beyond a reasonable doubt.[67]

As to the *second* due process argument, Justice White simply rejected the claim that the existence of dissenting jurors necessarily impeaches the verdict of the majority. He stated that disagreement itself does not establish reasonable doubt, especially where the majority continues to believe the defendant guilty. The fact that other jurors disagree does not prove, in the Court's view, that the state has failed to meet its heavy burden.

The other case dealing with less-than-unanimous verdicts, *Apodaca v. Oregon* (1972),[68] differed from its companion case of *Johnson* because it concerned a trial held after *Duncan v. Louisiana* (1968),[69] and hence was required to conform to the requirements of the Sixth Amendment. The justices seemed to agree that a somewhat higher standard of review was required in this case because no one opinion received even the five votes necessary for a majority, and seven justices felt obliged to write opinions explaining their separate views. Justice White wrote an opinion signed also by Justices Burger, Blackmun, and Rehnquist, which announced the Court's decision to uphold the constitutionality of nonunanimous verdicts in state courts. The opinions touch on a number of important facets of the jury and reveal some profound differences of understanding.

Justice White, applying the *functional* standard also used in *Williams v. Florida* (1970),[70] concluded that unanimity was not necessary. A jury reaching verdicts by a majority, he reasoned, will also serve the jury's *function* of standing between the defendant and the state and thwarting governmental oppression or prosecutorial excess. He rejected as unsupported by proof the assertion that less-than-unanimous verdicts would deny a voice to a segment of the community and would encourage the majority to ignore their colleagues. (Justice White was silent as to the minimum number of jurors constitutionally necessary to reach a verdict, but Justice Harry Blackmun, in a two-paragraph concurring opinion, said that although he agreed that a 9-3 verdict is constitutional he would have "great difficulty" with a 7-5 standard.)[71]

Justice Powell concurred with the White opinion but indicated that he would not agree if a *federal* court were to operate under a less-than-unanimous standard (the cases before the Court were from *state* courts). Although he agreed with the 1968 *Duncan* decision, which applied Sixth Amendment standards to the states, Powell did not believe that *all* the attributes of the federal jury were, by extension, imposed on state courts. Federalism, Powell stated, was intended to allow the states to experiment with processes and procedures different from those employed on the federal level; each state may thus become "a laboratory."[72] Justice Powell also observed that in an "unbroken line of cases reaching back into the late 1800s" the Supreme Court, almost without dissent, has recognized that unanimity is "indispensable" to federal jury trials, criminal and civil.[73] Thus, Powell held that *history* is the best guide for federal courts, but he agreed with White that the *functional* approach is appropriate to reviewing state trials and that this test does not require unanimous verdicts. The logic in this position is obscure.

The dissenting opinions in *Apodaca* point to the role of unanimous verdicts in ensuring representativeness and in preserving the government's strict burden of proof. Justice William Brennan's dissent argued that the Sixth Amendment *does* require unanimity and that all court verdicts therefore must be unanimous. Brennan pointed to the chilling effect of nonunanimous verdicts on the jury's capacity to represent the community, and for minority voices to be heard:

> In my opinion, the right of all groups in this nation to participate in the criminal process means the right to have their voices heard. A unanimous verdict vindicates that right. Majority verdicts could destroy it.[74]

Once a requisite majority of jurors agree, Brennan argued, they are unlikely to listen to the dissenters, who will be left out of the judging process.

In Justice Thurgood Marshall's view, the "functional" test allowed the Court to strip away almost all of the characteristics of the jury, leaving only the necessity that jurors be drawn from the entire community without the exclusion of any definable group. The Court's treatment of the reasonable doubt standard, he observes, lowers the burden the state must meet: The prosecutor no longer has to overcome *all* of the reasonable doubts of the jurors, only the doubts of 75 percent of the panel. Marshall also challenged a statement in Justice Powell's opinion that split verdicts may minimize hung juries caused by bribery or "juror irrationality," declaring that if jury-selection procedures have been fair, then every juror is competent and none can be called "irrational." In fact, what Powell calls "irrational," Marshall argues, is

> precisely the essence of the right of a jury trial. ... The juror whose dissenting voice is unheard may be a spokesman, not for any minority viewpoint, but simply for himself—and that, in my view, is enough. The doubts of a single juror are in my view evidence that the government has failed to carry its burden of proving guilt beyond a reasonable doubt.[75]

The emphasis of Justice William O. Douglas's dissenting opinion was his attempt to prove that the reliability of jury verdicts will be diminished by majority verdicts. The loss of credibility occurs because jurors are no longer obliged to deliberate fully. Once enough votes exist for a verdict, deliberation will cease; the *Apodaca* jury deliberated for only 41 minutes before voting 11-1 to convict Robert Apodaca of assault with a deadly weapon. The ability of jurors in the minority at the outset of deliberation to convince the majority to join their point of view, which the Chicago Jury Project reported occurred in roughly one case in ten,[76] will be erased. Furthermore, they will not have the opportunity of suggesting conviction on a lesser-included offense as a reasonable compromise.

Because less-than-unanimous verdicts increase the likelihood of conviction, Justice Douglas saw the majority decision as part of a " 'law and order' judicial mood" that diminished the basic Anglo-Saxon precept that it is better to err on the side of acquittal than on the side of guilt. Douglas wondered whether the next step was "the elimination of the presumption of innocence."[77]

It is now up to the states to decide whether to abandon the requirement for unanimity in their jury verdicts. The majority opinions in *Johnson* and *Apodaca*, although concluding that the

Constitution does not bar legislation authorizing less-than-unanimous verdicts, do not agree that such legislation should be favored. Indeed, Justice Blackmun (in a concurring opinion) stated: "Were I a legislator, I would disfavor [less-than-unanimous verdicts] as a matter of policy."[78] Since 1972, a few states have adopted less-than-unanimous verdicts for civil cases, but no new states have moved in that direction for felony trials, and only a very few have adopted a less-than-unanimous approach for misdemeanor trials (see Appendix E). No effort has been made to introduce a less-than-unanimous verdict into the federal system, apparently because of the strong case law that the Seventh Amendment requires a unanimous verdict[79] and because of Justice Powell's view that these still control federal courts.

States considering changing their system will have to weigh carefully the competing policy arguments. The reason most frequently cited for abolishing the requirement of unanimous verdicts is that the time and expense of trials would be reduced because fewer trials would result in hung juries. A second argument is that unanimity encourages juror corruption: because all jurors must agree on a verdict, unscrupulous persons can influence the outcome of a trial by bribing only one juror. In fact, the decision of the British Parliament to authorize jury verdicts of 10-2, if the jurors have debated for at least two hours, came after several notorious instances of jury tampering.[80] The ability of one stubborn juror to thwart the majority is also cited as a justification for eliminating unanimous verdicts. Unanimity is considered, in this view, antidemocratic because it enables one person to overcome the interests of others and prevents the majority from governing itself.[81]

How do these arguments stand up to the facts and theory of the jury system? On purely practical grounds, they are not very convincing. First, as to efficiency, the gains would be minimal. Kalven and Zeisel report that only 10 to 15 percent of all criminal defendants ask for jury trials,[82] and of this small percentage, only a few trials—5.6 percent—end in hung juries in states where unanimous verdicts are required.[83] Statistics from one jurisdiction, Multnomah County (Portland), Oregon, where a 10-2 verdict is accepted, show that hung juries occurred less than half as frequently as the national average—in only 2.5 percent of the 801 criminal jury trials held in 1970 and 1972.[84] This suggests that states in which unanimous verdicts are now required could reduce hung juries by 50 percent or more by moving to a majority system. But this reduction involves only about 3.1 percent of the 15 percent of the cases that are tried before a jury, or half of 1 percent of all cases. The economic argument thus becomes the savings that would result from not re-trying 0.5 percent of the cases. And even this figure is high because not every case ending in a hung jury is re-tried.

Second, although jury tampering is not unknown in the United States,[85] not enough of this type of criminal conduct occurs to warrant preventive measures as drastic as elimination of the unanimity principle. Less drastic alternatives are certainly available—namely, stricter enforcement of laws against jury tampering.

Finally, the premise that a single stubborn juror irrationally upsets the reasoned view of the other jurors was disproved by the Chicago Jury Project, which found that juries that begin with a large majority in either direction almost never hang.[86] Only if a sizable minority— four or five jurors—disagree with their colleagues on the first vote will a hung jury result. For one or two jurors to hold out to the end, they must have had companionship at the beginning of deliberations.[g]

But statistics should not be necessary to rebut these assertions. The jury was never meant to be efficient. The argument against permitting one "obstinate" juror to obstruct and delay proceedings fails to recognize the importance of the decision before a jury and the difference between a judicial and a legislative decision. The legislature makes policy decisions, and the majority view must prevail. The jury is asked to resolve a factual dispute and to decide whether the commission of certain acts justifies punishment, and it is entirely appropriate to require unanimity before the punishment can be meted out. Decisions made in the legislative branch rarely have such an immediate and devastating effect on an individual as does a verdict of guilt. Because of the implications of such a decision and the need for certainty, a different method of reaching the decision is required.[h]

An understanding of the nature of the jury system requires a rejection of the majority decisions in *Johnson* and *Apodaca*. Neither *history* nor—more important—*function* is in fact preserved by abol-

---

[g]These findings are supported by social psychologists, who report that when one person disagrees with a group of others in small group deliberations, that person will usually come to doubt their position and give up even strongly held perceptions if the others insist that he or she is mistaken. (Asch, "Effects of Group Pressure Upon the Modification and Distortion of Judgments," in Swanson, Newcombe, and Hartley, eds., *Readings in Social Psychology* (New York: Holt, 1952).)

[h]In civil trials, the standards of proof are less strict—juries being asked to render a verdict according to the "preponderance of evidence" rather than "beyond a reasonable doubt"—and the consequences of a civil verdict are less severe—a transfer of property rather than loss of freedom—so the impact of less-than-unanimous verdicts in civil trials may properly be assessed differently from criminal trials.

ishing unanimity. If we examine the effects of unanimity on the jury, we discover that the requirement for unanimous verdicts reinforces virtually every one of the jury's purposes:

• Unanimity is essential to the legitimacy of verdicts and to confidence in our legal system because it supports the fairness of verdicts.[87] The losing party is much less apt to complain if his or her story has failed to convince even a single juror among a group drawn from a cross-section of the community and holding diverse views. When defendants are convicted despite the objections of some jurors, on the other hand, the acceptability of the verdict may well be weakened. Indeed, one British commentator has suggested that split verdicts encourage dissenting jurors to state publicly their views and that the media will be encouraged to seek them out, stimulating dissatisfaction with the judicial system and a reduction of public confidence.[88] If the split is along racial or ethnic lines, then the verdict will tend to enhance divisions already existing in the community and may convince the losing party that prejudice played a part in her or his conviction. As Justice Potter Stewart declared in his dissent to *Johnson*:

> [C]ommunity confidence in the administration of criminal justice cannot but be corroded under a system in which a defendant who is conspicuously identified with a particular group can be convicted or acquitted by a jury split along group lines.[89]

• Unanimity is necessary to ensure careful weighing of the evidence in a dispute. When jurors know that they must all agree before their job is done, they are required to articulate their views rationally, to listen to each other, and to respond to the views of others. Justice White asserted in *Johnson* that:

> We have no grounds for believing that majority jurors . . . would simply refuse to listen to arguments presented to them in favor of acquittal, terminate discussion and render a verdict. . . .[90]

But Kalven and Zeisel, who studied majority verdicts, observed that "apparently the jury simply stops deliberating when it reaches the requisite majority."[91] (This observation was based on a finding that the number of 10-2 or 11-1 verdicts by juries in Oregon rose to 25 percent after that state abandoned the requirement of unanimity.)

• The need for unanimity reinforces the requirement that juries be selected from a representative cross-section of the community because it gives each juror, even members of small minorities, a voice. Nonunanimous verdicts might well have the effect of disenfranchising minority groups from effective participation in the legal system, erasing the gains of recent years and preventing further improvement. A minority group that comprises 10 percent of the population, Zeisel has explained, will have at least one representative on 72 percent of the 12-person juries impaneled, but that same minority group will have three or more representatives on only 11 percent of that jurisdiction's juries.[9 2] If the group has a distinctive viewpoint on any of the issues being tried, that viewpoint can be ignored or outvoted in 89 percent of the cases under a 10-2 system.

• Unanimity sustains the delicate power balance between the government and the defendant. To prevent oppression by the government, which has awesome power and resources that the individual defendant cannot hope to match, the defendant is protected by certain rights and procedures. Unanimity is one of those rights. Its importance was affirmed by Judge John R. Brown of the U.S. Court of Appeals for the Fifth Circuit, who described the role of unanimity's corollary, the hung jury:

> It is simply not legally correct that some jury must sometime decide that the defendant is "guilty" or "not guilty." The fact is, as history reminds us, a succession of juries may legitimately fail to agree until, at long last, the prosecution gives up. But such juries, perhaps more courageous than any other, have performed their useful, vital function in our system. This is the kind of independence which should be encouraged. *It is in this independence that liberty is secured. . . .*
>
> *I think a mistrial from a hung jury is a safeguard to liberty. In many areas it is the sole means by which one or a few may stand out against an overwhelming contemporary public sentiment.* Nothing should interfere with its exercise.[9 3]

Unanimity thus also protects a minority against oppression by the majority. In the words of this nation's eminent nineteenth-century constitutional scholar, Justice Joseph Story:

> The great object of a trial by jury in criminal cases is to guard against a spirit of oppression and tyranny on the part of rulers, and against a spirit of violence and vindictiveness on the part of the people. Indeed, it is often more important to guard against the latter than the former. . . .[9 4]

• Unanimity supports the social decision that "it is far worse to convict an innocent man than to let a guilty man go free."[9 5] Majority verdicts allow conviction despite disagreement by some of the jurors. The odds that innocent people will be convicted increase substantially under split-verdict rules. Data developed by Kalven and

Zeisel document that more people will be convicted if less-than-unanimous verdicts are adopted. In unanimous-verdict states, hung juries occur approximately 5.6 percent of the time;[96] in 56 percent of these hung juries, the vote is 11-1, 10-2, or 9-3; and among this group, the majority favors the prosecution 79 percent of the time.[97] By shifting to majority verdicts of 9-3, a state would reduce the number of hung juries by half and gain a conviction in almost four-fifths of the newly decided cases.

• Unanimity supports the constitutional requirement that no defendant be convicted except by proof beyond a reasonable doubt.[98] Depriving a person of liberty is a serious step, and our society has made the decision that it should not take place except when we have no reasonable doubt about its necessity. The unanimity requirement, like this rigorous standard of proof, enshrines the importance that freedom holds in our scale of values. Despite the fact that the two principles developed separately in history and under different circumstances,[99] they both support the same desire to safeguard individual rights and liberties:

> The unanimity of a verdict on a criminal case is inextricably interwoven with the required measure of proof. To sustain the validity of a verdict by less than all of the jurors is to destroy this test of proof beyond a reasonable doubt if one or more jurors remain reasonably in doubt as to guilt. It would be a contradiction in terms.[100]

Justice White's conclusion that "no reasonable doubt" exists when a jury fails to agree[101] is simply not supportable.

In upholding the constitutionality of juries of fewer than twelve and less-than-unanimous verdicts, the Supreme Court has opened the way for radical change in our system of justice. The legitimacy of the jury's verdict as an expression of the conscience of the community is brought into question by both these modifications. The ability of juries to reflect minority viewpoints is hampered by smaller juries, and will be erased in many cases where unanimity is not required. The opportunity for minority voices to be heard is diminished to an even greater extent in majority verdicts than in a jury of reduced size, as Hans Zeisel has explained:

> [T]he abandonment of the unanimity rule is but another way of reducing the size of the jury. *But it is reduction with a vengeance,* for a majority verdict requirement is far more effective in nullifying the potency of minority viewpoints than is the outright reduction of a jury to a size equivalent to the majority that is allowed to agree on a verdict. Minority viewpoints fare better on a jury of ten that must be unanimous than on a jury of twelve where ten members must agree on a verdict.[102]

The jury is a preserver of independence and freedom at the same time that it is a factfinder. Both these functions are threatened, as are the gains of recent years in making our juries truly democratic, by the Supreme Court's removal of the constitutional barriers to juries of less than twelve and less-than-unanimous verdicts. But the ultimate determination of the wisdom of abandoning these ancient safeguards rests in the hands of the legislators and the people.

## NOTES

1. 28 *U.S.C.* 1861-69.
2. *Williams v. Florida*, 399 U.S. 78 (1970).
3. *Colgrove v. Battin*, 413 U.S. 149 (1973).
4. *Johnson v. Louisiana*, 406 U.S. 356 (1972); *Apodaca v. Oregon*, 406 U.S. 404 (1972).
5. *Opinion of the Judges* 41 N.H. 550, 552 (1860) (emphasis added).
6. 399 U.S. 78.
7. *Ibid.*, p. 102.
8. *Ibid.*, p. 99.
9. *Ibid.*, p. 100.
10. *Ibid.*, p. 101.
11. *Ibid.*, pp. 100-101.
12. 413 U.S. 149.
13. *Ibid.*, p. 167 n.1 (emphasis added).
14. *Ibid.*, p. 166.
15. *People v. Feagley*, 14 Cal. 3d 346, 350; 121 Cal. Rptr. 509, 516, 14 P.2d 373, 380 (1975).
16. *Advisory Opinion to the Senate*, 108 R.I. 628, 278 A.2d 852 (1971).
17. *Gilbreath v. Wallace*, 292 Ala. 267, 292 So.2d 651 (1974).
18. *Alabama Constitution*, sec. 11.
19. *Gilbreath v. Wallace*, 292 So.2d at 656 (emphasis added).
20. Administrative Office of the U.S. Courts, *1974 Semi-Annual Report of the Director* (Washington: Government Printing Office, 1974), p. 77; and see Fisher, "The Seventh Amendment and the Common Law: No Magic in Numbers," 56 F.R.D. 507, at 535-42 (1972).
21. H.R. 8285, 93rd Cong., 2nd Sess. (1974).
22. *New York Times*, July 2, 1974, p. 15 (city ed.).
23. *Ibid.*, January 17, 1975, p. 1 (city ed.).
24. *Ibid.*, January 23, 1976, p. 12 (city ed.).
25. 399 U.S. 78, 102.
26. 413 U.S. 149, 167 n.1
27. See Hans Zeisel, ". . . And Then There Were None: The Diminution of the Federal Jury," *University of Chicago Law Review* 38 (1971): 716; *Colgrove v. Battin*, 413 U.S. 149, 167 n.1 (1973). See also Comment, "Florida's Six-Member Criminal Juries: Constitutional, But Are They Fair?" *University of Florida Law Review* 23 (1971): 404.
28. Institute of Judicial Administration, *A Comparison of Six- and Twelve-*

*Member Civil Juries in New Jersey Superior and County Courts* (New York: I.J.A., 1972), pp. 10, 14-15.

29. Subcommittee on Courts, Civil Liberties, and the Administration of Justice of the House Judiciary Com., *Hearings, Three-Judge Court and Six-Person Civil Jury*, 93rd Cong., 2nd Sess., Oct. 10, 1973, and Jan. 24, 1974, p. 20 (emphasis added).

30. *Ibid.*, p. 158 (emphasis added).

31. D.M. Johnson, *The Psychology of Thought and Judgment* (New York: Harper & Bros., 1955); and see generally, Albert M. and Julia C. Rosenblatt, "Six-Member Juries in Criminal Cases: Legal and Psychological Considerations," *St. John's Law Review* 47 (1973): 627-28.

32. "The Six-Man Jury," 59 F.R.D. 180, 200-201 (1972).

33. *Hearings, Three-Judge Court and Six-Person Civil Jury*, p. 159.

34. Zeisel, ". . . And Then There Were None," p. 717. The chart in note *c*, p. 199, is reprinted with the permission of the University of Chicago Law Review.

35. Note, "Six-Member and Twelve-Member Juries: An Empirical Study of Trial Results," *University of Michigan Journal of Law Reform* 6 (1973): 688.

36. *Ibid.*, p. 697.

37. *Ibid.*, p. 691.

38. Beiser and Varrin, "Six-Member Juries in the Federal Courts," *Judicature* (April 1975): See also Gordon Bermant and Rob Coppock, "Outcomes of Six- and Twelve-Member Jury Trials: An Analysis of 128 Civil Cases in the State of Washington," *Washington Law Review* 48 (1973): 595.

39. Note, "The Effect of Jury Size on the Probability of Conviction: An Evaluation of *Williams v. Florida*," *Case Western Reserve Law Review* 22 (1971): 544-47. The chart in note *d* is reprinted with permission of the Case Western Law Review.

40. Richard H. Nagasawa, Beth Eakin, and Richard L. Schuster, "The Six-Member Jury: Reform or Folly?" (unpublished, February 1974).

41. *New York Times*, May 17, 1971, p. 1.

42. Administrative Office of U.S. Courts, *Juror Utilization in United States Courts* (Washington: Government Printing Office, August 13, 1971).

43. *Hearings, Three-Judge Court and Six-Person Civil Jury*, p. 47.

44. *Ibid.*, pp. 39-47.

45. Illinois Judicial Conference, "Report of Committee to Study Less-Than-Unanimous Verdicts and the Use of Less than Twelve Jurors," *Illinois Judicial Conference Annual Report* (1962), pp. 62-72.

46. Note, "Six-Member and Twelve-Member Juries," p. 685.

47. Beiser and Varrin, "Six-Member Juries in the Federal Courts," p. 430.

48. D. Fox, I. Lorge, P. Weltz, and K. Herrold, "Comparison of Decisions Written by Large and Small Groups," *American Psychologist* 8 (1953): 351.

49. T.J. Bourchard, Jr., and M. Hare, "Size Performance and Potential in Brainstorming Groups," *Journal of Applied Psychology* 54 (1970): 51-55; and see J.R. Gibb, "The Effects of Group Size and of Threat Reduction upon Creativity in a Problem-Solving Situation," *American Psychologist* 6 (July 1951): 324; F. Frank and L.R. Anderson, "Effects of Task and Group Size Upon Group Productivity and Member Satisfaction," *Sociometry* 34 (March 1971): 135-49; R.F. Bales, F.L. Strodtbeck, T.M. Mills, and M.E. Rosenborough,

"Channels of Communication in Small Groups," *American Sociological Review* 16 (1951): 461-68; Frederick F. Stephen and Elliot G. Mishler, "The Distribution of Participation in Small Groups: An Exponential Approximation," *American Sociological Review* 17 (1952): 598-602; A.P. Hare, "Interaction and Consensus in Different Sized Groups," *American Sociological Review* 17 (1952): 261-67.

50. See A.P. Hare, *Handbook of Small Group Research* (New York: Free Press, 1962); C. Hawkins, *Interaction and Coalition Realignments in Consensus-Seeking Groups* (unpublished doctoral dissertation, Univ. of Chicago, 1960); J. James, "A Preliminary Study of the Size Determinant in Small Group Interaction," *American Sociological Review* 16 (1951): 474-77.

51. Nagasawa et al., "The Six-Member Jury," p. 13. See also, "Reducing the Size of Juries," 48 F.R.D. 79 (1969); *Hearings, Three-Judge Court and Six-Person Jury*, pp. 166-67 (testimony by Professor Hans Zeisel); Lloyd E. Moore, *The Jury: Tool of Kings, Palladium of Liberty* (Cincinnati: W.H. Anderson Co., 1973), p. 145; Hare, "A Study of Interaction and Consensus in Different Sized Groups," *American Sociological Review* 17 (June 1952): 261; Note, "Reducing the Size of Juries," *University of Michigan Journal of Law Reform* 5 (1971): 101, 103; Institute of Judicial Administration, *A Comparison of Six- and Twelve-Member Civil Juries* pp. 9, 10. To the contrary is R.F. Bales, *Personality and Interpersonal Behavior* (New York: Holt, Rinehart, & Winston, 1970).

52. Harry Kalven and Hans Zeisel, *The American Jury* (Boston: Little, Brown, 1966), p. 461.

53. Zeisel, ". . . And Then There Were None," p. 720.

54. *Ibid.*, p. 719.

55. Kalven and Zeisel, *The American Jury*, p. 462.

56. Frederick Pollack and Frederic W. Maitland, *History of English Law* (Cambridge, U.K.: Cambridge University Press, 1959), Vol. II, p. 626 (emphasis added).

57. *Williams v. Florida*, 399 U.S. 78, 98 n.45 (1970).

58. *Apodaca v. Oregon*, 406 U.S. at 408 n.3.

59. S. Mac Gutman, "The Attorney-Conducted Voir Dire of Jurors: A Constitutional Right," *Brooklyn Law Review* 39 (1972): 290, quoting from the *Journal of the House of Representatives*, compiled by The First Congress Project, Washington, D.C. (emphasis added); and see Fisher, "The Seventh Amendment and the Common Law," pp. 519-20.

60. *Thompson v. Utah*, 170 U.S. 343, 351 (1898); *Maxwell v. Dow*, 176 U.S. 581 (1900); *Andres v. United States*, 333 U.S. 740 (1948); *Patton v. United States*, 281 U.S. 276, 288 (1930).

61. *State v. Gann*, 254 Ore, 549, 463 P.2d 570 (1969); see Comment, "Should Jury Verdicts Be Unanimous in Criminal Cases?" *Oregon Law Review* 47 (1968): 417.

62. 406 U.S. 356. For a good analysis of the cases and the policy issues involved, see Note, "Divided They Stand: The Nonunanimous Criminal Jury," *Law and Social Order* (1973): 203.

63. 391 U.S. 145.

64. *In re Winship*, 397 U.S. 358 (1970), held that the due process clause of the Fourteenth Amendment requires the states to accept this high standard of proof.

65. Criminal Justice Act of 1967, c. 80, s. 13. Two Australian states have a similar rule. Lord Denning, "Address," *Australian Law Journal* 11 (1967): 226.

66. *Regina v. Adams* [1969] 1 W.L.R. 106, [1968] 3 All E.R. 437.

67. 406 U.S. at 361.

68. 406 U.S. 404.

69. 391 U.S. 145.

70. 399 U.S. 78.

71. 406 U.S. at 366.

72. *Ibid.*, p. 376.

73. *Ibid.*, p. 369.

74. *Ibid.*, p. 396.

75. *Ibid.*, pp. 402-3 (emphasis added).

76. Kalven and Zeisel, *The American Jury*, p. 490.

77. 406 U.S. at 393.

78. *Ibid.*, p. 366.

79. *American Publishing Co. v. Fisher*, 166 U.S. 464, 467-68 (1897); *Springville v. Thomas*, 166 U.S. 707 (1897).

80. Alec Samuels, "Criminal Justice Act," *Modern Law Review* 31 (1968): 24.

81. W. Haralson, "Unanimous Jury Verdicts in Criminal Cases," *Mississippi Law Journal* 21 (1950): 185.

82. Kalven and Zeisel, *The American Jury*, pp. 17-18.

83. *Ibid.*, p. 461.

84. Figures from James H. Murchison, Administrative Assistant, Multnomah County Circuit Court, Nov. 9, 1973.

85. See *Hoffa v. United States*, 385 U.S. 293 (1966).

86. Kalven and Zeisel, *The American Jury*, pp. 462-63.

87. Holtzoff, "Modern Trends in Trial By Jury," *Washington & Lee Law Review* 16 (1959): 27.

88. Samuels, "Criminal Justice Act," p. 25.

89. 406 U.S., at 397-98.

90. *Ibid.*, p. 361.

91. Kalven and Zeisel, *The American Jury*, p. 201.

92. Zeisel, ". . . And Then There Were None," p. 722.

93. *Huffman v. United States*, 297 F.2d 754, 759 (5th Cir. 1962) (emphasis added); and see *Green v. United States*, 309 F.2d 852 (5th Cir. 1962).

94. Joseph Story, *Commentaries on the Constitution of the United States*, (4th ed.; Boston, Little, Brown, 1873) Vol. 2, sec. 1780, p. 541.

95. Justice John Harlan in *In re Winship*, 397 U.S. 358, 372 (1970) (concurring opinion).

96. Kalven and Zeisel, *The American Jury*, p. 461.

97. *Ibid.*, p. 460.

98. *In re Winship*, 397 U.S. 358 (1970).

99. Note, "Unanimous Criminal Verdicts and Proof Beyond a Reasonable Doubt," *University of Pennsylvania Law Review* 112 (1964): 769; Note, "In the Wake of *Apodaca v. Oregon*: A Case for Retaining Unanimous Jury Verdicts," *Valparaiso Law Review* 7 (1973): 258-62.

100. *Hibdon v. United States*, 204 F.2d 834, 838 (6th Cir. 1953); *accord, Billeci v. United States*, 184 F.2d 394 (D.C. Cir. 1950); *United States v. Fioravanti*, 412 F.2d 407, 418 (3rd Cir. 1969).

101. *Johnson v. Louisiana*, 406 U.S. at 361.

102. Zeisel ". . . And Then There Were None," p. 722 (emphasis added).

*Chapter Nine*

# Conclusions

Our ability to maintain the jury as an institution of self-governance for 800 years is a powerful statement of our commitment to democratic solutions. The jury is the embodiment of the realization that only by gathering together persons from all sectors of society, presenting the evidence in a controversy to them, and asking them to deliberate on the issues involved can we be sure that all relevant perspectives have been considered and that the verdict represents the community's collective judgment on the controversy. Decision-making by citizens provides a level of common sense and a stamp of democratic legitimacy that cannot be attained by "experts" no matter how skilled they may be. Explicit guidelines for decision-making cannot be written for these most complicated disputes. Discretion and sound judgment must be exercised by some group, and it is most sensible to give that power to a group of ordinary persons with no personal ambition or stake in the matter. Only such a random sample of community members can render a verdict that is truly impartial, reflecting the community's norms and collective conscience.

Our commitment to the jury, and to the principle that it should be truly representative of the community, has, however, not been as firm as it might be. Substantial progress in broadening the base from which jurors are selected is impeded by a number of factors. The U.S. Congress and numerous state legislatures have in recent years passed significant reform statutes designed to increase the representativeness of juries, but bureaucratic decisions and apathy still conspire to delay the achievement of that goal.

Although the initial sources of jurors are generally much more representative than in the past, the process of jury selection in most courts steadily reduces the pool of prospective jurors in such a way as to create or increase disproportions among groups. The first stage of selection, in drawing names from the list of registered voters, leaves out many of the young, the poor, and the nonwhite. In the second state, liberal excuses to women, the aged and the young, and those who protest economic hardship eliminates still more prospective jurors. In the final step, including the voir dire and peremptory challenges, attorneys for one side or the other often attempt to shape a jury to their advantage by removing certain types of people from the jury panel.

Individuals summoned for jury duty almost invariably try to avoid their obligation because they know that much of their time will be wasted sitting in the jury room, that they will receive only a token payment for their appearance, that they may be subjected to extensive and embarrassing questioning before the trial, and that they may never actually sit on a jury at all. Because of the almost universal desire to avoid jury duty, and because of the usually lax attitude of jury commissioners and judges toward the granting of excuses, the juries that are impaneled are frequently not representative of the community. Defendants and litigants are all too often confronted with a jury that fails to include significant segments of the heterogeneous population.

In order to realize our commitment to representative juries, we must take a number of simple but important steps.

**The Wheel.** The lists from which jurors are selected must be as complete as is humanly possible. This initial step is fundamental to the success of a selection scheme because an unrepresentative source will inevitably produce unrepresentative juries.

States where individual discretion still governs the initial selection of prospective jurors must switch to a random scheme. These jurisdictions that permit jurors to be hand-picked by local officials or by specially selected citizens invariably impanel juries that are elite rather than representative. This method of selection is still used in some 16 states, in the South and in New England, and in a larger number of states—including New York, Texas, and California—for the selection of grand jurors. It is an anachronism today, when the importance of a representative jury is almost universally accepted.

Jurisdictions that use the list of registered voters as their exclusive source for jurors (all federal and most state courts) should seek to supplement it with the aim of giving all citizens an equal chance of becoming jurors. Because it can be demonstrated unequivocally that the exclusive use of the voter list skews the jury toward some sectors of society, research and experimentation with additional lists must be undertaken. Voter registration procedures should also be simplified to make it easier for people to vote. Even if voter lists were found to mirror society in some counties, supplementation would still be important as a means to spread the burden of jury duty to all citizens, not just voters, and ensure that jury service is not a penalty for voting. In most jurisdictions, a combination of voter lists and the list of holders of drivers' licenses will obtain a more representative jury wheel, but in others, these two will probably have to be used in connection with additional sources. A representative wheel could easily be assembled from census lists, if they were kept up to date for this purpose.

**Excuses.** No excuses should be granted to any person summoned for jury duty except in cases of medical hardship. The elimination of most excuses should be accomplished through a new attitude toward jury duty on the part of the courts and, eventually, the public. Serving on a jury should be seen as an obligation and responsibility to be shared by all citizens equally. A representative wheel will produce representative juries only if the persons randomly selected from that source are uniformly required to report for duty. No occupational excuses should be permitted because any such excuse means that one group will not be represented on the jury—whose strength comes from its role as a body representing us all. Automatic excuses for women, students, the aged, and other groups should be abolished for the same reason. Actual hardship excuses can be dealt with by allowing the person summoned to decide when, during the coming year, he or she would find it least inconvenient to serve.

In order to enable everyone who is summoned to serve on a jury, and obviate the need for excuses, the length of service should be reduced to one week (except in protracted trials), and the monetary compensation should be significantly increased. Reducing the length of service will also ensure that the jury resolves the issues in its case with a fresh approach, unencumbered by bits of information that jurors may have picked up in other trials. The wage for jury services should be equivalent to that of the average American worker or the average worker in the area. In 1977, this figure would be about $50 a day, but it would have to be adjusted regularly to keep up with inflation. Such a fair payment would ensure that the jury commissioner's office and the judges would use the time of the jurors more carefully, avoiding the long waits that are so common today, and would also make it impossible for any person to claim economic hardship as an excuse.

**Challenges.**   The questioning of jurors and, in particular, the use of peremptory challenges should be curtailed. Litigants have great power at the present time to alter the ultimate composition of their jury through the use of peremptory challenges. This power, which is supposed to compensate for the biased jury lists that are used, is a necessary tool when the source of jurors is not completely representative. But in the system we should be moving toward—in which the source of jurors is as complete as possible and virtually no excuses are granted—that power is less necessary. Given a representative jury panel, it would be improper to allow attorneys to challenge peremptorily large numbers of those persons not to the litigants' liking. The process of challenging alters a heterogeneous and diverse group and transforms it into a homogeneous body that may be less sensitive to some of the issues involved in the case. All persons are equally competent to be selected as jurors, and if they are randomly selected, they should be allowed to take their seats on the jury panel.

Questioning of jurors should, therefore, be limited to questions of actual familiarity with the litigants or their attorneys, or questions involving some unique bias that would make the juror inappropriate for the particular case at hand. Sometimes this will require questioning into racial prejudice or prejudice against a religion or some other aspect. But peremptory challenges should be strictly limited to no more than three (or five in the most serious of cases). In a criminal case, the accused should be given more peremptories than the prosecution.

**Political Trials.**   The special problems of impaneling juries for political trials should be addressed in such a way as to promote representativeness, which is especially important in cases where government power plays a large role. The effect of the government's advantages in such cases, which include publicity, selecting the trial site, and sequestration, should be carefully examined for their effect on the jury profile. A change of venue should be freely granted when an impartial jury cannot be impaneled without great difficulty, and excuses should be severely limited. With these changes, the increasingly widespread strategy of extensive voir dire based on a sociological and psychological examination of prospective jurors will be less necessary. These methods end by distorting the composition of a jury panel when it is representative and raise the specter of jury tampering even when it is not.

**Small Juries and Majority Verdicts.** We must insist on the preservation of the jury of twelve, rendering its decision by unanimous verdicts. The idea of the jury is one of a body that gathers together the collective wisdom of the community and applies it to the controversy at hand. Only if the body is large enough to include persons from all sectors of society can it serve that function, and only if the jurors are obliged to reach a unanimous verdict will they try to resolve the conflicting perspectives during their deliberations.

It may be appropriate to use a smaller jury in civil disputes involving only a small sum of money, but if the possible consequences of the trial include imprisonment for any period of time, then an accused must have the opportunity to present a defense to a significant collection of community members who must all agree before the punishment can be meted out. The verdicts of a jury of six appear to be more erratic and less reliable than the jury of twelve, and a verdict rendered with several jurors dissenting indicates that the matter was not proved beyond a reasonable doubt. The legitimacy of the jury's verdicts depends on the continued necessity of unanimous agreement among its diverse members.

**The Courts.** The burden of challenging jury selection procedures should be eased. At present, a litigant challenging the composition of the jury pool faces an almost impossible task. Even if the litigant shows that the jury pool is unrepresentative to a substantial degree, the court is likely to ignore the figures or to require further proof. The figures should be allowed to speak for themselves, as they do in numerous other areas of the law—school segregation, job discrimination, and reapportionment, to name three examples. If a jury pool is not representative, the reasons for the disparities should not determine the action taken. The fact of underrepresentation should be enough for the court to require a new selection scheme that will be representative. Persons challenging jury-selection procedures should be given ready access to jury files, and if an examination of those records shows that an important population group is underrepresented by 20 percent, or by 10 percent over a two-year period, then the selection procedure should be altered to correct the inequity.

The diversity of the jury is its strength. Only if we can ensure that our juries will reflect our diversity can we give to the jury the difficult task of resolving disputes. The jury expresses the community's judgment. If it truly represents a cross-section, its verdict should carry legitimacy. As an institution of the people rather than the government, and as a body that expresses the people's collective conscience rather than expert opinion, it is the essence of democracy. The jury serves as a reminder that we have a democratic government that derives its power from the people. The jury shows that harmony is possible if we listen to each other and seek a unified judgment from a diversity of viewpoints. But these benefits can be obtained only if the assembled jury is *representative* of the community so that the persons deliberating will have a legitimate claim to speak on behalf of the community.

# Postscript:
# Jury Nullification

Throughout this volume we have been analyzing questions concerning jury selection by referring to the jury's role as bringing the community's conscience into the deliberations and the ultimate verdict. What exactly should the jurors be told about their power to return a final and unreviewable verdict (final, at least, if the verdict is acquittal)? The jury has historically exercised the power to acquit even if the law and evidence would seem to justify a guilty verdict, and a debate has raged for hundreds of years whether jurors should be explicitly told they have this power. This question is somewhat tangential to the central questions of jury selection, and so this discussion is placed after the main text of this book, as a Postscript.

At the beginning of the Chicago trial of eight men alleged to have conspired to produce violence at the 1968 Democratic Convention, Federal District Judge Julius J. Hoffman told the jurors that they must always follow his instructions on matters of law. Defense lawyer Leonard Weinglass immediately objected: "The defense will contend that the jury is a representative of the moral conscience of the community. If there is a conflict between the judge's instructions and that of conscience, it should obey the latter." Judge Hoffman overruled the objection and the trial proceeded through the circus-like events that followed.[1]

Judge Hoffman's ruling was typical, and most American judges in recent years have insisted that they alone can evaluate and interpret the law, and that the role of the jury is simply to evaluate the evidence, decide what happened, and then apply the law—as enunciated by the judge—to the facts. In every criminal case in California, for instance, the jury is given the following instruction on the limitations of its power:

Ladies and Gentlemen of the Jury:

It becomes my duty as judge to instruct you concerning the law applicable to this case, and it is your duty as jurors to follow the law as I shall state it to you.

The function of the jury is to try the issues of fact that are presented by the allegations in the information filed in this court and the defendant's plea of "not guilty." This duty you should perform uninfluenced by pity for a defendant or by passion or prejudice against him. . . .

You are to be governed solely by the evidence introduced in this trial and the law as stated to you by me. The law forbids you to be governed by mere sentiment, conjecture, sympathy, passion, public opinion or public feeling. Both the People and the defendant have a right to demand, and they do demand and expect, that you will conscientiously and dispassionately consider and weigh the evidence and apply the law of the case, and that you will reach a just verdict, regardless of what the consequences may be. . . .[2]

Many defense lawyers and scholars have continued to argue, however, that the jury's role is broader, and juries have in fact continually arrived at verdicts that indicate they are considering more than just the facts. The Chicago Jury Project discovered that in a significant number of cases the jury returns a verdict of not guilty, despite strong evidence to the contrary, because they feel the application of the law would lead to an unjust result in the particular case at hand.[3] And in numerous recent cases with political overtones, the jury has brought in a verdict of not guilty although the evidence seemed to have required a guilty verdict. Everyone agrees that juries always have the *power* to acquit, and that a jury decision to acquit is not subject to review or reversal in any manner. But many lawyers and some commentators have argued that the jury has a *right* to acquit even when the evidence indicates that a crime has been committed, and that the jury should be specifically informed of that right.[4] The contention is not that jurors should be told that they can *make up* any law they want and apply it to the case at hand. Jurors certainly cannot, for instance, *convict* a defendant unless the defendant has committed acts that have previously been declared unlawful, because to convict in the absence of a specific statute is to deny an accused the due process of law in the most basic sense. But to acquit when special circumstances justify leniency is another matter.

Such action is basic to our notion of the jury as a body designed to stand between the accused and a sometimes oppressive or overzealous government.[5]

Jurors should not therefore be told by the trial judge, as they are told in California and in almost every other jurisdiction, that "it is your duty as jurors to follow the law as I shall state it to you."[6] Jurors should instead be told that although they are a public body bound to give respectful attention to the laws, they have the final authority to decide whether or not to apply a given law to the acts of the defendant on trial before them. More explicitly, jurors should be told that they represent their communities and that it is appropriate to bring into their deliberations the feelings of the community and their own feelings based on conscience. Finally, they should be told that despite their respect for the law, nothing would bar them from acquitting the defendant if they feel that the law, as applied to the factual situation before them, would produce an inequitable or unjust result.

Such an instruction will not permit persons to pick and choose with impunity the laws they will obey or disobey. Most jurors, because they were among those who elected the legislators who passed the laws, will apply the law as written to the facts of the case. In some cases, however, they will conclude that the legislators could not have intended the law to apply to their set of facts, or that it is time to review the wisdom of the law, and they will acquit a person who has broken a law. This is an important safeguard—fought for during several centuries—that should be recognized and strengthened.

## THE HISTORICAL RECORD

The first clear assertion and acceptance of the jury's position as an independent decision-making body came in the London trial of William Penn and William Mead in 1670, which is described in Chapter 1, page 5. The jury's refusal to follow the judge's instructions on the law that applied to the case, the willingness of several jurors to spend months in jail insisting on their right to make the final decision on the guilt or innocence of the accused, and the subsequent vindication of their position has been deemed to be such an important event in Anglo-Saxon jurisprudence that the trial is commemorated by a memorial hung in the Old Bailey courthouse in London—the only trial to be so remembered:

> Near this site William Penn and William Mead were tried in 1670 for preaching to an unlawful assembly in Gracechurch Street.
> This tablet commemorates the courage and endurance of the Jury,

Thomas Vere, Edward Bushell and ten others, who refused to give a verdict against them although they were locked up without food for two nights and were fined for their final verdict of Not Guilty.

The case of these jurymen was reviewed on a writ of Habeas Corpus and Chief Justice Vaughan delivered the opinion of the court *which established the Right of the Juries to give their Verdict according to their conviction.* [Emphasis added.]

The right of the jury to pass on questions of law as well as issues of fact quickly became accepted in England, and spread to the North American colonies where juries refused to convict for violations of the crown's laws. Colonial juries regularly refused, for instance, to enforce the Navigation Acts designed by the British Parliament to channel all colonial trade through the mother country. Ships impounded by the British for violations of trade restrictions were regularly released by juries in obvious disregard of law and fact. Because North American juries refused to follow the law in these cases the British established courts of vice-admiralty to try maritime cases (including violations of the Navigation Acts) without a jury, a source of great bitterness among the colonists and one of the many grievances that culminated in the Revolution.[7]

The most famous colonial example of jury nullification is the case of John Peter Zenger, who was the only printer in New York who would publish material not authorized by the British mayor. Under the British law that was then in force, the crime consisted in printing such material, and their truth was no defense to the charge. That Zenger had printed the material was not denied, but the jury nonetheless refused to convict. Zenger's lawyer, Andrew Hamilton, told the jurors that they "have the right beyond all dispute to determine both the law and the facts."[8] The jury followed his advice, acquitted Zenger, and once again insisted upon the jury's role as the ultimate arbiter of criminal disputes.

By the end of the eighteenth century this principle was quite firmly established in the minds of all the thinkers who helped form the colonies into a nation. John Adams, one of the more conservative leaders of this period, wrote in his diary in 1771 as follows:

Now, should the melancholy case arise that the judges should give their opinions to the jury against one of these fundamental principles, is a juror obliged to find his verdict generally, according to this direction, or even to find the fact specially and submit the law to the court? Every man of any feeling or conscience, will answer no. *It is not only his right, but his duty, in that case, to find the verdict according to his own best understanding, judgment, and conscience, though in direct opposition to the direction of the court.*[9]

After the American Revolution and the writing of the U.S. Constitution, this principle was repeated again and again. In a 1794 civil case heard before the United States Supreme Court (under its original jurisdiction), Chief Justice John Jay, after instructing the jury on the law and advising them that as a general rule they should take the law from the court, specifically told the jurors:

> But it must be observed that by the same law, which recognized the reasonable distribution of jurisdiction, *you have, nevertheless, a right to take upon yourselves to judge of both, and to determine the law as well as the fact in controversy.*[10]

Justices James Iredell and James Wilson, both on the Supreme Court in 1794, specifically expressed agreement, in another case, with the doctrine that the jurors can judge the law.[11] And even the politically repressive Sedition Law of 1798 stated that in prosecutions for seditious libels "the jury who shall try the cause shall have a right to determine the law and the fact, under the direction of the court, as in other cases."[12]

A parallel insistence on the right of the jury to pass on questions of law was occurring in England during this time, and the debates concerning Fox's Libel Act of 1792 are particularly instructive because they demonstrate that this right of jury freedom was designed to shift the law *in only one direction*—that of *mercy*. During the last half of the eighteenth century, the crown brought repeated prosecutions for libel, and the crown's judges tried to control the jury in the same way the colonial judge had tried to control John Peter Zenger's jury. In one celebrated case, the judge went so far as to tell the jurors that because the defendant did not deny he had published the document in question and because the judge ruled as a matter of law that the document was libelous, the jurors were obliged to return a verdict of guilty.[13] Such high-handed tactics caused an uproar, and in 1792, after much debate, Parliament passed Fox's Libel Act, which clearly articulated the jury's role in such cases.

The act stated that the judge could explain the law to the jurors, but that they were free to return either a special verdict, responding to each factual issue and leaving the law to the judge, or a general verdict, simply guilty or not guilty with no explanation of how the result was reached. As a protection against an overly aggressive jury, the defendant could ask the judge to reverse a jury verdict of guilty, and in any event the judge was authorized to reverse whenever he felt the jury's guilty verdict was unwarranted.[14] The jury's right to decide matters of law, therefore, moved in only one direction. The jurors could decide that the law did not apply to a defendant when a judge thought it did, and their decision would be final. If, however, they decided that the law did apply when the judge thought it did not, their decision would not be final. Because the jury could only mitigate the harshness of the law, and could not impose its own harsher view of the law to convict an unsuspecting person, this limited view of the jury's right to consider the law as well as the facts does not raise any problems of due process.

## THE NINETEENTH-CENTURY REVISION

In the nineteenth century, however, this right of the jury to consider the equities of the law was sharply curtailed in the United States, because some leading judges did not believe that a jury can logically be given the power to mitigate the law without also being given the power to create harsh and vindictive laws. The most forceful advocate of limiting the jury's function to fact-finding was Supreme Court Justice Joseph Story. While sitting as trial judge in a case involving the transportation of slaves along the coast of Africa, Justice Story was presented with the argument that the jury can judge the law as well as the facts. He conceded that the jurors have the "physical power to disregard the law, as laid down to them by the court." Nonetheless, Story maintained, they cannot decide the law, morally, on the basis of their own notions or whimsy.

> On the contrary, I hold it the most sacred constitutional right of every party accused of a crime, that the jury should respond as to the facts, and the court as to the law. It is the duty of the court to instruct the jury as to the law; and it is the duty of the jury to follow the law, as it is laid down by the court. This is the right of every citizen; and it is his only protection. If the jury were at liberty to settle the law for themselves, the effect would be, not only that the law itself would be most uncertain, from the different views, which different juries might take of it; but in case of error, there would be no remedy or redress by the injured party; for the court would not have any right to review the law as it had been settled by the jury.... Every person accused as a criminal has a right to be tried according to the law of the land; and not by the law as a jury may understand it, or choose, from wantoness, or ignorance, or accidental mistake, to interpret it. If I thought that the jury were the proper judges of the law in criminal cases, I should hold it my duty to abstain from the responsibility of stating the law to them upon any such trial. But believing, as I do, that every citizen has a right to be tried by the law, and according to the law; that it is my privilege and truest shield against oppression and wrong; I feel it is my duty to state my views fully and openly on the present occasion.[15]

Justice Story's language is strong, but an analysis of the case he was considering indicates that his reasoning should not apply to the current debates over jury nullification, i.e., the right of the jury to refuse to apply the law. He was dealing with an 1820 statute that provided the death penalty for any American citizen who should "seize any negro or mulatto" with the intent of making the person seized a slave. The defendant on trial before Justice Story had been a sailor on a ship that he had picked up and transported a number of slaves in Portuguese Africa. According to the Justice, before the statute could be applied to the defendant's acts, two questions of interpretation had to be resolved: (1) whether the statute applied to mere sailors who gained no title over slaves and no profit from their sale; and (2) whether it applied to the transportation of persons previously enslaved between two points both within a country practicing slavery. To both these questions, Justice Story's answer was no. His concern in depriving the jurors of the power to interpret the law was, therefore, to prevent them from convicting and executing the defendant out of vengeance when he was inclined to be merciful. He was worried about a jury punishing for a crime that had not been legislatively intended, rather than its acting mercifully and refusing to punish for the violation of a statute.

The argument being made today by lawyers defending persons who have committed crimes of conscience is very different from the one facing Justice Story. Leonard Weinglass argued only that the jurors have the power to temper the law with mercy. He was not saying that they had the power to interpret the law for any purpose beyond the confines of the courtroom. He certainly was not arguing that the jury should be empowered to hand down a harsher punishment than permitted under current law. If such discretion were given to the jury, some "patriotic" jurors would undoubtedly have sought to impose the death penalty on persons who protested against the Vietnam war.

Our judicial system already recognizes some distinctions between a jury acting vengefully and one acting mercifully. Appellate judges can reduce a sentence or refuse to uphold a conviction if they feel a jury has imposed too harsh a judgment on the accused. Appellate judges are, however, prevented from reviewing a judgment of acquittal no matter how irrational it seems. Although Justice Story did not specifically address himself to the jury's right to act mercifully, he apparently could not accept the seeming inconsistency of allowing a jury to reduce a punishment if it could not also increase it. He felt that if the jury's power to create laws was to be limited, its power to nullify them also had to be limited. Because we have recognized that a clear distinction can be drawn between a jury's mercy and its vengeance, we should not accept uncritically Justice Story's arguments, based, as they were, on an inability to draw this distinction.

Justice Story's successor in leading the judicial campaign to limit jury freedom was Supreme Court Justice Benjamin R. Curtis. In 1851 Justice Curtis was sitting as trial judge in a case involving a violation of the Fugitive Slave Act, a statute that was obnoxious to a large part of the population and hard to enforce because juries continually acquitted in cases of obvious violation. The defendant's lawyer began his summation to the jury by arguing that "this being a criminal case, the jury were rightfully the judges of the law as well as the fact."[16] If, he continued, any of the jurors believed the statute "to be unconstitutional, they were bound by their oaths to disregard any direction to the contrary which the court might give them."[17] Justice Curtis interrupted the argument at this point and gave a long opinion rejecting the assertion. Unlike Justice Story, Justice Curtis was squarely faced with the argument that the jury should be allowed to act mercifully to mitigate the effect of an unjust law. Like Justice Story, however, he refused to consider that proposition alone, and instead seems to have viewed the argument as something more—that the jurors should have total authority to pass on the law with the power to increase as well as decrease the penalties to be imposed. Justice Curtis, for instance, cites an 1802 congressional statute that said the decisions of the Supreme Court shall be final. If, as he noted, the jurors were permitted to decide questions of law, then they could overturn decisions of the Supreme Court; the purpose of this statute would be subverted, and uniform interpretations of the law would not be possible.[18] In making this argument, Curtis was raising a red herring, even within the context of his case. The argument is certainly inapplicable to the contentions raised by lawyers in today's cases of conscience and protest. No lawyer is asking that juries be allowed to reverse a decision of the Supreme Court, or even that any jury's decision should have effect beyond the limits of the specific case being tried. The contention is simply that within one courtroom and with regard to one set of facts, the impaneled jurors should have the discretion not to apply the law to one defendant.

The rulings of Justices Story and Curtis had wide impact throughout the country, but each was only the decision of an individual judge and hence was only as influential as it was persuasive. In 1895 the full Supreme Court finally considered the question and, quoting extensively from the Story and Curtis decisions, agreed with the conclusion of the individual judges by a vote of seven to two. The case, *Sparf and Hansen v. United States* (1895),[19] involved two sailors accused of having thrown a comrade overboard from an American vessel near Tahiti. The sailors were charged with murder, and their defense was that what they did constituted only the lesser offense of manslaughter. The defendants asked the trial judge to tell the jurors that it was within their power to return a verdict of either murder or manslaughter, but the judge refused, saying no evidence had been introduced that would support a verdict of manslaughter. The trial judge conceded that it was within the power of the jury to return a verdict of manslaughter, but maintained that such a conclusion would not be legally defensible. In response to a request for additional instruction, the trial judge told the jurors:

> In a proper case, a verdict for manslaughter may be rendered, as the district attorney has stated; and even in this case you have the physical power to do so; but as one of the tribunals of the country, a jury is expected to be governed by law, and the law it should receive from the court.[20]

The convicted defendants appealed to the Supreme Court, arguing that the jury had been improperly instructed, but the Court rejected the challenge. The majority opinion spent 42 pages reviewing earlier decisions and came to the conclusion that because jurors cannot be allowed to increase the penalties or create laws on their own, they cannot be allowed to reduce such penalties or nullify laws. The reasoning parallels that of Justices Story and Curtis and suffers from the same inability to distinguish between the two directions in which a jury can move. Even though no one before the Court argued that the jury should be allowed to create its own crimes or to render stiffer punishment than the law allows, the Court was haunted by that specter. Because the Court could not distinguish between a jury's lowering and raising the punishment, the Court deprived the jurors of the right to do either. In the Court's words:

> Any other rule than that indicated in the above observations would bring confusion and uncertainty in the administration of the criminal law. Indeed, if a jury may rightfully disregard the direction of the court in the matter of law, and determine for themselves what the law is in the particular case before them, it is difficult to perceive any legal ground upon which a verdict of conviction can be set aside by the court as being against the law. If it be the function of the jury to decide the law as well as the facts—if the function of the court be only advisory as to the law—why should the court interfere for the protection of the accused against what it deems an error of the jury in matter of law?[21]

Since *Sparf and Hansen* few courts have reviewed the basis for the decision and most states and all federal courts now tell their jurors that they must follow the law as given to them by the judge.

## JURY NULLIFICATION TODAY

In Indiana and Maryland, however, the judges still specifically tell jurors that they have the authority to nullify the law in appropriate cases.[22] The Indiana Constitution says that "[i]n all criminal cases whatsoever, the jury shall have the right to determine the law and the facts."[23] During the nineteenth and early twentieth century this provision was rarely cited, but recently it has come back into its own and has been interpreted to mean what it says and to be constitutional.[24] In 1967, the Indiana Supreme Court said:

> It appears to this court that Article I, section 19, taken in conjunction with the presumption of innocence is far from an outmoded, archaic anachronism. *Rather, despite its venerable age, it appears to be in the vanguard of modern thinking with regard to the full protection of the rights of the criminal defendant.*[25]

The Maryland Constitution contains a provision that reads as follows:

> In the trial of all criminal cases, the Jury shall be the Judges of Law, as well as of fact, except that the Court may pass upon the sufficiency of the evidence to sustain a conviction.[26]

This provision is important, and its interpretation is instructive, because it demonstrates how a jury can be given the power of mercy without also being given the power of vengeance. The following instruction is given to the jury in every Maryland criminal case:

> Members of the Jury, this is a criminal case and under the Constitution and the laws of the State of Maryland in a criminal case the jury are the judges of the law as well as of the facts in the case. So that whatever I tell you about the law, while it is intended to be helpful to you in reaching a just and proper verdict in the case, it is not binding upon you as members of the jury and you may accept the law as you apprehend it to be in the case.[27]

This instruction does not lead to a system of jurors magically creating crimes out of the blue or abusing their powers. Even critics of jury freedom concede that in Maryland "[c]riminal trials go on with fair success and justice."[28] To protect the accused against a jury that might be tempted to act improperly, a number of safeguards have been built into the trial process. The judge decides all questions concerning the admissibility of evidence. If either party requests the judge to do so, the judge must give the jury an advisory instruction on the law. If the trial judge thinks insufficient evidence exists to support a jury verdict of guilty, he or she is empowered to direct a verdict of acquittal. If the jury has misapplied the law to the prejudice of the accused, the trial judge can set the verdict aside and order a new trial. Similarly, the Maryland Supreme Court can review the sufficiency of the evidence if the defendant argues on appeal that the jury has convicted improperly.[29] The defendant, therefore, has the benefit of a jury determination on the applicability of the law, but is protected from a jury that might use its power to his or her detriment.

In other states, the jury is not told they have the power to nullify, but they do so nonetheless, according to the findings of the Chicago Jury Project, in cases involving a sympathetic defendant or one who is perceived to have been punished enough, and in cases involving an unpopular law such as drunk driving or gaming laws.[30]

## THE MODERN DEBATE OVER JURY NULLIFICATION

Since the publication of the results of the Chicago Jury Project in 1966, the question of jury nullification has been debated in the context of political trials, and although most judges continue to resist telling the jurors that they have the power to refuse to enforce a law, more and more juries seem to be asserting their ancient power to do so.

In *United States v. Moylan* (1969),[31] the defendants, known as the Catonsville Nine, had burned draft files with homemade napalm to protest the war in Vietnam. They claimed their acts were morally justified because of the illegal and immoral nature of the war, and they asked the trial judge to instruct the jurors that they could find the defendants not guilty because their law-breaking acts were based on conscience. In rejecting this claim the U.S. Court of Appeals for the Fourth Circuit noted that judges had been giving jurors a nullification instruction until the middle of the nineteenth century. The court further conceded that the jury does have the *power* to nullify, and stated that this power has "not always [been] contrary to the interest of justice."[32] But the court refused to recognize that the jurors should be told they have the power to nullify for to do so would encourage the jurors in their "lawlessness."[33]

*United States v. Simpson* (1972)[34] similarly involved a defendant who destroyed draft files as a protest against the war in Vietnam, and who asked his trial judge to instruct the jurors that they had the right to acquit him regardless of the evidence of his guilt if in good conscience they believed he should not be punished for his conduct. The trial judge refused and the U.S. Court of Appeals for the Ninth Circuit affirmed the conviction, holding that they were obliged to follow *Sparf and Hansen v. United States* (1895). In the course of its opinion, the appelate court again conceded that jury nullification has frequently been beneficial: "We acknowledge the truth that all such verdicts, especially when viewed in hindsight, cannot reasonably be said to have been undesirable."[35] The footnote of the court refers to the cases of William Penn and John Peter Zenger and notes that they "illustrate how well our society's interests have been served by acquittals resulting from application by the jurors of their collective conscience and sense of justice."[36] But if the doctrine works so well, and many verdicts resulting from it have not been undesirable, why does the court disallow the defendant's instruction to the jury? The court reasons that the combination of (1) the jurors' knowledge that they can return "conscience verdicts" without being specifically instructed, and (2) the inability of the trial judge to compel the jury to convict even where the evidence is quite clear, provides enough protection for the defendant.

Jurors are, however, frequently unaware of their power to acquit and they are not infrequently coerced into a verdict they do not personally believe in. After the 1968 trial of Dr. Benjamin Spock, Rev. William Sloane Coffin, and three others in Boston,[37] for instance, several jurors reported that they felt they had no choice but to come in with a guilty verdict after the trial judge's narrow instructions. One juror noted: "I knew they were guilty when we were charged by the judge. I did not know prior to that time—I was in full agreement with the defendants until we were charged by the judge. That was the kiss of death!"[38] Not everyone impaneled as a juror remembers the lessons of their American history courses when they learned about John Peter Zenger.

*United States v. Dougherty* (1972)[39] gives further amplification to the position adopted by the Ninth Circuit. In this case, nine members of the Catholic clergy broke into the offices of the Dow Chemical Company and destroyed the premises, as a protest against Dow's manufacture of napalm. The defendants, known as the "D.C.-9," requested a jury nullification instruction at the trial. Their request was refused. On appeal, the U.S. Court of Appeals for the District of Columbia upheld by a 2-1 vote the trial judge's refusal to give the nullification instruction.

Once again, the majority conceded that the "pages of history shine on instances of the jury's exercise of its prerogative to disregard uncontradicted evidence and instructions of the judge,"[40] mentioning specifically the John Peter Zenger case and the nineteenth-century acquittals in fugitive slave cases. But then, after acknowledging the value of jury nullification, Judge Harold Leventhal (writing for the majority) says he fears that the "way the jury operates may be radically altered if there is alteration in the way it is told to operate."[41] Judge Leventhal asserts that jurors already know of their power to nullify through "informal communication from the total culture," citing literature, television, newspapers, conversations, and readings of history.[42] These informal sources convey the idea that jurors are free to depart from the judge's instruction in rare cases. But what functions well as an informal procedure may become completely unworkable if institutionalized.

Consider, Judge Leventhal suggests, the analogy to speed limits. A posted speed limit of 60 mph produces speeds of 10 or 15 miles an hour in excess of that limit. Some of this greater speed is tolerated, as motorists know, even though they are not officially told about it. But if the speed limit were raised to include the speeds now tolerated, motorists would drive at even greater speeds, and the tolerance factor would have to be raised accordingly. According to the majority opinion: "But can it be supposed that the speeds would stay substantially the same if the speed limit were put: Drive as fast as you think appropriate, without the posted limit as an anchor, a point of departure?"[43] And similarly, Judge Leventhal concludes, in cases of high conscience the jury will exercise its strong preference for freedom, without being told to do so, but the jury should not be encouraged to deviate from the norm. Any other rule would make the juror feel that "it is he who fashions the rule that condemns."[44]

It is significant that Judge Leventhal does not carefully define what he understands jury nullification to be. The use of the speed limit example indicates that he feels he is considering the question whether the jury can decide what in fact the law is. Jury nullification proponents would respond that the speed limit sign should say that the posted limit is 60 mph, but if emergency conditions exist, persons who drive faster will not be punished. Jury nullification does not ask the jury to make up the law, but rather to refuse to apply it where to do so would be unjust.

In a dissenting opinion that reflects an understanding of the jury as a source of our freedoms, Chief Judge David Bazelon directs his attention to the weak spots in the majority opinion. Judge Bazelon condemns the inconsistent view that appreciates nullification as enhancing the "over-all normative effect of the rule of law"[45] but that at the same time says that the nullification doctrine must be concealed from jurors, and perhaps even denounced in their presence—as was done in this case. Jurors should be told, says Judge Bazelon, that part of their job is to pass judgment on the equity of applying the law to the defendant charged in this particular case:

> *The [jury nullification] doctrine permits the jury to bring to bear on the criminal process a sense of fairness and particularized justice.* The drafters of legal rules cannot anticipate and take account of every case where a defendant's conduct is "unlawful" but not blameworthy, any more than they can draw a bold line to mark the boundary between an accident and negligence. It is the jury—as spokesman for the community's sense of values—that must explore that subtle and elusive boundary. . . . *The very essence of the jury's function is its role as spokesman for the community conscience in determining whether or not blame can be imposed.*[46]

## THE 1973 CAMDEN-28 TRIAL

Although the federal appellate decisions have all rejected the argument that jurors should be told they have the right to nullify the law, defendants are increasingly allowed to make full and complete statements to the jury about motivation and justification, and sometimes direct appeals have been made to juries to exercise the ancient right of nullification. In the spring of 1973, 28 persons were put on trial in the Camden, New Jersey, federal court for destroying the records of the local selective service office.[47] These individuals had been caught red-handed by the F.B.I. immediately after the act, and it was later revealed that the F.B.I. had been told of their planning activities and had in fact supplied the anti-war activists with the tools and knowledge required to carry out their act of civil disobedience. At the trial, Judge Clarkson S. Fisher permitted the defendants to make statements about their purposes and political feelings, and allowed the jury to hear testimony about the *Pentagon Papers* and the nature of the Vietnam war. But even more significantly, Judge Fisher (who was appointed to the bench in 1970 by President Nixon) allowed defense attorney David Kairys to make an impassioned closing argument to their jury about their right to acquit in these circumstances. The judge had previously told the jury that they did not have even the power to nullify, but after argument he was persuaded otherwise. He told the jury that his earlier comment had been incorrect, and specifically told the jury "if you find that the overreaching participation by Government agents or informers in the activities as you have heard them here was so fundamentally unfair to be offensive to the basic standards of decency, and shocking to the universal sense of justice, then you may acquit any defendant to whom this defense applies."[4][8]

The closing argument made by attorney Kairys is a forceful summary of the justifications for nullification, and, because it is unusual for a judge to permit such an argument to be made, it is presented here with only slight editorial alterations:

Now, I'd like to move on—and I am almost done now—to the second reason why I think this case is not simple and why I think these defendants should be acquitted. And that's jury nullification.

Now, the term "nullification" I think is a bad term. It's used to describe the power of a jury to acquit if they believe that a particular law is oppressive, or if they believe that a law is fair but to apply it in certain circumstances would be oppressive.

Now, the second situation might be something like the Boston Tea Party. No one would say that breaking into a ship shouldn't be criminal, shouldn't be a crime. But in those particular circumstances, should people be convicted of doing that? That's the question.

This power that jurors have is the reason why we have you jurors sitting there instead of computers. Because you are supposed to be the conscience of the community. You are supposed to decide if the law, as the Judge explains it to you, should be applied or if it should not. Nothing the Judge would say to you is inconsistent with this power.

It's not a request on our part that you show any disrespect for the law. It's part of the law.... It's as essential as reasonable doubt. It's the same kind of function.

... You decide, considering the circumstances of the case, should you brand the defendants as criminal. And it's very important in that regard, that you are only required to say guilty or not guilty. That's what people call the general verdict. You don't have to give reasons. You don't have to give specifics. You don't have to justify what you did; and if you say not guilty, it can't be reviewed by any Court.

... Are they deserving of the community's scorn—you being the community—or are they not deserving of the community's scorn? That's what the question is.

Now, the defendants have violated the law, and they've destroyed property, and they've explained to you how they did this, to preserve life and to preserve liberty.

Now, as I indicated in my opening statement, that may sound radical, but I submit that it's in the best American tradition. And it starts, of course, with George Washington, Thomas Jefferson, and Benjamin Franklin, all of whom violated the law to preserve life and liberty.

The Boston Tea Party, the people who did that violated the law to preserve life and liberty, and I explained some New Jersey Tea Parties that were here. One of them involving someone from Cumberland County [New Jersey] to whom there is a statue in a square in a town in Cumberland County. He became the Governor after he did that and after a jury refused to indict him or convict him.

The underground railroad was [a] violation of the Fugitive Slave Act and you've heard testimony that the Selective Service Act is slavery. Well the underground railroad was in clear violation of Federal law. It was also done in darkness, in the middle of the night. People didn't stand up and say, "Arrest me for it."

We talked about Rosa Parks who violated the law. She sat in the back of the bus to preserve life and liberty, the beginning of the Civil Rights Movement. We talked about Martin Luther King and Daniel Ellsberg, both of whom violated law to preserve life and liberty, all of whom are called radical, all of whom are condemned particularly in their own times.

[The next several paragraphs described the defendants on trial and their particular decision to commit an act of civil disobedience.]

The Vietnamese are not less deserving of our concern. And acquittal in this case will not undermine the society. It will enrich it, just as we are all proud and we all feel our society was enriched by those American jurors who refused to convict people for violating the Fugitive Slave Act. That was an act in which I think everybody in this courtroom can say, "I'm proud that Americans did that."

We also live in a time where our highest Government officials are accused—we don't know if they are guilty—of violating the law, not to preserve life or liberty, but for personal gain. Not to further the democratic process, but a perversion of the democratic process, for personal gains.

Our times reminded me of a quote of a woman named Mother Jones, you heard her birthday commemorated here. She was an organizer around 1900, a labor organizer.

She said in 1900: "I asked a man in prison once how he happened to be there, and he said he had stolen a pair of shoes. I told him if he had stolen a railroad, he would be a United States Senator."

I ask you to consider if this society cannot tolerate the tearing up of papers or the violation of law, how can it tolerate the napalming of a child? How can we reconcile that? Last Christmas [1972] we heard our Government proclaim Peace on Earth while they were bombing Bach Mai Hospital in Hanoi.

And I submit it's in the best tradition of this country, of every country, to resist this non-violently, not to stand by. And that's what these defendants did.

You must judge who went too far. Did the Government go too far in prosecuting the war? Did the defendants go too far? Did the F.B.I. go too far? And I think those kinds of judgments really require you to look at and in some sense judge yourself. The prosecution is asking you to publicly brand these people as criminals; and if that's done it will be done in your name. No one else's.

I urge you to say no to the prosecution, say no to this horrible war, say no to the F.B.I.'s manufacture of a crime, and say yes to some hope for the future. Say yes for life. Thank you.[49]

The jury acquitted the defendants on all counts.

## THE KANSAS JURY NULLIFICATION INSTRUCTION

An equally remarkable assertion of the validity of the jury nullification principle was the 1971 decision of the trial judges of Kansas to authorize judges to instruct their jurors that they have the power to consider the equity of the law as it applies to the case at hand. The following instruction was printed in the official book on jury instructions as one which could—at the discretion of the judge but not over the objections of the defendant—be given to juries in criminal cases:

> It is presumed that juries are the best judges of fact. Accordingly, you are the sole judges of the true facts in this case.
>
> I think it requires no explanation, however, that judges are presumed to be the best judges of the law. Accordingly, you must accept my instruction as being correct statements of the legal principles that generally apply in a case of the type you have heard.
>
> The order in which the instructions are given is no indication of their relative importance. You should not single out certain instructions and disregard others but should construe each one in the light of and in harmony with the others.
>
> These principles are intended to help you in reaching a fair result in this case. You should give them due respect. Moreover, justice will ordinarily be done by applying them as a whole to the facts which you find have been proven. You should do just that if, by so doing, you can do justice in this case.
>
> Even so, it is difficult to draft legal statements that are so exact that they are right for all conceivable circumstances. Accordingly, you are entitled to act upon your conscientious feeling about what is a fair result in this case, and acquit the defendant if you believe that justice requires such a result.
>
> Exercise your judgment without passion or prejudice, but with honesty and understanding. Give respectful regard to my statements of the law for what help they may be in arriving at a conscientious determination of justice in this case. That is your highest duty as a public body and as officers of this court.[50]

When they authorized the use of this instruction, the judges appended "Notes on Use" to act as an explanation of its meaning. These notes describe this instruction as a "more honest statement" of the jury's role than is the traditional instruction that orders the jurors to adhere rigidly to the judge's explanation of the law.

> Arguably, the above instruction should bring into play the underlying value of trial by jury; the application of community conscience. If extenuating circumstances make an otherwise culpable act excusable, a jury should feel empowered to so find. Community standards are more apt

to be applied if the jurors are told they are free to do what, overall, seems right to them.[51]

The Kansas instruction recognized that nullification is a mercy doctrine that allows the jury to suspend the law and acquit despite technical guilt under the letter of the law. After having been used only a few times, however, this nullification instruction was disapproved in 1973 by the Kansas Supreme Court.[52] Although recognizing the power of the jury to return any verdict whatsoever, the court said, "power is one thing and proper function and legal duty is another."[53] The court reviewed the reasoning of Justice Story and of the U.S. Supreme Court in *Sparf and Hansen* (1895), failing to recognize that the carefully phrased trial judge's instruction did not give the jury the right to change the law, but only to refuse to apply it in exceptional cases that warranted mercy. The crux of the Kansas opinion is contained in the following language:

> The administration of justice cannot be left to community standards or community conscience but must depend upon the protection afforded by the rule of law. The jury must be directed to apply the rules of law to the evidence even though it must do so in the face of public outcry and indignation. Disregard for the principles of established law creates anarchy and destroys the very protection which the law affords an accused.[54]

The court thus seems to have misunderstood the instruction entirely. It does not authorize the jury to proceed lawlessly, but instead tries to impress upon the jury, in as careful a fashion as possible, the jury's role as the ultimate decision-maker on the question of whether a general law can be equitably applied to the particular fact situation presented to the jury.

## THE U.S. SUPREME COURT AND JURY NULLIFICATION

The United States Supreme Court has not considered the jury nullification doctrine directly since the 1895 decision in *Sparf v. Hansen*, but the Court has in a number of recent cases recognized the jury's role as the community's conscience and has recognized its importance as a law-making body. In the 1968 case of *Duncan v. Louisiana*,[55] the Court ruled that the Constitution requires states to provide jury trials for all defendants facing a possible punishment of six months or more. The justification for this ruling was not that juries are more efficient or more reliable as finders of fact than judges, but rather that they bring to the controversy the community's common-sense approach to the matter and can mitigate the harshness of the law in appropriate cases. The key passage in Justice Byron R. White's majority opinion is reprinted below, because even though it is quite long it provides as persuasive an argument in favor of jury nullification as can be found anywhere:

> The guarantees of jury trial in the Federal and State Constitutions reflect a profound judgment about the way in which law should be enforced and justice administered. *A right to jury trial is granted to criminal defendants in order to prevent oppression by the Government.* Those who wrote our constitutions knew from history and experience that it was necessary to protect against unfounded criminal charges brought to eliminate enemies and against judges too responsive to the voice of higher authority. The framers of the constitutions strove to create an independent judiciary but insisted upon further protection against arbitrary action. *Providing an accused with the right to be tried by a jury of his peers gave him an inestimable safeguard against the corrupt or overzealous prosecutor and against the compliant, biased or eccentric judge.* If the defendant preferred the common-sense judgment of a jury to the more tutored but perhaps less sympathetic reaction of a single judge, he was to have it. Beyond this, the jury trial provisions in the Federal and State Constitutions reflect a fundamental decision about the exercise of official power—a reluctance to entrust plenary powers over the life and liberty of the citizen to one judge or to a group of judges. Fear of unchecked power, so typical of our State and Federal Government in other respects, found expression in the criminal law in *this insistence upon community participation in the determination of guilt or innocence.* The deep commitment of the Nation to the right of jury trial in serious criminal cases as a defense against arbitrary law enforcement qualifies for protection under the Due Process Clause of the Fourteenth Amendment, and must therefore be respected by the States.[56]

Justice White did not specifically say what the jury should be told about its obligations, but one cannot help but feel that he believed a fairly constituted jury might well have exercised the power of nullification in this case. Gary Duncan, a black 19-year-old, was given a 60-day jail sentence because he jostled a white youth after a discussion in which Duncan attempted to act as peacemaker between whites and blacks. A representative jury, containing blacks as well as whites, might well have refused to send Duncan to jail for this act.

A second Supreme Court decision, *Witherspoon v. Illinois* (1968),[57] rendered two weeks after *Duncan*, confirmed the notion that the Court is conscious of the jury's political role and is willing to strengthen that role. Witherspoon was sentenced to death by a jury from which all persons who harbored any doubt over imposing the death penalty were excluded. The procedure followed an Illinois statute that said the judge should excuse every juror who states that "he has conscientious scruples against capital punishment or that he is opposed to the same."[58] The statute was clearly designed to ensure that juries in capital cases would return the death penalty as often as possible.

The Court declared this procedure unconstitutional as a violation of Witherspoon's right to due process of law, because the court had inpaneled a "hanging jury" and had thus "stacked the deck" against the defendant.[59] The Court must feel that it is the essence of a jury trial that a jury be able to exercise its power of nullification, subject of course to each juror's willingness at least to pay respectful attention to the law as ordained by the legislature and as explained by the court. The most telling clue to the Supreme Court's view of the jury's role is contained in the following passage from *Witherspoon*:

> [O]ne of the most important functions any jury can perform in making such a selection [between life and death] is to maintain a link between contemporary community values and the penal system—a link without which the determination of punishment could hardly reflect "the evolving standards of decency that mark the progress of a maturing society."[60]

If the jury is to maintain this link, it must be given the authority to reject judicial instructions when they conflict with the values of the community. Justice Hugo Black, in a dissenting opinion, criticized the Court for ignoring the decision made by the Illinois Legislature that a jury in a capital case should be biased toward capital punishment, and argued that the jury should not be restructured to alter the legislature's decision. It is conceivable that the majority did mistakenly fail to consider the intent of the Illinois Legislature, but it is much more likely that they believed it to be an unconstitutional act for a legislature to deprive a jury of its power to nullify, because such a power is inherent in the American concept of a jury. The Court tempered the jury's power of nullification by demanding that each juror be willing to say that he or she would at least consider imposing the penalty desired by the legislature and by allowing the exclusion of those prospective jurors who had formulated a firm and unyielding determination to disobey the law. Only Justice William O. Douglas would go one step further and say that even those persons unalterably opposed to the death penalty should be allowed to participate in the determination of whether the death penalty should be imposed.[61]

Three years after *Witherspoon*, in 1971, the Supreme Court acknowledged the importance of jury nullification as a force in shaping the law, in a case challenging the constitutionality of the death penalty. In explaining why many states left the question whether to impose the death penalty to the jury, the Court noted that the juries were making such decisions anyway, by refusing to convict in cases with sympathetic defendants or mitigating circumstances:

> In order to meet the problem of jury nullification, legislatures did not try, as before, to refine further the definition of capital homicides. Instead they adopted the method of forthrightly granting juries discretion which they had been exercising in fact.[62]

Still more recently, in 1974, the Court once again acknowledged the role of the jury as representing the community's conscience by stating that it was appropriate to allow the jurors to decide—based solely on their individual views—what constitutes the contemporary community standards of obscenity.[63]

Rather than confining the jury to a strait-jacket fact-finding role, the Supreme Court has thus in recent years specifically acknowledged the role of the jury as a repository of community wisdom. The jury brings community standards to bear on any number of legal questions, and the act of refusing to convict some defendants in special circumstances is consistent with that role.

## CRIMES OF CONSCIENCE AND CRIMES OF VIOLENCE

Some people who are sympathetic toward the idea of telling a jury it has the right to nullify in crimes of conscience recoil at the idea of giving the same instruction in a case involving a crime of violence. Certainly the need for the instruction seems more evident in crimes of conscience, and it is in this realm that most of the debate over jury nullification has taken place. In a case of conscience, the defendant is being prosecuted because she or he has protested against the policy of the state. The victims of the crime are the persons who are in power at the time and who are making policy for the government. Cases of seditious libel and draft card burning are obvious examples. The jury stands between the policy-makers and the defendant and consequently can repudiate the state's policy with a verdict of acquittal.

Those who argue against the instruction being given in a crime of violence point to southern juries that have acquitted white defendants despite strong evidence that the defendants killed black persons. This is a troubling example, but it is not ultimately persuasive, because the line between crimes of conscience and crimes of violence cannot be neatly drawn in advance *and is really a line that must be drawn by the jury in deciding whether mitigating factors justify the defendant's actions.*

Two direct answers can be offered to the example of southern juries. First, southern juries acquit white defendants even without being told they have the power to do so, and no evidence exists that they would acquit more often if they were explicitly told they had the power. The passage of Fox's Libel Law in 1792 did not, for instance, make it significantly more difficult for the English Government to obtain criminal convictions.[64] Second the solution to the problem of southern juries is not to deprive them of their power to nullify but to make them more representative of the community, i.e., to have more blacks on the jury rolls.

In a non-southern context, juries will not ordinarily be tempted to exercise their power to nullify the law in a crime of violence. The jury is unlikely to ignore the law and the judge's instructions, because the people—and the jurors as representatives of the people— are victims of these crimes. Sometimes, however, the power to nullify does become important with regard to a crime of violence. Juries have recurringly nullified the law by acquitting a defendant charged with murder when the evidence shows that she or he ended the life of a relative or patient whose suffering from an incurable illness had become unendurable. Most lawyers and judges have therefore recognized that the concept of jury nullification should apply to crimes of violence if it applies at all, as is evidenced by *Sparf and Hansen, Duncan, Witherspoon, Moylan, Simpson, Dougherty,* and *Camden 28*, all involving acts of violence.

## CONCLUSION

After an earlier version of this Postscript was published in *The Center Magazine*,[65] a publication of the Center for the Study of Democratic Institutions in Santa Barbara, California, the *American Bar Association Journal* ran a lead editorial denouncing the arguments presented here. Before summarizing the Postscript, it seems appropriate to present that editorial in its entirety:

### Nihilism at Santa Barbara

The work of institutions such as the Center for the Study of Democratic Institutions at Santa Barbara certainly deserves to be encouraged. The nation needs organizations, not connected with either local or national government, in which impartial and objective research is done on the manner in which our governments are operating. Now and then, however, proposals are made that are not only on the silly side but also dangerous to the fundamental principles on which our system of government is based.

This is illustrated by a position taken by Jon M. Van Dyke, a visiting fellow at the center, in a discussion on "The Jury as a Political Institution." According to the center's magazine of July, 1970, Professor Van Dyke urged that jurors be given full authority to disregard the instructions of the judge as to what the law is, stating: "We should tell the jurors that they have the power to acquit, even if the accused's activities have violated the law as it is articulated by the trial judge."

Certainly no principle of law could survive if a jury were free to disregard it, substituting only the jury's own sense, which might be rational or emotional, of what fairness and justice require. As a participant in the same panel at which Professor Van Dyke made his proposal, Abe Fortas, the former United States Supreme Court Justice, put his finger on the vice of the proposal by pointing out:

> In effect, it is an attack upon law itself. In effect, it is an assertion of the right of the individual to determine for himself what the standard of his conduct shall be. What is being proposed is not merely that jurors should be given the power to determine what is the law, but that they should be instructed that they may acquit a defendant even though they believe that he did something the law forbids. This goes to the heart of our society because it says that this shall not be a society in which there are general rules of law and conduct which apply to everybody and to which everybody is held accountable.

Another participant, Judge Simon H. Rifkind, put the finishing touch to the argument.

> Mr. Van Dyke asks why, if I am in favor of some kind of departures by the jury, I am afraid to make that universal. The answer is that one can have a fine musical composition with variations, but if you had a composition made up entirely of variations you would have discord. His proposal would create law-less society, not a lawless society, but a law-less society, a society without law, without regulations. That is a monstrosity. No such society has ever existed or ever will exist.[66]

This editorial misunderstands the argument. Persons supporting jury nullification do not favor an abandonment of law, or a return to the law of the jungle. Instead they favor informing the jury that it is their responsibility—in addition to reviewing the evidence and deciding what happened—to decide whether it is appropriate to enforce the law as to the defendant on trial in their case.

Whenever a criminal act occurs, the police officer investigating the matter has discretion whether to make an arrest. If an arrest is made, the prosecutor has discretion to bring the matter to court or not. The trial judge then has discretion to allow the matter to proceed to trial or not. All these public officials know of their discretion and usually use it with the understanding that they are acting for the public. Jurors are also acting on behalf of the public, and they also have discretion in deciding whether to convict the accused. The jurors, however, frequently do not know they have this discretion, and hence in many cases the accused is deprived of an important safeguard.

The added safeguard of jury discretion is particularly important in three situations: (1) the prosecutor may be overzealous in bringing a prosecution because a particularly prominent or controversial person is involved or because of some personal relationship he or she has to one of the parties; (2) the trial judge may not be able to view the case objectively because of some personal eccentricity or deep-seated bias,[6][7] and (3) the government may be the victim of the crime in a way that makes it impossible for the prosecutor not to prosecute or for the judge to dismiss the matter.

In each of these three situations, but most particularly in the third, the jury can act mercifully when the police officer, the prosecutor, and judge are unable to be merciful, because the jury will not be called to answer for its acts. As Judge Learned Hand put it:

> [T]he institution of trial by jury—especially in criminal cases—has its hold upon public favor chiefly for two reasons. The individual can forfeit his liberty—to say nothing of his life—only at the hands of those who, unlike any official, are in no wise accountable, directly or indirectly, for what they do, and who at once separate and melt anonymously in the community from which they came. Moreover, since if they acquit their verdict is final, *no one is likely to suffer of whose conduct they do not morally disapprove*; and *this introduces a slack into the enforcement of law, tempering its rigor by the mollifying influence of current ethical conventions*. A trial by any jury, however small, preserves both these fundamental elements and a trial by a judge preserves neither, at least to anything like the same degree.[68]

Some jurors are aware of their power to nullify or mitigate the law and others act unconsciously to reach compromises that the law permits but does not encourage. Many jurors are not aware of this power, however, and do not review an accusation to decide whether it is appropriate to apply the law to the accused before them. The defendant is then inadequately protected against injustice.

## NOTES

1. *New York Times*, Sept. 26, 1969, p. 25 (city ed.); Judge Hoffman's ruling on this issue was upheld in *United States v. Dellinger*, 472 F.2d 340, 408 (7th Cir. 1972).

2. *California Jury Instructions, Criminal* (CALJIC), No. 1, p. 28.

3. Harry Kalven, Jr., and Hans Zeisel, *The American Jury* (Boston: Little, Brown, 1966), pp. 55-347.

4. For general reference see Scheflin, "Jury Nullification: The Right to Say No," *Southern California Law Review* 45 (1972): 168; Van Dyke, "The Jury as a Political Institution," *Catholic Lawyer* 16 (1970): 224; Sax, "Conscience and Anarchy: The Prosecution of War Resisters," *Yale Review* 57 (1968): 481; Howe, "Juries as Judges of Criminal Law," *Harvard Law Review* 52 (1939): 582.

5. See *Duncan v. Louisiana*, 391 U.S. 145, 155-56 (1968), discussed below.

6. *California Jury Instructions*, note 2, above.

7. Charles M. Andrews, *The Colonial Period of American History*, (New Haven: Yale University Press, 1934) Vol. 4, pp. 140ff., 152ff., 222-27, 251ff. One of the grievances listed in the Declaration of Independence is the denial of the right of trial by jury in certain cases, an apparent reference to, among other things, the courts of vice-admiralty. See *ibid.*, p. 270, and see generally Lloyd E. Moore, *The Jury: Tool of Kings, Palladium of Liberty* (Cincinnati: W.H. Anderson Co., 1973) pp. 107-13.

8. James Alexander, ed., *A Brief Narration of the Case and Trial of John Peter Zenger* (Cambridge, Mass.: Harvard University Press, 1963), p. 78.

9. C.F. Adams, ed., *The Works of John Adams* (Boston: Little and Brown, 1850) Vol. 2, pp. 253-55 (emphasis added).

10. *Georgia v. Brailsford*, 3 U.S. (3 Dall.) 1, 4 (1794) (emphasis added).

11. *Bingham v. Cabot*, 3 U.S. (3 Dall.) 18, 33 (1795).

12. 1 Stat. 596 (1798).

13. *The Dean of St. Asaph's Case*, 21 Howell's State Trials 847, 870 (1783).

14. See *Sparf and Hansen v. United States*, 156 U.S. 51, 135 (1895) (Gray, J., dissenting).

15. *United States v. Battiste*, 24 F. Cas. 1042, 1043 (No. 14,545) (C.C.D. Mass. 1835).

16. *United States v. Morris*, 26 F. Cas. 1323, 1331 (No. 15,815) (C.C.D. Mass. 1851).

17. *Ibid.*

18. *Ibid.*, p. 1334.

19. 156 U.S. 51.

20. *Ibid.*, pp. 61-62 n.1.

21. *Ibid.*, p. 101.

22. Georgia's constitution also preserves the right of jury nullification ("On the trial of all criminal cases the jury shall be the judges of the law and the facts, and shall give a general verdict of 'guilty' or 'not guilty.' "... Art. I, sec. 2-201), but this provision has been interpreted otherwise by the courts of Georgia. See *Brown v. State*, 40 Ga. 689 (1870).

23. Art. I, sec. 19.

24. *Holliday v. State*, 254 Ind. 85, 257 N.E.2d 679 (1970).

25. *Pritchard v. State*, 248 Ind. 566, 230 N.E.2d 416, 421 (1967) (emphasis added).

26. Art. 15, sec. 5.

27. *Wyley v. Warden*, 372 F.2d 742, 743 n.1 (4th Cir. 1967).

28. Dennis, "Maryland's Antique Constitutional Thorn," *University of Pennsylvania Law Review* 92 (1943): 39.

29. *Slansky v. State*, 192 Md. 94, 108, 63 A.2d 599, 606 (1949); *Giles v. State*, 229 Md. 370, 384-85, 183 A.2d 359, 366, *appeal dismissed* (for want of a federal question), 372 U.S. 967 (1963). Cf. *Brady v. Maryland*, 373 U.S. 83 (1963).

30. Kalven and Zeisel, *The American Jury*, pp. 286-312.

31. 417 F.2d 1002 (4th Cir. 1969).

32. *Ibid.*, p. 1006.

33. *Ibid.*

34. 460 F.2d 515 (9th Cir. 1972).

35. *Ibid.*, p. 519.

36. *Ibid.*

37. 416 F.2d 165 (1st Cir. 1969).

38. Jessica Mitford, *The Trial of Dr. Spock* (New York: Knopf, 1970), p. 232.

39. 473 F.2d 1113 (D.C.Cir. 1972).

40. *Ibid.*, p. 1130.

41. *Ibid.*, p. 1135.

42. *Ibid.*

43. *Ibid.*, p. 1134.

44. *Ibid.*, p. 1136.

45. *Ibid.*, p. 1143.

46. *Ibid.* p. 1142 (emphasis added). The U.S. Court of Appeals for the Seventh Circuit agreed with the result reached in the *Moylan, Simpson,* and *Dougherty* cases in *United States v. Dellinger*, 472 F.2d 340, 408 (7th Cir. 1972).

47. *United States v. Anderson et al.*, Crim. No. 602-71 (D.N.J. 1973).

48. *Ibid.*, Transcript, p. 8729.

49. *Ibid.*, pp. 8386-94.

50. *Pattern Instructions for Kansas* 51.03 (1971), pp. 36-37, as quoted in Frederick Woleslagel, *Jury* (Reno, Nevada: National College of the State Judiciary, 1973), pp. 112-13.

51. *Ibid.*, p. 113.

52. *State v. McClanahan*, 212 Kan. 208, 510 P.2d 153 (1973).

53. *Ibid.*, p. 158.

54. *Ibid.*, p. 159.

55. 391 U.S. 145.

56. *Ibid.*, pp. 155-56 (emphasis added) (see also p. 8, above).

57. 391 U.S. 510.

58. *Ibid.*, p. 512, quoting Ill. Rev. Stat., ch. 38, sec. 115-4(d) (Supp. 1967).

59. *Ibid.*, p. 523.

60. *Ibid.*, p. 519 n.15.

61. See generally Note, "Trial by Jury in Criminal Cases," *Columbia Law Review* 69 (1969): 419-32.

62. *McGautha v. California*, 402 U.S. 183, 199 (1971).

63. *Jenkins v. Georgia*, 418 U.S. 153 (1974).

64. See Sax, "Conscience and Anarchy," pp. 491-92.

65. Van Dyke, "The Jury as a Political Institution," *Center Magazine* 3

(March 1970): 17; excerpts from a discussion of the article in which former Justice Abe Fortas and former federal district judge Simon H. Rifkind participated appeared in "Follow-Up/The Jury," *Center Magazine* 3 (July 1970): 59-68.

66. *American Bar Association Journal*, 57 (1971): 999. Reprinted with the permission of the American Bar Association Journal.

67. See references to these two problems in the quote from *Duncan*, above, at footnote 56.

68. *United States v. Adams*, 126 F.2d 774, 775-76 (2d Cir. 1942) (emphasis added).

# Appendixes

*Part I*

**Jury Selection Methods
in the United States**

# Appendix A:
# Trial Juries

| State | Selection Process | Source(s) of Names | Age Requirements | Other Special Requirements |
|---|---|---|---|---|
| Alabama | Discretion, exercised by a 3-member citizen jury commission. | List of voters, tax rolls, telephone directories, city directories, civic organizations. | 21-65 | "Esteemed in their community for their integrity, good character, and sound judgment." Must read English or be a householder (Ala. Code, Title 30, sec. 21). |
| Alaska | Random selection. | List of actual voters, tax rolls, list of persons with trapping, hunting, and fishing licenses, and sometimes drivers' license lists. | 19- | None |
| Arizona | Random selection. | List of registered voters. | 18- | None |
| Arkansas | Discretion exercised by a 3 to 12 member citizen jury commission appointed by a circuit judge. | List of registered voters. | 18- | "Good character or approved integrity," "sound judgment or reasonable information," "good behavior" (Ark. Stat., sec. 39-102). |
| California | Random selection. | List of registered voters, supplemented in some counties with the drivers' license lists. | 18- | "Fair character and approved integrity," "sound judgment" (C.C.P., sec. 205). |
| Colorado | Random selection (Uniform Jury Selection Act) | Registered voters lists, lists of drivers' licenses, city directories. | 18- | None |
| Connecticut | Discretion, exercised by town civil servants. | List of registered voters and city directories. | 21- | "Esteemed in their community as persons of good character, approved integrity, sound judgment and fair education" (Conn. Stat., sec. 51-217). |
| Delaware | Random selection, but from districts that are not uniform, and favor rural areas over urban areas. | List of registered voters; volunteers are accepted. | 18- | "Sober and judicious" (10 Del. C., sec. 4505). |
| District of Columbia (the federal system) | Random selection. | List of registered voters. | 18- | None |
| Florida | Discretion, exercised by county commissioner or 2-citizen jury commissions. (In Dade County [Miami] | No particular source. | 18- | "Law abiding citizens of approved integrity, good character, sound judgment and intelligence" (Fla. Stat. Ann., sec. 40.01). |

*(Va. Code Ann., sec. 59-106 [1965]).*

...selection, including the tax digest and personal acquaintances.

| State | Selection method | Age | Source lists | Qualifications |
|---|---|---|---|---|
| | | | | None |
| Hawaii | sion, appointed by a judge. Random selection. | 18- | Lists of registered voters, plus optional supplemental lists, including taxpayers' and drivers' license lists. In Honolulu, the voter list is supplemented with a small selection from the telephone book. | None |
| Idaho | Random selection (Uniform Jury Selection Act). | 18- | Registered voters list, drivers' license lists, electric utility's list. | None |
| Illinois | Random selection. | 18- | List of registered voters. | "Of fair character, of approved integrity, of sound judgment, well-informed" (*Ill. Rev. Stat.*, Ch. 78, sec. 2 [1965]). |
| Indiana | Random selection. | 18- | List of registered voters, occasionally supplemented by the tax rolls. The legislature passed the Uniform Jury Selection Act (which required supplementation) for Lake County (Gary) in 1973, but the state supreme court interpreted the statute to eliminate the requirement of supplementation. | Jurors must be free-holders (*Ind. Stat. Ann.*, sec. 4-7115 [1968]), "good repute and honesty" (*Ind. Stat. Ann.*, sec. 4-7101). |
| Iowa | Random selection. | 18- | List of actual voters. | "Good moral character, sound judgment" (*Iowa Code Ann.*, sec. 607.1). |
| Kansas | Random selection. | 18- | Lists of registered voters or state census rolls, or both. | None |
| Kentucky | Discretion, exercised by a 3-member citizens' jury commission appointed by a judge. | 18- | List of registered voters and tax lists. | "Sober, temperate, discreet, and of sound demeanor" (*Ken. Rev. Stat.*, sec. 29.025). |
| Louisiana | Discretion, exercised by a 5-member citizen jury commission appointed by a judge. (In Orleans Parish, they are appointed by the governor.) | 18- | No particular source. | None |
| Maine | Random selection. | 18- | List of registered voters. | None |
| Maryland | Random selection. | 18- | List of registered voters. | None |

| State | Selection Process | Source(s) of Names | Age Requirements | Other Special Requirements |
|---|---|---|---|---|
| Massachusetts | Discretion, exercised by town officials and county officials followed by personal interviews. | Police census lists. | 18-70 | "Sound judgment," "good moral character" (*Mass. Gen. Laws. Ann.*, Ch. 234, sec. 4 [Supp. 1972]). |
| Michigan | Random selection. | List of registered voters. | 18- | None |
| Minnesota | Random selection. | List of registered voters and sometimes the city directory. | 18- | None |
| Mississippi | Random selection. | Lists of registered voters. | 21- | None |
| Missouri | Random selection in the major cities, discretion in the less populated counties. | List of registered voters, tax rolls, other sources. | 21- | "Sober and intelligent, of good reputation" (*Vernon's Ann. Mo. Stat.*, sec. 494.010). |
| Montana | Random selection. | Tax rolls. | 18- | None |
| Nebraska | Random selection. | List of actual or registered voters. | 21-70 | "Of fair character, of approved integrity, well-informed . . . of sound mind and discretion" (*Neb. Stat*, sec. 25-1601). |
| Nevada | Random selection. | List of registered voters, sometimes supplemented. | 18- | None |
| New Hampshire | Discretion, exercised by town selectmen. | No particular sources. | 18- | None |
| New Jersey | Random selection. | List of registered voters. | 21-75 | "Impartial," "best qualified" (*N.J.S.A.*, sec. 2A:75-2). |
| New Mexico | Random selection. | List of registered voters. | 18- | None |
| New York | A permanent jury list is maintained, added to by Random Selection, followed by a personal interview. | Lists of registered voters, telephone books, tax rolls, and other sources. Volunteers are accepted. | (21-75 in counties with fewer than 100,000 and New York City; 21-72 elsewhere). | "Intelligent, of sound mind and good character; well-informed" (*Judiciary Law.*, sec. 596). |
| North Carolina | Discretion, exercised by a 3-member citizen jury commis- | Lists of registered voters and tax rolls. | 18- | None |

| | Jury Selection Act). | licenses. | | |
|---|---|---|---|---|
| Ohio | Random selection, followed by personal interviews conducted by a 2-member citizen jury commission, appointed by judges and representing the 2 major political parties. | List of registered voters. | 18- | None |
| Oklahoma | Discretion, exercised by a jury commission composed of civil servants, *or*—at the discretion of the presiding judge—random selection. Oklahoma and Tulsa counties now both select randomly from the voter list. | List of registered voters. | 18- | "Sound mind and discretion," "good moral character" (*Okla. Stat.*, sec. 38-28). |
| Oregon | Random selection. | List of registered voters. (Statute also authorizes use of tax lists.) | 18- | "Most competent" (*Ore. Rev. Stat.*, sec. 10.110). |
| Pennsylvania | Random selection, followed (in Philadelphia) by some personal interviews. | List of registered voters. | 18- | "Mentally fit and morally strong" (*Pa. Stat.*, sec. 1252). "Sober, intelligent and judicious" (17 *Penn. Stat.*, sec. 942). |
| Rhode Island | Random selection, followed by personal interviews. | List of registered voters. | 21- | "Good moral character," "sound judgment" (*Gen. Law. R.I.*, sec. 9.9-23). |
| South Carolina | Discretion, exercised by a jury commission composed of civil servants. | List of registered voters. | 21-65 | "Good moral character," "sound judgment" (*S.C. Code*, sec. 38-52). |
| South Dakota | Random selection. | List of registered voters. | 18-70 | None |
| Tennessee | Discretion, exercised by a jury commission composed of civil servants. | Various lists. | 18- | "Upright and intelligent persons known for their integrity, fair character and sound judgment" (*Tenn. Code Ann.*, sec. 22-228). |
| Texas | Random selection. | List of registered voters. | 18- | "Of good moral character, of sound judgment, well-informed" (*V. Ann. Civ. St.*, Art. 2110). |
| Utah | Random selection. | List of registered voters. | 21- | "Sound mind and discretion," "must be a taxpayer" (*Utah Code Ann.*, 78-46-8). |

| State | Selection Process | Source(s) of Names | Age Requirements | Other Special Requirements |
|---|---|---|---|---|
| Vermont | Discretion, exercised by town officials. | Various lists. | 18- | "Mentally, morally and physically qualified" (*Vt. Stat.*, sec. 12-1401). |
| Virginia | Discretion, exercised by 2 to 9 member citizen jury commission, appointed by a judge. Counties can use a random selection method at the discretion of the chief judge of the circuit court. | No particular sources. | 18- | "Well qualified" (*Code Va.*, sec. 8-208.10). |
| Washington | Random selection. | List of registered voters. | 18- | Must be a taxpayer (Sec. 1, ch. 57, *Laws of 1911*, as amended, 1975). |
| West Virginia | Discretion, exercised by a 2-member citizen jury commission (representing the 2 major political parties). | No particular sources. | 18-65 | "Sound judgment," "good moral character." Paupers are excluded. (*W. Vir. Code*, ch. 52, art 1, sec. 24 [Michie 1966].) |
| Wisconsin | Random selection, followed by personal interviews conducted by a 3-member citizen jury commission. | List of registered voters. | 18- | "Esteemed in their community as of good character and sound judgment" (*Wisc. Stat.*, sec. 225.01). |
| Wyoming | Random selection. | List of registered voters. | 18-72 | "Competent and well-qualified" (*Wyo. Stat.*, sec. 1-83). |
| The Federal Courts | Random selection. | List of registered voters. | 18- | None |

# Appendix B:
# Grand Juries

| State | Grand Jury Selection Process | Size of Grand Jury | Number of Grand Jurors Needed to Indict | Scope of Grand Jury Activities | Is a grand jury indictment essential for all felony prosecutions (unless waived by the accused)? |
|---|---|---|---|---|---|
| Federal Courts | Random selection from registered voters followed by questioning by a judge and the U.S. Attorney. | 23 | 12 | Criminal indictments and investigation into organized crime and conspiratorial criminal activity. | Yes (all with a potential sentence of more than a year) |
| Alabama | Discretion, exercised by a 3-member citizen jury commission. | 18 | 12 | Criminal indictments and investigations of local governmental affairs. | Yes |
| Alaska | Random selection from the lists of actual voters, tax rolls, and lists of trapping, hunting, and fishing licenses. | 12-18 | Majority | Criminal indictments and investigations of local government affairs. | Yes |
| Arizona | Randomly selected from registered voter lists then questioned and selected by judges. Statute authorizes statewide grand juries. | 12-16 (16 in Mariposa County [Phoenix]) | 9 | Criminal indictments. | No |
| Arkansas | Discretion exercised by a 3 to 12 member citizen commission appointed by a circuit judge. | 16 | 12 | Criminal indictments and investigations of local governmental affairs. | Yes |
| California | Discretion exercised by the superior court judges, except in a few counties, including San Francisco, where the selection is random from the list of registered voters. | 19 in all counties except Los Angeles, where it is 23. | 12/19-14/23 | Investigates local governmental affairs and considers indictments in fewer than 5 percent of all felony matters. Serves one year. | No |
| Colorado | Random selection from the list of registered voters, driver's license lists and city directories, followed by questioning | Usually 12, occasionally as large as 23. | 9/12-12/23 | Investigate controversial crimes, like police shootings and governmental corruption. | No |

| | | | | | |
|---|---|---|---|---|---|
| | Discretion, exercised by the county sheriff. | 18 | 12 | All crimes with sentence of death or life imprisonment, occasional investigations. | Yes (but only for crimes with a potential sentence of death or life imprisonment). |
| Delaware | Discretion, exercised by jury commissioners who pick grand jurors according to geographical districts. | 10-15 | 7/10-9/15 | Criminal indictments, investigations; serves for one year. | Yes (with certain constitutional and statutory exceptions). |
| District of Columbia | Random selection from the list of registered voters, followed by questioning by a judge and sometimes by the U.S. Attorney. | 23 | 12 | Criminal indictments. Serves at least 2 months. Frequently 9 or 10 are operating at once. | Yes (all crimes with a potential sentence of a year or more). |
| Florida | Discretion, exercised by county commissions or jury commission (appointed by governor). Statewide grand juries can be impaneled. | 15-18 | 12 | Criminal indictments, investigations of county offices. | Capital offenses only. |
| Georgia | Discretion, exercised by commissioners, appointed by judge. | 16-23 | Majority | Criminal indictments, investigations of local government affairs, inspections; sets salary for certain jobs. | Yes |
| Hawaii | Random selection from the list of registered voters, which may be supplemented with some names from other lists. | 18-23 | 12 | Criminal indictments. | No. |
| Idaho | Random selection from registered voter list, utility list, and drivers' license list. | 16 | 12 | Public offenses. | No. |
| Illinois | Usually, random selection from the registered voter list, followed by questioning about the time involved. | 23 (20 on supplemental panel). | 12 | Criminal indictments and investigations of official misconduct. | Yes |

| State | Grand Jury Selection Process | Size of Grand Jury | Number of Grand Jurors Needed to Indict | Scope of Grand Jury Activities | Is a grand jury indictment essential for all felony prosecutions (unless waived by the accused)? |
|---|---|---|---|---|---|
| Indiana | Random selection from the registered voter list, followed by questioning by a judge and prosecutor for bias and time. | 6 | 5 | Criminal indictments (major felony cases). | No |
| Iowa | Random selection from the list of actual voters. | 7 | 5 | Criminal indictments, investigations of prisons, conduct of public officials, highways. | Yes |
| Kansas | Random selection from the list of registered voters and/or census list. | 15 | 12 | All public offenses. | No |
| Kentucky | Discretion, exercised by a 3-member citizen commission appointed by a judge. | 12 | 9 | Criminal indictments. | Yes |
| Louisiana | Discretion, exercised by citizen jury commission. | 12 | 9 | Criminal indictments. | Capital offenses only. |
| Maine | Random selection from voter registration lists followed by questioning by a judge and the district attorney. | 13-23 | 12 | Criminal indictments. In Cumberland County (Portland), the grand jury serves for one year and meets for 5-10 days three times a year. | Yes |
| Maryland | Random selection from voter registration lists screened to see who can spare the time. | 23 | 12 | Criminal indictments. Also inspects government agencies. Meets every day for four months. | No |
| Massachusetts | 35 names are randomly drawn from the trial jury list, which is assembled by discretion, then a judge selects 23 persons. | 23 | 12 | Criminal indictments. | Yes |
| Michigan | Random selection from the list of registered voters. | 13-17 (Also 1 person [judge] | 9 | Criminal indictments (infrequently) and investigations. | No |

| | | | | | |
|---|---|---|---|---|---|
| | ...from the list of registered voters (separate list maintained). | 16-23 | 16 | Criminal indictments, investigations of prisons and public officials. | No |
| Mississippi | Discretion, exercised by the local boards of supervisors. | 15-20 | 12 | Criminal indictments and investigations of local governmental affairs. | No |
| Missouri | Randomly selected names are screened carefully by the judges who make the final selection. | 12 | 9 | Criminal indictments, investigations, inspections, inquiries into government fiscal matters. | No |
| Montana | Random selection from tax rolls. | 11 | 10 | Criminal indictments, investigations, public officials, prisons. | No |
| Nebraska | Random selection of 40 names from the list of actual or registered voters, and from that list of 40, 16 are picked by the judge and jury commissioner. | 16 | 12 | Criminal indictments, county jail. | No |
| Nevada | 36 persons are nominated by the county commissioners and one judge; 17 are then drawn by lot. | 17 | 12 | Criminal indictments and investigations of local governmental affairs. | No |
| New Hampshire | Random selection from the trial jury list, which is assembled by the discretion of town officials. | 23 | 12 | Criminal indictments and investigations of subversive activities. Meets about 4 days every 2-3 months. | Yes |
| New Jersey | Random selection from the list of registered voters. Statute authorizes statewide grand juries.[a] | 23 | 12 | Criminal indictments, investigations. | Yes |
| New Mexico | Random selection from the voter registration list followed by questioning by a judge. | 12 | 8 | Criminal indictments, investigations. In Bernalillo County (Albuquerque), grand juries meet once a week for a 6-month term. Elsewhere, they are called infrequently. | No |

| State | Grand Jury Selection Process | Size of Grand Jury | Number of Grand Jurors Needed to Indict | Scope of Grand Jury Activities | Is a grand jury indictment essential for all felony prosecution (unless waived by the accused)? |
|---|---|---|---|---|---|
| New York | Specially selected from persons who have been qualified as trial jurors and who pass a police investigation. | 16-23 | 12 | Criminal indictments, investigations into prisons and misconduct of public officials. Serves for one month. | Yes |
| North Carolina | Discretion, exercised by a 3-member citizen jury commission, appointed by 3 local officials. | 9 | Majority | Criminal indictments, inspections. | Yes |
| North Dakota | Random selection from lists of actual voters and holders of drivers' licenses. | 8-11 | 6 | Criminal indictments, prisons, public officials. Only rarely assembled. | No |
| Ohio | Random selection from the registered voter list followed by questioning. | 9 | 7 | Criminal indictments. | Yes |
| Oklahoma | Varies by county. | 12 | 9 | Criminal indictments and investigations of local governmental affairs. Can be called by petition of citizens. | No |
| Oregon | Random selection from list of registered voters. | 7 | 5 | Criminal indictments and investigations of public prisons and offices pertaining to courts of justice. | No |
| Pennsylvania | Selected from voter registration lists, and sometimes interviewed by jury clerk, and jury masters. | 15-23 | 12 | Criminal indictments and investigations. | Counties are authorized to abolish indicting grand juries and many have done so. |
| Rhode Island | Random selection from voter registration list followed by an interview. Statewide grand juries are authorized. | 13-23 | 12 | Criminal indictments. | Only for offenses punishable by death or life imprisonment. |

| State | Selection | | | Function | |
|---|---|---|---|---|---|
| South Carolina | Discretion, exercised by a jury commission composed of civil servants. | 18 | 12 | Criminal indictments. | Yes |
| South Dakota | Random selection from the list of registered voters. | 8 | 5 | Criminal indictments, investigations of governmental misconduct. | No |
| Tennessee | Randomly selected from the trial jury lists which are compiled by jury commissioners without guidelines. Same person may serve as foreperson for several years. | 13 | 12 | Criminal indictments and investigations of prisons, elections, and governmental affairs. | Yes |
| Texas | Discretion exercised by citizen jury commissioners, appointed by a judge. | 12 | 9 | Criminal indictments, investigations. | Yes |
| Utah | Random selection from voter registration list; potential grand jurors are screened by the judges. | 7 | 5 | Criminal indictments, investigations, inspections (public prisons, willful and corrupt misconduct of public officials). | No |
| Vermont | Jury commissioners select names. | 18 | 12 | Criminal indictments. | Only for offenses punishable by death or life imprisonment. |
| Virginia | Judges choose names. | 5-7 | 4 | Criminal indictments. | Yes |
| Washington | Random selection from voter registration list. | 12-18; 17-18 in King County (Seattle) | 3/4 | Criminal indictments and investigations of governmental affairs. | No |
| West Virginia | Discretion, exercised by a 2-member citizen jury commission (representing the 2 major political parties). | 16 | 12 | Criminal indictments. | Yes |
| Wisconsin | Names selected by jury commissioners and then screened by the judges. In Milwaukee County, random selection from the registered voter list. | 17 | 12 | Criminal indictments. | No |

| State | Grand Jury Selection Process | Size of Grand Jury | Number of Grand Jurors Needed to Indict | Scope of Grand Jury Activities | Is a grand jury indictment essential for all felony prosecutions (unless waived by the accused)? |
|---|---|---|---|---|---|
| Wyoming | Random selection from the voter registration list. Statewide grand juries can be assembled. | 12-16 | 9 | Criminal indictments, inspections, investigations. | No |

aThe U.S. Court of Appeals for the Third Circuit, in *Zicarelli v. New Jersey*, said that the use of statewide grand juries in New Jersey was unconstitutional because it deprived defendants of their right to a grand jury selected from the local vicinity. *New York Times*, Nov. 21, 1975, pp. 1, 45 (city ed.).

# Appendix C:
# Statutory Excuses

| | *Alabama* | *Alaska* | *Arizona* | *Arkansas* | *California* | *Colorado* |
|---|---|---|---|---|---|---|
| Attorneys | X | X | | X | | |
| Doctors, Dentists | X | X | | X | | |
| Nurses | X | | | X | | |
| Pharmacists | X | | | X | | |
| Optometrists | X | | | X | | |
| Morticians | X | | | X | | |
| Veterinarians | X | | | | | |
| Hospital Employees | X | | | | | |
| Clergy | | X | | X | | |
| Employees of Federal State, or Local Government[a] | J,P,PG, S,US | X | | E,F,M,P | | |
| National Guardsmen on Active Duty | X | | | X | | |
| Teachers | X | X | | | | |
| Transportation-Related Employee[b] | B,R,S,T | | | | | |
| Communications-Related Employee[c] | N,R,TG, TP | | | | | |
| Financial Hardship | | X | | X | | |
| Personal Bad Health | X | X | | X | | X |
| Over a Given Age | 65 | | | 65 | | |
| Females w/Small Children (age limit if specified)[d] | | | | | | |
| Persons Caring for the Disabled | | X | | X | | |
| Previous Jury Service | | 1 yr. | | 2 yr. | | |
| Felony Conviction | X | X | | X | | |
| Vague Clause about Public Necessity or Undue Hardship[e] | | | X | X | X | U |
| All Women | X | | | | | |
| Residency Requirement | 1 yr. | | | | | |

| Connecticut | Delaware | District of Columbia | Florida | Georgia | Hawaii | Idaho | Illinois |
|---|---|---|---|---|---|---|---|
| x | x | x | x | x | x | | x |
| x | x | x | | x | x | | x |
| x | | x | | x | | | |
| | x | | | x | | | |
| | x | | | | | | |
| | x | | | | | | |
| | | | | x | | | |
| | x | x | | | x | | x |
| E,F | x | M,F,P,E,J | J,P,S, US | F,J,E, P,L | E,J,F, P,M | | E,J,F, P |
| x | . | | | | x | | x |
| | x | x | | x | | | |
| | | | | | | | N |
| x | | | | | x | | |
| | | 70 | | 65 | | | |
| 16 | | 7 | 15 | 15 | | | |
| x | | | | | | | |
| | 1 yr. | 2 yr. | | | 1 yr. | | |
| | | | | | x | x | |
| x | | | | x | | U | |
| | | | | x | | | |
| | | 1 yr. | 1 yr. | 6 mo. | | | |

| | Indiana (Lake County) | Indiana (Rest of State) | Iowa | Kansas | Kentucky |
|---|---|---|---|---|---|
| Attorneys | | | x | | |
| Doctors, Dentists | | x | x | | |
| Nurses | | | x | | |
| Pharmacists | | | x | | |
| Optometrists | | | | | |
| Morticians | | | x | | |
| Veterinarians | | x | x | | |
| Hospital Employees | | | | | |
| Clergy | | | x | | |
| Employees of Federal State, or Local Government[a] | M,E,J | E,P,F | F,US | | |
| National Guardsmen on Active Duty | | x | | x | |
| Teachers | | | x | | |
| Transportation-Related Employee[b] | | | | | |
| Communications-Related Employee[c] | | | | | |
| Financial Hardship | | | | | |
| Personal Bad Health | x | | x | x | |
| Over a Given Age | | 65 | 65 | | |
| Females w/Small Children (age limit if specified)[d] | | | | | |
| Persons Caring for the Disabled | | | x | | |
| Previous Jury Service | 1 yr. | 1 yr. | | 1 yr. | 1 yr. |
| Felony Conviction | x | | | x within last 10 yrs. | x |
| Vague Clause about Public Necessity or Undue Hardship[e] | U | | | x | x |
| All Women | | | | | |
| Residency Requirement | | | | | 1 yr. |

| Louisiana | Maine | Maryland | Massachusetts | Michigan | Minnesota | Mississippi | Missouri |
|---|---|---|---|---|---|---|---|
| x | x |  | x | x | x | x | x |
| x | x |  | x | x | x | x | x |
|  |  |  | x |  |  |  |  |
| x |  |  |  |  | x | x |  |
| x |  |  |  |  |  |  |  |
|  |  |  | x |  |  |  |  |
| x |  |  | x |  |  | x | x |
| x | E,J,P, US | M | x | L,S | x | x | J,L,M, S,US |
| x |  | x |  |  | x |  | x |
|  |  |  |  |  |  | x F,R | x |
|  |  |  |  |  |  | TG,TP | S |
|  |  |  |  |  |  | x | x |
|  | x | x |  |  |  | x | x |
|  |  | 70 | 70 | 70 |  | 65 | 65 |
|  |  |  | 16 |  |  |  |  |
| 2 yr. | 5 yr. | 3 yr. |  | 1 yr. | 1 yr. | 2 yr. | 1 yr. |
|  | x | x |  | x |  | x | x |
|  | x | x | x |  | x |  | x |
|  |  |  | x |  |  |  | x |

|  | Montana | Nebraska | Nevada | New Hampshire | New Jersey |
|---|---|---|---|---|---|
| Attorneys | x | x | x | x | |
| Doctors, Dentists | x | x | x | x | x |
| Nurses | x | | x | | |
| Pharmacists | x | x | x | | |
| Optometrists | | | | | |
| Morticians | x | x | | | |
| Veterinarians | | | | | |
| Hospital Employees | x | | | | x |
| Clergy | x | x | | | |
| Employees of Federal State, or Local Government[a] | J,E,PG,F, Mail | S,L,Mail | x | E,J,P,F | S,P,F,M |
| National Guardsmen on Active Duty | x | x | | | x |
| Teachers | x | x | | | x |
| Transportation-Related Employee[b] | R | | R | | |
| Communication-Related Employee[c] | TG | | | | TG,TP |
| Financial Hardship | | | | | |
| Personal Bad Health | x | x | x | | |
| Over a Given Age | | 70 | 65 | 70 | 75 |
| Females w/Small Children (age limit if specified)[d] | x* | x | | 12 | x* |
| Persons Caring for the Disabled | | | | | |
| Previous Jury Service | | 2 yr. | | | 1 yr. |
| Felony Conviction | x | x | x | | x |
| Vague Clause about Public Necessity or Undue Hardship[e] | | | | | |
| All Women | | | | | |
| Residency Requirement | 1 yr. | | | | 2 yr. |

| New Mexico | New York | North Carolina | North Dakota | Ohio | Oklahoma | Oregon |
|---|---|---|---|---|---|---|
| | x | | | x | x | x |
| | x | | | x | x | x |
| | | | | x | | |
| | x | | | | | |
| | x | | | | | x |
| | x | | | | | x |
| | | | | | | |
| | x | | | x | x | |
| | x | | | x | L,E,Mail,J, P,PG | S,US, J,F |
| | x | | | | x | x |
| | | | | x | | |
| | S | | | | | |
| | N | | | | N | |
| | | | | | | |
| | | | x | x | x | x |
| | 70-75 | | | 70 | 65 | 70 |
| | | | | | x* | |
| | | | | | | |
| | 2 yr. | 2 yr. | 2 yr. | 1 yr. | | 1 yr. |
| | x | x | x | x | x | x |
| x | | x | U | x | | x |

|  | Pennsylvania | Rhode Island | South Carolina | South Dakota | Tennessee |
|---|---|---|---|---|---|
| Attorneys | x | x | x | x | x |
| Doctors, Dentists | x |  | x |  | x |
| Nurses | x |  | x |  |  |
| Pharmacists | x |  | x |  | x |
| Optometrists |  |  | x |  |  |
| Morticians | x |  | x |  |  |
| Veterinarians |  |  | x |  |  |
| Hospital Employees |  |  | x |  | x |
| Clergy | x | x | x |  | x |
| Employees of Federal State, or Local Government[a] | x | S,US, E,J,F, P | L,S,US | PG,J,E | S,US,F |
| National Guardsmen on Active Duty | x | x |  |  | x |
| Teachers | x | x |  |  | x |
| Transportation-Related Employee[b] |  |  | R |  | R |
| Communication-Related Employee[c] | TG |  |  |  |  |
| Financial Hardship | x |  |  |  |  |
| Personal Bad Health |  |  | x | x |  |
| Over a Given Age |  |  | 65 | 70 | 65 |
| Females w/Small Children (age limit if specified)[d] |  |  | 7 |  |  |
| Persons Caring for the Disabled |  |  |  |  |  |
| Previous Jury Service | 3 yr. | 2 yr. | 1 yr. | 2-4 yr. | 4 yr. |
| Felony Conviction |  |  | x | x | x |
| Vague Clause about Public Necessity or Undue Hardship[e] | x |  | x |  |  |
| All Women |  |  |  |  | x |
| Residency Requirement |  |  |  |  | 1 yr. |

[a]Employees of Federal, State or Local Government:
    x  —  indicates most employees are covered.
    E  —  elected officials.
    F  —  firemen.
    J  —  judicial officials.
    L  —  local officials.
    M  —  members of the military forces.
 Mail  —  postal employees.
    P  —  police & members of other law-enforcement agencies.
  PG  —  prison guards.
    S  —  state officials.
  US  —  officers of the United States.

| Texas | Utah | Vermont | Virginia | Washington | West Virginia | Wisconsin | Wyoming |
|-------|------|---------|----------|------------|---------------|-----------|---------|
|  | x | x | x | x |  | x | x |
|  | x | x | x | x |  | x | x |
|  |  | x |  |  |  |  |  |
|  | x |  | x |  |  | x | x |
|  |  |  | x |  |  |  |  |
|  |  |  | x | x |  |  |  |
|  |  |  | x |  |  |  |  |
|  | x |  | x |  |  |  | x |
|  |  | x | x |  |  | x | x |
|  | x | S,US,P,F | x | US,S,F,P |  | E,L,P,S,F | x |
|  |  |  |  |  |  |  |  |
|  | x |  | x |  |  |  | x |
|  |  |  |  |  |  |  |  |
|  | x | x | x | x |  | x | x |
|  | R |  | R,A,S,F |  |  |  | R |
|  | TG, TP, N,F |  |  | TG |  |  | TG,TP |
| 65 |  | 70 | 70 | 60 | 65 | 65 | 72 |
| 10 | 10 |  | 16* |  |  |  | x |
|  | x |  | x |  |  |  |  |
| 6 mo. | 1 yr. | 2 yr. |  |  | 2 yr. | 2 yr. |  |
| x | x | x | x | x | x |  | x |
| x |  | x |  |  | x | x | x |
|  | 6 mo. |  | 1 yr. | 1 yr. |  |  | 1 yr. |

bTransportation-Related Employees:
      A  —  airline pilots or other employees.
      B  —  bus drivers.
      F  —  ferry boat operators.
      R  —  railroad employees.
      S  —  officers & employees of ships.
      SB —  school bus drivers.
      T  —  truck drivers.

cCommunications-Related Employees:
      N  —  newspaper reporter.
      R  —  radio broadcast engineers & announcers.
      TG —  telegraph operator.

Communications-Related Employees (cont.)

    TP   —  telephone operator.

    TV   —  television news gatherer.

[d]An asterisk (*) indicates that the statute is sex-neutral and applies to any person charged with caring for a minor child.

[e]Vague Clause about "Public Necessity" or "Undue Hardship":

    U   —  The language in the Uniform Jury Selection and Service Act is "Undue hardship, extreme inconvenience or public necessity," and is meant to be a strict clause.

Other Categories: Alabama: actuaries; Delaware: cashiers at incorporated banks; District of Columbia: sole proprietor of a business; Louisiana: chiropractors; Mississippi: cashiers at incorporated banks, millers; Rhode Island: students; Texas: students; Utah: millers; Virginia: persons participating in the harvest, students while school is in session; Wisconsin: medical students and law students.

Appendix D:
Number of Peremptory
Challenges and Method
of Voir Dire

Number of Peremptory Challenges

| State | Capital Cases State | Capital Cases Defense | Felonies State | Felonies Defense | Misdemeanors State | Misdemeanors Defense | Civil Cases Plaintiff | Civil Cases Defense | Method of Voir Dire[g] |
|---|---|---|---|---|---|---|---|---|---|
| Alabama | 4(s) | 8(s) | 4(s) | 8(s) | 4(s) | 8(s) | 4 or 6(s) | 4 or 6(s) | Attorney |
| Alaska | 6 | 10 | 6 | 10 | 3 | 3 | 3 | 3 | Judge |
| Arizona | 10 | 10 | 6 | 6 | 2 | 2 | 4 | 4 | Civil: judge; criminal: judge plus attorney |
| Arkansas | 10 | 12 | 6 | 8 | 3 | 3 | 3(s) | 3(s) | Judge |
| California | 26[a] | 26[a] | 13 | 13 | 13 | 13 | 8 | 8 | Attorney |
| Colorado | 15 | 15 | 10 | 10 | 3 | 3 | 4/3 | 4/3 | Judge plus attorney |
| Connecticut | 25/15[b] | 25/15[a] | 6[b] | 6[b] | 3[b] | 3[b] | 3[b] | 3[b] | Attorney |
| Delaware | 12 | 20 | 6 | 6 | 6 | 6 | 3 | 3 | Judge |
| Florida | 10 | 10 | 6[b] | 6[b] | 3[b] | 3[b] | 3[b] | 3[b] | Civil: attorney; criminal: judge plus attorney |
| Georgia | 10[c] | 20[c] | 6 | 12 | 6 | 12 | 6(s) | 6(s) | Civil: attorney; criminal: judge plus attorney |
| Hawaii | 12[a] | 12[a] | 3 | 3 | 3 | 3 | 3 | 3 | Attorney |
| Idaho | 10[a] | 10[a] | 6 | 6 | 6 | 6 | 4 | 4 | Attorney |
| Illinois | 20 | 20 | 10 | 10 | 5 | 5 | 5 | 5 | Judge plus attorney |
| Indiana | 20 | 20 | 10 | 10 | 3 | 3 | 6 | 6 | Judge plus attorney |
| Iowa | 8 + 2(s)[a] | 8 + 2(s)[a] | 4 + 2(s) | 4 + 2(s) | 2 + 2(s) | 2 + 2(s) | 3 + 2(s) | 3 + 2(s) | Attorney |
| Kansas | 12/8[a] | 12/8[a] | 6 | 6 | 4 | 4 | 3 | 3 | Attorney |
| Kentucky | 5 | 15 | 5 | 15 | 3 | 3 | 3 | 3 | Civil: judge; criminal: judge plus attorney |
| Louisiana | 12 | 12 | 12 | 12 | 6 | 6 | 6 | 6 | Attorney |
| Maine | 10 | 20 | 8 | 8 | 4 | 4 | 4 | 4 | Civil: judge; criminal: judge plus attorney |
| Maryland | 10 | 20 | 10 | 20 | 4 | 4 | 4(s) | 4(s) | Judge |
| Massachusetts | 12[a] | 12[a] | 4 | 4 | 4 | 4 | 4 | 4 | Judge |

| | | | | | | | | |
|---|---|---|---|---|---|---|---|---|
| Minnesota | 10[a] | 20[a] | 3 | 5 | 3 | 5 | 2 | 2 | Judge plus attorney |
| Mississippi | 12 | 12 | 6 | 6 | 6 | 6 | 4 | 4 | Attorney |
| Missouri: | | | | | | | | | |
|   Cities over 200,000 | 15/10[a] | 20/12[a] | 4 | 8 | 4 | 8 | 3 | 3 | Judge |
|   Elsewhere: | 6[a] | 12[a] | 4 | 8 | 3 | 8 | 3 | 3 | |
| Montana | 10/8[a] | 10/8[a] | 6 | 6 | 4 | 6 | 2 | 2 | Attorney |
| Nebraska | 10[a] | 12[a] | 6 | 6 | 3 | 6 | 6(s) | 6(s) | Attorney |
| Nevada | 8[a] | 8[a] | 4 | 4 | 4 | 4 | 4 | 4 | Judge |
| New Hampshire | 10 | 20 | 3 | 3 | 3 | 3 | 3 | 3 | Judge |
| New Jersey | 12 | 20 | 10 | 10 | 10 | 10 | 6 | 6 | Judge |
| New Mexico | 8[a] | 12[a] | 3 | 5 | 3 | 5 | 5 | 5 | Judge plus attorney |
| New York | 20 | 20 | 15 | 15 | 10 | 15 | 3[b] | 3[b] | Attorney |
| North Carolina | 9 | 14 | 4 | 6 | 4 | 6 | 8 | 8 | Judge plus attorney |
| North Dakota | 15 | 15 | 10 | 10 | 6 | 10 | 6 | 6 | Attorney |
| Ohio | 6 | 6 | 4 | 4 | 4 | 4 | 3[d] | 3[d] | Judge plus attorney |
| Oklahoma | 9 | 9 | 5 | 5 | 3 | 5 | 3 | 3 | Judge plus attorney |
| Oregon | 6[a] | 12[a] | 3 | 6 | 3 | 6 | 3 | 3 | Civil: attorney; criminal: judge plus attorney |
| Pennsylvania | 20[e] | 20[e] | 8 | 8 | 6 | 8 | 4 | 4 | Judge plus attorney |
| Rhode Island | 1 out of 4 | 1 out of 4 | 1 out of 4 | 1 out of 4 | 1 out of 4 | 1 out of 4 | 1 out of 4 | 1 out of 4 | Judge plus attorney |
| South Carolina | 5 | 10 | 5 | 10 | 5 | 10 | 4(s) | 4(s) | Judge |
| South Dakota | 20[a] | 20[a] | 10 | 10 | 3 | 10 | 3 | 3 | Attorney |
| Tennessee | 6 | 15 | 4 | 8 | 3 | 8 | 4 | 4 | Judge |
| Texas | 15 | 15 | 10 | 10 | 5 | 10 | 6 | 6 | Attorney |
| Utah | 10 | 10 | 4 | 4 | 3 | 4 | 3 | 3 | Judge |
| Vermont | 6 | 6 | 6 | 6 | 6 | 6 | 6 | 6 | Attorney |
| Virginia | 4 | 4 | 4 | 4 | 3 | 4 | 3(s)[f] | 3(s)[f] | Judge plus attorney |
| Washington | 12 | 12 | 6 | 6 | 3 | 6 | 3 | 3 | Civil: judge plus attorney; criminal: attorney |

*Number of Peremptory Challenges*

| State | Criminal Cases | | | | | | Civil Cases | | Method of Voir Dire[g] |
| | Capital Cases | | Felonies | | Misdemeanors | | | | |
| | State | Defense | State | Defense | State | Defense | Plaintiff | Defense | |
|---|---|---|---|---|---|---|---|---|---|
| West Virginia | 2(s) | 6(s) | 2(s) | 6(s) | 2(s) | 6(s) | 4 | 4 | Attorney |
| Wisconsin | 6[a] | 6[a] | 4 | 4 | 4 | 4 | 3 | 3 | Attorney |
| Wyoming | 12 | 12 | 8 | 8 | 4 | 4 | 3 | 3 | Attorney |
| Federal Courts | 12 | 12 | 5 | 5 | 2 | 2 | 3 | 3 | Judge |

Note: (s) indicates that the struck-jury method is used (see pp. 146-49). Also, if more than one figure is given (i.e., 4/3), the first refers *to 12-person juries and the second to 6-person juries.*

[a]This figure also applies to trials involving possible life imprisonment.

[b]6-person juries.

[c]Applies to all trials involving a possible punishment of over 4 years in prison.

[d]8-person juries.

[e]Applies to all of the more serious felonies.

[f]5- and 7-person juries.

[g]*Judge*—indicates that the judge has unfettered control of the questioning of jurors. Attorneys may submit questions to the judge, which the judge may or may not ask the jurors, and the judge can in his or her discretion allow the attorneys to ask questions directly of the jurors after concluding questioning.
*Attorney*—indicates that the attorneys have primary control of the questioning of the jurors, subject to judicial control only for abuse.
*Judge plus attorney*—indicates the judge will generally begin the questioning with standard questions on bias, but that the attorneys will then have a right to question the jurors directly at the conclusion of the judge's questions. Local practices differ and many judges have their own individual approaches to this problem.

Appendix E:
Size of Trial Juries and
Vote Required for a
Jury Verdict

## SIZE OF TRIAL JURIES AND VOTE REQUIRED FOR A JURY VERDICT (IN PARENTHESES)

| State | Criminal Trials | | Civil Trials |
| --- | --- | --- | --- |
| | Felonies | Misdemeanors | |
| Alabama | 12 (U) | 12 (U) | 12 (U) |
| Alaska | 12 (U) | 6 (U) | 12; 6 if the amount in controversy is less than $3,000 (5/6) |
| Arizona | 12 in capital cases and if the potential punishment is 30 years or more; 8 in all other cases (U) | 8 (U) | 8 (3/4); 6 in courts not of record (5/6) |
| Arkansas | 12 (U) | 12; 6 in Justice-of-the-Peace courts (U) | 12 (3/4) |
| California | 12 (U) | 12 (U) | 12 (3/4) |
| Colorado | 12 (U) | 12 in the most serious misdemeanors; 6 in all others (U) | 6 in district courts; 3 in county courts (controversy concerns less than $500) (U) |
| Connecticut | 12 in capital cases or if the potential punishment is life imprisonment; 6 in all other cases (U) | 6 (U) | 6 (U) |
| Delaware | 12 (U) | 12 (U) | 12 (U) |
| Dist. of Columbia (and Federal Courts generally) | 12 (U) | 12 (U) | 6 (U) |
| Florida | 12 in capital cases; 6 in all others (U) | 6 (U) | 6 (U) |
| Georgia | 12 (U) | 5 to 12 depending on the county (U) | 12 (U) |
| Hawaii | 12 (U) | 12 (U) | 12 (5/6) |
| Idaho | 12 (U) | 6 (5/6) | 12; 6 if the amount in controversy is $500 or less (3/4) |
| Illinois | 12 (U) | 12 (U) | 12 (U) |
| Indiana | 12 (U) | 12 (U) | 12; 6 if the amount in controversy is $500 or less (U) |
| Iowa | 12 (U) | 12; 6 in municipal courts which have jurisdiction over crimes punishable by one year or less or | 12; 6 if the amount in controversy is $500 or less (U) |

| | | | |
|---|---|---|---|
| Kansas | 12 (U) | 12; 6 in magistrate courts (U) | 12; 6 if the amount in controversy is $3,000 or less (U) |
| Kentucky | 12 (U) | 12; 6 in inferior courts with jurisdiction over crimes punishable by one year or $500 fine (U) | 12 (3/4); 6 in inferior courts that have jurisdiction over controversies of $500 or less (5/6) |
| Louisiana | 12 (capital crimes: U; other felonies: 3/4) | 5 (U) | 12 (3/4) |
| Maine | 12 (U) | 12 (U) | 6 (3/4) |
| Maryland | 12 (U) | 12 (U) | 12 (U) |
| Massachusetts | 12 in superior courts; 6 in district courts (trials de novo) (U) | 12 in superior courts; 6 in district courts (trials de novo) (U) | 12 (5/6) |
| Michigan | 12 (U) | 12 (U) | 6 (5/6); but 12 in cases involving civil commitment (U) |
| Minnesota | 12 (U) | 12 for "gross misdemeanors"; 6 for others (U) | 6 (A 5/6 verdict can be accepted, but only after 6 hours of deliberation) |
| Mississippi | 12 (U) | 6 if punishable in county jail; otherwise 12 (U) | 12; 6 if amount in controversy is less than $200 (3/4) |
| Missouri | 12 (U) | 12 (U, except for courts not of record: 2/3) | 12 (courts of record: 3/4; courts not of record: 2/3) |
| Montana | 12 (U) | 12; 6 in Justice-of-the Peace courts or police courts (2/3) | 12; 6 if matter in controversy is less than $10,000 (2/3) |
| Nebraska | 12 in district courts; 6 in county courts (U) | 12 in district courts; 6 in county courts and police magistrate's courts—maximum punishment of 6 months in jail (U) | 12 in district courts; 6 in county courts—less than $2,000 in controversy (5/6 verdict can be accepted, but only after 6 hours of deliberation) |
| Nevada | 12 (U) | 12 (U) | 8 (3/4) |
| New Hampshire | 12 (U) | 12; 6 if no prison term over one year can result from conviction (U) | 12 (U) |
| New Jersey | 12 (U) | 12 (U) | 12 (5/6) |
| New Mexico | 12 (U) | 12; 6 in magistrate's courts—maximum punishment of 6 months in jail (U) | 12 (5/6) |

| State | Criminal Trials | | Civil Trials |
| --- | --- | --- | --- |
| | *Felonies* | *Misdemeanors* | |
| New York | 12 (U) | 6 (U) | 6 (5/6) |
| North Carolina | 12 (U) | 12; 6 in justices' courts (U) | 12; 6 in justices' courts (U) |
| North Dakota | 12 (U) | 12 (U) | 12; 6 if amount in controversy is $200 or less (U) |
| Ohio | 12 (U) | 8 (U) | 8; 6 in municipal and county courts (3/4) |
| Oklahoma | 12 (U) | 12; 6 for violations of city ordinances (3/4) | 12; 6 if amount in controversy is less than $2,500 (3/4) |
| Oregon | 12; 6 in district and county courts—maximum punishment of one year or less (1st degree murder: U, all others: 5/6) | 12; 6 in district and county courts—maximum punishment of one year or less (5/6) | 12; 6 in district and county courts (3/4) |
| Pennsylvania | 12 (U) | 12 (U) | 12; 6 before Justices of the Peace (5/6) |
| Puerto Rico | 12 (3/4) | | |
| Rhode Island | 12 (U) | 12 (U) | 12 (U) |
| South Carolina | 12 (U) | 12; 6 in magistrate's courts which have jurisdiction over crimes with a potential punishment of less than 30 days in jail or $100 fine (U) | 12; 6 in county courts—which have jurisdiction over controversies involving $1,000 or less (U) |
| South Dakota | 12 (U) | 12; 6 in matters before Justices of the Peace (U) | 12 (5/6); 6 in matters before Justices of the Peace (3/4) |
| Tennessee | 12 (U) | 6 (U) | 6 (U) |
| Texas | 12 (U) | 12 in district courts; 6 in county courts (3/4) | 12; 6 in matters before Justices of the Peace (3/4) |
| Utah | 12 in capital cases; 8 in all others (U) | 8; 4 in inferior courts (U) | 8; 4 in inferior courts (3/4) |
| Vermont | 12 (U) | 12; 6 in justices' courts (U) | 12; 6 in justices' courts (U) |
| Virginia | 12 (U) | 5 (U) | 12 in "special" cases; 7 in most others; 5 if the amount in controversy is less than $300 (U) |

| | | | |
|---|---|---|---|
| Washington | 12 (U) | 12; 6 in Justice-of-the-Peace courts—maximum punishment of 6 months in jail (U) | 12; 6 in Justice-of-the-Peace courts—$3,000 or less (5/6) |
| West Virginia | 12 (U) | 12 (U) | 12; 6 in Justice-of-the-Peace courts (U) |
| Wisconsin | 12 (U) | 12 (U) | 12 (5/6) |
| Wyoming | 12 (U) | 12 in district courts; 6 in county courts (U) | 12 in district courts; 6 in county courts (U) |

*The information in parentheses refers to the vote required for a jury verdict; U means that a unanimous vote is needed for verdict.

Note: In many states, the number of jurors listed here can be reduced by agreement of all the parties involved in the litigation.

# Part II

# Demographic Data:
# Jury Composition

# Appendixes F-I:
# The Demographic Data—An
# Explanatory Statement

Appendixes F-I provide demographic data on the juries of courts throughout the country and illustrate the under-representation of persons in lower socioeconomic groups, nonwhites, the young and the elderly, and women.

## SOURCES FOR THE DATA

**The Federal Courts.** The federal courts have offered themselves as a model of fairness and have undertaken statistical studies on their own, so it is appropriate to start with the federal courts when analyzing discrimination. Each district court was asked in 1971 and again in 1974 to conduct a study of jurors on its master wheel (which is assembled randomly from the voter registration list) and of the actual jurors that appeared for service. These samples were given to Professor Henry Moore, a retired member of the University of Alabama faculty, and he compared them to figures, prepared by the Bureau of the Census, of the appropriate adult populations for each federal district and division. Professor Moore submitted the results to the Committee on the Operation of the Jury System, composed of federal judges, which is instructed to monitor the federal jury system. The judges have never released these figures to the public, because Professor Moore's report "consisted of raw information which might easily be misinterpreted."[1] The samples were, however, assembled under the careful supervision of the Federal Judicial Center and the Administrative Office of the U.S. Courts, and can be accepted as generally accurate.

I have been able to obtain the raw data directly from about two-thirds of the federal districts across the country and present them here, in conjunction with 1970 census data that I have computed. The lists that follow include all the federal districts that have made their data available, except those whose sample number of jurors is smaller than 100, because the statistical significance lowers dramatically for such a small sample. In Table G-1, Race, only those districts whose nonwhite population exceeds 4 percent are included, because the statistical comparison is less persuasive when the population base is smaller. Some districts with Asian and Native-American populations that are smaller are included in the later tables in Appendix G, however, because these population groups are generally only a small minority of a district's population.

The term "nonwhite" as used in the federal tables includes all races other than Caucasian, but *does not* include persons of Hispanic origin, because the federal government classifies them as "white."

**The State Courts.** The data for state courts come from a wide variety of sources, as the explanatory remarks indicate. Where the explanatory remarks are less detailed, the data have been prepared either directly by me or by students working closely under my supervision. Much of the data have been prepared for litigation, and when it is included here it has been undisputed by the opposing side and thus can be accepted as essentially accurate. The data obtained by visual observation are, of course, less accurate than the data obtained from questionnaires, but I have used some of these data when no other method of obtaining the information was available. I have tried to use large enough samples so that some error would not alter the basic information provided by this data.

## A WORD OF CAUTION ON THE CENSUS DATA

**Race.** One problem in dramatizing underrepresentation on juries is the impossibility of obtaining accurate census statistics. The Bureau of the Census has admitted that its 1970 count missed 7.7 percent of all blacks (1.88 million blacks) and only 1.9 percent of all whites (3.45 million),[2] but it has been unable to pinpoint where the missing persons might be. Presumably they are in the large metropolitan ghettos where people are frequently unidentified because of housing code violations and general apprehension about any questions from the government. The 1970 census figures used in these tables have *not* been adjusted to reflect these errors, but it should always be remembered that the relative census figures for nonwhites are about *6 percent lower* than they should be. In addition, the black population continues to grow faster than the white population; the black population rose 5 percent between 1970 and 1973, while the white population rose only 2 percent.[3]

**The Socioeconomic Statistics.** Inflation has raised most of our incomes since the 1970 census. And educational levels have also been rising steadily, especially among the young. Comparing these jury figures to those of the census is thus useful for showing trends, but the differences cannot be given an absolute interpretation.

The occupational figures are, on the other hand, relatively stable, and have been accepted as the most appropriate for showing real differences between interest groups in this country. Occupation statistics are significant even though some blue-collar workers make more money than some white-collar workers—compare, for instance, an experienced plumber's salary to that of a young school teacher. The blue-collar worker, even if he or she has reached a level of relative prosperity, still tends to identify with other blue-collar workers. The basic distinction is between persons who work primarily with their hands and those who work primarily with their minds. The distinction is certainly crude, but it has proved useful in identifying differences in attitude and approach. For the purpose of these tables, agricultural workers have been included as blue-collar.

Clerical workers are in something of a hybrid category. The setting and the trappings of the clerk's job tend to be closer to that of the manager, the technician, and the professional, and hence we have classified clerical workers as white-collar employees.

## THE RATE OF ERROR

The term "Rate of Error" has been used in all of the following charts to indicate the extent of under- or over-representation that exists on the juries surveyed. The rate of error is obtained by taking the difference between the percentage a given demographic group has on a jury and the percentage that demographic group has in the population of the community, and then dividing that figure by the demographic group's percentage of the population of the community. Thus, if males constituted 50 percent of a county's adult population, but held 80 percent of the seats on a jury, the rate of error would be +60 (80 − 50 = 30, 30 ÷ 50 = 60). In this example, the rate of error for females would be −60 (20 − 50 = −30, −30 ÷ 50 = −60). If the figure is preceded by a plus (+) sign, that population is *over*-represented, and if the figure is preceded by a minus (—) sign, the population group is *under*-represented. As explained in Chapter Four, pp. 93-98, this method of computation has been used by a number of courts in recent years. As Chapter Four also explains, any over- or under-representation of more than 20 percent should be viewed as "substantial" and thus a violation of our responsibility to impanel juries that constitute a fair cross-section of the community.

## NOTES

1. Letter from Arthur J. Stanley, Senior District Judge for the District of Kansas and chairperson of the Committee on the Operation of the Jury System, dated December 26, 1973.

2. Jacob S. Siegel, "Estimates of Coverage of the Population by Sex, Race, and Age in the 1970 Census," *Demography* 11 (Feb. 1974): 1; U.S. Bureau of the Census, *Census of Population and Housing: 1970 Evaluation and Research Program PHC(E)-4*, "Estimates of Coverage of Population by Sex, Race and Age: Demographic Analysis" (Washington: Government Printing Office, 1973).

3. San Francisco *Chronicle*, May 9, 1974, p. 8, quoting a Census Bureau report.

**Appendix F:
Occupation, Income, and
Education Statistics**

**Table F-1. Federal Courts: Occupation Studies Conducted by the District Courts (only those divisions using samples of 100 or more are listed). Number in Parentheses Indicates Size of Sample.**

| State and District | Percentage (of those employed) of blue-collar workers in the division | Percentage (of those employed) of blue-collar workers on the jury | Rate of error: over- (+) or under- (−) representation | Date |
|---|---|---|---|---|
| Alabama: Middle District | 62.1% | 58.2% (376)<br>52.8 (345) | − 6.3%<br>−15.0 | 1968-1971<br>1971 |
| Alabama: Northern District | 58.4 | 50.5 (398) | −13.5 | 1971 |
| Alabama: Southern District | 63.1 | 60.5 (430)<br>71.5 (340) | − 4.1<br>+13.3 | 1971<br>1973 |
| Arizona: Phoenix Division | 47.5 | 38.5 (278) | −18.9 | 1971 |
| Tucson-Globe Division | 48.4 | 39.4 (193) | −18.6 | 1971 |
| Arkansas: Western District: Fort Smith Division | 62.9 | 55.4 (112) | −11.9 | 1971 |
| California: Central District | 45.3 | 34.0 (356) | −24.9 | 1971 |
| California: Eastern District: Fresno Division | 53.8 | 38.0 (108) | −29.4 | 1971 |
| Sacramento Division | 39.5 | 49.1 (289) | − 0.8 | 1971 |
| California: Northern District: San Francisco Division | 39.4 | 20.4 (647) | −48.2 | 1971 |
| California: Southern District | 44.9 | 38.9 (312)<br>32.1 (256) | −13.4<br>−28.5 | 1971<br>1972 |
| Colorado: Denver Division | 42.5 | 36.6 (235) | −13.9 | 1971 |
| Connecticut: Bridgeport Division | 43.3 | 38.1 (278) | −12.0 | 1971 |
| Hartford Division | 45.6 | 45.8 (238) | + 0.4 | 1971 |
| New Haven Division | 50.8 | 45.8 (299) | − 9.8 | 1971 |
| Delaware | 42.0 | 34.3 (137)<br>36.3 (438) | −18.3<br>−13.6 | 1971<br>1973 |
| District of Columbia | 42.1 | 43.2 (373) | + 2.6 | 1971 |
| Florida: Middle District: Ft. Myers Division | 57.9 | 34.8 (141) | −39.9 | 1971 |

| |  | | | | |
|---|---|---|---|---|---|
| | Jacksonville Division | 50.6 | 32.7 (202) | −39.3 | 1971 |
| | Ocala Division | 59.5 | 36.4 (176) | −38.8 | 1971 |
| | Orlando Division | 45.2 | 20.9 (316) | −53.8 | 1971 |
| | Tampa Division | 51.5 | 39.0 (236) | −24.3 | 1971 |
| Georgia: | Northern District: | | | | |
| | Atlanta Division | 43.2 | 39.6 (355) | − 8.3 | 1971 |
| | Newnan Division | 67.1 | 58.8 (114) | −12.4 | 1971 |
| | Rome Division | 65.7 | 67.7 (189) | + 3.0 | 1971 |
| Georgia: | Southern District: | | | | |
| | Augusta Division | 59.7 | 52.4 (309) | −12.2 | 1971 |
| | Brunswick Division | 62.8 | 55.0 (231) | −12.4 | 1971 |
| | Dublin Division | 69.0 | 60.3 (277) | −12.6 | 1971 |
| | Savannah Division | 57.0 | 56.9 (390) | − 0.2 | 1971 |
| | Swainsboro Division | 73.1 | 53.1 (213) | −27.4 | 1971 |
| | Waycross Division | 69.1 | 62.0 (171) | −10.3 | 1971 |
| Hawaii | | 50.2 | 31.6 (158) | −37.1 | 1971 |
| Idaho | | 56.8 | 56.7 (231) | − 0.2 | 1971 |
| Illinois: | Northern District: | | | | |
| | Eastern Division | 52.9 | 40.7 (351) | −23.1 | 1971 |
| Indiana: | Southern District | 57.0 | 50.8 (435) | −10.9 | 1971 |
| Iowa: | Northern District: | | | | |
| | Cedar Rapids Division | 56.7 | 56.0 (116) | − 1.2 | 1971 |
| Iowa: | Southern District: | | | | |
| | Central Division | 48.6 | 46.5 (271) | − 4.3 | 1971 |
| Kansas: | Kansas City-Leavenworth Division | 55.8 | 50.0 (176) | −10.4 | 1971 |
| | Topeka Division | 43.6 | 47.7 (155) | + 9.4 | 1971 |
| | Witchita-Hutchinson Division | 46.9 | 37.7 (175) | −19.6 | 1971 |
| Louisiana: | Eastern District: | | | | |
| | New Orleans Division | 53.2 | 48.6 (391) | − 8.6 | 1971 |
| Maryland | | 42.2 | 40.7 (403) | − 3.6 | 1970 |
| Massachusetts | | 47.3 | 44.2 (511) | − 6.6 | 1973 |
| Mississippi: | Southern District: | | | | |
| | Eastern Division | 64.1 | 53.2 (263) | −17.0 | 1971 |
| | Hattiesburg Division | 61.9 | 60.4 (346) | − 2.4 | 1971 |

| State and District | Percentage (of those employed) of blue-collar workers in the division | Percentage (of those employed) of blue-collar workers on the jury | Rate of error: over- (+) or under- (−) representation | Date |
|---|---|---|---|---|
| Jackson Division | 56.6 | 50.1 (371) | −11.5 | 1971 |
| Southern Division | 56.5 | 56.3 (371) | − 0.3 | 1971 |
| Western Division | 61.0 | 54.7 (194) | −10.3 | 1971 |
| Missouri: Eastern District: | | | | |
| Eastern Division | 48.3 | 50.3 (326) | + 4.1 | 1971 |
| Montana: | | | | |
| Billings Division | 48.2 | 34.5 (142) | −28.4 | 1971 |
| Great Falls Division | 52.7 | 42.3 (104) | −19.7 | 1971 |
| Havre-Glasgow Division | 62.3 | 51.1 (137) | −18.0 | 1971 |
| New Hampshire | 56.5 | 32.1 (106) | −43.2 | 1971 |
| New Jersey: | | | | |
| Camden Division | 51.6 | 50.0 (110) | − 3.1 | 1971 |
| Newark Division | 45.9 | 39.2 (388) | −14.6 | 1971 |
| Trenton Division | 47.7 | 53.5 (114) | +12.2 | 1971 |
| New Mexico | 47.7 | 60.1 (318) | +26.0 | 1974 |
| New York: Eastern District | 41.8 | 27.8 (291) | −33.5 | 1971 |
| North Carolina: Eastern District: | | | | |
| Elizabeth City Division | 64.6 | 37.5 (120) | −42.0 | 1971 |
| Fayetteville Division | 64.4 | 50.5 (222) | −21.6 | 1971 |
| New Bern Division | 61.7 | 41.9 (191) | −32.1 | 1971 |
| Raleigh Division | 50.9 | 34.8 (247) | −31.6 | 1971 |
| Wilmington Division | 64.2 | 53.9 (154) | −16.0 | 1971 |
| Wilson Division | 64.2 | 49.6 (224) | −22.7 | 1971 |
| North Dakota: Northeastern Division | 57.3 | 61.8 (102) | + 7.9 | 1971 |
| Northwestern Division | 55.2 | 61.5 (104) | +11.4 | 1971 |
| Oklahoma: Eastern District | 61.6 | 58.1 (260) | − 5.7 | 1971 |
| Oregon: Portland Division | 45.9 | 43.9 (171) | − 4.4 | 1971 |
| Pennsylvania: Eastern District | 51.8 | 39.4 (457) | −23.9 | 1971 |
| South Carolina: Area A Division | 63.2 | 61.2 (188) | − 3.2 | 1971 |
| Area B Division | 46.1 | 48.6 (278) | + 5.4 | 1971 |
| Area C Division | 55.5 | 58.3 (240) | + 5.0 | 1971 |

| | | | | |
|---|---|---|---|---|
| Tennessee: | Eastern District: | | | |
| | Northeastern Division | 63.1 | 63.3 (281) | + 0.3 | 1971 |
| | Northern Division | 58.5 | 45.3 (309) | −22.6 | 1971 |
| | Southern Division | 65.3 | 57.1 (389) | −12.6 | 1971 |
| Tennessee: | Western District: | 52.0 | 59.0 (134) | +13.5 | 1971 |
| Texas: | Southern District: | | | |
| | Brownsville Division | 59.1 | 27.6 (105) | −53.3 | 1971 |
| | Corpus Christi Division | 54.3 | 46.8 (111) | −13.8 | 1971 |
| | Galveston Division | 55.9 | 51.0 (100) | − 8.8 | 1971 |
| | Houston Division | 47.8 | 52.8 (322) | +10.5 | 1971 |
| Texas: | Western District: | | | |
| | Austin Division | 47.4 | 38.5 (148) | −18.8 | 1971 |
| | Del Rio Division | 58.2 | 40.3 (134) | −30.8 | 1971 |
| | El Paso Division | 48.5 | 27.3 (105) | −43.7 | 1971 |
| | San Antonio Division | 50.2 | 39.2 (286) | −21.9 | 1971 |
| Utah: | Central Division | 48.9 | 53.9 (128) | +10.2 | 1971 |
| | Northern Division | 42.7 | 29.8 (104) | −30.2 | 1971 |

Note: The Administrative Office discontinued their official sampling of the occupational breakdown of federal jurors (as of late 1973) for no publicly annouced reason. See Gewin, "An Analysis of Jury Selection Decisions," 506 F.2d 805, at 825 (1975).

**Table F-2.   Federal Courts: Additional Occupation Studies**

| | Percentage (of those employed) Blue-Collar Workers in the District | Percentage (of those employed) Blue-Collar Workers on the Jury | Rate of Error | Source and Date |
|---|---|---|---|---|
| California: Northern District (entire district) | 42.9% | 26.0% | −39.4% | Study supervised by the author of the 396 employed persons who served on 23 grand juries between 1969 and 1975, for the case of *United States v. Rafofsky,* No. CR 74-687 OJC (N.D. Cal. 1975). |
| North Carolina: Eastern District (entire district) | 47.8 | 24.5 | −48.7 | Sample of 800 examined by Ruth Astle for the defense in the case of *United States v. MacDonald,* Nos. 75-1870, 75-1871 (E.D. N.C. 1975). |
| Rhode Island | 54.5 | 50.3 | − 7.7 | Sample of 399 qualified jurors examined in 1970. (Edward N. Beiser, "Are Juries Representative?" *Judicature* 57 [1973]: 194, 196.) |

**Table F-3.   State Courts: Occupation Studies**

| State Court | Percentage (of those employed) Blue-Collar Workers in the County | Percentage (of those employed) Blue-Collar Workers on the Jury | Rate of Error | Source and Date |
|---|---|---|---|---|
| *Arizona* | | | | |
| Maricopa County | 57.0% | 45.5% | −20.2% | 429 actual jurors, studied in April & May, 1972, as reported in "Juries and Jurors in Maricopa County," *Law & Social Order* (1973): 188. |
| *California* | | | | |
| Los Angeles County Central District | 44.8 | 26.9 | −40.0 | 1000 actual jurors, questioned in January and February 1973 by Leo Breiman for *People v. Taylor*, No. A-277-425 (Los Angeles Superior Court, 1974). |
| Los Angeles County Grand Jury | | 1.1 | −97.5 | A study of the 720 persons nominated for the grand jury between 1971 and 1976, conducted by Prof. Peter Sperlich, U. of California, Berkeley, for *People v. Harris* (Los Angeles Superior Court, 1976). |
| Marin County | 29.7 | 19.5 | −34.3 | 383 juror questionnaires examined in 1975 by Ruth Astle and Anita Oppenheimer. |
| Orange County | 41.9 | 21.7 | −48.2 | 207 jurors questioned in 1974 by Harvey Grody, Mike Kinney, and Jim Wisley, Calif. State Univer., Fullerton. |
| Sacramento County | 40.2 | 32.6 | −18.9 | 493 cards filled out by persons sent juror questionnaires, summer 1972. |
| San Bernadino County | 52.2 | 45.0 | −13.8 | 456 cards filled out by actual jurors, July 1972. |
| San Francisco County: Trial Jurors | 38.4 | 28.4 | −26.0 | 2,150 jurors examined in 1972-73. |
| Grand Jurors | | 3.0 | −92.2 | The six 19-person grand juries between 1970 and 1975-76. |
| Santa Clara County | 40.9 | 28.4 | −30.6 | List of 915 qualified jurors, 1972-73. |

| State Court | Percentage (of those employed) Blue-Collar Workers in the County | Percentage (of those employed) Blue-Collar Workers in the Jury | Rate of Error | Source and Date |
|---|---|---|---|---|
| Colorado | | | | |
| Denver County | 41.5 | 31.9 | −23.1 | Examination of court records on 440 qualified jurors, summer 1972. |
| | | 32.9 | −20.7 | Examination of court records on 425 employed, qualified jurors, June 1974. |
| El Paso County (Colorado Springs) | 44.4 | 29.1 | −34.5 | 889 cards filled out by actual jurors, 1972-73. |
| Pueblo County | 55.6 | 48.7 | −12.4 | Cards filled out by 464 actual jurors, 1972-74. |
| Massachusetts | | | | |
| Suffolk County (Boston) | 45.3 | 46.3 | + 2.2 | A count of 1,538 qualified jurors from official data in 1972. |
| | | 43.9 | − 3.1 | A count of 387 actual jurors from juror questionnaires in January and May 1974. |
| Nevada | | | | |
| Washoe County (Reno) | 47.5 | 38.9 | −18.1 | 835 cards filled out by actual jurors, 1972-73. |
| New Mexico | | | | |
| Bernalillo County (Albuquerque) | 39.3 | 25.9 | −34.1 | Questionnaires of 367 employed actual jurors examined at different times, 1972, 1973, 1974. |
| New York | | | | |
| Queens County: Grand Jury | 39.6 | 18.5 | −53.3 | An examination of the list of 1,500 potential grand jurors in 1973 by sociologist Eric Single for the Queen's County Legal Aid Society. |
| Rhode Island (statewide) | 54.5 | 51.4 | − 5.7 | 359 qualified jurors, 1970. Edward N. Beiser, "Are Juries Representative?" *Judicature* 57 (1973): 196. |

| | | | | |
|---|---|---|---|---|
| *Texas* | | | | |
| Harris County: | | | | |
| Trial Jurors | 46.0 | 40.1 | −12.8 | A count of the listed occupations for 1,380 qualified jurors, October 1971. |
| Grand Jurors | | 17.3 | −62.4 | Survey of 156 grand jurors who served between 1969 and 1972. *Dumont v. Estelle*, 377 F. Supp. 374, 386 (S.D. Texas, 1974). |
| *Utah* | | | | |
| Salt Lake County | 44.3 | 41.8 | − 5.6 | 267 cards filled out by actual jurors in July and October 1972. |
| *Virginia* | | | | |
| Arlington County | 20.9 | 20.2 | − 3.3 | An examination of lists of 163 qualified employed jurors in 1972 and 1973. |
| | | 12.0 | −42.6 | An examination of the lists of 308 qualified employed jurors in 1974. |

Note: All the census data used in these occupational statistics cover all persons 16 and over who are employed.

**Table F-4.   Income Statistics: State Courts**

| State | Percentage of Persons Living in Families Making Less Than $10,000 in the County | Percentage of Persons Living in Families Making Less Than $10,000 on the Jury | Rate of Error | Date and Source |
|---|---|---|---|---|
| *California* | | | | |
| Los Angeles County: Central District | 55.6% | 30.2% | −45.7% | 1,000 jurors questioned in January & February 1973 by Leo Breiman for *People v. Taylor*, No. A-277425 (L.A. Sup. Ct., 1974). |
| Orange County[a] | 29.4 | 14.0 | −52.4 | 606 jurors questioned in 1974 by Harvey Grody, Mike Kinney and Jim Wisley, Calif. State Univ., Fullerton. |
| Sacramento County | 46.2 | 35.1 | −24.0 | 493 cards filled out by persons sent juror questionnaires, summer 1972. |
| San Bernardino County | 54.0 | 39.8 | −26.3 | 673 cards filled out by actual jurors, summer 1972. |
| *Colorado* | | | | |
| El Paso County | 57.0 | 29.5 | −48.2 | 888 cards filled out by actual jurors, 1972-73. |
| Pueblo County | 63.3 | 45.4 | −28.3 | Cards filled out by 524 actual jurors, 1972-74. |
| *Nevada* | | | | |
| Washoe County (Reno) | 42.4 | 36.0 | −14.6 | 835 cards filled out by actual jurors, 1972-73. |
| *Texas* | | | | |
| Harris County (Grand Jurors) | 47.0 | 4.0 | −91.5 | Survey of 156 grand jurors who served between 1969 and 1972. *Dumont v. Estelle*, 377 F. Supp. 374, 386 (S.D. Tex. 1974). |
| *Utah* | | | | |
| Salt Lake County | 51.9 | 44.0 | −15.2 | 267 cards filled out by actual jurors in July and October 1972. |

aThe figures for Orange County only use $9,000

| Jurisdiction | Less Than High School | | | A High School Degree | | | Some College Education | | | Source and Date |
|---|---|---|---|---|---|---|---|---|---|---|
| | Percent in District | Percent on Jury | Rate of Error | Percent in District | Percent on Jury | Rate of Error | Percent in District | Percent on Jury | Rate of Error | |
| U.S. District Court for the Eastern District of California: Northern Division | Not available | | | Not available | | | 25.7% | 49.1% | +91.9% | An examination of 448 randomly drawn questionnaire from the 1975 draw by Prof. Peter Sperlich, U. California at Berkeley, for the case of *United States v. Soliah* (1976). |
| U.S. District Court for the Northern District of California | 34.2 | 9.1 | −73.4 | 32.5 | 36.4 | +12.0 | 33.3 | 54.5 | +63.7 | An examination of the questionnaires of 529 persons who served on 23 grand juries between 1969 and 1975. The study was done under the author's supervision for the case of *United States v. Rafofsky*, R74-687 OJC (N.D. Cal., 1975). The educational background of 7 grand jurors could not be determined and they have been omitted. |
| U.S. District Court for the District of Massachusetts | 41.5 | 29.7 | −28.4 | 34.9 | 38.0 | + 8.9 | 23.6 | 32.2 | +36.4 | An examination of 1,150 qualified juror questionnaires in 1970 by M.I.T. political scientists Hayward A. Alker, J., Carl Hosticka, and Michael Mitchell. |
| | 41.5 | 18.7 | −45.1 | 34.9 | 41.8 | +19.8 | 23.6 | 39.5 | +67.4 | Official statistics collected by the court for 615 actual jurors, Nov. 21, 1973. |

| Jurisdiction | Less Than High School | | | A High School Degree | | | Some College Education | | | Source and Date |
|---|---|---|---|---|---|---|---|---|---|---|
| | Percent in District | Percent on Jury | Rate of Error | Percent in District | Percent on Jury | Rate of Error | Percent in District | Percent on Jury | Rate of Error | |
| U.S. District Court for the District of New Jersey: Camden Division | 49.9 | 39.4 | −21.0 | 33.0 | 45.5 | +28.8 | 17.1 | 18.1 | + 5.8 | Examination of jury venire containing 315 names, supervised by attorney David Kairys in 1972. |
| U.S. District Court for the District of Rhode Island | 53.6 | 37.3 | −30.4 | 29.0 | 42.6 | +46.9 | 17.4 | 20.1 | +15.5 | 300 qualified jurors, 1970. Edward N. Beiser, "Are Juries Representative?" *Judicature* 57 (1973): 196. |
| U.S. District Court for the Eastern District of North Carolina | *8 Years of Schooling or Less* 35.5 { | 20.2 / 17.7 | −43.1 / −50.1 | Not available | Not available | | Not available | Not available | | Sample of 796 jurors examined by the defendant. Sample of 701 jurors examined by the prosecution in 1975 for the case of *United State v. Mac-Donald*, Nos. 75-1870, 75-1871 (E.D. N.C. 1975). |

| Jurisdiction | Less Than High School | | | A High School Degree | | | Some College Education | | | Source and Date |
|---|---|---|---|---|---|---|---|---|---|---|
| | Percent in District | Percent on Jury | Rate of Error | Percent in District | Percent on Jury | Rate of Error | Percent in District | Percent on Jury | Rate of Error | |
| *California* | | | | | | | | | | |
| Los Angeles County | 38.0% | 9.8% | −74.2% | 32.7% | 33.2% | + 1.5% | 29.3% | 57.0% | +94.5% | 1,000 actual jurors questioned in January and February 1973 by Leo Breiman for *People v. Taylor*, No. A-277-425 (Los Angeles Sup. Ct., 1974). |
| Orange County | 29.4 | 6.1 | −79.3 | 35.0 | 19.0 | −45.7 | 35.6 | 74.5 | +109.3 | 606 jurors questioned in 1974 by Harvey Grody, Mike Kinney, and Jim Wisley, Calif. State Univ., Fullerton. |
| Sacramento County | 33.2 | 10.2 | −69.3 | 36.4 | 45.7 | +25.5 | 30.4 | 44.1 | +45.1 | 493 cards filled out by persons sent juror questionnaires, summer 1972. |
| San Bernardino County | 42.5 | 21.4 | −49.6 | 33.4 | 40.0 | +19.8 | 24.1 | 38.6 | +60.2 | 673 cards filled out by actual jurors, summer 1972. |
| *Colorado* | | | | | | | | | | |
| Denver County | 38.3 | 21.3 | −44.4 | 31.8 | 31.9 | + 0.3 | 29.5 | 46.9 | +59.0 | Officially collected data on 1,440 qualified jurors, June-August 1972. |
| El Paso County | 27.1 | 8.1 | −70.1 | 39.8 | 34.0 | −14.6 | 33.1 | 58.0 | +75.8 | 888 cards filled out by actual jurors, 1972-73. |
| Pueblo County | 47.9 | 24.3 | −49.3 | 32.2 | 45.6 | +41.2 | 19.8 | 30.1 | +52.0 | Cards filled out by 555 actual jurors, 1972-74. |
| *Maryland* | | | | | | | | | | |
| Prince George's County | 32.9 | 15.5 | −52.9 | 36.8 | 34.4 | − 6.5 | 30.3 | 50.0 | +65.0 | 264 questionnaires filled out by actual jurors in October 1973 for Bird Engineering—Research Associates, Vienna, Va. |

| Jurisdiction | Less Than High School | | | A High School Degree | | | Some College Education | | | Source and Date |
|---|---|---|---|---|---|---|---|---|---|---|
| | Percent in District | Percent on Jury | Rate of Error | Percent on Jury | Percent in District | Rate of Error | Percent in District | Percent on Jury | Rate of Error | |
| **Nevada** | | | | | | | | | | |
| Washoe County (Reno) | 30.9 | 13.8 | −55.3 | 37.7 | 39.5 | + 4.8 | 31.4 | 46.7 | +48.7 | 815 cards filled out by actual jurors, 1972-73. |
| **New Mexico** | | | | | | | | | | |
| Bernalillo County (Albuquerque) | 33.8 | 12.4 | −63.3 | 33.5 | 41.4 | +23.6 | 32.7 | 46.2 | +41.3 | Questionnaires of 565 jurors examined at different periods in 1972, 1973 and 1974. |
| **Rhode Island** | 53.6 | 45.0 | −16.0 | 29.0 | 38.0 | +31.0 | 17.4 | 17.0 | − 2.3 | 359 qualified jurors, 1970. Edward N. Beiser, "Are Juries Representative?" *Judicature* 57 (1973): 196. |
| **Texas** | | | | | | | | | | |
| Harris County (Houston) Grand Jury | 47.0 | 3.0 | −93.6 | 25.0 | 8.0 | −36.7 | 28.0 | 89.0 | +217.9 | Survey of 156 grand jurors who served between 1969 and 1972. *Dumont v. Estelle*, 377 F. Supp. 374, 386 (S.D. Tex. 1974). |
| **Utah** | | | | | | | | | | |
| Salt Lake County | 32.5 | 17.2 | −47.1 | 35.5 | 42.3 | +19.2 | 32.0 | 40.4 | +26.3 | 267 cards collected from actual jurors in July & October, 1972. |

Note: The census figures used for comparison purposes cover only those persons 25 and over. No other comparable statistic is available.

## Appendix G:
## Racial Statistics

Table G-1 provides information assembled by the court clerks of the federal district courts at the request of the Administrative Office of the Courts in Washington, D.C. These figures include all nonwhites (except where indicated), but in nearly all of these districts, the nonwhites are almost exclusively black. The federal government makes no separate classification for people of Hispanic origin, and they are included in the white category in Table G-1. In Tables G-3 and G-4, however, Hispanic jurors are isolated, and their underrepresentation on our juries is illustrated. Tables G-5 through G-8 focus on Asian-Americans and Native-Americans.

I obtained the official surveys directly from about three-fourths of the district courts and have reproduced in Table G-1 all the data I obtained for those divisions or districts whose over-18 population is at least 4 percent nonwhite, but only if the survey included at least 100 jurors.

Table G-1.   Racial Make-up of Federal District Court Juries (Number in parentheses is size of sample)

| State | District | Division | Year | Percentage of Nonwhites | | | Rate of Error[a] | |
|---|---|---|---|---|---|---|---|---|
| | | | | 1970 Census* | Master Wheel | Actual Jurors | Master Wheel | Actual Jurors |
| Alabama | Middle | | 1968-71 | 26.3 | — | 17.7 (475) | — | -32.7 |
| | | | 1971 | | 21.2 (430) | 16.4 (427) | -19.4 | -37.6 |
| | | | 1974 | | 22.5 (494) | 20.5 (278) | -14.4 | -22.1 |
| | Northern | | 1971 | 18.1 | 16.9 (514) | 15.9 (561) | - 6.6 | -12.2 |
| | | | 1974 | | 14.6 (500) | 16.7 (515) | -19.3 | - 7.7 |
| | Southern | | 1971 | 32.2 | 25.9 (505) | 25.3 (768) | -19.6 | -21.4 |
| | | | 1973 | | 29.3 (198) | 29.0 (710) | - 9.0 | - 9.9 |
| Alaska[b] | | Fairbanks | 1974 | 4.3** | 1.8 (443) | 2.0 (152) | -58.1 | -53.5 |
| Arizona | | Phoenix | 1971 | 5.4*** | 5.0 (499) | 2.7 (401) | - 7.4 | -50.0 |
| | | | 1974 | | 4.1 (341) | 2.0 (1,729) | -24.1 | -63.0 |
| | | Prescott | 1971 | 27.5** | 9.2 (443) | — | -66.5 | — |
| | | | 1974 | | 19.9 (322) | 6.4 (298) | -27.6 | -68.7 |
| | | Tucson-Globe | 1971 | 5.8** | 2.4 (464) | 2.1 (330) | -58.6 | -63.8 |
| | | | 1974 | | 3.5 (341) | 3.9 (1,565) | -39.7 | -32.8 |
| Arkansas | Western | El Dorado | 1971 | 27.3 | 27.1 (314) | — | - 0.7 | — |
| | | Hot Springs | 1971 | 9.7 | 16.8 (202) | — | +73.2 | — |
| | | Texarkana | 1971 | 22.3 | 27.5 (218) | 20.0 (150) | +23.3 | -10.3 |
| California | Central | | 1971 | 10.4** | 11.8 (498) | 9.8 (500) | +13.5 | - 5.8 |
| | | | 1974 | | 11.5 (496) | 11.5 (496) | +10.6 | +10.6 |
| | Eastern | Fresno | 1971 | 7.8** | 6.6 (212) | 4.8 (187) | -15.4 | -38.5 |
| | | | 1974 | | 7.1 (465) | 3.2 (187) | - 9.0 | -59.0 |
| | | Sacramento | 1971 | 7.3** | 5.7 (281) | 6.9 (434) | -21.9 | - 5.5 |
| | | | 1974 | | 4.3 (492) | 6.6 (483) | -41.1 | - 9.6 |
| | Northern | Oakland | 1971 | 15.1 | 12.6 (475) | 8.9 (1,077) | -16.5 | -52.7 |
| | | San Francisco | 1971 | 18.8 | 7.8 (564) | 10.0 (668) | -58.5 | -29.1 |
| | | S.F./Oakland/Eureka | 1974 | 14.1** | 16.5 (816) | | +17.0 | |
| | | San Jose | 1971 | 6.2 | 5.5 (473) | | -11.3 | — |
| | | | 1974 | 6.4** | 9.2 (403) | | +43.8 | — |
| Colorado | | Denver | 1971 | 4.3** | 3.8 (393) | 2.9 (314) | -11.6 | -32.6 |
| | | | 1974 | | 2.4 (451) | 2.7 (490) | -44.2 | -37.2 |
| Connecticut | | Bridgeport | 1971 | 6.5 | 2.5 (401) | 4.5 (398) | -61.5 | -30.8 |
| | | | 1974 | | 3.1 (446) | | -52.3 | — |

| State / Region | Location | Year | | | | | |
|---|---|---|---|---|---|---|---|
| | Hartford | 1971 | 4.6 | 2.0 (386) | 2.1 (290) | −36.3 | −34.5 |
| | New Haven | 1974 | 5.5 | 2.2 (500) | 2.5 (160) | −52.2 | −45.7 |
| | | 1969-73 | | 3.5 (395) | 3.7 (361) | −36.4 | −32.7 |
| | | 1974c | | 3.3 | | −40.0 | — |
| | | | | 2.7 (445) | 2.7 (113) | −50.9 | −50.9 |
| Delaware | | 1971 | 13.2** | 9.5 (280) | 11.7 (231) | −28.0 | −11.4 |
| | | 1974 | 13.2** | 8.5 (312) | 12.7 (321) | −35.6 | − 3.8 |
| District of Columbia | | 1971 | 65.1 | 56.4 (351) | 77.7 (495) | −13.4 | +19.4 |
| | | 8/72 to 2/73d | | 66.3 (14,552) | — | + 1.8 | — |
| | | 6/73d | | | | | |
| | | 6/17/74e | | 66.6 (286) | 76.6 (252) | + 2.3 | +17.7 |
| Florida — Middle | Ft. Myers | 1971 | 7.5 | | 5.2 (305) | — | — |
| | | 1974 | | 3.6 (2,835) | | −52.0 | −30.7 |
| | Jacksonville | 1971 | 18.2 | | 13.3 (310) | — | −26.9 |
| | | 1974 | | 15.4 (6,267) | 26.0 (500) | −15.4 | +42.9 |
| | Ocala | 1971 | 16.2 | | 13.5 (297) | — | −16.7 |
| | | 1974 | | 9.4 (2,353) | 8.3 (228) | −42.0 | −48.8 |
| | Orlando | 1971 | 10.5 | | 6.2 (465) | — | −41.0 |
| | | 1974 | | 6.6 (5,294) | 7.2 (484) | −37.1 | −31.4 |
| | Tampa | 1971 | 8.5 | | 6.4 (327) | — | −24.7 |
| | | 1974 | | 5.0 (11,768) | 5.7 (389) | −41.2 | −32.9 |
| Florida — Northern | Gainesville | 1974 | 17.0** | 9.5 (349) | 12.7 (165) | −44.1 | −25.3 |
| | Marianna | 1974 | 15.3** | 12.6 (350) | | −17.6 | — |
| | Pensacola | 1974 | 14.5** | 10.2 (500) | 17.7 (130) | −29.7 | +22.1 |
| | Tallahassee | 1974 | 29.6** | 24.1 (498) | | −18.6 | — |
| Florida — Southern | Ft. Lauderdale | 1974 | 9.7** | 5.9 (541) | 7.1 (241) | −39.2 | −26.8 |
| | Ft. Pierce | 1974 | 17.5** | 9.7 (535) | | −44.6 | — |
| | Key West | 1974 | 8.2** | 3.2 (526) | 3.7 (136) | −61.0 | −54.9 |
| | Miami | 1974 | 12.2** | 7.4 (552) | 15.7 (1,436) | −39.3 | +28.7 |
| | W. Palm Beach | 1974 | 14.7** | 10.3 (552) | 8.0 (187) | −29.9 | −45.6 |
| Georgia — Middle | Albany | 1974 | 34.5** | 27.7 (274) | 18.6 (143) | −19.7 | −47.2 |
| | Americus | 1974 | 39.0** | 30.8 (276) | | −20.8 | — |
| | Athens | 1974 | 20.7** | 14.8 (277) | | −28.5 | — |
| | Columbia | 1974 | 28.6 | 25.3 (336) | 24.6 (138) | −11.5 | −14.0 |
| | Macon | 1974 | 32.2** | 26.9 (316) | 23.6 (140) | −16.5 | −26.7 |
| | Thomasville | 1974 | 31.1** | 20.6 (277) | | −33.8 | — |
| | Valdosta | 1974 | 23.5** | 19.3 (275) | 13.1 (283) | −17.9 | −44.3 |

| State | District | Division | Year | Percentage of Nonwhites | | | Rate of Error[a] | |
|---|---|---|---|---|---|---|---|---|
| | | | | 1970 Census* | Master Wheel | Actual Jurors | Master Wheel | Actual Jurors |
| Georgia | Northern | Atlanta | 1971 | 18.4 | 17.0 (400) | 15.3 (567) | − 7.6 | −16.8 |
| | | | 1974 | | 14.4 (494) | 13.8 (723) | −21.7 | −25.0 |
| | | Gainesville | 1971 | 6.5 | 3.4 (290) | — | −47.7 | — |
| | | | 1974 | | 2.6 (344) | — | −60.0 | — |
| | | Newnan | 1971 | 22.3 | 14.4 (299) | 14.5 (138) | −35.4 | −35.0 |
| | | | 1974 | | 12.6 (341) | — | −43.5 | — |
| | | Rome | 1971 | 6.9 | 4.1 (296) | 7.6 (223) | −40.6 | +10.1 |
| | | | 1974 | | 6.9 (348) | 5.1 (157) | 0.0 | −26.1 |
| | Southern | Augusta | 1971 | 31.3 | 34.1 (490) | 29.9 (412) | + 8.9 | − 4.5 |
| | | | 1974 | | 27.8 (317) | — | −11.2 | — |
| | | Brunswick | 1971 | 23.3 | 28.0 (480) | 47.1 (291) | +20.0 | +102.1 |
| | | | 1974 | | 19.7 (315) | — | −15.5 | — |
| | | Dublin | 1971 | 25.9 | 32.2 (466) | 28.4 (380) | +24.4 | + 9.7 |
| | | | 1974 | | 18.7 (316) | — | −27.8 | — |
| | | Savannah | 1971 | 30.4 | 31.1 (474) | 28.2 (500) | + 2.3 | − 7.2 |
| | | | 1974 | | 26.7 (491) | — | −12.2 | — |
| | | Swainsboro | 1971 | 30.5 | 31.7 (477) | 19.4 (283) | + 3.9 | −36.4 |
| | | | 1974 | | 20.2 (317) | — | −33.8 | — |
| | | Waycross | 1971 | 19.2 | 29.2 (487) | 24.3 (230) | +52.1 | +26.6 |
| | | | 1974 | | 14.2 (316) | — | −26.0 | — |
| Hawaii | | | 1971 | 61.3 | 71.8 (404) | 70.9 (210) | +17.1 | +15.7 |
| | | | 1973 | | 66.5 (332) | 69.3 (199) | + 8.5 | +13.1 |
| Illinois | | Eastern | 1971 | 15.7 | 10.5 (1,995) | 13.5 (463) | −33.1 | −14.0 |
| | | | 1974 | | 17.5 (489) | 16.7 (448) | +11.5 | + 6.4 |
| Indiana | Northern | Hammond (at Hammond) | 1974 | 16.5** | 30.4 (483) | 20.0 (300) | +84.2 | +21.2 |
| | | South Bend | 1974 | 4.1** | 2.5 (500) | 3.5 (283) | −39.0 | −14.6 |
| | Southern | | 1971 | 5.7 | 12.8 (485) | 15.2 (500) | +124.6 | +166.7 |
| | | | 1974 | | 4.4 (475) | 2.7 (475) | −22.8 | −52.6 |
| Kansas | | Kansas City-Leavenworth | 1971 | 8.1 | 4.4 (475) | 9.6 (228) | −45.7 | +18.5 |
| | | | 1974 | | 6.3 (495) | 9.7 (218) | −22.2 | +19.8 |
| | | Topeka | 1971 | 5.4 | 3.3 (471) | 3.0 (229) | −38.9 | −44.4 |
| | | | 1974 | | 2.1 (486) | 2.1 (146) | −61.1 | −61.1 |
| | | Witchita-Hutchinson | 1971 | 4.7 | 3.5 (471) | 4.7 (230) | −25.5 | 0 |
| | | | 1974 | | 2.2 (496) | 3.0 (198) | −53.2 | −36.2 |

| | | | | | | | | |
|---|---|---|---|---|---|---|---|---|
| Louisiana | Eastern | New Orleans | 1971 | [illegible] | [illegible] | [illegible] | [illegible] | [illegible] |
| | | Baton Rouge | 1971 | 29.3 | – | 32.0 (100) | – | + 9.2 |
| | Eastern | | 1974 | 26.6** | 21.8 (500) | 21.8 (500) | –18.0 | –18.0 |
| | Middle | | 1974 | 30.3** | 21.4 (350) | 24.9 (209) | –29.4 | –17.8 |
| | Western | Alexandria | 1974 | 23.8** | 15.0 (341) | 18.6 (279) | –37.0 | –21.8 |
| | | Lafayette | 1974 | 22.6** | 15.1 (350) | 17.6 (318) | –33.2 | –22.1 |
| | | Lake Charles | 1974 | 17.3** | 15.8 (341) | 17.3 (225) | – 8.7 | 0 |
| | | Monroe | 1974 | 31.3** | 25.5 (341) | – | –18.5 | – |
| | | Opelousas | 1974 | 32.4** | 30.7 (322) | – | – 5.2 | – |
| | | Shreveport | 1974 | 31.5** | 22.9 (350) | – | –27.3 | – |
| Maryland | | | 1971 | 16.7** | 7.1 (410) | 10.8 (500) | –57.5 | –35.3 |
| | | | 1974 | | 13.8 (500) | 11.0 (500) | –17.4 | –34.1 |
| Michigan | Eastern | Southern (Detroit) | 1974 | 15.9** | 14.2 (506) | 16.8 (417) | –10.7 | + 5.7 |
| | | Southern (Flint) | 1974 | 9.2** | 7.0 (300) | – | –23.9 | – |
| Mississippi | Northern | Delta | 1974 | 48.5** | 35.6 (500) | – | –26.6 | – |
| | | Eastern | 1974 | 22.6** | 15.2 (500) | 14.0 (114) | –32.7 | –38.1 |
| | | Greenville | 1974 | 51.8** | 38.0 (500) | – | –26.6 | – |
| | | Western | 1974 | 27.0** | 16.2 (500) | – | –40.0 | – |
| | Southern | Eastern | 1971 | 30.3 | 15.8 (486) | 17.7 (369) | –47.9 | –41.6 |
| | | | 1974 | | 21.8 (500) | – | –28.1 | – |
| | | Hattiesburg | 1971 | 23.3 | 13.1 (482) | 13.7 (476) | –43.8 | –41.2 |
| | | | 1974 | | 19.4 (500) | 10.4 (115) | –16.7 | –55.4 |
| | | Jackson | 1971 | 34.2 | 23.5 (481) | 22.2 (500) | –31.3 | –35.1 |
| | | | 1974 | | 22.6 (500) | 23.2 (315) | –33.9 | –32.2 |
| | | Southern | 1971 | 14.5 | 8.8 (477) | 11.6 (500) | –39.3 | –20.0 |
| | | | 1974 | | 11.0 (500) | 10.5 (275) | –24.1 | –27.6 |
| | | Western | 1971 | 47.3 | 28.2 (248) | 24.5 (482) | –40.4 | –48.2 |
| | | | 1974 | | 34.8 (500) | – | –26.4 | – |
| Missouri | Eastern | Eastern | 1971 | 13.3 | 12.6 (532) | 18.7 (450) | – 5.3 | +40.6 |
| | | | 1974 | | 14.8 (500) | 15.4 (364) | +11.3 | +15.8 |
| | | Southeastern | 1971 | 5.8 | 2.9 (311) | – | –50.0 | – |
| | | | 1974 | | 2.9 (341) | – | –50.0 | – |
| | Western | Central | 1974 | 4.8** | 0.8 (500) | 2.0 (351) | –83.3 | –58.3 |
| | | Western | 1974 | 11.2** | 14.6 (500) | 10.5 (535) | +30.4 | – 6.7 |
| New Jersey | | Camden | 1971 | 10.7 | 10.9 (229) | 11.3 (150) | + 1.9 | + 5.6 |
| | | | 1974 | 11.0** | 9.1 (493) | 7.8 (385) | –17.3 | –29.1 |
| | | Newark | 1971 | 10.9 | 6.5 (479) | 8.0 (500) | –40.4 | –26.6 |
| | | | 1974 | 11.1** | 7.2 (483) | 10.2 (498) | –35.1 | – 8.1 |

| State | District | Division | Year | Percentage of Nonwhites 1970 Census* | Percentage of Nonwhites Master Wheel | Percentage of Nonwhites Actual Jurors | Rate of Error[a] Master Wheel | Rate of Error[a] Actual Jurors |
|---|---|---|---|---|---|---|---|---|
| New Jersey | | Trenton | 1971 | 6.7 | 8.3 (228) | 6.0 (150) | +23.9 | −10.4 |
| | | | 1974 | 6.9** | 9.6 (471) | 10.3 (349) | +39.1 | +49.3 |
| New Mexico | | Albuerque-Santa Fe | 1971 | 10.1 | 1.5 (f) | 1.0 (f) | −85.1 | −90.1 |
| | | Roswell | 1971 | 4.3 | 3.5 (f) | 2.2 (f) | −18.6 | −44.2 |
| | | Statewide | 1974 | 8.3** | 1.3 (1,274) | 0 (384) | −84.3 | −100.0 |
| New York | Eastern | | 1971 | 13.1 | 6.8 (458) | 10.0 (500) | −48.1 | −23.7 |
| | | | 1974 | 13.4** | 9.3 (425) | 12.2 (500) | −30.6 | − 9.0 |
| | Southern | | 1974 | 18.5** | 17.3 (498) | 19.3 (514) | − 6.5 | + 4.3 |
| | Western | Buffalo | 1974 | 6.3** | 3.6 (500) | 9.2 (500) | −42.9 | +46.0 |
| | | Rochester | 1974 | 4.7** | 2.8 (500) | 3.6 (449) | −40.4 | −23.4 |
| North Carolina | Eastern | Elizabeth City | 1971 | 36.1 | 21.3 (319) | 18.7 (216) | −41.0 | −48.2 |
| | | | 1974 | 37.4** | 23.3 (330) | — | −37.7 | — |
| | | Fayetteville | 1971 | 31.8 | 53.4 (448) | 18.9 (383) | +67.9 | −40.6 |
| | | | 1974 | 31.7** | 22.8 (368) | 26.7 (101) | −28.1 | −15.8 |
| | | New Bern | 1971 | 21.4 | 12.8 (299) | 14.0 (317) | −40.2 | −34.6 |
| | | | 1974 | 20.9** | 15.4 (370) | — | −26.3 | — |
| | | Raleigh | 1971 | 24.3 | 12.9 (349) | 12.9 (385) | −46.9 | −46.9 |
| | | | 1974 | 24.9** | 12.4 (356) | 14.9 (114) | −50.2 | −40.2 |
| | | Washington | 1971 | 33.6 | 17.9 (309) | 45.6 (150) | −46.7 | +35.7 |
| | | | 1974 | 33.8** | 19.5 (328) | — | −42.3 | — |
| | | Wilmington | 1971 | 26.5 | 17.9 (296) | 17.9 (283) | −32.5 | −32.5 |
| | | | 1974 | 27.1** | 15.5 (368) | 22.2 (126) | −42.8 | −18.1 |
| | | Wilson | 1971 | 34.9 | 15.9 (358) | 18.0 (380) | −54.4 | −48.4 |
| | | | 1974 | 35.8** | 21.0 (328) | — | −41.3 | — |
| | Western | Asheville | 1974 | 5.5** | 3.9 (459) | 5.0 (101) | −29.0 | − 9.1 |
| | | Bryson City | 1974 | 5.3** | 4.5 (466) | — | −15.1 | — |
| | | Charlotte | 1974 | 19.3** | 15.7 (445) | 16.5 (103) | −18.7 | −14.5 |
| | | Shelby | 1974 | 10.5** | 8.9 (463) | — | −15.2 | — |
| | | Statesville | 1974 | 9.3** | 5.4 (442) | — | −41.9 | — |
| Ohio | Northern | Eastern (Cleveland) | 1974 | 11.7** | 10.0 (489) | 9.6 (356) | −14.5 | −18.0 |
| | | Western | 1974 | 5.0** | 4.8 (290) | 3.9 (312) | − 4.0 | −22.0 |
| Oklahoma | Eastern | | 1971 | 13.1 | 8.6 (769) | 7.3 (355) | −34.1 | −44.3 |
| | | | 1973 | | 11.9 (436) | 9.0 (412) | − 9.2 | −31.3 |
| | Western | | 1974 | 7.7** | 5.6 (450) | — | −27.3 | — |

| State | Region | Location | Year | (%) | | | | |
|---|---|---|---|---|---|---|---|---|
| Pennsylvania | Eastern | | 1974 | | 11.2 (498) | 10.2 (499) | -18.8 | -26.1 |
| South Carolina | | Area A | 1969 | 19.0 | 17.1 (973) | | -10.0 | -15.3 |
| | | | 1971 | | 16.5 (438) | 16.1 (235) | -13.2 | -32.6 |
| | | | 1974 | | 13.5 (460) | 12.8 (273) | -28.9 | |
| | | Area B | 1969 | 29.5 | 18.9 (973) | | -35.9 | +42.7 |
| | | | 1971 | | 26.8 (441) | 42.1 (316) | - 9.2 | - 9.8 |
| | | | 1974 | | 23.5 (459) | 26.6 (783) | -20.3 | |
| | | Area C | 1969 | 34.3 | 21.1 (964) | | -38.5 | -18.1 |
| | | | 1971 | | 34.6 (449) | 28.1 (338) | + 0.9 | - 8.5 |
| | | | 1974 | | 29.4 (452) | 31.4 (395) | -14.3 | |
| South Dakota | Western | | 1971 | 9.9 | | 6.4 (110) | | -35.4 |
| Tennessee | Eastern | Northern | 1971 | 8.1 | 2.5 (435) | 2.9 (382) | -69.1 | -64.2 |
| | | | 1974 | | 5.3 (492) | | -34.6 | |
| | | Southern | 1971 | 16.0 | 13.2 (433) | 13.5 (483) | -17.5 | -15.6 |
| | | | 1974 | | 10.2 (498) | 4.1 (194) | -36.3 | -74.4 |
| | Middle | Winchester | 1971 | 5.8 | 5.0 (438) | 1.9 (107) | -13.8 | -67.2 |
| | | | 1974 | | 6.3 (322) | | + 8.6 | |
| | | Columbia | 1971 | 8.0 | 8.6 (163) | | + 7.5 | |
| | | | 1974 | | 8.4 (453) | | + 5.0 | |
| | | Nashville | 1971 | 14.4 | 12.4 (210) | 17.2 (116) | -13.9 | +19.4 |
| | | | 1974 | | 13.8 (427) | 15.6 (160) | - 4.2 | + 8.3 |
| | Western | Eastern | 1971 | 15.3 | 15.9 (258) | | + 3.9 | +19.0 |
| | | | 1974 | | 12.0 (333) | 18.2 (148) | -21.6 | + 9.4 |
| | | Western | 1971 | 31.9 | 34.6 (422) | 34.9 (175) | + 8.5 | + 4.1 |
| | | | 1974 | | 26.6 (500) | 33.2 (208) | -16.6 | |
| Texas | Eastern | Beaumont | 1974 | 19.1** | 15.6 (614) | 17.6 (176) | -18.3 | - 7.9 |
| | | Marshall | 1974 | 28.3** | 22.3 (507) | 19.2 (104) | -21.2 | -32.2 |
| | | Paris | 1974 | 11.9** | 11.1 (579) | | - 6.7 | |
| | | Sherman | 1974 | 6.6** | 3.8 (644) | | -42.4 | |
| | | Texarkana | 1974 | 17.6** | 15.9 (618) | | - 9.6 | |
| | | Tyler | 1974 | 19.1** | 19.1 (572) | 14.5 (304) | 0 | -24.1 |
| | Northern | Abilene | 1974 | 4.5** | 1.7 (481) | 1.9 (522) | -62.2 | -57.8 |
| | | Dallas | 1974 | 15.2** | 13.2 (432) | 13.1 (580) | -13.2 | -13.8 |
| | | Fort Worth | 1974 | 9.2** | 7.4 (433) | 6.0 (698) | -19.6 | -34.8 |
| | | Lubbock | 1974 | 5.5** | 1.8 (546) | | -67.3 | |
| | | Witchita Falls | 1974 | 6.2** | 2.5 (481) | | -59.7 | |
| | Southern | Galveston | 1971 | 15.0 | 21.4 (491) | 12.4 (121) | +15.7 | -17.3 |
| | | Houston | 1971 | 18.5 | 20.4 (475) | 28.5 (411) | +10.3 | +54.1 |
| | | | 1974 | | | 17.2 (483) | | - 7.0 |

| State | District | Division | Year | Percentage of Nonwhites | | | Rate of Error[a] | |
|---|---|---|---|---|---|---|---|---|
| | | | | 1970 Census* | Master Wheel | Actual Jurors | Master Wheel | Actual Jurors |
| Texas | Western | Austin | 1971 | 9.9 | 13.5 (430) | 12.1 (190) | +36.4 | +22.2 |
| | | | 1974 | | 5.0 (557) | 3.8 (316) | −49.5 | −61.6 |
| | | Midland-Odessa | 1971 | 6.0 | 4.3 (439) | 6.7 (120) | −28.3 | +11.7 |
| | | | 1974 | | 5.0 (558) | 0.6 (318) | −16.7 | −90.0 |
| | | San Antonio | 1971 | 6.0 | 7.2 (458) | 5.8 (382) | +20.0 | − 3.3 |
| | | | 1974 | | 4.6 (609) | 6.2 (500) | −23.3 | + 3.3 |
| | | Waco | 1971 | 11.8 | 17.5 (457) | — | +48.0 | — |
| | | | 1974 | | 13.6 (500) | — | +15.3 | — |
| Virginia | Western | Charlottesville | 1974 | 16.6** | 8.9 (501) | 8.6 (117) | −46.4 | −48.2 |
| | | Danville | 1974 | 25.1** | 20.0 (365) | 17.4 (265) | −20.3 | −30.7 |
| | | Lynchburg | 1974 | 17.5** | 15.9 (465) | 9.1 (247) | − 9.1 | −48.0 |
| | | Roanoke | 1974 | 4.6 | 7.8 (404) | 7.7 (247) | +69.6 | +67.4 |
| Washington | Eastern | Yakima | 1974 | 4.9 | 1.6 (322) | 2.5 (127) | −67.3 | −49.0 |
| West Virginia | Southern | Beckley | 1971 | 7.7 | 6.8 (249) | — | −11.7 | — |
| | | | 1974 | | 4.3 (278) | — | −44.2 | — |
| | | Bluefield | 1971 | 9.6 | 10.8 (185) | — | +12.5 | — |
| | | | 1974 | | 7.9 (278) | — | −17.7 | — |

*Over-21 population, unless marked by two asterisks [**] which indicate that the over-18 population has been computed.

aUnder- (−) or over- (+) representation (see pp. 295-96).

bThese figures for the Fairbanks Division include blacks only, and do not include other nonwhites (see also Tables G-6 and G-7).

cUnited States v. Jenkins, 496 F.2d 57 (2nd Cir. 1974).

dThese two figures were obtained directly from the jury commissioner's office rather than from the official survey submitted to the Administrative Office.

eVisual observation of jurors in both the superior and district courts.

fSize of sample not available.

**Table G-2. Blacks on State Court Juries**

| State | Percentage of Blacks in the County | Percentage of Blacks on the Jury[a] | Rate of Error | Date and Source |
|---|---|---|---|---|
| *Alabama* | | | | |
| Jefferson County | 27.6 (21-65) | Ranges from low of 16.0 (week of Oct. 12, 1970) to high of 35.7 (week of May 31, 1971) | −42.0 to +29.3 | *Bryant v. State*, 6 Div. 339, 272 So.2d 286, 293 (Ala. Crim. App. 1972). |
| Lawrence County | 15.4 (over 21) | Approx. 4.9 | −68.2 | Analysis of 1,000 persons on the 1972 jury list. *Beecher v. State*, 320 So.2d 716, 721 (Ala. Crim. App. 1974). |
| | | Approx. 5.2 | −66.2 | Analysis of 3,000 persons on the 1973 jury list. *Id.* at 720. |
| | | 6.0 | −61.0 | Analysis of 150 names on jury venires in April and June 1973. *Id.* at 721. |
| Montgomery County | 31.6 (between 21 and 65) | 8.8 | −72.2 | Survey of 320 jurors summoned in Jan.-Feb. 1972 by the Southern Poverty Law Center. *Penn. v. Eubanks*, 360 F. Supp. 699 (N.D. Ala. 1973). |
| *Arkansas* | | | | |
| Miller County | 19.7 (over 21) | 7.3 | −62.9 | December 1971, 800 jurors on venire. *Murrah v. Arkansas*, 532 F.2d 105 (8th Cir. 1976). |
| *California* | | | | |
| Alameda County | 13.4 (over 18) | 12.9 | − 3.7 | 1972 and 1973. Visual observation at Oakland Courthouse of 499 jurors. |
| Los Angeles County | 9.5 (over 18) | 6.7 | −29.5 | 1,000 actual jurors questioned in January and February, 1973, by Leo Breiman for *People v. Taylor*, No. A-277-425 (Los Angeles Superior Court, 1974). |
| Sacramento County | 4.8 (over 18) | 2.2 | −54.2 | 493 cards filled out during the summer of 1972 by persons selected as prospective jurors by the court. |
| San Francisco County: Trial Jurors | 10.9 (over 18) | 12.5 | +14.7 | Visual observation of 1,207 jurors in 1972-73. |

| State | Percentage of Blacks in the County | Percentage of Blacks on the Jury[a] | Rate of Error | Date and Source |
|---|---|---|---|---|
| Grand Jurors | 10.9 (over 18) | 10.5 | -3.7 | Survey of the 114 grand jurors who served between 1970 and 1976. Plaintiffs' brief in *Quadra v. Superior Court, Hastings Law Journal* 27 (1976): 616-19, 633. |
| San Diego County | 4.0 (over 18) | 3.9 | -2.5 | Visual observation of 307 jurors, May 21, 1973. |
| *Colorado* | | | | |
| Denver County | 7.5 (over 18) | 4.1 | -45.3 | Visual observation of 221 jurors in June 1972. |
| | | 7.4 | -1.3 | Visual observation of 176 jurors, June 24, 1974. |
| El Paso County | 4.9 (over 18) | 2.0 | -59.2 | 883 cards filled out by actual jurors 1972-73. |
| *Florida* | | | | |
| Levy County | 20.7 | 1969–12.8 | -38.2 | *Marshall v. Holmes*, 365 F.Supp. 613, 616, (N.D. Fla. 1973). |
| | | 1970–14.5 | -30.0 | |
| | (over 18) | 1971– 7.6 | -63.3 | |
| | | 1972–14.4 | -30.4 | |
| | | 1973–18.0 | -13.0 | |
| *Georgia* | | | | |
| Coweta County: Trial Jury | 28.3 (over 18) | 10.9 | -61.5 | *White v. State*, 230 Ga. 327, 331, 196 S.E.2d 849, 853 (1973) *appeal dismissed* 414 U.S. 886 (1973); *Gould v. State*, 131 Ga. App. 811, 207 S.E.2d 519 (1974). |
| Grand Jury | | 14.3 | -49.5 | *Gould, supra*, at 523. |
| DeKalb County: Grand Jury | 12.0 (over 21) | 3.4 | -71.7 | Grand jury pool of 1,581 persons. *Julian v. State*, 134 Ga. App. 592, 215 S.E.2d 496 (1975). |
| Dougherty County: Trial Jurors | 30.2 (over 21) | 19.2 | -36.4 | 1972 lists: *Thompson v. Sheppard*, 490 F.2d 830 (5th Cir. 1974). |
| Grand Jurors | | 16.4 | -45.7 | Ibid. |
| Quitman County: Trial Jurors | 51.3 (over 18) | 34.6 | -32.6 | 1973 lists: *Foster v. Sparks*, 506 F.2d 805, 808 (5th Cir. 1975). |
| Grand Jurors | | 36.7 | -28.5 | |

| Location | % (age) | | % deviation | Source |
|---|---|---|---|---|
| *Illinois* <br> Cook County (Chicago) | 18.6 (over 18) | 19.7 | + 5.9 | Visual observation of 461 jurors at the Civic Center Courthouse and the criminal court at 26th and California, on June 4, 1974. |
| *Maryland* <br> Baltimore City | 40.8 (over 18) | 9/69 - 8/70 = 34.4 <br> 9/70 - 8/71 = 40.7 <br> 1972 = 45.5 <br> 1973 = 46.7 <br> Jan. 1974 = 45.0 | -15.7 <br> - 0.2 <br> +11.5 <br> +14.5 <br> +10.3 | Official courthouse records of all persons qualified as jurors. |
| *Massachusetts* <br> Suffolk County (Boston) | 11.3 (over 21) | 6.9 | -38.9 | Visual observation of 130 jurors on June 10, 1974. |
| *Missouri* <br> City of St. Louis | 34.4 (over 21) | 38.4 | +11.6 | Visual observation of 242 jurors during the week of March 26, 1973. |
| *Nevada* <br> Washoe County (Reno) | 1.6 (over 18) | 0.8 | -50.0 | 835 cards filled out by jurors as they reported, 1972-73. |
| *New Mexico* <br> Bernalillo County (Albuquerque) | 1.9 (Over 18) | 1.0 | -47.4 | A count of 618 juror questionnaires at different times, 1972-74. |
| *New York* <br> Albany County | 4.4 (over 21) | Approximately 2 | -54.4 | March 1973. *Anderson v. Casscles*, 531 F.2d 682, 685 (2nd Cir. 1976). |
| Erie County (Buffalo) | 8.4 (21-74) | 5.5 | -34.5 | Attica Bros. Defense Fund Study of 1,199 qualified jurors in early 1974. (Subsequently found unconstitutional for other reasons.) *People v. Attica Bros.*, June 27, 1974; *The Conspiracy*, Vol. 4, No. 11 (Sept. 1974). |
| Brooklyn (Kings Co.) | 21.5 (over 21) | 11.4 | -47.0 | Visual observation of 176 jurors, Dec. 20, 1972. |
| | | 15.7 | -27.0 | Visual observation of 229 jurors, June 7, 1974. |

| State | Percentage of Blacks in the County | Percentage of Blacks on the Jury[a] | Rate of Error | Date and Source |
|---|---|---|---|---|
| Manhattan (N.Y. Co.) | 21.8 (over 21) | 21.3 | – 2.3 | Visual observation of 253 jurors, Dec. 20, 1972. |
| | | 22.8 | + 4.6 | Visual observation of 426 jurors, June 6, 1974. |
| Queens County: Grand Jury | 10.6 (over 21) | 4.4 | –58.5 | Survey of the 1971 Grand Jury Rolls by the New York Legal Aid Society. |
| *North Carolina* | | | | |
| Beaufort County | 30.2 | 12.0 | –60.3 | April 1975. Figures prepared prior to the Joan Little murder case. *Washington Post*, April 23, 1975, p. A29. |
| Forsythe County | Approximately 20 | Approximately 10 | –50.0 | 1970-71. *State v. Cornell*, 281 N.C. 20, 187 S.E.2d 768, 777 (1972). |
| *South Carolina* | | | | |
| Edgefield County | 51.6 | 19.1 | –63.0 | 1968-71. *Bright v. Thurmond*, Civ. No. 71-459 (D.S.C. 1971. |
| Marion County: Trial Jurors | 44 (between 21 and 65) | 1970:35 | –20.5 | *Blackwell v. Thomas*, 476 F.2d 443, 446 (4th Cir. 1973). |
| | | 1971:32 | –27.3 | Ibid. |
| | | 1972:29 | –34.1 | Ibid. |
| Grand Jurors | | 1970:22 | –50.0 | Ibid. |
| | | 1971:33 | –25.0 | Ibid. |
| | | 1972:28 | –36.4 | Ibid. |
| Spartanburg County | 21.1 | 12.4 | –41.2 | Survey of the 401 persons called as jurors in 1970 and 1971. *McKinney v. Walker*, 394 F.Supp. 1015, 1017 (D.S.C. 1974). |
| | | 5.7 | –73.0 | Survey of the 228 persons who sat as jurors in 1970 and 1971. *Id.* |
| *Texas* | | | | |
| Harris County (Houston): Grand Jurors | 20.0 | 15.0 | –25.0 | Survey of 156 grand jurors who served between 1969 and 1972. *Dumont v. Estelle*, 377 F.Supp. 374, 386 (S.D. Texas 1974). |

[a]Figures refer to *trial* juries unless otherwise indicated.

**Table G-3.    Hispanic-Americans on Federal Court Juries**

| Federal Courts | Percentage Spanish-surnamed in Division | Percentage Spanish-surnamed on Jury | Rate of Error | Date and Source |
|---|---|---|---|---|
| U.S. District Court for the District of Colorado: | | | | |
| Denver Division | 8.9 | 4.9 | −44.9 | Sample of 723, Jan. 1972 to June 1973, *United States v. Test*, 399 F. Supp. 683, 687 (D. Colo. 1975). |
| | | 6.7 | −24.7 | Sample of 2,020, Jan. 1973 to Dec. 1974. Ibid. |
| | | 6.2 | −30.3 | Sample of 2,111, July 30, 1973 to May 29, 1974. Ibid. |
| Grand Junction Division | 8.9 | 4.8 | −46.1 | Sample of 832 on July 2, 1973. Ibid. |
| Pueblo Division | 16.3 | 12.8 | −21.5 | Sample of 872 on July 6, 1973. Ibid. |
| U.S. District Court for the Northern District of California | 11.2 | 6.3 | −43.8 | 23 grand juries assembled between 1969 and 1975, surveyed for *United States v. Rafofsky*, No. CR-74-687 OJC (N.D. Cal., Feb. 11, 1975). See *Hastings Law Journal* 28 (1976): 61. |

**Table G-4. Hispanic-Americans on State Court Juries**

| State Courts | Percentage Spanish-surnamed in County | Percentage Spanish-surnamed on Jury | Rate of Error | Date and Source |
|---|---|---|---|---|
| *California* | | | | |
| Alameda County | 11.1 (over 18) | 0.7 | −93.7 | Visual observation of 449 jurors in 1972 and 1973. |
| Los Angeles County[a] | 11.7 (over 18) | 8.6 | −26.5 | 1,000 actual jurors questioned in January and February, 1973 by Leo Breiman for *People v. Taylor*, No. A-277-425 (Los Angeles Superior Court, 1974). |
| Marin County | 5.4 (over 18) | 2.8 | −48.1 | 460 randomly selected eligible jurors examined in February 1975 by Ruth Astle and Anita Oppenheimer. |
| Orange County | 9.5 (over 18) | 1.2 | −87.4 | 606 jurors questions by Harvey Grody, Mike Kinney and Jim Wisley, Calif. State Univ., Fullerton, January-June 1974. |
| Sacramento County | 8.1 (over 18) | 4.0 | −50.6 | 493 forms filled out by prospective jurors in 1972 and returned to the jury commissioner. |
| San Bernardino County | 13.2 (over 18) | 10.1 | −23.5 | 724 forms filled out by prospective jurors as they reported for jury duty in July 1972. |
| San Diego County | 10.4 (over 21) | 5.2 | −50.0 | An examination of the names of 1,000 persons selected for jury duty on January 14, 1972. |
| San Francisco County: Trial Jurors | 12.1 (over 18) | 8.5 | −18.3 | Visual observation of 307 jurors, May 21, 1973. |
| | | 4.6 | −62.0 | Visual observation of 1,207 jurors at various times, 1972-73. |
| Grand Jurors | | 3.5 | −71.1 | Survey of the 114 grand jurors who served between 1970 and 1976. Plaintiffs' brief in *Quadra v. Superior Court, Hastings Law Journal* 27 (1976): 616-19,633. |
| Santa Clara County | 13.6 (over 21) | 6.1 | −55.1 | Examination of list of 1,261 persons seated as jurors, Sept. 4, 1969 to Sept. 7, 1970, by attorney Richard Such. (*People v. Rios*, No. 48220 [Santa Clara Superior Court, 1970].) |
| | | 6.8 | −50.0 | Examination of list of 3,200 qualified jurors, late 1971, by Angela Davis's defense team. |
| | | 7.4 | −45.6 | Examination of another list of 5,273 qualified jurors, early 1972, by Angela Davis's defense team. |

| | | | | |
|---|---|---|---|---|
| *Colorado* | | | | |
| Denver County | 16.8 (all persons) | 8.9 | −34.6 | Visual observation of 481 jurors, fall 1972. |
| | | 8.1 | −51.8 | An examination of the names of 1,440 persons summoned for jury duty, June-August 1972. |
| | | 8.6 | −48.8 | An examination of the names of 753 persons summoned for jury duty, May-June 1974. |
| El Paso County (Colorado Springs) | 7.2 (over 18) | 9.7 | −42.3 | Visual observation of 176 jurors, June 24, 1974. |
| | | 3.0 | −58.3 | 888 cards filled out by persons reporting for jury duty in 1972 and 1973. |
| Pueblo County | 31.3 | 27.4 | −12.5 | 551 cards filled out by persons reporting for jury duty in 1972, 1973, and 1974. |
| *Nevada* | | | | |
| Washoe County (Reno) | 4.4 (over 18) | 3.4 | −22.7 | 835 cards filled out by persons reporting for jury duty in 1972 and 1973. |
| *New Mexico* | | | | |
| Bernalillo County (Albuquerque) | 34.7 (over 18) | 20.8 | −40.1 | An examination of the names of 668 qualified jurors in September, October, and December 1971. |
| | | 18.8 | −45.8 | An examination of 618 juror questionnaires from different periods in 1972, 1973, and 1974. |
| *New York* | | | | |
| King's County (Brooklyn) | 7.5[b] (over 21) | 0 | −100.0 | Visual observation of 176 jurors, Dec. 20, 1972. |
| | | 0.4 | −94.7 | Visual observation of 229 jurors, June 7, 1974. |
| New York County (Manhattan) | 14.8[b] (over 21) | 3.7 | −75.0 | An examination of the names of 1,232 persons summoned for jury duty, December 1972. |
| | | 0.8 | −94.6 | Visual observation of 253 jurors, Dec. 20, 1972. |
| | | 3.5 | −76.4 | Visual observation of 426 jurors, June 6, 1974. |
| *Texas* | | | | |
| Harris County (Houston): Trial Jurors | 8.7 (21 & over) | 2.3 | −73.6 | An examination of the names of 1,382 persons called for jury duty in October 1971. |

| State Courts | Percentage Spanish-surnamed in County | Percentage Spanish-surnamed on Jury | Rate of Error | Date and Source |
|---|---|---|---|---|
| Grand Jurors[c] | 11.0 | 3.0 | −72.7 | Survey of 156 grand jurors who served between 1969 and 1972. *Dumont v. Estelle*, 377 F. Supp. 374, 386 (S.D. Texas, 1974). |
| Hidalgo County: Grand Jurors[c] | 79.2 | 45.5 | −42.6 | 1969-72. *Partida v. Castaneda*, 524 F.2d 481, 483-84 (5th Cir. 1975). |
| *Utah* | | | | |
| Salt Lake County | 3.8 (21 & over) | 2.6 | −31.6 | 267 cards filled out by prospective jurors as they reported for duty in 1972. |

[a]The figures for Los Angeles refer to persons whose mother tongue is Spanish, instead of whether they have a Spanish surname.

[b]Between 1970 and 1973, the Hispanic population in New York City rose by 11.5 percent. *New York Times*, Dec. 22, 1974, p. 32. The given figures of 7.5 and 14.8 percents are, however, the 1970 census figures unaltered, as are all the other census figures in these charts.

[c]The court used the category "Mexican-American race," which may be somewhat different from the category "Spanish-surnamed."

**Table G-5. Asian-Americans on Federal Court Juries**

| Federal Court | Percentage of Asians in Division (computed to approximate over-18) | Percentage of Asians | | Rate of Error | |
|---|---|---|---|---|---|
| | | Master Wheel | Actual Jurors | Master Wheel | Actual Jurors |
| *Alaska* | | | | | |
| Juneau Division | 1.5 | 0.9 (447) | — | −40.0 | — |
| Ketchikan Division | 1.1 | 1.4 (436) | — | +27.3 | — |
| *California: Eastern District* | | | | | |
| Fresno Division | 3.0 | 2.0 (465) | 1.6 (187) | −33.3 | −46.7 |
| Sacramento Division | 3.0 | 1.8 (492) | 4.1 (483) | −40.0 | +36.7 |
| *California: Northern District* | | | | | |
| San Francisco-Oakland-Eureka Division | 5.1 | 5.5 (816) | 2.1 (668) | + 7.8 | −58.8 |
| San Jose Division | 4.0 | 4.7 (403) | — | +17.5 | — |
| *California: Southern Division* | 1.6 | 1.2 (500) | 0.6 (500) | −25.0 | −62.5 |
| Hawaii | 58.8 | 66.1 (332) | 68.8 (199) | +12.4 | +17.0 |
| *New York: Eastern District* | 1.0 | 0.7 (425) | 1.0 (500) | −30.0 | 0 |

Note: Number in parentheses indicates size of sample.

Source: Federal surveys conducted by court clerks in 1973 and 1974.

**Table G-6.  Asian-Americans on State Court Juries**

| Jurisdiction | Percentage of Asians in County | Percentage of Asians on Jury | Rate of Error | Date and Source |
|---|---|---|---|---|
| *California* | | | | |
| Alameda County (Oakland) | 4.6 | 0.9 | −80.4 | Visual observation of 449 jurors in 1972. |
| Sacramento County | 4.1 | 3.7 | − 9.8 | Cards sent to 493 prospective jurors during summer of 1972. |
| San Diego County | 2.6 | 0.3 | −88.5 | Visual observation of 307 jurors, May 21, 1973. |
| San Francisco County: | | | | |
| Trial Jurors | 13.2 | 6.3 | −52.3 | Visual observation of 1,207 jurors, 1972-73. |
| Grand Jurors | | 8.8 | −33.2 | Survey of the 114 grand jurors who served between 1970 and 1976. Plaintiffs' brief in *Quadra v. Superior Court, Hastings Law Journal* 27 (1976): 616-19, 633. |
| *New York* | | | | |
| King's County (Brooklyn) | 1.3 (over 21) | 0 | −100.0 | Visual observation of 176 jurors, Dec. 20, 1972. |
| | | 0 | −100.0 | Visual observation of 229 jurors, June 7, 1974. |
| New York County (Manhattan) | 3.8 (over 21) | 0.2 | −94.7 | An examination of the names of 1,232 jurors summoned in December 1972. |
| | | 0.4 | −90.0 | Visual observation of 253 jurors, Dec. 20, 1972. |
| | | 1.6 | −60.0 | Visual observation of 426 jurors, June 6, 1974. |

Table G-1. Native-Americans on Federal Court Juries (Number in Parentheses is the Size of the Sample)

| Federal Courts | Percent of Native-Americans in the division (computed to approximate the over-18 population) | Percent of Native-Americans on the Jury | | Rate of Error | |
|---|---|---|---|---|---|
| | | Master Wheel | Actual Jurors | Master Wheel | Actual Jurors |
| *District of Alaska*[a] | | | | | |
| Anchorage Division | 7.4 | 4.6 (456) | 5.2 (252) | –37.8 | – 29.7 |
| Fairbanks Division | 18.3 | 20.8 (443) | 7.2 (152) | +13.7 | – 60.7 |
| Juneau Division | 15.8 | 14.1 (447) | — | –10.8 | — |
| Ketchikan Division | 15.6 | 18.3 (436) | — | +17.3 | — |
| Nome Division | 75.8 | 77.0 (466) | — | + 1.6 | — |
| *District of Arizona* | | | | | |
| Phoenix Division | 1.5 | 0.8 (341) | 0 (1,729) | –46.7 | –100.0 |
| Prescott Division | 25.8 | 19.3 (322) | 4.7 (298) | –25.2 | – 81.8 |
| Tucson Division | 2.6 | 1.5 (341) | 1.5 (1,565) | –42.3 | – 42.3 |
| *District of Montana* | | | | | |
| Billings Division | 3.7 | 2.5 (275) | 1.1 (285) | –32.4 | – 70.3 |
| Great Falls Division | 3.5 | 2.9 (276) | 1.6 (187) | –17.1 | – 54.3 |
| Havre-Glasgow Division | 6.6 | 5.0 (278) | — | –24.2 | — |
| Helena Division | 1.1 | 1.1 (278) | — | 0 | — |
| Missoula Division | 2.1 | 3.2 (278) | 1.4 (213) | +52.4 | – 33.3 |
| *Eastern District of North Carolina* | | | | | |
| Fayetteville Division | 8.0 | 5.7 (368) | 5.9 (101) | –28.8 | – 26.3 |
| *Western District of North Carolina* | | | | | |
| Bryson City Division | 3.7 | 3.6 (466) | — | – 2.7 | — |
| *District of North Dakota* | | | | | |
| Northeastern Division | 3.4 | 1.9 (1,970) | 2.9 (103) | –44.1 | – 14.7 |
| Northwestern Division | 1.6 | 1.1 (1,962) | 0 (140) | –31.3 | –100.0 |
| | | — | 0.6 (174)[b] | — | – 62.5 |
| Southwestern Division | 1.8 | 1.4 (1,967) | 1.6 (122) | –22.2 | – 11.1 |
| *Eastern District of Oklahoma* | 6.3 | 4.6 (436) | 2.4 (412) | –27.0 | – 61.9 |
| *Western District of Oklahoma* | 1.9 | 1.1 (450) | — | –42.1 | — |

Source: These federal surveys were conducted by the clerks of the federal district courts in 1974 (except where noted). Only those districts and divisions with at least a 1 percent Native-American population and at least 100 persons in their samples are listed.

aMost of the Native-Americans in Alaska are Aleuts or Eskimos.

bThis survey was of the actual jurors who reported for the trial of Kenneth Freeman, a Native-American, in September 1974. (*United States v. Freeman*, 514 F.2d 171, 173 (8th Cir. 1975)).

**Table G-8. Native-Americans on State Court Juries**

| | Percent of Native-Americans in the County (computed to approximate the over-18 population) | Percent of Native-Americans on the Jury | Rate of Error | Date and Source |
|---|---|---|---|---|
| *Arizona* | | | | |
| Maricopa County | 1.0 (over 18) | 0.2 | −80.0 | 438 questionnaires by jurors. "Juries and Jurors in Maricopa County," *Law & the Social Order* (1973), pp. 183, 191. |
| *Nevada* | | | | |
| Washoe County (Reno) | 1.4 (over 18) | 2.3 | +64.3 | 835 cards filled out by prospective jurors, 1972-73. |
| *New Mexico* | | | | |
| Bernalillo County (Albuquerque) | 1.8 (over 18) | 1.1 | −38.9 | 618 questionnaires, examined at different times in 1972, 1973, and 1974. |

**Appendix H:
Age Statistics**

| Age | Percent Population (1970 Census) | Percent on Jury | Rate of Error | Date and Source |
|---|---|---|---|---|
| **Federal Courts** | | | | |
| *Central District of California* | | | | |
| 21-29 | 22.2 | 13.7 | -38.3 | Study by Leo Breiman of jurors eligible in December 31, 1969. |
| 30 and over | 77.8 | 86.3 | +10.9 | |
| *Eastern District of California* | | | | |
| 18-29 | 28.5 | 14.8 | -48.1 | Random survey of 441 jury questionnaires conducted by Professor Peter Sperlich, Univ. California, Berkeley, for *United States v. Soliah*, Jan. 7, 1976. |
| 30 and over | 71.5 | 85.2 | +19.2 | |
| *Northern District of California* | | | | |
| 21-24 | 10.6 | 2.8 | -73.6 | Examination of 2203 questionnaires of jurors found to be qualified, conducted by Attorney Robert Henn in 1970 and 1971. |
| 25-34 | 21.3 | 15.0 | -29.6 | |
| 35-44 | 17.6 | 18.4 | + 4.5 | |
| 45-54 | 18.7 | 28.1 | +50.3 | |
| 55-64 | 15.5 | 24.1 | +55.5 | |
| 65 and over | 16.5 | 11.5 | -30.3 | |
| 18-29 | 29.9 | 14.6 | -51.2 | An examination of the 529 questionnaires filled out by grand jurors who served on 23 grand juries impaneled between 1969 and 1975 for the case of *United States v. Rafofsky*, No. CR 74-687 OJC, Feb. 11, 1975. |
| 30 and over | 70.1 | 85.4 | +21.8 | |
| *Southern District of California* | | | | |
| 21-24 | 13.0 | 1.2 | -90.8 | Examination of 8,640 juror questionnaires conducted by Attorney Alfred P. Knoll in 1971. |
| 25-30 | 12.0 | 8.5 | -29.2 | |
| 31 and over | 75.0 | 90.9 | +21.2 | |
| *District of Columbia* | | | | |
| 18-20 | 8.7 | 3.9 | -55.2 | Court records of all 12,110 persons deemed qualified jurors based on questionnaires returned during Aug. 12, 1972 to Feb. 11, 1973. |
| 21-25 | 14.5 | 9.4 | -35.2 | |
| 26-35 | 20.2 | 18.8 | - 6.9 | |
| 36-45 | 15.9 | 18.0 | +13.2 | |

| 46-55 | 15.6 | 22.6 | +44.9 |
| 56-65 | 12.8 | 18.7 | +46.1 |
| 66-69 | 3.7 | 5.3 | +43.2 |
| 70 and over | 8.5 | 3.3 | −61.2 |

Court records of all 1997 persons deemed qualified jurors in June 1973.

| 18-20 | 8.7 | 2.7 | −69.0 |
| 21-25 | 14.5 | 8.3 | −42.8 |
| 26-35 | 20.2 | 17.3 | −14.4 |
| 36-45 | 15.9 | 19.9 | +25.2 |
| 46-55 | 15.6 | 20.8 | +33.3 |
| 56-65 | 12.8 | 20.9 | +63.3 |
| 66-69 | 3.7 | 5.4 | +45.9 |
| 70 and over | 8.5 | 4.7 | −44.7 |

*Northern District of Illinois: Eastern District*

| 21-24 | 8.7 | 2.3 | −73.6 |
| 25 and over | 91.3 | 97.7 | + 7.0 |

*Chase v. United States*, 468 F.2d 141, 143 (1972) (May 1970 venire).

*Northern District of Indiana: Hammond Division (at Hammond)*

| 18-25 | 19.8 | 19.3 | − 2.5 |
| 26-35 | 19.4 | 18.0 | − 7.2 |
| 36-45 | 19.4 | 20.0 | + 3.1 |
| 46-55 | 18.6 | 25.0 | +34.4 |
| 56-65 | 12.6 | 16.0 | +27.0 |
| Over 65 | 10.2 | 1.7 | −83.3 |

Sample of 300 jurors reporting for service taken by the clerk of the court in 1974 (within nine months after the master wheel had been refilled).

*District of Massachusetts*

| 21-25 | 12.6 | 5.0 | −60.3 |
| 26-29 | 8.4 | 5.7 | −32.1 |
| 30-39 | 16.9 | 16.6 | − 1.8 |
| 40-49 | 19.2 | 26.9 | +40.1 |
| 50-59 | 17.6 | 24.0 | +36.4 |

1970 Study of 1,150 jurors by M.I.T. political scientists Hayward R. Alker, Jr., Carl Hosticka, and Michael Mitchell (unpublished).

| Age | Percent Population (1970 Census) | Percent on Jury | Rate of Error | Date and Source |
|---|---|---|---|---|
| 60-69 | 13.1 | 17.4 | +32.8 | |
| 70 and over | 12.2 | 4.4 | -63.9 | |
| *Eastern District of Michigan* | | | | |
| 21-24 | 7.2 | 1.9 | -73.6 | Examination of 850 juror questionnaires conducted by Attorney Neal Bush in 1970 for *U.S. v. Sinclair*, Crim. No. 44395 (E.D. Mich. 1970). |
| 25-29 | 10.4 | 6.9 | -33.7 | |
| 30-34 | 12.3 | 7.9 | -35.8 | |
| 35-39 | 12.8 | 10.8 | -15.6 | |
| 40-44 | 11.6 | 14.2 | +22.4 | |
| 45-49 | 10.3 | 17.4 | +68.9 | |
| 50-54 | 8.7 | 13.9 | +59.8 | |
| 55-59 | 7.9 | 11.5 | +45.6 | |
| 60-64 | 6.4 | 7.9 | +23.4 | |
| 65 and over | 12.4 | 7.6 | -38.7 | |
| *Eastern District of North Carolina* | | | | |
| 18-34 | 40.8 | [1] 27.4 | -32.8 | [1] Sample of 880 jury questionnaires examined by the defendant in *United States v. MacDonald*, Nos. 75-1870, 75-1871 (E.D.N.C. 1975). [2] Sample of 701 jury questionnaires examined by the prosecution in the same case. |
| | | [2] 33.9 | -16.9 | |
| *District of New Jersey: Camden Division* | | | | |
| 21-24 | 12.3 | 0 | -100.0 | An examination of 485 juror questionnaires by attorney David Kairys in 1972 for *United States v. Anderson, et al.*, Crim No. 602-71 (D.N.J. 1973). |
| 25-29 | 10.3 | 4.6 | -55.3 | |
| 30-34 | 8.9 | 6.6 | -25.8 | |
| 35-39 | 9.1 | 6.8 | -25.3 | |
| 40-44 | 10.1 | 15.1 | +49.5 | |
| 45-49 | 10.3 | 17.2 | +67.0 | |
| 50-54 | 9.0 | 18.0 | +100.0 | |
| 55-59 | 7.9 | 12.2 | +54.4 | |
| 60-64 | 6.5 | 10.1 | +55.4 | |

| | | | | |
|---|---|---|---|---|
| 65-69 | 5.4 | 7.3 | +35.2 | |
| 70 and over | 10.2 | 2.3 | −77.5 | |
| *District of Rhode Island* | | | | |
| 21-29 | 21.5 | 12.6 | −41.9 | Edward N. Beiser, "Are Juries Representative?" *Judicature* 57 (1973): 194. (Study of 399 jurors, made in 1970.) |
| 30-39 | 16.0 | 16.5 | + 3.1 | |
| 40-49 | 19.6 | 27.3 | +39.3 | |
| 50-59 | 17.9 | 25.8 | +44.1 | |
| 60-69 | 13.3 | 15.6 | +17.3 | |
| 70 and over | 11.7 | 2.3 | −80.3 | |
| $m_1$ | **State Courts** | | $mmm$ | |
| *Arizona* | | | | |
| Maricopa County (Phoenix) | | | | |
| 18-24 | 18.1 | 6.9 | −61.8 | Study of 360 qualified jurors by Arizona State Law Students in April and May 1972, *Law & Soc. Order* (1973): 187. |
| 25-34 | 19.6 | 23.6 | +20.4 | |
| 35-49 | 26.7 | 36.7 | +37.5 | |
| 50-64 | 21.1 | 28.3 | +34.1 | |
| 65 and over | 14.5 | 4.4 | −69.7 | |
| *California* | | | | |
| Los Angeles County: Trial Jurors | | | | |
| 18-19 | 5.0 | 1.2 | −76.0 | Questionnaires filled in by 1,000 jurors in January and February 1973, processed by Leo Breiman for *People v. Taylor*, No. A277-425 (L.A. Superior Ct., Oct. 11, 1974). |
| 20-29 | 23.4 | 19.1 | −18.4 | |
| 30-39 | 17.6 | 20.2 | +14.8 | |
| 40-49 | 18.7 | 26.4 | +41.2 | |
| 50-59 | 15.9 | 23.4 | +47.2 | |
| 60-69 | 10.6 | 7.5 | −29.2 | |
| 70 and over | 9.0 | 2.2 | −75.6 | |
| Grand Jurors | | | | |
| 18-29 | 28.2 | 1.7 | −94.0 | Examination of the 1,079 persons nominated as grand jurors between 1971 and 1976, by Professor Peter Sperlich, U. California, Berkeley, for the case of *People v. Harris*, Jan. 22, 1976. |
| 30 and over | 71.8 | 98.3 | +36.9 | |

| Age | Percent Population (1970 Census) | Percent on Jury | Rate of Error | Date and Source |
|---|---|---|---|---|
| Marin County | | | | |
| 18-29 | 26.7 | 27.2 | + 2.6 | A random survey of 400 juror questionnaires conducted in February 1975 by Ruth Astle and Anita Oppenheimer. |
| 30-39 | 21.0 | 16.5 | −21.4 | |
| 40-49 | 20.6 | 18.0 | −12.6 | |
| 50-59 | 15.4 | 19.8 | +28.6 | |
| 60 and over | 16.1 | 18.5 | +14.9 | |
| Orange County (Municipal and Superior Courts) | | | | |
| 18-20 | 7.9 | 2.9 | −63.3 | Official court records of 16,517 jurors for 1972. |
| 21-29 | 22.1 | 14.1 | −36.2 | |
| 30-39 | 21.2 | 22.8 | + 7.5 | |
| 40-49 | 21.0 | 26.8 | +27.6 | |
| 50-59 | 13.2 | 18.4 | +39.4 | |
| 60 and over | 14.6 | 15.0 | + 2.7 | |
| 18-20 | 7.9 | 4.7 | −40.5 | Official court records of 8,154 potential jurors, 1974. |
| 21-29 | 22.1 | 17.1 | −22.6 | |
| 30-39 | 21.2 | 18.5 | −12.7 | |
| 40-49 | 21.0 | 24.0 | +14.3 | |
| 50-59 | 13.2 | 20.2 | +53.0 | |
| 60 and over | 14.6 | 15.6 | + 6.8 | |
| Riverside County | | | | |
| 18-34 | 34.1 | 22.6 | −33.5 | Survey of 5,148 juror questionnaires (before excuses were granted) conducted by attorneys Len Holt and Franklin P. Glenn and law student Doug Elliott working on the case of People v. Lawton and Gardner, CR 9138 and CR 9485, August 21, 1974. |
| 35-64 | 46.0 | 49.6 | + 7.8 | |
| 65 and over | 19.9 | 27.9 | +40.2 | |
| Sacramento County | | | | |
| 18-20 | 7.8 | 2.0 | −74.4 | Cards filled out by 493 prospective jurors, summer 1972. |
| 21-24 | 10.6 | 8.3 | −21.7 | |

| | | | |
|---|---|---|---|
| 25-29 | 10.7 | 10.5 | – 1.9 |
| 30-34 | 9.2 | 10.3 | +12.0 |
| 35-39 | 9.1 | 9.3 | + 2.2 |
| 40-44 | 9.9 | 12.6 | +27.3 |
| 45-49 | 10.4 | 15.0 | +44.2 |
| 50-54 | 8.8 | 10.5 | +19.3 |
| 55-59 | 7.1 | 7.7 | + 8.5 |
| 60-64 | 5.4 | 7.1 | +31.5 |
| 65-69 | 4.0 | 3.7 | – 7.5 |
| 70-74 | 3.0 | 2.2 | –26.7 |
| Over 75 | 4.0 | 0.4 | –90.0 |

San Bernardino County

| | | | |
|---|---|---|---|
| 21-24 | 11.4 | 3.4 | –70.2 |
| 25-29 | 11.5 | 8.2 | –28.7 |
| 30-34 | 10.0 | 10.0 | 0 |
| 35-39 | 9.6 | 9.6 | 0 |
| 40-44 | 9.6 | 12.0 | +25.0 |
| 45-49 | 9.6 | 14.5 | +51.0 |
| 50-54 | 8.6 | 13.8 | +60.5 |
| 55-59 | 7.5 | 12.2 | +62.7 |
| 60-64 | 6.5 | 6.1 | – 6.2 |
| 65-69 | 5.7 | 6.3 | +10.5 |
| 70-74 | 4.5 | 3.0 | –33.3 |
| Over 75 | 5.6 | 1.0 | –82.1 |

Cards filled out by 732 jurors reporting for service, summer 1972.

San Francisco County (Superior Court)

| | | | |
|---|---|---|---|
| 18-20 | 6.5 | 0.2 | –96.9 |
| 21-24 | 11.0 | 5.2 | –52.7 |
| 25-34 | 19.4 | 22.8 | +17.5 |
| 35-44 | 14.4 | 24.9 | +72.9 |

Visual observations of 1,207 trial jurors, 1972-73.

| Age | Percent Population (1970 Census) | Percent on Jury | Rate of Error | Date and Source |
|---|---|---|---|---|
| 45-54 | 15.6 | 23.0 | +47.4 | |
| 55-59 | 7.7 | 11.5 | +49.4 | |
| 60-64 | 7.5 | 7.4 | – 1.3 | |
| 65-74 | 11.2 | 5.0 | –55.4 | |
| Over 75 | 6.7 | 0 | –100.0 | |
| 18-20 | 6.5 | 0 | –100.0 | 114 grand jurors who served between 1970 and 1976. Plaintiffs' briefs in *Quadra* |
| 21-24 | 11.0 | 0 | –100.0 | *v. Superior Court, Hastings L.J.* 27 (1976): 603-606, 632. |
| 25-34 | 19.4 | 10.5 | –45.9 | |
| 35-44 | 14.4 | 11.4 | –26.3 | |
| 45-54 | 15.6 | 36.8 | +135.9 | |
| 55-59 | 7.7 | 15.8 | +105.2 | |
| 60-64 | 7.5 | 11.4 | +52.0 | |
| 65-74 | 11.2 | 13.2 | +17.9 | |
| Over 75 | 6.7 | 0.9 | –86.6 | |
| San Francisco County (Municipal Courts) | | | | |
| 21-30 | 25.5 | 21.4 | –16.1 | Court records of 5,174 jurors for 1971. |
| 31-40 | 16.0 | 18.2 | +13.8 | |
| 41-50 | 16.6 | 22.8 | +37.3 | |
| 51-60 | 16.4 | 22.7 | +38.4 | |
| 61-70 | 14.1 | 12.1 | –14.2 | |
| Over 70 | 11.4 | 2.9 | –74.6 | |
| Santa Clara County | | | | |
| 18-20 | 8.1 | 2.3 | –71.6 | Visual observation of 486 jurors, fall, 1972. |
| 21-24 | 11.2 | 5.1 | –54.5 | |
| 25-34 | 24.2 | 26.3 | + 8.7 | |

| | | | |
|---|---|---|---|
| 35-44 | 19.7 | 30.8 | +56.3 |
| 45-54 | 17.1 | 18.1 | + 5.8 |
| 55-59 | 5.7 | 5.1 | −10.5 |
| 60-64 | 4.3 | 6.4 | +48.8 |
| 65-74 | 5.6 | 4.1 | −26.8 |
| Over 75 | 3.8 | 1.6 | −57.9 |

*Colorado*

Denver County — Court records of all 9,646 persons summoned to serve as jurors in 1972.

| | | | |
|---|---|---|---|
| 18-20 | 8.5 | 1.5 | −82.4 |
| 21-29 | 22.9 | 20.8 | − 9.2 |
| 30-39 | 14.9 | 16.9 | +13.4 |
| 40-49 | 16.0 | 20.9 | +30.6 |
| 50-59 | 14.8 | 20.9 | +41.2 |
| 60-69 | 11.7 | 12.9 | +10.3 |
| 70 and over | 11.0 | 6.3 | −42.7 |

Court records of all 9,615 persons summoned to serve as jurors in 1973.

| | | | |
|---|---|---|---|
| 18-20 | 8.5 | 5.3 | −37.6 |
| 21-29 | 22.9 | 30.2 | +31.9 |
| 30-39 | 14.9 | 17.4 | +16.8 |
| 40-49 | 16.0 | 15.7 | − 1.9 |
| 50-59 | 14.8 | 16.8 | +13.5 |
| 60-69 | 11.7 | 9.6 | −17.9 |
| 70 and over | 11.0 | 4.9 | −55.5 |

El Paso County — 800 cards collected from actual jurors in 1973.

| | | | |
|---|---|---|---|
| 18-20 | 11.3 | 2.8 | −75.2 |
| 21-24 | 18.3 | 7.5 | −59.0 |
| 25-29 | 11.5 | 12.9 | +12.2 |
| 30-34 | 9.4 | 9.0 | − 4.3 |
| 35-39 | 9.5 | 11.8 | +24.2 |
| 40-44 | 8.3 | 13.1 | +57.8 |
| 45-49 | 7.6 | 12.6 | +65.8 |

| Age | Percent Population (1970 Census) | Percent on Jury | Rate of Error | Date and Source |
|---|---|---|---|---|
| 50-54 | 6.3 | 11.0 | +74.6 | |
| 55-59 | 4.7 | 7.3 | +55.3 | |
| 60-64 | 3.8 | 6.2 | +63.2 | |
| 65-69 | 3.0 | 3.8 | +26.7 | |
| 70-74 | 2.6 | 1.4 | −46.2 | |
| Over 75 | 3.7 | 0.5 | −86.5 | |
| **Pueblo County** | | | | |
| 18-20 | 8.7 | 4.0 | −54.0 | 556 cards filled out by actual jurors, 1972-74. |
| 21-24 | 9.2 | 8.3 | − 9.8 | |
| 25-29 | 9.0 | 11.7 | +30.0 | |
| 30-34 | 8.4 | 10.8 | +28.6 | |
| 35-39 | 8.6 | 9.0 | + 4.7 | |
| 40-44 | 9.2 | 10.3 | +12.0 | |
| 45-49 | 9.2 | 10.4 | +13.0 | |
| 50-54 | 8.6 | 11.7 | +36.0 | |
| 55-59 | 7.9 | 9.0 | +13.9 | |
| 60-64 | 6.4 | 7.0 | + 9.4 | |
| 65-69 | 5.1 | 5.2 | + 2.0 | |
| 70-74 | 3.7 | 2.0 | −45.9 | |
| Over 75 | 6.0 | 0.7 | −88.3 | |
| **Georgia** | | | | |
| Coweta County (Trial Jury Lists) | | | | |
| 18-30 | 26.1 | 3.1 | −88.2 | 400 from grand jury list; 2,138 from trial jury list. *White v. State*, 230 Ga. 327, 196 S.E.2d 849 (1973); *appeal dismissed* 414 U.S. 886 (1973); *Gould v. State*, 131 Ga. App. 811, 207 S.E.2d 519 (1974). |
| 31 and over | 73.9 | 96.9 | +31.1 | |

| Coweta County (Grand Jury Lists) | | | |
|---|---|---|---|
| 18-30 | 26.1 | 1.3 | −95.0 |
| 31 and over | 73.9 | 98.7 | +33.6 |

*Maryland*

City of Baltimore

| | | | |
|---|---|---|---|
| 21-29 | 21.4 | 15.5 | −27.6 |
| 30-39 | 16.5 | 17.5 | + 6.1 |
| 40-49 | 19.1 | 24.9 | +30.4 |
| 50-59 | 18.2 | 23.4 | +28.6 |
| 60-69 | 14.0 | 14.8 | + 5.7 |
| 70-79 | 7.9 | 3.7 | −53.2 |
| Over 80 | 2.9 | 0.2 | −93.1 |

Official court records, 2,219 jurors, Sept. 1969 – Aug. 1970.

| | | | |
|---|---|---|---|
| 21-29 | 21.4 | 16.9 | −20.6 |
| 30-39 | 16.5 | 17.1 | + 3.6 |
| 40-49 | 19.1 | 25.6 | +34.0 |
| 50-59 | 18.2 | 23.0 | +26.4 |
| 60-69 | 14.0 | 14.2 | + 2.1 |
| 70-79 | 7.9 | 2.9 | −63.3 |
| Over 80 | 2.9 | 0.2 | −93.1 |

Official court records, 2,543 jurors, Sept. 1970 – Aug. 1971.

| | | | |
|---|---|---|---|
| 21-29 | 21.4 | 21.0 | − 1.9 |
| 30-39 | 16.5 | 17.0 | + 3.0 |
| 40-49 | 19.1 | 24.0 | +25.7 |
| 50-59 | 18.2 | 21.6 | +18.7 |
| 60-69 | 14.0 | 14.0 | 0.0 |
| 70-79 | 7.9 | 2.3 | −70.1 |
| Over 80 | 2.9 | 0.1 | −96.6 |

Official court records, 2,664 jurors, in 1972.

| | | | |
|---|---|---|---|
| 18-20 | 7.7* | 3.6 | −53.2 |
| 21-29 | 19.7* | 22.5 | +14.2 |

Official court records, 1,958 jurors, May-Dec. 1973.

| Age | Percent Population (1970 Census) | Percent on Jury | Rate of Error | Date and Source |
|---|---|---|---|---|
| 30-39 | 15.2* | 17.5 | +15.1 | |
| 40-49 | 17.6* | 20.0 | +13.6 | |
| 50-59 | 16.8* | 21.1 | +25.6 | |
| 60 and over | 22.9* | 15.2 | -33.6 | Official court records, 1,375 jurors, Jan. 1974. |
| 18-20 | 7.7* | 4.9 | -36.4 | |
| 21-29 | 19.7* | 25.2 | +27.9 | |
| 30-39 | 15.2* | 18.3 | +20.4 | |
| 40-49 | 17.6* | 18.7 | + 6.2 | |
| 50-59 | 16.8* | 19.6 | +16.7 | |
| 60 and over | 22.9* | 13.3 | -41.9 | |
| *18 and over. | | | | |
| Prince George's County | | | | |
| 18-19 | 5.9 | 0.0 | -100.0 | Questionnaires filled out by 272 jurors in October 1973 for Bird Engineering—Research Associates, Inc., Vienna, Va. |
| 20-29 | 32.1 | 20.2 | -37.1 | |
| 30-39 | 21.6 | 23.9 | +10.6 | |
| 40-49 | 18.0 | 28.3 | +57.2 | |
| 50-59 | 12.2 | 17.3 | +41.8 | |
| 60-69 | 6.2 | 10.3 | +66.1 | |
| 70 and over | 4.0 | 0.0 | -100.0 | |
| Missouri | | | | |
| City of St. Louis | | | | |
| 21-24 | 9.8 | 0.8 | -91.8 | Visual observation of 242 jurors, March 1973. |
| 25-34 | 16.4 | 11.1 | -32.3 | |
| 35-44 | 15.3 | 27.7 | +81.0 | |
| 45-54 | 17.0 | 37.7 | +121.8 | |
| 55-59 | 9.1 | 12.8 | +40.7 | |

| | | | |
|---|---|---|---|
| 60-64 | 9.1 | 7.4 | −18.7 |
| 65-74 | 14.2 | 2.1 | −85.2 |
| Over 75 | 9.1 | 0.4 | −95.6 |

*Nevada*
  Washoe County (Reno)

| | | | |
|---|---|---|---|
| 18-20 | 7.5 | 2.5 | −66.7 |
| 21-24 | 9.7 | 7.4 | −23.7 |
| 25-29 | 10.7 | 11.4 | + 6.5 |
| 30-34 | 9.2 | 10.3 | +12.0 |
| 35-39 | 8.6 | 8.6 | 0 |
| 40-44 | 9.4 | 9.5 | + 1.1 |
| 45-49 | 9.8 | 10.1 | + 3.1 |
| 50-54 | 8.9 | 12.7 | +42.7 |
| 55-59 | 7.7 | 13.7 | +77.9 |
| 60-64 | 5.9 | 7.8 | +32.2 |
| 65-69 | 4.3 | 4.6 | + 7.0 |
| 70-74 | 4.2 | 1.1 | −73.8 |
| Over 75 | 4.1 | 0.4 | −90.2 |

835 cards filled out by jurors, 1972-73.

*New Mexico*
  Bernalillo County
    (Albuquerque)

| | | | |
|---|---|---|---|
| 18-20 | 9.1 | 4.6 | −49.5 |
| 21-24 | 11.5 | 10.0 | −13.0 |
| 25-29 | 11.7 | 10.6 | − 9.4 |
| 30-34 | 10.0 | 10.2 | + 2.0 |
| 35-39 | 9.6 | 10.6 | +10.4 |
| 40-44 | 9.6 | 12.0 | +25.0 |
| 45-49 | 9.6 | 13.4 | +39.6 |
| 50-54 | 7.9 | 12.4 | +57.0 |

Examination of 501 juror questionnaires, 1973-74.

| Age | Percent Population (1970 Census) | Percent on Jury | Rate of Error | Date and Source |
|---|---|---|---|---|
| 55-59 | 6.5 | 8.2 | +26.2 | |
| 60-64 | 5.1 | 5.2 | + 2.0 | |
| 65-69 | 3.7 | 2.2 | -40.5 | |
| 70-74 | 2.7 | 0.8 | -70.4 | |
| Over 75 | 3.1 | 0 | -100.0 | |
| *New York State* | | | | |
| New York County (Manhattan) | | | | |
| 21-25 | 13.3 | 3.1 | -76.7 | 2,014 jurors; study conducted by the Subcommittee on the Jury System of the Departmental Committees for Court Administration of the Appellate Division, First and Second Department, in April 1972. |
| 26-30 | 12.9 | 10.6 | -17.8 | |
| 31-40 | 19.9 | 22.9 | +15.1 | |
| 41-50 | 18.3 | 25.0 | +36.6 | |
| 51-60 | 17.0 | 20.9 | +22.9 | |
| 61-70 | 13.2 | 16.0 | +21.2 | |
| 71-75 | 5.4 | 1.4 | -74.1 | |
| Bronx County | | | | |
| 21-25 | 13.5 | 5.7 | -57.8 | 459 jurors; Ibid. |
| 26-30 | 11.9 | 10.9 | - 8.4 | |
| 31-40 | 19.1 | 12.6 | -34.0 | |
| 41-50 | 17.9 | 24.2 | +35.2 | |
| 51-60 | 17.4 | 21.8 | +25.3 | |
| 61-70 | 15.0 | 21.8 | +45.3 | |
| 71-75 | 5.1 | 3.1 | -39.2 | |
| Kings County (Brooklyn) | | | | |
| 21-25 | 13.2 | 4.5 | -65.9 | 759 jurors; Ibid. |
| 26-30 | 11.3 | 7.7 | -31.9 | |
| 31-40 | 18.4 | 13.9 | -24.5 | |

| | | | |
|---|---|---|---|
| 41-50 | 19.0 | 24.0 | +26.3 |
| 51-60 | 18.5 | 27.1 | +46.5 |
| 61-70 | 14.7 | 20.7 | +40.8 |
| 71-75 | 4.9 | 2.1 | -57.1 |
| **Queens County** | | | |
| 21-25 | 11.8 | 0.7 | -94.1 |
| 26-30 | 10.2 | 3.2 | -68.6 |
| 31-40 | 16.8 | 10.4 | -38.1 |
| 41-50 | 20.2 | 23.8 | +17.8 |
| 51-60 | 20.4 | 33.2 | +62.7 |
| 61-70 | 15.6 | 25.4 | +57.7 |
| 71-75 | 5.1 | 3.4 | -33.3 |

1,492 jurors; Ibid.

| | | | |
|---|---|---|---|
| **Richmond County (Staten Island)** | | | |
| 21-25 | 13.1 | 1.3 | -90.1 |
| 26-30 | 12.2 | 3.3 | -73.0 |
| 31-40 | 20.8 | 21.1 | + 1.4 |
| 41-50 | 21.2 | 29.4 | +38.7 |
| 51-60 | 17.5 | 26.8 | +53.1 |
| 61-70 | 11.5 | 17.7 | +53.9 |
| 71-75 | 3.9 | 0.3 | -92.3 |

299 jurors; Ibid.

| | | | |
|---|---|---|---|
| **Erie County (Buffalo)** | | | |
| 21-29 | 20.7 | 3.4 | -83.6 |
| 30-39 | 18.3 | 19.6 | + 7.1 |
| 40-49 | 22.3 | 27.3 | +22.4 |
| 50-59 | 20.0 | 31.8 | +59.0 |
| 60-69 | 13.8 | 16.3 | +18.1 |
| 70-74 | 4.9 | 1.6 | -67.3 |

1,650 juror questionnaires randomly selected from 16,976 persons summoned for jury duty in 1974. Attica Brothers Defense Challenge, March 27, 1974. Erie County selection procedure was subsequently found improper, *New York Times*, July 4, 1974, p. 1.

*North Dakota*

| | | | |
|---|---|---|---|
| **Cass County (Fargo)** | | | |
| 21-30 | 27.9 | 16.0 | -42.6 |
| 31-40 | 17.3 | 23.1 | +33.5 |

212 jurors in 1972, from the records of the clerk of the district court, Theodore H. Hanson.

| Age | Percent Population (1970 Census) | Percent on Jury | Rate of Error | Date and Source |
|---|---|---|---|---|
| 41-50 | 17.5 | 23.1 | +32.0 | 144 jurors in 1973, from the records of the clerk of the district court, Theodore L. Hanson. |
| 51-60 | 15.2 | 18.4 | +20.8 | |
| 61-70 | 11.4 | 11.3 | − 0.9 | |
| Over 70 | 10.6 | 8.0 | −24.5 | |
| 21-30 | 27.9 | 31.9 | +14.3 | |
| 31-40 | 17.3 | 22.2 | +28.3 | |
| 41-50 | 17.5 | 16.7 | − 4.6 | |
| 51-60 | 15.2 | 18.8 | +23.7 | |
| 61-70 | 11.4 | 7.6 | −33.3 | |
| Over 70 | 10.6 | 2.8 | −73.6 | |
| *Rhode Island* (Statewide) | | | | |
| 25-29 | 11.5 | 5.3 | −53.9 | Edward N. Beiser, "Are Juries Representative?" *Judicature* 57 (1973):194. (Study of 359 jurors made in 1970; persons under 25 were ineligible to serve as jurors at the time of the survey.) |
| 30-39 | 18.1 | 15.9 | −12.2 | |
| 40-49 | 22.2 | 36.0 | +62.2 | |
| 50-59 | 20.3 | 25.1 | +23.6 | |
| 60-69 | 14.8 | 13.7 | − 7.4 | |
| 70 and over | 13.1 | 4.2 | −67.9 | |
| *Texas* | | | | |
| Harris County (Houston) | | | | Compiled from 1,380 juror questionnaires, October 1971. |
| 21-24 | 11.8 | 8.1 | −31.4 | |
| 25-29 | 14.1 | 11.3 | −19.9 | |
| 30-34 | 11.5 | 7.8 | −32.2 | |
| 35-39 | 10.6 | 10.4 | − 1.9 | |
| 40-44 | 10.9 | 14.3 | +31.2 | |
| 45-49 | 10.2 | 16.0 | +56.9 | |
| 50-54 | 8.2 | 13.8 | +68.3 | |
| 55-59 | 7.0 | 10.0 | +42.9 | |

| | | | |
|---|---|---|---|
| 60-64 | 5.5 | 7.3 | +32.7 |
| 65-69 | 4.0 | 0.7 | −82.5 |
| 70-74 | 2.7 | 0.3 | −88.9 |
| Over 75 | 3.4 | 0.1 | −97.1 |

*Utah*

Salt Lake County

| | | | |
|---|---|---|---|
| 18-20 | 8.9 | 0.4 | −95.5 |
| 21-24 | 11.5 | 1.5 | −87.0 |
| 25-29 | 12.2 | 10.1 | −17.2 |
| 30-34 | 9.6 | 6.4 | −33.3 |
| 35-39 | 8.5 | 13.9 | +63.5 |
| 40-44 | 8.6 | 14.6 | +69.8 |
| 45-49 | 8.4 | 15.7 | +86.9 |
| 50-54 | 7.7 | 9.4 | +22.1 |
| 55-59 | 6.4 | 11.6 | +81.3 |
| 60-64 | 5.6 | 8.6 | +53.6 |
| 65-69 | 4.3 | 3.4 | −20.9 |
| 70-74 | 3.4 | 2.6 | −23.5 |
| Over 75 | 4.9 | 1.9 | −61.2 |

Cards filled out by 267 jurors, 1972.

*Virginia*

Arlington County

| | | | |
|---|---|---|---|
| 21-24 | 15.3 | 1.1 | −92.8 |
| 25-34 | 23.2 | 8.5 | −63.4 |
| 35-44 | 15.1 | 14.5 | − 4.0 |
| 45-54 | 19.6 | 26.0 | +32.7 |
| 55-59 | 8.9 | 16.4 | +84.3 |
| 60-64 | 6.9 | 15.2 | +120.3 |
| 65-74 | 7.3 | 14.7 | +101.4 |
| Over 75 | 3.7 | 3.5 | − 5.4 |

Survey of the 1,222 jurors on the fall 1972 jury venire by attorney William B. Moore.

# Appendix I:
# Sex Statistics

Table I-1.  Women on Federal Court Juries (Figures in parentheses indicate size of sample)

| Federal Courts[a] | Percent Women in the Division | Percent Women on Master Wheel | Rate of Error | Percent Women on Juries | Rate of Error | Discrimination | Excuse[b] | Date of Survey |
|---|---|---|---|---|---|---|---|---|
| **ALABAMA** | | | | | | | | |
| *Middle District* | 51.5 | 48.6 (430) | - 5.6 | 37.0 (427) | -28.2 | | -23.0 | 1971 |
| | | – | | 36.0 (475) | -30.1 | | -25.9 | 1968-71 |
| | | 51.6 (494) | + 0.2 | 43.5 (278) | -15.5 | | -15.7 | 1974 |
| *Northern District* | 51.9 | 46.1 (514) | -11.2 | 41.4 (561) | -20.2 | | -10.2 | 1971 |
| | | 48.8 (500) | - 6.0 | 38.1 (515) | -26.6 | | -21.9 | 1974 |
| *Southern District* | 51.0 | 50.0 (505) | - 2.0 | 51.0 (768) | 0 | | + 2.0 | 1971 |
| | | 53.0 (198) | + 3.9 | 51.5 (710) | - 1.0 | | - 2.8 | 1973 |
| **ALASKA** | | | | | | | | |
| Anchorage Division | 44.4** | 49.6 (456) | +11.7 | 43.3 (252) | - 2.5 | | -12.5 | 1974 |
| Fairbanks Division | 40.1** | 46.2 (444) | +15.2 | 50.7 (152) | +26.4 | | + 9.7 | 1974 |
| Juneau Division | 47.7** | 51.9 (447) | + 8.8 | – | – | – | – | 1974 |
| Ketchikan Division | 45.1** | 47.7 (436) | + 5.8 | – | – | | – | 1974 |
| Nome Division | 43.7** | 47.2 (466) | + 8.0 | – | – | | – | 1974 |
| **ARIZONA** | | | | | | | | |
| Phoenix Division | 51.9** | 56.1 (499) | + 8.1 | 44.9 (401) | -13.4 | | -20.4 | 1971 |
| | | 55.4 (341) | + 6.7 | 62.8 (1,729) | +21.0 | | +13.4 | 1974 |
| Prescott Division | 50.7** | 49.7 (433) | - 2.0 | – | – | | – | 1971 |
| | | 50.6 (322) | - 0.2 | 56.0 (298) | +10.5 | | +10.7 | 1974 |
| Tucson-Globe | 51.7** | 51.5 (464) | - 0.4 | 46.7 (330) | - 9.7 | | - 9.3 | 1971 |
| | | 46.0 (341) | -10.6 | 49.3 (1,565) | - 4.6 | | + 7.2 | 1974 |
| **ARKANSAS** | | | | | | | | |
| *Western District* | | | | | | | | |
| El Dorado Division | 52.0 | 52.0 (314) | 0 | – | – | | – | 1971 |
| Fort Smith Division | 49.0 | 55.0 (245) | +12.2 | 41.0 (178) | -16.3 | | -25.5 | 1971 |
| Harrison Division | 51.0 | 49.0 (175) | - 3.9 | – | – | | – | 1971 |
| Hot Springs Division | 48.0 | 46.0 (202) | - 4.2 | – | – | | – | 1971 |
| Texarkana Division | 53.0 | 53.0 (218) | 0 | 43.0 (150) | -18.9 | | -18.9 | 1971 |

| | | | | | | | |
|---|---|---|---|---|---|---|---|
| **CALIFORNIA** | | | | | | | |
| *Central District* | 52.4** | 49.0 (498) | – 6.5 | 45.0 (500) | –14.1 | – 8.2 | 1971 |
| *Eastern District* | 51.4** | 59.9 (212) | +16.5 | 47.1 (187) | – 8.4 | –21.4 | 1971 |
| Fresno Division | | 59.6 (500) | +16.0 | 42.0 (205) | –18.3 | –29.6 | 1974 |
| Sacramento Division | 51.1* | 48.8 (281) | – 4.5 | 46.1 (434) | – 9.8 | – 5.5 | 1971 |
| | | 49.4 (500) | – 3.3 | 53.8 (500) | + 5.3 | + 8.9 | 1974 |
| *Northern District* | | | | | | | |
| Eureka Division | 50.2 | 52.5 (421) | + 4.6 | — | — | — | 1971 |
| Oakland Division | 52.1 | 52.1 (475) | 0 | — | — | — | 1971 |
| San Francisco Division | 45.3 | 56.3 (564) | +24.3 | 46.2 (1,077) | + 2.0 | –17.9 | 1971 |
| S.F.-Oakland-Eureka Division | 51.9** | 48.0 (835) | – 7.5 | 49.6 (690) | – 4.4 | + 3.3 | 1974 |
| San Jose Division | 50.6*** | 53.7 (473) | + 6.1 | — | — | — | 1971 |
| | | 47.2 (424) | – 6.7 | — | — | — | 1974 |
| *Southern District* | 50.1* | 56.3 (373) | +12.4 | 47.9 (474) | – 4.4 | –14.9 | 1971 |
| | | 54.5 (473) | + 8.8 | 51.1 (476) | + 2.0 | – 6.2 | 1972 |
| | | 51.2 (500) | + 2.1 | 52.8 (500) | + 5.4 | + 3.1 | 1974 |
| **COLORADO** | | | | | | | |
| Denver Division | 52.3 | 52.4 (393) | + 0.2 | 49.7 (314) | – 5.2 | – 5.2 | 1972 |
| | | 52.3 (451) | 0 | 43.5 (490) | –17.0 | –17.0 | 1974 |
| Grand Junction Division | 51.0** | 48.0 (227) | – 5.9 | — | — | — | 1971 |
| | | 52.9 (263) | + 3.7 | — | — | — | 1974 |
| Pueblo Division | 49.2** | 55.7 (262) | +13.2 | — | — | — | 1971 |
| | | 52.1 (288) | + 5.8 | — | — | — | 1974 |
| **CONNECTICUT** | | | | | | | |
| Bridgeport Division | 53.3 | 48.7 (482) | – 8.6 | 43.3 (398) | –18.8 | –11.1 | 1971 |
| | | 51.9 (451) | – 2.6 | | | — | 1974 |
| Hartford Division | 53.0 | 52.7 (485) | – 0.7 | 41.5 (327) | –21.7 | –21.3 | 1971 |
| | | 50.4 (500) | – 4.9 | 36.9 (160) | –30.4 | –26.8 | 1974 |
| New Haven Division | 53.1 | 49.3 (471) | – 7.2 | 40.5 (405) | –23.7 | –17.8 | 1971 |
| | | 52.1 (445) | – 1.9 | 36.3 (113) | –31.6 | –30.3 | 1974 |
| **DELAWARE** | 52.4** | 46.4 (280) | –11.5 | 46.3 (231) | –11.6 | – 0.2 | 1971 |
| | | 50.9 (316) | – 2.9 | 44.1 (322) | –15.8 | –13.4 | 1974 |

| Federal Courts[a] | Percent Women in the Division | Percent Women on Master Wheel | Rate of Error | Percent Women on Juries | Rate of Error | Excuse Discrimination[b] | Date of Survey |
|---|---|---|---|---|---|---|---|
| DISTRICT OF COLUMBIA | 53.5 | 54.7 (351) | + 2.2 | 56.6 (495) | + 5.7 | − 3.5 | 1971 |
|  |  | 59.2 (28,738) | +10.7 | — | — | — | 1972-73 |
| **FLORIDA** |  |  |  |  |  |  |  |
| *Middle District* |  |  |  |  |  |  |  |
| Fort Meyers Division | 51.0 | 52.6 (3,130) | + 2.9 | 48.0 (322) | − 5.9 | — | 1971 |
|  |  | — |  | — | — | — | 1974 |
| Jacksonville Division | 50.0 | 52.9 (6,834) | + 5.8 | 51.0 (350) | + 2.0 | — | 1971 |
|  |  | — |  | 46.0 (500) | − 8.0 | −13.0 | 1974 |
| Ocala Division | 52.0 | 51.9 (2,562) | − 0.2 | 44.0 (322) | −15.4 | — | 1971 |
|  |  | — |  | 49.6 (228) | − 4.6 | − 4.4 | 1974 |
| Orlando Division | 51.0 | 49.8 (5,440) | − 2.4 | 49.0 (500) | − 3.9 | — | 1971 |
|  |  | — |  | 48.4 (500) | − 5.1 | − 2.8 | 1974 |
| Tampa Division | 52.0 | 54.5 (12,759) | + 4.8 | 47.0 (350) | − 9.6 | — | 1971 |
|  |  | — |  | 42.2 (389) | −18.8 | −22.6 | 1974 |
| *Northern District* |  |  |  |  |  |  |  |
| Gainesville Division | 50.9** | 51.6 (350) | + 1.2 | 47.3 (165) | − 7.1 | − 8.3 | 1974 |
| Marianna Division | 52.3*** | 50.6 (350) | − 3.3 | — | — | — | 1974 |
| Pensacola Division | 50.8** | 56.0 (500) | +10.2 | 50.8 (130) | 0 | − 9.3 | 1974 |
| Tallahassee Division | 53.1** | 53.0 (500) | − 0.2 | — | — | — | 1974 |
| *Southern District* |  |  |  |  |  |  |  |
| Ft. Lauderdale Division | 53.6** | 53.0 (541) | − 1.1 | 48.1 (241) | −10.3 | − 9.2 | 1974 |
| Ft. Pierce Division | 52.5*** | 53.3 (535) | + 1.5 | — | — | — | 1974 |
| Key West Division | 45.7*** | 49.6 (526) | + 8.5 | 44.1 (136) | − 3.5 | −11.1 | 1974 |
| Miami Division | 53.8** | 53.8 (552) | 0 | 52.7 (1,436) | − 2.0 | − 2.0 | 1974 |
| West Palm Beach Div. | 53.3** | 56.2 (552) | + 5.4 | 52.4 (187) | − 1.7 | − 6.8 | 1974 |
| **GEORGIA** |  |  |  |  |  |  |  |
| *Middle District* |  |  |  |  |  |  |  |
| Albany Division | 53.2** | 53.7 (274) | + 0.9 | 44.1 (143) | −17.1 | −17.9 | 1974 |

| | | | | | | | |
|---|---|---|---|---|---|---|---|
| Americus Division | 54.9** | 51.1 (276) | − 6.9 | — | — | — | 1974 |
| Athens Division | 52.5** | 48.4 (277) | − 7.6 | — | — | — | 1974 |
| Columbia Division | 48.8** | 56.0 (336) | +14.8 | 47.8 (138) | − 2.0 | −14.6 | 1974 |
| Macon Division | 54.0** | 53.5 (316) | − 0.9 | 40.7 (140) | −24.6 | −23.9 | 1974 |
| Thomasville Division | 54.0** | 54.2 (277) | + 0.4 | — | — | — | 1974 |
| Valdosta Division | 52.4** | 54.9 (275) | + 4.8 | 43.8 (283) | −16.4 | −20.2 | 1974 |
| *Northern District* | | | | | | | |
| Atlanta Division | 53.1** | 57.0 (400) | + 7.3 | 40.0 (567) | −24.7 | −29.8 | 1971 |
| | | 51.0 (494) | − 4.0 | 41.1 (723) | −22.6 | −19.4 | 1974 |
| Gainesville Division | 52.5** | 44.2 (290) | −15.8 | — | — | — | 1971 |
| | | 49.4 (344) | − 5.9 | — | — | — | 1974 |
| Newnan Division | 53.7** | 51.8 (299) | − 3.5 | 43.5 (138) | −19.0 | −16.0 | 1971 |
| | | 51.3 (341) | − 4.5 | — | — | — | 1974 |
| Rome Division | 52.9** | 51.0 (296) | − 3.6 | 40.8 (223) | −22.9 | −20.0 | 1971 |
| | | 52.3 (348) | − 1.1 | 44.6 (157) | −15.7 | −14.7 | 1974 |
| *Southern District* | | | | | | | |
| Augusta Division | 47.0** | 42.4 (490) | − 9.8 | 39.8 (412) | −15.3 | − 6.3 | 1971 |
| | | 53.9 (317) | +14.7 | — | — | — | 1974 |
| Brunswick Division | 52.2** | 49.8 (480) | − 4.6 | 26.2 (291) | −49.8 | −47.4 | 1971 |
| | | 50.0 (316) | − 4.2 | — | — | — | 1974 |
| Dublin Division | 53.2** | 48.8 (466) | − 8.3 | 38.7 (380) | −27.3 | −20.7 | 1971 |
| | | 49.4 (316) | − 7.1 | — | — | — | 1974 |
| Savannah Division | 51.7** | 53.8 (474) | + 4.1 | 41.2 (500) | −20.3 | −23.4 | 1971 |
| | | 54.4 (491) | + 5.2 | — | — | — | 1974 |
| Swainsboro Division | 53.6** | 49.3 (477) | − 8.0 | 31.5 (283) | −41.2 | −36.1 | 1971 |
| | | 45.7 (317) | −14.7 | — | — | — | 1974 |
| Waycross Division | 52.6** | 51.3 (487) | − 2.5 | 42.1 (230) | −20.0 | −17.9 | 1971 |
| | | 49.4 (316) | − 6.1 | — | — | — | 1974 |
| HAWAII | 48.0* | 53.5 (404) | +11.5 | 55.0 (210) | +14.6 | + 2.8 | 1971 |
| | | 43.5 (322) | − 9.4 | 44.7 (199) | − 6.9 | + 2.8 | 1973 |
| IDAHO | 50.0 | 50.0 (404) | 0 | 44.0 (361) | −12.0 | −12.0 | 1971 |
| | | 53.0 (468) | + 6.0 | 48.3 (118) | − 3.4 | − 8.9 | 1974 |

| Federal Courts[a] | Percent Women in the Division | Percent Women on Master Wheel | Rate of Error | Percent Women on Juries | Rate of Error | Discrimination[b] | Excuse | Date of Survey |
|---|---|---|---|---|---|---|---|---|
| **ILLINOIS** | | | | | | | | |
| *Northern District* | | | | | | | | |
| Eastern Division | 52.5 | 54.4 (1,995) | + 3.6 | 39.7 (463) | −24.4 | −27.0 | | 1971 |
| | | 54.8 (491) | + 4.4 | 48.9 (454) | − 6.9 | − 8.9 | | 1974 |
| Western Division | 52.2 | 53.3 (298) | + 2.1 | — | — | — | | 1971 |
| | | 54.6 (335) | + 4.6 | — | — | — | | 1974 |
| **INDIANA** | | | | | | | | |
| *Northern District* | | | | | | | | |
| Fort Wayne Division | 52.6** | 53.0 (498) | + 0.8 | 60.4 (250) | +14.8 | +14.0 | | 1974 |
| Hammond at Hammond Division | 51.7** | 55.4 (487) | + 7.2 | 45.3 (300) | −12.4 | −18.2 | | 1974 |
| Hammond at Lafayette Division | 50.1** | 54.2 (478) | + 8.2 | — | — | — | | 1974 |
| South Bend Division | 52.2** | 51.0 (500) | − 2.3 | 44.2 (283) | −15.3 | −13.3 | | 1974 |
| *Southern District* | 52.9** | 45.6 (485) | −13.8 | 40.8 (500) | −22.9 | −10.5 | | 1971 |
| | | 45.3 (475) | −14.4 | 36.8 (475) | −30.4 | −19.2 | | 1974 |
| **IOWA** | | | | | | | | |
| *Northern District* | | | | | | | | |
| Cedar Rapids Division | 52.6* | 51.9 (160) | − 1.3 | 47.9 (148) | − 8.9 | − 7.7 | | 1971 |
| | | 54.8 (347) | + 4.2 | — | — | — | | 1974 |
| Central Division | 52.8** | 47.1 (350) | −10.8 | — | — | — | | 1974 |
| Fort Dodge | | 50.9 (165) | − 3.6 | 41.1 (124) | −22.2 | −19.3 | | 1971 |
| Mason City | | 53.6 (151) | + 1.5 | — | — | — | | 1971 |
| Eastern Division | 52.6** | 50.9 (517) | − 3.2 | — | — | — | | 1974 |
| Dubuque | | 51.2 (160) | − 2.7 | — | — | — | | 1971 |
| Waterloo | | 48.6 (138) | − 7.6 | — | — | — | | 1971 |
| Western Division | 53.0** | 46.7 (197) | −11.9 | 39.0 (133) | −26.4 | −16.5 | | 1971 |
| | | 50.8 (354) | − 4.2 | 48.9 (135) | − 7.7 | − 3.7 | | 1974 |
| *Southern District* | | | | | | | | |
| Central Division | 52.6** | 50.4 (464) | − 4.2 | 47.9 (409) | − 9.0 | − 5.0 | | 1971 |
| | | 53.0 (500) | + 0.8 | 48.9 (656) | − 7.0 | − 7.7 | | 1973 |

| Division | | % (n) | Diff | % (n) | Diff | Diff | Year |
|---|---|---|---|---|---|---|---|
| Davenport Division | 53.3 | 52.7 (215) | 8.8 | 50.4 (115) | − 3.6 | − 6.3 | 1973 |
| | | 53.8 (500) | + 2.9 | 46.6 (116) | −11.9 | −21.3 | |
| Western Division | 52.9** | 59.2 (233) | +11.9 | — | — | — | 1971 |
| | | 54.7 (450) | + 3.4 | — | — | — | 1973 |
| **KANSAS** | | | | | | | |
| Dodge City Division | 53.4* | 45.6 (235) | −14.5 | — | — | — | 1971 |
| | | 57.3 (246) | + 7.3 | — | — | — | 1974 |
| Fort Scott Division | 54.5* | 49.5 (239) | − 9.2 | — | — | — | 1971 |
| | | 48.5 (196) | −11.0 | — | — | — | 1974 |
| Kansas City-Leavenworth Division | 51.5* | 54.5 (475) | + 5.8 | 41.2 (228) | −20.0 | −24.4 | 1971 |
| | | 56.2 (495) | + 9.1 | 44.5 (218) | −13.6 | −20.8 | 1974 |
| Salina Division | 55.0* | 56.3 (251) | + 2.4 | — | — | — | 1971 |
| | | 54.3 (245) | − 1.3 | — | — | — | 1974 |
| Topeka Division | 52.4* | 50.9 (471) | − 2.9 | 46.6 (227) | −11.1 | − 8.4 | 1971 |
| | | 53.7 (486) | + 2.5 | 58.9 (146) | +12.4 | + 9.7 | 1974 |
| Witchita-Hutchinson Division | 52.2* | 54.6 (471) | + 4.6 | 41.3 (230) | −20.9 | −24.4 | 1971 |
| | | 52.2 (496) | 0 | 49.5 (198) | − 5.2 | − 5.2 | 1974 |
| **LOUISIANA** | | | | | | | |
| *Eastern District* | | | | | | | |
| New Orleans Division | 53.0 | 51.0 (500) | − 3.8 | 43.6 (500) | −17.7 | −14.5 | 1971 |
| | | 51.0 (500) | − 3.8 | 49.6 (500) | − 6.4 | − 2.7 | 1974 |
| Baton Rouge Division | 51.0 | — | — | 43.0 (100) | −15.7 | — | 1971 |
| *Middle District* | 51.6** | 45.4 (350) | −12.0 | 41.6 (209) | −19.4 | − 8.4 | 1974 |
| *Western District* | | | | | | | |
| Alexandria Division | 53.1** | 46.9 (341) | −11.7 | 46.2 (279) | −13.0 | − 1.5 | 1974 |
| Lafayette Division | 52.4*** | 46.9 (350) | −10.5 | 40.6 (318) | −22.5 | −13.4 | 1974 |
| Lake Charles Division | 45.7*** | 27.9 (341) | −38.9 | 24.9 (225) | −45.5 | −10.8 | 1974 |
| Monroe Division | 53.7*** | 54.3 (341) | + 1.1 | — | — | — | 1974 |
| Opelousas Division | 53.1** | 42.5 (322) | −20.0 | — | — | — | 1974 |
| Shreveport Division | 54.2** | 51.7 (350) | − 4.6 | 49.8 (227) | − 8.1 | − 3.7 | 1974 |
| **MAINE** | | | | | | | |
| Northern Division | 51.7* | 48.4 (213) | − 6.4 | — | — | — | 1971 |

| Federal Courts[a] | Percent Women in the Division | Percent Women on Master Wheel | Rate of Error | Percent Women on Juries | Rate of Error | Excuse Discrimination[b] | Date of Survey |
|---|---|---|---|---|---|---|---|
| Southern Division | 53.2* | 48.0 (371) | − 9.8 | 39.5 (172) | −26.5 | −17.7 | 1971 |
| MARYLAND | 52.2** | 50.5 (410) | − 3.3 | 40.2 (500) | −23.0 | −20.4 | 1971 |
| | | 52.4 (500) | + 0.4 | 47.6 (500) | − 8.8 | − 9.2 | 1974 |
| MASSACHUSETTS | 53.8** | 54.1 (c) | + 0.6 | 42.6 (c) | −20.8 | −21.2 | 1971 |
| **MICHIGAN** | | | | | | | |
| *Eastern District* | | | | | | | |
| Northern Division (Bay City) | 51.9** | 52.8 (299) | + 1.7 | — | — | — | 1974 |
| Southern Division (Detroit) | 52.3** | 56.1 (508) | + 7.3 | 51.7 (418) | − 1.1 | − 7.8 | 1974 |
| Southern Division (Flint) | 51.8** | 51.3 (300) | − 1.0 | — | — | — | 1974 |
| **MINNESOTA** | | | | | | | |
| First & Third Division | 52.7** | 49.4 (500) | − 6.3 | 46.4 (306) | −12.0 | − 6.1 | 1974 |
| Second & Fourth Division | 52.7** | 49.0 (500) | − 7.0 | 42.2 (268) | −19.9 | −13.9 | 1974 |
| Fifth Division | 51.4** | 45.1 (350) | −12.3 | — | — | — | 1974 |
| Sixth Division | 50.5** | 45.2 (341) | −10.5 | — | — | — | 1974 |
| **MISSISSIPPI** | | | | | | | |
| *Northern District* | | | | | | | |
| Eastern Division | 53.0** | 50.6 (500) | − 4.5 | 46.5 (114) | −12.3 | − 8.1 | 1974 |
| Delta Division | 53.7** | 53.2 (500) | − 0.9 | — | — | — | 1974 |
| Greenville Division | 53.9** | 57.4 (500) | + 6.5 | — | — | — | 1974 |
| Western Division | 52.6** | 46.6 (500) | −11.4 | — | — | — | 1974 |
| *Southern District* | | | | | | | |
| Eastern Division | 53.3** | 45.7 (486) | −14.2 | 46.3 (369) | −13.1 | + 1.3 | 1971 |
| | | 47.6 (500) | −10.7 | — | — | — | 1974 |
| Hattiesburg Division | 53.3** | 40.0 (482) | −25.0 | 44.3 (476) | −16.9 | +10.8 | 1971 |
| | | 45.2 (500) | | | | | |

| Division | % | Year | Value (N) | Δ | Value (N) | Δ | Δ |
|---|---|---|---|---|---|---|---|
| Jackson Division | 54.0** | 1971 | 46.4 (481) | −14.1 | 46.2 (500) | −14.4 | − 0.4 |
|  |  | 1974 | 49.4 (500) | − 8.5 | 50.8 (315) | − 5.9 | + 2.8 |
| Southern Division | 49.0** | 1971 | 39.8 (477) | −18.8 | 45.0 (500) | − 8.2 | +13.1 |
|  |  | 1974 | 43.8 (500) | −10.6 | 33.5 (275) | −31.6 | −23.5 |
| Western Division | 54.7** | 1971 | 40.2 (248) | −26.5 | 35.1 (482) | −35.8 | −12.7 |
|  |  | 1974 | 49.2 (500) | −10.0 | — | — | — |

### MISSOURI

*Eastern District*

| Division | % | Year | Value (N) | Δ | Value (N) | Δ | Δ |
|---|---|---|---|---|---|---|---|
| Eastern Division | 53.9** | 1971 | 53.6 (532) | − 0.5 | 36.7 (450) | −31.9 | −31.5 |
|  |  | 1974 | 50.2 (500) | − 6.9 | 42.9 (364) | −20.4 | −14.5 |
| Northern Division | 52.0* | 1971 | 54.3 (256) | + 4.4 | — | — | — |
|  |  | 1974 | 41.0 (322) | −21.2 | — | — | — |
| Southeastern Division | 50.0* | 1971 | 52.1 (311) | + 4.2 | — | — | — |
|  |  | 1974 | 47.5 (341) | − 5.0 | — | — | — |

*Western District*

| Division | % | Year | Value (N) | Δ | Value (N) | Δ | Δ |
|---|---|---|---|---|---|---|---|
| Central Division | 52.0** | 1974 | 56.8 (500) | + 9.2 | 37.9 (351) | −27.1 | −33.3 |
| St. Joseph Division | 53.2** | 1974 | 55.0 (500) | + 3.4 | 39.9 (348) | −25.0 | −27.5 |
| Southern Division | 48.9** | 1974 | 42.4 (500) | −13.3 | 49.2 (537) | + 0.6 | +16.0 |
| Southwestern Division | 53.7** | 1974 | 57.6 (500) | + 7.3 | 44.3 (368) | −17.5 | −23.1 |
| Western Division | 53.6** | 1974 | 53.0 (500) | + 1.1 | 39.8 (535) | −25.7 | −24.9 |

### MONTANA

| Division | % | Year | Value (N) | Δ | Value (N) | Δ | Δ |
|---|---|---|---|---|---|---|---|
| Billings Division | 51.6** | 1971 | 55.2 (279) | + 7.0 | 52.3 (235) | + 1.4 | − 5.3 |
|  |  | 1974 | 53.2 (278) | + 3.1 | 52.6 (285) | + 1.9 | − 1.1 |
| Butte Division | 50.3** | 1971 | 47.0 (272) | − 6.6 | 48.3 (116) | − 4.0 | + 2.8 |
|  |  | 1974 | 53.2 (278) | + 5.8 | 47.9 (165) | − 4.8 | −10.0 |
| Great Falls Division | 50.2** | 1971 | 55.5 (281) | +10.6 | 42.8 (187) | −14.8 | −22.9 |
|  |  | 1974 | 49.6 (278) | − 1.2 | 45.5 (187) | − 9.4 | − 8.3 |
| Havre-Glasgow Division | 49.9** | 1971 | 51.2 (283) | + 2.6 | 48.2 (222) | − 3.5 | − 5.9 |
|  |  | 1974 | 46.4 (278) | − 7.0 | — | — | — |
| Helena Division | 51.9** | 1971 | 52.7 (264) | + 1.5 | — | — | — |
|  |  | 1974 | 51.8 (278) | − 0.2 | — | — | — |

| Federal Courts[a] | Percent Women in the Division | Percent Women on Master Wheel | Rate of Error | Percent Women on Juries | Rate of Error Discrimination[b] | Excuse Discrimination[b] | Date of Survey |
|---|---|---|---|---|---|---|---|
| Missoula | 50.2** | 52.7 (275) | + 5.0 | 41.6 (154) | −17.1 | −21.0 | 1971 |
|  |  | 52.9 (278) | + 5.4 | 53.5 (213) | + 6.6 | + 1.1 | 1974 |
| **NEW HAMPSHIRE** | 51.1 | 39.9 (459) | −21.9 | 38.2 (178) | −25.2 | − 4.3 | 1971 |
|  |  | 54.9 (494) | + 7.4 | — | — | — | 1974 |
| **NEW JERSEY** |  |  |  |  |  |  |  |
| Camden Division | 52.6* | 50.2 (229) | − 4.6 | 40.0 (150) | −24.0 | −20.3 | 1971 |
|  |  | 51.1 (493) | − 2.9 | 47.3 (385) | −10.1 | − 7.4 | 1974 |
| Newark Division | 53.6** | 50.1 (479) | − 6.5 | 45.4 (500) | −15.3 | − 9.4 | 1971 |
|  |  | 54.8 (491) | + 2.2 | 47.8 (500) | −10.8 | −12.8 | 1974 |
| Trenton Division | 51.7** | 47.8 (228) | − 7.5 | 46.0 (150) | −11.0 | − 3.8 | 1971 |
|  |  | 52.6 (473) | + 1.7 | 41.7 (350) | −19.3 | −20.7 | 1974 |
| **NEW MEXICO** |  |  |  |  |  |  |  |
| Entire District | 51.6** | 40.7 (1,274) | −21.1 | 42.2 (384) | −18.2 | + 3.7 | 1974 |
| Albuquerque-Santa Fe Division |  | 49.0 (c) | − 5.0 | 45.0 (c) | −12.8 | − 8.2 | 1971 |
| Las Cruces Division |  | 36.0 (c) | −30.2 | 29.1 (c) | −43.6 | −19.2 | 1971 |
| Roswell Division |  | 49.6 (c) | − 3.9 | 33.3 (c) | −35.5 | −32.9 | 1971 |
| **NEW YORK** |  |  |  |  |  |  |  |
| Eastern District | 53.9** | 51.1 (458) | − 5.2 | 43.0 (500) | −20.2 | −15.9 | 1971 |
|  |  | 56.9 (425) | + 5.6 | 44.6 (500) | −17.3 | −21.6 | 1974 |
| Southern District | 54.2** | 54.0 (498) | − 0.4 | 53.5 (514) | − 1.3 | − 0.9 | 1974 |
| Western District |  |  |  |  |  |  |  |
| Buffalo Division | 53.2** | 52.0 (500) | − 2.3 | 46.6 (500) | −12.4 | −10.4 | 1974 |
| Rochester Division | 53.1** | 51.2 (500) | − 3.6 | 43.2 (449) | −18.6 | −15.6 | 1974 |
| **NORTH CAROLINA** |  |  |  |  |  |  |  |
| Eastern District |  |  |  |  |  |  |  |
| Elizabeth City Division | 53.0* | 43.0 (263) | −18.9 | 45.6 (182) | −14.0 | + 6.0 | 1971 |
|  | 52.8** | 53.3 (330) | + 0.9 | — | — | — | 1974 |

| | | | | | | | |
|---|---|---|---|---|---|---|---|
| Fayetteville Division | 48.2* | 17.5 (292) | −63.7 | 46.3 (322) | − 3.9 | +164.6 | 1971 |
| | 45.7** | 54.3 (368) | +18.8 | 58.4 (101) | +27.8 | + 7.6 | 1974 |
| New Bern Division | 48.4* | 48.7 (265) | + 0.6 | 43.2 (278) | −10.7 | −11.3 | 1971 |
| | 44.3** | 54.6 (371) | +23.3 | — | — | — | 1974 |
| Raleigh Division | 52.4* | 47.9 (309) | − 8.6 | 48.1 (341) | − 8.2 | + 0.4 | 1971 |
| | 52.2** | 51.4 (356) | − 1.5 | 44.7 (114) | −14.4 | −13.0 | 1974 |
| Washington Division | 53.6* | 48.1 (262) | −10.3 | 41.7 (103) | −22.2 | −13.3 | 1971 |
| | 53.4** | 52.1 (328) | − 2.4 | — | — | — | 1974 |
| Wilmington Division | 53.3* | 50.2 (251) | − 5.8 | 44.6 (240) | −16.3 | −11.2 | 1971 |
| | 52.8** | 48.1 (368) | − 8.9 | 46.8 (126) | −11.4 | − 2.7 | 1974 |
| Wilson Division | 53.5* | 49.2 (309) | − 8.0 | 42.2 (322) | −21.1 | −14.2 | 1971 |
| | 52.9** | 49.7 (328) | − 5.0 | — | — | — | 1974 |
| *Western District* | | | | | | | |
| Asheville Division | 53.2** | 43.3 (459) | −18.4 | 41.6 (101) | −21.8 | − 4.1 | 1973 |
| Bryson City Division | 51.7** | 46.4 (466) | −10.3 | — | — | — | 1973 |
| Charlotte Division | 53.7** | 53.3 (445) | − 0.7 | 47.6 (103) | −11.4 | −10.7 | 1973 |
| Shelby Division | 53.0** | 38.0 (463) | −28.3 | — | — | — | 1973 |
| Statesville Division | 52.7** | 33.9 (442) | −35.7 | — | — | — | 1973 |
| **NORTH DAKOTA** | | | | | | | |
| Northeastern Division | 49.0 | 50.3 (1,970) | + 2.7 | 40.0 (140) | −18.4 | − 9.3 | 1971 |
| | | | | 45.6 (103) | − 6.9 | | 1974 |
| Northwestern Division | 49.2 | 51.7 (1,962) | + 5.1 | 44.2 (147) | −10.2 | − 8.9 | 1971 |
| | | | | 47.1 (140) | − 4.3 | | 1974 |
| Southeastern Division | 49.7 | 49.4 (1,967) | − 0.6 | 45.8 (142) | − 7.3 | − 7.3 | 1974 |
| Southwestern Division | 50.3 | 49.6 (1,967) | − 1.4 | 42.5 (134) | −15.5 | + 4.0 | 1971 |
| | | | | 51.6 (122) | + 2.6 | | 1974 |
| **OHIO** | | | | | | | |
| *Northern District* | | | | | | | |
| Eastern Division (Cleveland) | 53.0** | 43.6 (491) | −17.7 | 40.2 (358) | −24.2 | − 7.8 | 1974 |
| Western Division | 52.7** | 57.2 (292) | + 8.5 | 51.1 (313) | − 3.0 | −10.7 | 1974 |

| Federal Courts[a] | Percent Women in the Division | Percent Women on Master Wheel | Rate of Error | Percent Women on Juries | Rate of Error | Excuse Discrimination[b] | Date of Survey |
|---|---|---|---|---|---|---|---|
| **OKLAHOMA** | | | | | | | |
| Eastern District | 52.0* | 41.4 (769) | −20.4 | 38.3 (355) | −26.3 | − 7.5 | 1971 |
|  |  | 43.8 (461) | +15.8 | 33.7 (412) | −35.2 | −23.1 | 1973 |
| Western District | 52.0* | 50.4 (450) | − 3.1 | — | — | — | 1974 |
| **OREGON** | | | | | | | |
| Coquille Division | 49.5 | 45.4 (163) | − 8.3 | — | — | — | 1971 |
|  |  | 50.3 (193) | + 1.6 | — | — | — | 1973 |
| Eugene Division | 51.1 | 61.6 (172) | +20.5 | — | — | — | 1971 |
|  |  | 55.5 (200) | + 8.6 | — | — | — | 1973 |
| Medford Division | 52.2 | 58.3 (156) | +11.7 | — | — | — | 1971 |
|  |  | 52.9 (204) | + 1.3 | — | — | — | 1973 |
| Pendleton Division | 52.1 | 55.9 (170) | + 7.3 | — | — | — | 1971 |
|  |  | 57.5 (200) | +10.4 | — | — | — | 1973 |
| Portland Division | 53.8 | 54.8 (400) | + 1.9 | 56.3 (247) | + 4.6 | + 2.7 | 1971 |
|  |  | 54.2 (467) | + 0.9 | 47.0 (117) | −12.6 | −13.4 | 1972 |
| **PENNSYLVANIA** | | | | | | | |
| Eastern District | 52.1 | 59.5 (484) | +14.2 | 35.0 (500) | −32.8 | −41.2 | 1971 |
|  |  | 54.4 (500) | + 4.4 | 47.4 (500) | − 9.0 | −12.9 | 1974 |
| RHODE ISLAND | 51.8** | 51.4 (173) | − 0.8 | 51.4 (173) | − 0.8 | 0 | 1971 |
|  |  | 44.3 (350) | −14.5 | 37.7 (350) | −27.2 | −14.2 | 1974 |
| **SOUTH CAROLINA** | | | | | | | |
| A Division | 53.8 | 47.2 (438) | −12.3 | 45.1 (235) | −16.2 | − 4.4 | 1971 |
|  |  | 46.7 (460) | −13.2 | 42.9 (273) | −20.3 | − 8.1 | 1974 |
| B Division | 47.5 | 50.6 (449) | + 6.5 | 43.2 (338) | − 9.1 | −14.6 | 1971 |
|  |  | 56.9 (459) | +19.8 | 39.0 (783) | −17.9 | −31.5 | 1974 |

| | | | | | | |
|---|---|---|---|---|---|---|
| C Division | 50.5 | 47.2 (441) | − 6.5 | 41.5 (316) | −17.8 | −12.1 | 1971 |
| | | 51.8 (452) | + 2.6 | 37.2 (395) | −26.3 | −28.2 | 1974 |
| **SOUTH DAKOTA** | | | | | | | |
| Western Division | 49.4 | — | — | 46.4 (110) | − 6.1 | — | 1971 |
| **TENNESSEE** | | | | | | | |
| *Eastern District* | | | | | | | |
| Northeastern Division | 51.3 | 48.1 (395) | − 6.2 | 42.6 (366) | −17.0 | −11.4 | 1971 |
| | | 44.3 (341) | −13.6 | 38.1 (139) | −25.7 | −14.0 | 1974 |
| Northern Division | 51.1 | 46.4 (435) | − 9.2 | 37.4 (382) | −26.8 | −19.4 | 1971 |
| | | 45.7 (492) | −10.6 | — | — | — | 1974 |
| Southern Division | 57.1 | 49.0 (433) | −14.2 | 38.3 (483) | −32.9 | −21.8 | 1971 |
| | | 49.6 (498) | −13.1 | 51.0 (194) | −10.7 | + 2.8 | 1974 |
| Winchester Division | 51.1 | 51.4 (438) | + 0.6 | 38.3 (107) | −25.0 | −25.5 | 1971 |
| | | 47.5 (322) | − 7.0 | — | — | — | 1974 |
| *Middle District* | | | | | | | |
| Columbia Division | 51.5 | 49.7 (163) | − 3.5 | — | — | — | 1971 |
| | | 51.0 (453) | − 1.0 | — | — | — | 1974 |
| Nashville Division | 50.2 | 54.8 (210) | + 9.2 | 50.0 (116) | − 0.4 | − 8.8 | 1971 |
| | | 50.4 (427) | + 0.4 | 47.5 (160) | − 5.4 | − 5.8 | 1974 |
| Northeastern Division | 50.8 | 47.7 (199) | − 6.1 | — | — | — | 1971 |
| | | 46.7 (443) | − 8.1 | — | — | — | 1974 |
| *Western District* | | | | | | | |
| Eastern Division | 53.4** | 49.6 (258) | − 7.1 | 49.3 (148) | − 7.7 | − 6.1 | 1971 |
| | | 52.5 (333) | − 1.7 | | | | 1974 |
| Western Division | 54.0** | 50.2 (422) | − 7.0 | 38.9 (175) | −28.0 | −22.5 | 1971 |
| | | 56.6 (500) | + 4.8 | 58.2 (208) | + 7.8 | + 2.8 | 1974 |
| **TEXAS** | | | | | | | |
| *Eastern District* | | | | | | | |
| Beaumont Division | 52.4** | 49.7 (614) | − 5.2 | 47.7 (176) | − 9.0 | − 4.0 | 1974 |

| Federal Courts[a] | Percent Women in the Division | Percent Women on Master Wheel | Rate of Error | Percent Women on Juries | Rate of Error | Excuse Discrimination[b] | Date of Survey |
|---|---|---|---|---|---|---|---|
| Marshall Division | 53.6** | 42.4 (507) | −20.9 | 42.3 (104) | −21.1 | − 0.2 | 1974 |
| Paris Division | 53.6** | 52.2 (579) | − 2.6 | — | — | — | 1974 |
| Sherman Division | 53.2** | 51.6 (644) | − 3.0 | — | — | — | 1974 |
| Texarkana Division | 53.4** | 40.9 (618) | −23.4 | — | — | — | 1974 |
| Tyler Division | 53.0** | 50.0 (572) | − 5.7 | 43.1 (304) | −18.7 | −13.8 | 1974 |
| *Northern District* | | | | | | | |
| Abilene Division | 52.6** | 52.9 (488) | + 0.6 | 42.2 (529) | −19.8 | −20.2 | 1974 |
| Amarillo Division | 52.3** | 49.2 (488) | − 5.9 | — | — | — | 1974 |
| Dallas Division | 53.2** | 49.9 (473) | − 6.2 | 46.3 (587) | −13.0 | − 7.2 | 1974 |
| Fort Worth Division | 51.9*** | 42.8 (439) | −17.5 | 43.8 (703) | −15.6 | + 2.3 | 1974 |
| Lubbock Division | 51.8*** | 47.8 (546) | − 7.7 | — | — | — | 1974 |
| San Angelo Division | 52.8*** | 50.9 (436) | − 3.6 | — | — | — | 1974 |
| Witchita Falls Division | 51.7*** | 49.2 (488) | − 4.8 | — | — | — | 1974 |
| *Southern District* | | | | | | | |
| Brownsville Division | 54.5*** | 56.4 (234) | + 3.5 | 40.6 (128) | −25.5 | − 7.5 | 1971 |
| | | — | | 37.5 (136) | −31.2 | −33.5 | 1974 |
| Corpus Christi Division | 51.9*** | 51.8 (164) | − 0.2 | 30.0 (130) | −42.2 | −32.3 | 1971 |
| | | — | | | | | 1974 |
| Galveston Division | 50.8** | — | | 31.4 (121) | −38.2 | −35.0 | 1971 |
| Houston Division | 51.7** | 48.5 (491) | − 6.2 | 41.4 (411) | −19.9 | −14.6 | 1971 |
| | | 49.3 (475) | − 4.6 | 48.2 (485) | − 6.8 | − 2.2 | 1974 |
| Laredo Division | 54.0** | 53.0 (117) | − 1.8 | — | — | — | 1971 |
| | | 50.9 (226) | − 5.7 | — | — | — | 1974 |
| *Western District* | | | | | | | |
| Austin Division | 51.6** | 55.3 (430) | + 7.2 | 40.0 (190) | −22.5 | −27.7 | 1971 |
| | | 47.8 (557) | − 7.4 | 37.3 (316) | −27.7 | −22.0 | 1974 |

| Division | | | | | | | Year |
|---|---|---|---|---|---|---|---|
| Del Rio Division | 52.1** | 49.7 (435) | − 4.6 | 52.0 (196) | − 0.2 | + 4.6 | 1971 |
| | | 46.6 (500) | −10.6 | — | — | — | 1974 |
| El Paso Division | 51.9** | 46.5 (449) | −10.4 | 39.3 (201) | −24.3 | −15.5 | 1971 |
| | | 52.4 (553) | + 1.0 | 52.3 (555) | + 0.8 | − 0.2 | 1974 |
| Midland-Odessa Division | 51.8** | 51.0 (439) | − 1.5 | 40.8 (120) | −21.2 | −20.0 | 1971 |
| | | 47.2 (558) | − 8.9 | 47.8 (318) | − 7.7 | + 1.3 | 1974 |
| Pecos Division | 51.0** | 49.6 (468) | − 2.7 | 34.5 (113) | −32.4 | −30.4 | 1971 |
| | | 54.4 (500) | + 6.7 | 38.9 (126) | −23.7 | −28.5 | 1974 |
| San Antonio Division | 52.0** | 48.0 (458) | − 7.7 | 49.5 (382) | − 4.8 | + 3.1 | 1971 |
| | | 53.2 (609) | + 2.3 | 41.6 (500) | −20.0 | −21.8 | 1974 |
| Waco Division | 49.1** | 48.6 (457) | − 1.0 | — | — | — | 1971 |
| | | 46.8 (500) | − 4.7 | — | — | — | 1974 |
| **UTAH** | | | | | | | |
| Central Division | 52.1** | 55.7 (271) | + 6.9 | 45.3 (181) | −13.0 | −18.7 | 1971 |
| Northern Division | 51.0** | 47.3 (264) | − 7.2 | 50.3 (173) | − 1.4 | + 6.3 | 1971 |
| **VERMONT** | (Statewide) | | | | | | |
| Brattleboro Division | 52.5** | 55.6 (295) | + 5.9 | 46.3 (322) | −11.8 | −16.7 | 1974 |
| Burlington Division | 52.5** | 53.1 (322) | + 1.1 | 46.3 (322) | −11.8 | −12.8 | 1974 |
| Montpelier Division | 52.5** | 51.6 (318) | − 1.7 | 47.8 (322) | − 9.0 | − 7.4 | 1974 |
| Rutland Division | 52.5** | 55.1 (303) | + 5.0 | 53.7 (322) | + 2.3 | − 2.5 | 1974 |
| **VIRGINIA** | | | | | | | |
| *Western District* | | | | | | | |
| Abingdon Division | 52.1** | 44.3 (351) | −15.0 | 40.9 (264) | −21.5 | − 7.7 | 1974 |
| Charlottesville Division | 48.5** | 55.1 (501) | +13.6 | 53.0 (117) | + 9.3 | − 3.8 | 1974 |
| Danville Division | 51.4** | 42.2 (365) | −17.9 | 46.4 (265) | − 9.7 | +10.0 | 1974 |
| Harrisonburg Division | 51.7** | 44.7 (369) | −13.5 | 49.2 (177) | − 4.8 | +10.1 | 1974 |
| Lynchburg Division | 51.4** | 47.5 (465) | − 7.6 | 47.1 (329) | − 8.4 | − 0.8 | 1974 |
| Roanoke Division | 50.2** | 50.2 (424) | 0 | 56.3 (247) | +12.2 | +12.2 | 1974 |

| Federal Courts[a] | Percent Women in the Division | Percent Women on Master Wheel | Rate of Error | Percent Women on Juries | Rate of Error | Discrimination | Excuse[b] | Date of Survey |
|---|---|---|---|---|---|---|---|---|
| **WASHINGTON** | | | | | | | | |
| *Eastern District* | | | | | | | | |
| Spokane Division | 51.0 | 40.5 (341) | −20.6 | 48.5 (167) | − 4.9 | | +19.8 | 1974 |
| Richland-Walla Walla Division | 50.6 | 46.8 (109) | − 7.5 | — | — | | — | 1971 |
| | | 54.3 (278) | + 7.3 | — | — | | — | 1974 |
| Yakima Division | 52.1 | 52.8 (322) | + 1.3 | 52.0 (127) | − 0.2 | | − 1.5 | 1974 |
| **WEST VIRGINIA** | | | | | | | | |
| *Southern District* | | | | | | | | |
| Beckley Division | 51.5 | 54.2 (249) | + 5.2 | — | — | | — | 1971 |
| | | 53.2 (278) | + 3.3 | — | — | | — | 1974 |
| Bluefield Division | 51.9 | 53.5 (185) | + 3.1 | — | — | | — | 1971 |
| | | 53.6 (278) | + 3.3 | — | — | | — | 1974 |
| Charleston Division | 51.7 | 51.1 (266) | − 1.2 | 45.3 (139) | −12.4 | | −11.4 | 1971 |
| | | 54.0 (322) | + 4.4 | — | | | — | 1974 |
| Huntington Division | 51.7 | 52.2 (228) | + 1.0 | 50.0 (124) | − 3.3 | | − 4.2 | 1971 |
| | | 55.0 (322) | + 6.4 | — | | | — | 1974 |
| **WISCONSIN** | | | | | | | | |
| *Western District* | | | | | | | | |
| Eau Claire Division | 50.4 | 47.5 (200) | − 5.8 | — | — | | — | 1971 |
| | | 52.0 (254) | + 3.2 | — | — | | — | 1972 |
| | | 50.7 (268) | + 0.6 | — | — | | — | 1973 |
| La Crosse Division | 50.4 | 50.0 (200) | − 0.8 | — | — | | — | 1971 |
| | | 45.4 (249) | − 9.9 | — | — | | — | 1972 |
| | | 58.2 (263) | +15.5 | — | — | | — | 1973 |
| Madison Division | 50.8 | 61.0 (200) | +20.1 | — | — | | — | 1971 |
| | | 52.7 (256) | + 3.7 | — | — | | — | 1972 |
| | | 50.0 (252) | − 1.6 | — | — | | — | 1973 |

| | | | | | |
|---|---|---|---|---|---|
| Superior Division | 50.0 | 47.5 (200) | − 5.0 | — | 1971 |
| | | 46.9 (262) | − 6.2 | — | 1972 |
| | | 50.6 (253) | + 1.2 | — | 1973 |
| Wasau Division | 50.8 | 48.0 (200) | − 5.5 | — | 1971 |
| | | 51.3 (263) | + 1.0 | — | 1972 |
| | | 51.6 (270) | + 1.6 | — | 1973 |
| WYOMING | | | | | |
| Casper Division | 51.5** | 45.0 (100) | −12.6 | — | 1974 |
| Sheridon Division | 49.8** | 56.0 (100) | +12.4 | — | 1974 |

Note: Census figures—*indicates the over-21 figure is used; **indicates the over-18 figure is used.

aThese surveys were all conducted by the clerks of the federal district courts.
bSee pp. 122 and 392.

cSize of sample not available.

**Table I-2.   Women on State Court Juries**

| State and County | Percent of Women in County | Percent of Women on Juries | Rate of Error | Source and Date |
|---|---|---|---|---|
| **Alabama** | | | | |
| Montgomery County | 53.8 (between 21 and 65) | 16.0 | −70.3 | 1972. *Penn v. Eubanks*, 360 F. Supp. 699 (N.D. Ala. 1973). |
| **Arizona** | | | | |
| Maricopa County (Phoenix) | 51.2 | 55.6 | + 8.6 | 439 jurors examined by Arizona State law students in April-May 1972. *Law & Social Order* (1973): 187. |
| **California** | | | | |
| Alameda County | 51.9 (over 18) | 47.3 | − 8.9 | Visual observation of 450 jurors, Oct. 1972-April 1973. |
| Los Angeles County | 52.7 (over 18) | 42.9 | −18.6 | 1,000 questionnaires filled out by jurors in January-February 1973 for *People v. Taylor*, No. A-277425 (L.A. Sup. Ct., Oct. 11, 1974). |
| Marin County | 50.3 | 50.9 | + 1.2 | Survey of 444 juror questionnaires randomly selected in February 1975 by Ruth Astle and Anita Oppenheimer. |
| Orange County | 51.9 (over 18) | 49.3 | − 5.0 | 23,001 jurors, selected for 1970. |
| | | 48.4 | − 6.7 | 26,410 jurors, selected for 1971. |
| | | 50.2 | − 3.3 | 16,517 jurors, selected for 1972. |
| | | 51.9 | 0 | 20,753 jurors, selected for 1974 (all from court figures). |
| Sacramento County | 52.0 (over 18) | 55.2 | + 6.2 | Cards filled out by 493 jurors in summer of 1972. |
| | | 47.4 | − 8.8 | 268 grand jury nominees—1972. |

| | | | | |
|---|---|---|---|---|
| San Bernardino | 51.6 (over 21) | 50.9 | − 1.4 | Cards filled out by 734 jurors in July 1972. |
| San Diego | 48.0 (over 18) | 50.1 | + 4.4 | A count of the names of 1,000 jurors, Jan. 1972. |
| San Francisco: Trial Jurors | 52.4 (over 18) | 51.5 | + 7.3 | Visual observation of 266 jurors, May 21, 1973. |
| | | 50.9 | − 2.9 | Visual observation of 1,207 jurors, 1972-73. |
| Grand Jurors | | 17.5 | −66.6 | All 114 grand jurors, 1970-76. Plaintiffs' brief, *Quadra v. Superior Court, Hastings Law Journal* 27 (1976): 601-602, 631. |
| Santa Clara: Trial Jurors | 51.7 (over 18) | 49.4 | − 4.4 | Visual observation of 486 jurors, Fall-Winter 1972. |
| Grand Jurors | | 11.6 | −77.9 | Survey of the 95 grand jurors who served between 1969 and 1973. *People v. Peraza,* No. 57,546 (Santa Clara Superior Ct., Sept. 13, 1974). See also, *People v. Navarette,* 54 Cal. App.3d 1064, 127 Cal. Rptr. 55 (1976). |
| *Colorado* | | | | |
| Adams County | 50.9 | 42.0 | −17.5 | 137 questionnaires filled out by jurors in 1973 for Bird Engineering—Research Associates, Inc. |
| Denver County | 54.1 (over 18) | 53.4 | − 1.3 | Count of 1,800 jurors, June-August 1972. |
| | | 46.3 | −14.4 | Count of 700 jurors, June 1974. |
| El Paso County (Colorado Springs) | 54.0 | 55.6 | + 3.0 | 887 cards filled out by jurors, Oct., 1972 to May 1973. |
| Jefferson County | 51.6 (over 18) | 35.0 | −32.2 | 200 questionnaires filled out by jurors in 1973 for Bird Engineering—Research Associates, Inc. |
| Pueblo County | 50.9 | 47.8 | − 6.1 | 559 cards filled out by jurors, 1972-74. |
| *Florida* | | | | |
| Levy County | 52.2 (over 21) | 46.1 | −11.7 | *Marshall v. State,* 365 F. Supp. 613, 616 (N.D. Fla. 1973); August 1970 survey. |
| | | 48.3 | − 7.5 | *Marshall v. Holmes,* 365 F. Supp. 1356 (N.D. Fla. 1973); 1972 survey. |

| State and County | Percent of Women in County | Percent of Women on Juries | Rate of Error | Source and Date |
|---|---|---|---|---|
| *Georgia* | | | | |
| Coweta County: Trial Jury | 53.3 | 16.2 | −69.6 | 1960-71; *White v. Georgia*, 230 Ga. 327, 196 S.E.2d 849, *appeal dismissed*, 414 U.S. 886 (1973); *Gould v. State*, 131 Ga. App. 811, 207 S.E.2d 519 (1974), 209 Ga. 844, 209 S.E.2d 312 (1974). |
| Grand Jury | 53.3 | 4.5 | −91.6 | *Id.* |
| DeKalb County: Grand Jury | 53.2 | 4.1 | −92.3 | Survey of 1,581 names in grand jury pool, *Julian v. State*, 134 Ga. App. 592, 215 S.E.2d 496 (1975). |
| Dougherty County: | 52.7 (over 21) | 37.9 | −28.1 | *Thompson v. Sheppard*, 490 F.2d 830 (5th Cir. 1974). |
| Quitman County Trial Jury | 54.2 (over 18) | 48.8 | −10.0 | 1973. *Foster v. Sparks*, 506 F.2d 805, 808 (5th Cir. 1975). |
| Grand Jury | | 27.9 | −48.5 | Ibid. |
| *Kansas* | | | | |
| Barton County | 52.9 (over 18) | 52.5 | −0.8 | 61 cards collected, spring 1974. |
| *Louisiana* | | | | |
| St. Tammany | 53.0 (over 18) | 0.6 | −98.9 | 1,800 jurors summoned between Dec. 8, 1971 and Nov. 3, 1972. *Taylor v. Louisiana*, 95 S. Ct. 692, 695 (1975). |
| Washington | 53.7 (over 18) | Less than 1 | Greater than −98.1 | *Edwards v. Healy*, 363 F. Supp. 1110 (E.D. La. 1973). |
| *Maryland* | | | | |
| Baltimore City | 54.3 | 57.0 | +5.0 | Court records, Sept. 1969 to Aug. 1970 (2,229 jurors). |
| | | 56.7 | +4.4 | Sept. 1970 to Aug. 1971 (2,536 jurors). |
| | | 56.6 | +4.2 | 1972 (2,658 jurors). |

| Location | | | | Source / Notes |
|---|---|---|---|---|
| | | 54.9 | +1.1 | 1973 (3,122 jurors). |
| | | 55.3 | +1.8 | Jan. 1974 (1,375 jurors). |
| Montgomery County | 53.0 (over 18) | 49.1 | −7.4 | Observation of jury orientation session, Dec. 15, 1972. |
| Prince George's County | 51.6 | 43.9 | −14.9 | 264 questionnaires filled out by jurors, October 1973, for Bird Engineering–Research Associates, Inc. |
| *Massachusetts* | | | | |
| Suffolk County (Boston) | 53.8 | 28.9 | −46.3 | Count of 1,538 juror names, March-Sept. 1972. |
| | | 37.2 | −30.8 | Count of 387 jurors who served in Jan. and May 1974. |
| | | 36.9 | −31.4 | Visual observation of 130 jurors, June 10, 1974. |
| *Minnesota* | | | | |
| Hennepin County (Minneapolis) | 53.9 | 45.0 | −16.5 | 200 questionnaires filled out for Bird Engineering–Research Associates, Inc. in 1973. |
| *Missouri* | | | | |
| City of St. Louis | 56.7 | 43.0 | −24.2 | Visual observation of 242 jurors, March 1973. |
| *Nevada* | | | | |
| Washoe County (Reno) | 50.8 | 46.3 | −8.9 | 835 cards filled out by jurors, 1972-73. |
| *New Mexico* | | | | |
| Bernalillo County (Albuquerque) | 52.6 (over 18) | 53.8 | +2.3 | Count of 651 juror questionnaire, 1972-74. |
| *New York* | | | | |
| Bronx County | 55.2 | 8.6 | −84.4 | Court survey of 444 jurors in April 1972. Appellate Division Committee on Court Administration, "The Juror in New York City." |
| Erie County (Buffalo) | 53.0 (21-74) | 16.8 | −68.3 | 1973-74 study of 1,651 jurors by the Attica Defense Fund (this selection scheme was declared unconstitutional in *People v. Attica Brothers*, Erie County Supreme Court, June 27, 1974). |

| State and County | Percent of Women in County | Percent of Women on Juries | Rate of Error | Source and Date |
|---|---|---|---|---|
| King's County (Brooklyn) | 54.6 | 12.1 | −77.8 | Court survey of 742 jurors in April 1972. |
| New York County (Manhattan) | 54.1 | 16.8 | −68.9 | Complete list of 107,000 eligible jurors, *New York Times*, Jan. 22, 1975. |
| Queens County: | 54.0 | 3.4 | −93.7 | Court survey of 1,438 jurors in April 1972. |
| Grand Jury | 54.0 | 13.1 | −75.7 | 1,500 persons on the grand jury rolls in 1972. |
|  |  | 2.9 | −95.0 | A count of 69 grand jurors in May and June 1973 by grand juror Monique Golden. |
| Richmond County (Staten Island) | 52.2 | 15.2 | −67.0 | Court survey of 283 jurors in April 1972. |
| *North Dakota* |  |  |  |  |
| Cass County (Fargo) | 50.8 | 45.8 | − 9.8 | 212 jurors selected in Dec. 1971. |
|  |  | 50.7 | − 0.2 | 144 jurors selected in 1973. |
| *Rhode Island* |  |  |  |  |
| (Statewide) | 51.8 (over 18) | 44.0 | −15.1 | 359 jurors examined by Prof. Edward N. Beiser, Brown University in 1970. *Judicature* 57 (1973): 196. |
| *South Carolina* |  |  |  |  |
| Dillon County | 54.2 | 42.0 | −22.5 | 1971 jury list, *Blackwell v. Thomas*, 476 F.2d 443 (4th Cir. 1973). |
| *Tennessee* |  |  |  |  |
| Henry County | 53.2 (over 21) | 0.9 (jury lists) | −98.3 | 2,280 persons summoned for duty, July, 1961, to January, 1972. Briefs filed for *Stubblefield v. Tennessee*, 420 U.S. 903 (1975). |
|  |  | 0.0 (actually served) | −100.0 |  |
| Shelby County (Memphis) | 52.0 | 4.0 | −92.3 | Examination of the jury lists for May-July, 1972. |

| | | | | |
|---|---|---|---|---|
| | | 2.9 | −94.4 | 480 jurors watched by reporter James Cole, fall 1972, *Memphis Commercial Appeal*, Dec. 24, 1972. |
| *Texas* | | | | |
| Harris County (Houston): Trial Jurors | 51.1 | 41.0 | −19.8 | 1,410 jurors impaneled in October 1971. |
| Grand Jurors | | 22.0 | −56.9 | Survey of 156 persons who served as grand jurors between 1969 and 1972. *Dumont v. Estelle*, 377 F. Supp. 374 (W.D. Texas, 1974). |
| *Utah* | | | | |
| Salt Lake County | 51.3 | 48.7 | − 7.0 | Cards filled out by 267 jurors, July and October, 1972. |
| *Virginia* | | | | |
| Arlington County | 53.7 | 15.7 | −70.8 | 1972 jury venire containing 1,500 names examined by attorney William B. Moore. |
| | | 37.9 | −29.4 | A count of 261 jurors, April to June 1974. |

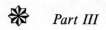 *Part III*

# Additional Background
# Material

## Appendix J:
## Jury Composition and
## Jury Verdicts: Studies
## from Baltimore and
## Los Angeles

In Chapter Two, a survey is provided of the extent of underrepresentation on U.S. juries, and studies concerning the effect of that underrepresentation on jury verdicts are discussed. Two jurisdictions have changed their jury selection procedure in recent years, producing results that strongly indicate that jury composition does affect jury verdicts (see pp. 33-35).

The city of Baltimore, Maryland, changed its method of selecting jurors from a personal-selection or "key-man" approach in September 1969 to a random-selection system from the voter registration lists. Figures on jury verdicts have been hard to assemble, but the somewhat incomplete figures do indicate a definite trend toward a lower rate of conviction following the change. The court administrators did not keep careful conviction-acquittal information prior to the September 1969 change. What they did keep was a log of each day's court events that tells how many trials were held in each crime category and the results of all the trials combining jury with nonjury trials. In other words, on a given day there may have been six robbery trials before judges and three robbery trials before juries, resulting in seven convictions and two acquittals. If that were the case, we would not be able to tell what the conviction rate is in the jury trials—except that at least one resulted in a conviction. On other days, the results are less ambiguous—one murder trial before a jury, one conviction. The tables that follow provide figures for all felony trials between 1965 and 1974. The tables also distribute all the uncertain trials throughout the years in a 2-1 conviction-acquittal ratio, which seems like the most neutral estimate to make, and which provides a less fluctuating and perhaps more reliable figure.

**Table J-1.  Rate of Conviction, City of Baltimore: All Felonies**

| | 1965 | 1966 | 1967 | 1968 | Jan.-Aug. 1969 | Sept.-Dec. 1969 | 1970 | 1971 | 1972 (except for May)a | '1973b | Jan.-Jun. 14, 1974 | Totals Before Sept. 1969 | Totals After Sept. 1969 |
|---|---|---|---|---|---|---|---|---|---|---|---|---|---|
| Total | 72 | 134 | 94 | 128 | 176 | 132 | 256 | 355 | 267 | 372 | 178 | 604 | 1560 |
| Convictions | 43 | 85 | 62 | 75 | 108 | 64 | 148 | 199 | 187 | 238 | 109 | 373 | 945 |
| Acquittals | 8 | 15 | 12 | 22 | 16 | 34 | 56 | 83 | 80 | 134 | 69 | 73 | 456 |
| Uncertain | 21 | 34 | 20 | 31 | 52 | 34 | 52 | 73 | – | – | – | 158 | 159 |
| Rate of Conviction Excluding the Uncertains | 84.3% | 85.0% | 83.8% | 77.3% | 87.1% | 65.3% | 72.5% | 70.6% | 70.0% | 64.0% | 61.2% | 83.6% | 67.5% |

*If the Uncertains are distributed in 2-1 Convictions-Acquittals ratio:*

| | 1965 | 1966 | 1967 | 1968 | Jan.-Aug. 1969 | Sept.-Dec. 1969 | 1970 | 1971 | 1972 (except for May)a | '1973b | Jan.-Jun. 14, 1974 | Totals Before Sept. 1969 | Totals After Sept. 1969 |
|---|---|---|---|---|---|---|---|---|---|---|---|---|---|
| Convictions | 57 | 108 | 76 | 96 | 143 | 87 | 183 | 248 | 187 | 238 | 109 | 480 | 1052 |
| Acquittals | 15 | 26 | 18 | 32 | 33 | 45 | 73 | 107 | 80 | 134 | 69 | 124 | 508 |
| Rate of Conviction | 79.2% | 80.6% | 80.9% | 75.0% | 81.3% | 65.9% | 71.5% | 69.9% | 70.0% | 64.0% | 61.2% | 79.5% | 67.4% |

aThe figures for May 1972 are missing from the court files. The court began compiling totals for jury trials in 1972, thus eliminating the "uncertains" from this chart.

bIn April 1973 the court started keeping these figures by individual defendant, rather than by case, as they had during the previous 18 months.

Los Angeles County, California, provides another laboratory that illustrates the effect of increasing and then decreasing the number of nonwhites on juries. The jurors in the populous Central District of Los Angeles have generally been selected from throughout the county, but for a year and a half—from July 1970 to January 1972—the jurors in that district were selected exclusively from among the 1.5 million residents of the district.

First, the demographic figures should be presented. The population breakdown for the Central District is as follows:

| | |
|---|---|
| Blacks: | 31.5 percent |
| Chicanos: | 18.3 percent |
| Anglo-Europeans: | 50.2 percent |

When the residents of the Central District are put into the county-wide draw their relative strength (22 percent of the county's population) falls off dramatically for reasons detailed in other sections of this book—excessive mobility, economic reasons for being excused, a high rate of nonresponse to the summons, and so on. Rather than comprising 22 percent of the county's juries, residents of the Central District—according to the jury commissioner's figures—comprise only 11 percent. This reduces the nonwhite impact on the countywide juries still further, and the actual figures for the countywide juries are as follows:

| | |
|---|---|
| Blacks: | 8 percent |
| Chicanos: | 7 percent |
| Anglo-Europeans: | 85 percent |

Perhaps the most authoritative body of statistics are those kept by Frank S. Zolin, the Executive Officer of the Los Angeles County Superior Court. His statistics on the rate of conviction for the jury trials held in the Central District's Superior Court are seen on p. 380.[1] The rate of conviction slipped a bit in 1970 and then plummeted almost 20 points in 1971. A conviction ratio less than 50 percent is almost unheard of, but it happened during the year that the Central District was selecting its jurors exclusively from the residents of that area. To demonstrate that 1971 was not simply a very unusual year in Los Angeles County, the figures for the rest of the County are offered for purposes of comparison (see p. 380).

**Table J-2.   Rate of Conviction, City of Baltimore: By Crime Category**

| | 1965 | 1966 | 1967 | 1968 | Jan.-Aug. 1969 | Sept.-Dec. 1969 | 1970 | 1971 | 1972 | 1973 | Jan.-Jun. 14, 1974 | Totals Before Sept. 1969 | Totals After Sept. 1969 |
|---|---|---|---|---|---|---|---|---|---|---|---|---|---|
| *Assault, Assault to Murder, Assault on an Officer* | | | | | | | | | | | | | |
| Convictions | 3 | 5 | 10 | 7 | 6 | 7 | 13 | 25 | 33 | 42 | 17 | 31 | 137 |
| Acquittals | 0 | 1 | 0 | 3 | 5 | 1 | 3 | 20 | 14 | 24 | 4 | 9 | 66 |
| Uncertain | 5 | 12 | 6 | 10 | 8 | 5 | 10 | 13 | 22 | 11 | 3 | 41 | 64 |
| Conviction Rate | 100 | 83.3 | 100 | 70.0 | 54.6 | 87.5 | 81.3 | 55.6 | 70.2 | 63.6 | 81.0 | 77.5 | 67.5 |
| Conviction Rate % if Uncertains Are Distributed 2-1 | 79.2 | 72.2 | 87.5 | 68.4 | 59.6 | 79.5 | 75.7 | 58.0 | 69.1 | 64.1 | 79.2 | 72.0 | 67.3 |
| *Burglary* | | | | | | | | | | | | | |
| Convictions | 3 | 2 | 1 | 1 | 1 | 2 | 4 | 10 | 10 | 9 | 5 | 8 | 40 |
| Acquittals | 1 | 0 | 0 | 0 | 1 | 0 | 0 | 3 | 0 | 2 | 1 | 2 | 6 |
| Uncertain | 1 | 3 | 3 | 2 | 5 | 1 | 7 | 4 | 9 | 3 | 6 | 14 | 30 |
| Conviction Rate | 75.0 | 100 | 100 | 100 | 50.0 | 100 | 100 | 76.9 | 100 | 81.8 | 83.3 | 80.0 | 87.0 |
| Conviction Rate % if Uncertains Are Distributed 2-1 | 73.4 | 80.0 | 75.0 | 77.8 | 61.9 | 88.9 | 78.8 | 74.5 | 84.2 | 78.6 | 75.0 | 72.2 | 78.9 |
| *Conspiracy* | | | | | | | | | | | | | |
| Convictions | 0 | 0 | 0 | 0 | 13 | 8 | 6 | 3 | 2 | 6 | 4 | 13 | 29 |
| Acquittals | 0 | 1 | 0 | 0 | 0 | 4 | 4 | 1 | 0 | 1 | 0 | 1 | 10 |
| Uncertain | 0 | 0 | 0 | 0 | 1 | 1 | 0 | 0 | 0 | 1 | 0 | 1 | 20 |
| Conviction Rate | | 0 | | | 100 | 66.7 | 60.0 | 75.0 | 100 | 85.7 | 100 | 92.9 | 74.4 |
| Conviction Rate % if Uncertains Are Distributed 2-1 | | 0 | | | 97.6 | 66.7 | 60.0 | 75.0 | 100 | 83.3 | 100 | 91.1 | 74.0 |

*Murder*

| | | | | | | | | | | | | | |
|---|---|---|---|---|---|---|---|---|---|---|---|---|---|
| Convictions | 6 | 13 | 10 | 17 | 9 | 8 | 18 | 34 | 50 | 64 | 20 | 55 | 194 |
| Acquittals | 0 | 4 | 2 | 2 | 5 | 6 | 10 | 8 | 19 | 20 | 8 | 13 | 71 |
| Uncertain | 1 | 1 | 0 | 4 | 2 | 2 | 5 | 9 | 13 | 9 | 4 | 8 | 42 |
| Conviction Rate | 100 | 76.5 | 83.3 | 89.5 | 64.3 | 57.1 | 64.3 | 81.0 | 72.5 | 76.2 | 71.4 | 80.9 | 73.2 |
| Conviction Rate % if Uncertains Are Distributed 2-1 | 95.3 | 75.9 | 83.3 | 85.5 | 64.6 | 58.3 | 64.6 | 78.4 | 71.5 | 75.3 | 70.8 | 79.4 | 72.3 |

*Rape*

| | | | | | | | | | | | | | |
|---|---|---|---|---|---|---|---|---|---|---|---|---|---|
| Convictions | 0 | 10 | 4 | 4 | 5 | 1 | 5 | 11 | 8 | 13 | 11 | 23 | 49 |
| Acquittals | 1 | 0 | 3 | 0 | 0 | 2 | 6 | 15 | 10 | 12 | 7 | 4 | 52 |
| Uncertain | 0 | 0 | 0 | 2 | 2 | 0 | 0 | 2 | 4 | 1 | 1 | 4 | 8 |
| Conviction Rate | 0 | 100 | 57.1 | 100 | 100 | 33.3 | 45.5 | 42.3 | 44.4 | 52.0 | 61.1 | 85.2 | 48.5 |
| Conviction Rate if Uncertains Are Distributed 2-1 | 0 | 100 | 57.1 | 88.9 | 90.5 | 33.3 | 45.5 | 44.0 | 48.5 | 52.6 | 61.4 | 82.8 | 49.8 |

*Robbery*

| | | | | | | | | | | | | | |
|---|---|---|---|---|---|---|---|---|---|---|---|---|---|
| Convictions | 13 | 14 | 17 | 14 | 21 | 6 | 37 | 58 | 68 | 93 | 33 | 79 | 295 |
| Acquittals | 2 | 0 | 1 | 4 | 0 | 3 | 8 | 5 | 8 | 19 | 10 | 7 | 53 |
| Uncertain | 9 | 13 | 9 | 11 | 16 | 11 | 15 | 37 | 33 | 48 | 10 | 58 | 154 |
| Conviction Rate | 86.7 | 100 | 94.4 | 77.8 | 100 | 66.7 | 82.2 | 92.1 | 89.5 | 83.0 | 76.7 | 91.9 | 84.8 |
| Conviction Rate if Uncertains Are Distributed 2-1 | 79.7 | 84.0 | 85.2 | 73.6 | 85.6 | 66.7 | 78.3 | 82.7 | 82.6 | 78.1 | 74.8 | 81.7 | 79.2 |

**Conviction Rate in the Central
District of Los Angeles**

|  | Acquittals | Convictions | Rate of Conviction |
|---|---|---|---|
| 1967 | 203 | 535 | 72.5% |
| 1968 | 190 | 453 | 70.5 |
| 1969 | 189 | 383 | 67.0 |
| 1970 | 220 | 402 | 64.6 |
| 1971 | 252 | 225 | 47.2 |
| 1972 | 157 | 313 | 66.6 |
| 1973 | 294 | 478 | 61.9 |

**Conviction Rate for All of Los Angeles
County**

| District | 1971 | | | 1972 | | |
|---|---|---|---|---|---|---|
|  | Acq. | Conv. | Rate of Conv. | Acq. | Conv. | Rate of Conv. |
| Central | 252 | 225 | 47.2 | 157 | 313 | 66.6 |
| East (Pomona) | 19 | 46 | 70.8 | 10 | 67 | 87.0 |
| NE (Pasadena) | 9 | 43 | 82.7 | 17 | 30 | 63.8 |
| NW (Van Nuys) | 13 | 51 | 79.7 | 19 | 55 | 74.3 |
| S (Long Beach) | 27 | 91 | 77.1 | 15 | 65 | 81.3 |
| SE (Norwalk) | 24 | 81 | 77.1 | 25 | 99 | 79.8 |
| SW Torrance) | 26 | 79 | 75.2 | 19 | 59 | 75.6 |
| W (Santa Monica) | 12 | 51 | 81.0 | 16 | 76 | 82.6 |
| Totals | 382 | 667 | 63.6 | 278 | 763 | 73.3 |
| Total without the Central District | 130 | 442 | 77.3 | 121 | 451 | 78.8 |

The Los Angeles District Attorney's Office keeps its own informal figures for its own internal use, which differ in some
respects, but show the same trend. These figures are kept by
separate cases (which may include more than one defendant)
rather than by individual defendants, hence the discrepancy. For
the Central District the jury trial statistics are as follows:

|  | Convictions | Acquittals | Rate of Conviction |
|---|---|---|---|
| 1969 | 158 | 325 | 67.3 |
| 1970 | 174 | 326 | 65.2 |
| 1971 | 137 | 167 | 54.9 |
| 1972 (Jan.-July) | 38 | 152 | 80.0 |

Somewhat smaller figures, but the same unmistable change in 1971.

A final set of figures appears in a study put together by the Rand Corporation examining the flow of arrested persons through the District Attorney's Office and then through the courts. These figures show only the rate of conviction without listing the number of trials, and they cover only 1970 and 1971, but they do break down the trials by type of felony and thus give us some further insight into the nature of the juror rebellion in the Central District. The figures extracted from that study pertinent to this discussion are given in Table J-3. The rate of conviction dropped in the Central District in every crime category examined by the Rand Corporation, even though the rate was rising or holding steady in the rest of the county. The office of the district attorney, one must assume, was operating in the usual way, but the juror in the Central District—50 percent nonwhite and largely poor—were more skeptical of the prosecution's evidence than were jurors in other parts of the county. These Central District jurors were performing the function that has traditionally justified our reliance on the somewhat cumbersome and expensive jury system—they were bringing the community's conscience into the courtroom and were concluding more frequently that the government had not proved a case that would justify putting a fellow human being behind bars.

## NOTE

1. These are collected from the official reports put out by the Superior Court. See, e.g., Frank Zolin, *Executive Officer's Report—1972/73*, (Los Angeles: Superior Court, 1974), pp. 44-45.

**Table J-3. Conviction Rate, Central District of California**

| District | All Felonies | | Possession of Marijuana | | Possession of Dangerous Drugs | | Forgery | | Possession of Narcotics | | Sale of Narcotics | | Burglary | | Robbery | | Assault | |
|---|---|---|---|---|---|---|---|---|---|---|---|---|---|---|---|---|---|---|
| | 1970 | 1971 | 1970 | 1971 | 1970 | 1971 | 1970 | 1971 | 1970 | 1971 | 1970 | 1971 | 1970 | 1971 | 1970 | 1971 | 1970 | 1971 |
| Central | 63.3 | 48.6 | 40.0 | 20.0 | 58.8 | 39.3 | 76.9 | 0.0 | 57.1 | 50.0 | 81.6 | 70.6 | 69.5 | 42.9 | 69.1 | 59.2 | 50.9 | 35.7 |
| East (Pomona) | 76.1 | 67.2 | 33.3 | 33.3 | 100.0 | 100.0 | 100.0 | 100.0 | 100.0 | – | 100.0 | 83.3 | 66.7 | 54.6 | 71.4 | 54.6 | 0.0 | 71.4 |
| NE (Pasadena) | 70.2 | 86.1 | 0.0 | 100.0 | – | – | 100.0 | – | – | 100.0 | 100.0 | 100.0 | 60.0 | 100.0 | 53.9 | 85.7 | – | 83.3 |
| NW (Van Nuys) | 79.8 | 76.9 | 57.1 | 100.0 | 100.0 | 33.3 | 100.0 | – | 100.0 | – | 100.0 | 93.8 | 69.6 | 87.5 | 100.0 | 71.4 | 87.5 | 57.1 |
| S (Long Beach) | 73.7 | 83.1 | 75.0 | 77.8 | 100.0 | 85.7 | 50.0 | 100.0 | 100.0 | 0.0 | 83.3 | 71.4 | 66.7 | 82.8 | 70.0 | 90.9 | 20.0 | 100.0 |
| SE (Norwalk) | 72.0 | 69.8 | 57.1 | 60.0 | 81.3 | 65.2 | 100.0 | 50.0 | 100.0 | 100.0 | 87.5 | 90.4 | 75.0 | 37.5 | 88.9 | 80.0 | 61.1 | 46.2 |
| SW (Torrance) | 75.3 | 77.1 | 100.0 | 50.0 | 83.3 | – | 100.0 | 66.7 | – | 100.0 | 80.0 | 100.0 | 66.7 | 63.6 | 73.7 | 81.5 | 50.0 | 75.0 |
| W (Santa Monica) | 83.2 | 77.5 | 57.1 | 33.3 | 100.0 | 66.7 | 100.0 | 75.0 | 100.0 | 100.0 | 86.7 | 90.9 | 78.6 | 75.0 | 90.0 | 100.0 | 66.7 | 54.6 |
| Countywide | 69.8 | 64.9 | 50.0 | 42.0 | 76.0 | 57.4 | 85.2 | 58.8 | 85.0 | 71.4 | 86.1 | 83.8 | 69.7 | 62.2 | 72.6 | 73.3 | 53.2 | 55.6 |

Source: Reprinted by permission of the publisher, from *Prosecution of Adult Felony Defendants* by Peter N. Greenwood, Sorrel Wildhorn, Eugene C. Poggio, Michael J. Strumwasser and Peter De Leon, by Rand Corporation (Lexington, Mass.: Lexington Books, D.C. Heath and Company, 1976).

## Appendix K:
## Illustrations of
## Discriminatory Effects
## of the Excusing Process

Chapter Five explains how excuses are granted and suggests that the results of the excusing process may favor some demographic groups over others on jury panels. Poorer people, blue-collar workers, the elderly, the young, and particularly young women, all are excused at a disproportionately high rate and as a result they fill fewer seats on our juries than do the middle-aged, middle-class white-collar workers. This appendix is designed to illustrate how this process works.

### EVALUATING EXCUSES—A CENSUS-BASED MODEL

Before examining how jury commissioners actually handle excuses, we should look at a profile of the population to determine how many people fall into the various excuse categories according to information put together by the U.S. Bureau of the Census. The Census Bureau makes an intensive study of 1 percent of the population throughout the country to provide additional information about the habits of our people. This 1 percent is carefully chosen to represent the population at large. Three political scientists at the Massachusetts Institute of Technology took the computer tape for Eastern Massachusetts (covering Barnstable, Bristol, Dukes, Essex, Middlesex, Nantucket, Norfolk, Plymouth, Suffolk, and Worcester Counties) and programmed a computer to pick out all the people who might be disqualified, exempt, or excused under the federal statute.[1] The over-21 population for the area in 1970 was 3,129,700, and so the 1 percent sample includes 31,297 persons. The results are given in Table K-1. This computer exercise assumes that

Table K-1.  Census-Based Model

| | | | | |
|---|---|---|---|---|
| Total Sample | | | 31,297 | |
| *Potentially Disqualified:* | | | | |
| Not a citizen | 1,032 | ( 3.3%) | | |
| Disabled | 1,534 | ( 4.9%) | | |
| In jail | 35 | ( 0.1%) | | |
| Total | | | 2,601 | ( 8.3%) |
| *Potentially Exempt:* | | | | |
| In Armed Forces | 398 | ( 1.3%) | | |
| Fireman or Police Officer | 244 | ( 0.8%) | | |
| Judge or Public Officer | 60 | ( 0.2%) | | |
| Total | | | 702 | ( 2.3%) |
| *Potentially Excused:* | | | | |
| Over 70 years | 3,090 | ( 9.9%) | | |
| Clergy | 37 | ( 0.1%) | | |
| Care of child | 5,567 | (17.8%) | | |
| Doctor or Nurse | 556 | ( 1.8%) | | |
| Teacher | 1,093 | ( 3.5%) | | |
| Attorney | 42 | ( 0.1%) | | |
| Sole Proprietor | 1,676 | ( 5.4%) | | |
| Total | | | 12,064 | (38.6%) |
| *Total Potentially Unqualified, Exempt, Excused* | | | 15,367 | (49.1%) |
| *Total Qualified* | | | 15,930 | (50.9%) |

everyone who is eligible for an excuse will claim one, and so it overstates the number of persons excused. Despite this overstatement, the computer study indicates that at least one-half of all persons receiving questionnaires should be qualified for jury duty under the federal jury statute which contains more excuses and exemptions than do many of the states. As we shall see, however, it is rare for a court to obtain 50 percent service from the persons returning jury questionnaires, and usually the number is much lower.

## THE FEDERAL COURTS

The clerical staff in the federal courts tends to be more highly paid and somewhat more professional in their operation, so it is appropriate to examine their procedures first. Excuses are granted at three different points—first, when persons selected from the master wheel are sent their first questionnaires; second, if they pass the first hurdle and are put onto the qualified wheel, when they are sent a summons for jury duty; and third, when they actually come into the courthouse on the day they are called. The final step is particularly informal, and it is hard to obtain specific statistics, but the data in Table K-2 attempt to chronicle the flow of potential jurors through the process. Table K-2 provides information about the first stage—

names are selected from the master wheel, questionnaires are sent and returned, and they are processed.

Several interesting facts can be found in this data, even though the figures are not in every case directly comparable to each other. Some courts have a rate of nonresponse that is three times that of other courts, indicating that lists used may have become outdated quickly or that no vigorous follow-up is employed. Wide variations are also seen in the types of excuses granted. The federal clerks in Camden, N.J. and Washington, D.C. seem to be less willing to grant excuses than the clerks in Maine, Los Angeles, and San Francisco. Excuses on the ground of health show a particularly wide fluctuation, and differences in excuses based on transportation difficulty of course reflect the different geographical areas concerned. The Camden, N.J., figures were prepared by David Kairys, an attorney preparing a challenge, and he discovered that the Camden clerk denied 32.5 percent of all the requests for excuses. The jury clerk in the Sacramento Division of the Eastern District of California has said, in contrast, that she grants virtually every request for an excuse.[2]

After jurors have been qualified by the federal clerks, they are then put on the "qualified wheel" and they can request an excuse at this stage as well. The Bird Engineering—Research Associates, Inc., have examined the jury selection procedures in a number of courts in recent years, under a grant from the Law Enforcement Assistance Agency, and they have produced the data shown in Tables K-3 and K-4, which compare the procedure in the federal courts of Denver, Colorado, and New York City (Manhattan).

As shown in Tables K-3 and K-4, the Denver federal court winds up with 24.2 percent of the persons who receive questionnaires as actual jurors, but the federal court in Manhattan obtains only 8.8 percent of those who originally receive a qualifying questionnaire. This disparity is even more remarkable because the Denver clerks excuse everyone who asks for an excuse, automatically, without question.[3] It may be, therefore, that heavily urban districts have more difficulty inducing their residents to serve as jurors, partly because the cost of living is higher (and the fee paid to jurors is relatively less), partly because people in large metropolitan areas are more mobile and harder to track down, and partly because urban courts may not be able or willing to devote the resources needed to pursue reluctant jurors.

## STATE COURTS

The practices in the state courts show even greater variation than those of the federal courts, and it is difficult to know exactly how to

**Table K-2.   Federal Court Excuses**

| | Central District of California | Northern District of California San Francisco Division | District of Columbia | District of Columbia | Maine Northern Division | Maine Southern Division | District of N.J. Camden Division |
|---|---|---|---|---|---|---|---|
| Number of Questionnaires Mailed | 41,628 | 7,658a | 24,430 | 4,403 | 250 | 450 | 1,000 |
| Percent Undeliverable or No Response | 7.5 | N.A. | 22.7 | 27.4 | 14.8 | 13.7 | 21.0 |
| Percent Completed and Returned | 92.5 | N.A. | 77.3 | 72.6 | 85.2 | 86.3 | 79.0 |
| Total Percent Disqualified, Exempt or Excused | 56.5 | 71.2 | 26.9 | 26.4 | 50.4 | 46.3 | 29.8 |
| Exempt or Excused for Occupational Reasons: | | | | | | | |
| Teacher | | 2.8 | 2.2 | 2.0 | 1.6 | 0.7 | 1.2 |
| Government Employee, Armed Forces, Police, Fire, etc. | | 1.9 | 1.1 | 1.0 | 3.2 | 2.3 | 0.9 |
| Professional (Dr., Atty., Minister, etc.) | | 4.0 | 1.9 | 1.8 | 2.0 | 1.2 | 1.0 |
| Total | 6.3 | | | | | | |
| Excused for Occupational Hardship: | | | | | | | |
| Self-Employed | 3.3 | 1.7 | | | | | 2.3 |
| Other Hardship | 8.5 | 4.0 | | | 5.2 | 3.5 | 8.5 |
| Student | | 1.0 | | | | | |
| Mother of Small Children | 7.5 | 11.0 | 1.7 | 1.8 | 6.4 | 5.8 | 3.1 |
| Sole Caretaker of Invalid | 0.9 | | | | | | |
| Poor Health | 14.6 | 11.0 | 3.8 | 4.2 | 6.0 | 5.3 | |
| Over 70 | 3.8 | 12.4 | 5.3 | 5.8 | 7.6 | 12.3 | 7.1 |
| Transportation Difficulties | 7.3 | 7.4 | | | 9.6 | 6.3 | 3.7 |

| | Court statistics, 1972. | Questionnaires examined by legal worker Nicolas de Lancie, 1971-1972. | Court statistics, Aug. 1972-Fall 1973. | Court statistics, June 1973. | Court statistics, 1971. | Court statistics, 1971. | Figures prepared by attorney David Kairys, Fall 1972. |
|---|---|---|---|---|---|---|---|
| Previous Jury Service | 0.5 | 2.0 | 0.8 | 0.8 | 1.6 | 0.9 | |
| Felony Conviction | 0.1 | 0.1 | 0.4 | 0.5 | | | |
| Moved from the Jurisdiction | 2.3 | 8.4 | 7.0 | 5.9 | 1.6 | 3.0 | 0.2 |
| Deceased | 0 | 2.3 | 2.0 | 2.3 | 4.8 | 4.7 | 1.8 |
| Other | 1.4 | 1.3 | 0.6 | 0.4 | 2.4 | 0.2 | |
| Percent Added to the Qualified Wheel | 36.1 | 28.8 | 50.4 | 46.2 | 34.8 | 40.0 | 48.5 |
| Source & Date | Court statistics, 1972. | Questionnaires examined by legal worker Nicolas de Lancie, 1971-1972. | Court statistics, Aug. 1972-Fall 1973. | Court statistics, June 1973. | Court statistics, 1971. | Court statistics, 1971. | Figures prepared by attorney David Kairys, Fall 1972. |

[a]This figure is the number of questionnaires returned. No information is available on the number that were mailed. Percentages for the Northern District of California are thus based on the number of questionnaires returned.

**K-3.  Excusing Process: Federal District Court, Colorado, Denver Division, 1974**

*Qualification Process*
*2600 Questionnaires Sent*

| | |
|---|---|
| 22%<br>Undelivered<br>or no<br>Response | |
| 32%<br>Disqualified<br>Exempt<br>Excused | |
| 46%<br>Qualified | |

| | |
|---|---|
| Disqualified[a] | 4.6% |
| Exempt, excluded[b] | 6.8% |
| Excused | 20.6% |

| | |
|---|---|
| Age | 6.8% |
| Woman/custody | 3.4% |
| Sole prop. | 4.3% |
| Attys, M.D.'s | 1.2% |
| Teachers | 1.2% |
| Transportation | 0.8% |
| Sole care | 1.2% |
| Jury duty | 1.0% |
| Clergy | 0.6% |
| | 20.5% |

*Summoning Process*
*100 Summonses Sent*

| | |
|---|---|
| 6%<br>Undelivered<br>or no<br>Response | |
| 41.3%<br>Disqualified<br>Exempt<br>Excused | |
| 52.7%<br>Serve | |

| | |
|---|---|
| Disqualified[a] | 7.4% |
| Exempt, excluded[b] | 1.5% |
| Excused | 32.4% |

| | |
|---|---|
| Work conflict | 10.1% (temporary) |
| Financial hardship | 3.1% |
| Woman/custody | 3.8% |
| Student | 3.7% |
| Transportation | 1.8% |
| Sole prop. | 1.4% |
| Teacher | 1.3% |
| Jury duty | 0.5% |
| Age | 0.1% |
| Atty. | 0.2% |
| Sole care | 1.6% |
| Vacation | 4.0% (temporary) |
| C.O. | 0.5% |
| Unknown | 0.2% |
| | 32.3% |

| | | | |
|---|---|---|---|
| [a]Disqualified: | Under 18 years<br>Residence<br>Citizenship<br>Language<br>Health<br>Felony conviction | [b]Exempt, excluded: | Armed Forces<br>Fire/Police<br>Public officers<br>Deceased<br>Moved<br>Prior service |

**K-4. Excusing Process: Federal Court for the Southern District of New York, 1974**

*Qualification Process*
*37,081 Questionnaires Sent*

| | |
|---|---|
| 6.4%<br>Not Returned | |
| 19.4%<br>Undeliverable | |
| 44.8%<br>Disqualified<br>Exempt<br>Excused | |
| 29.4%<br>Qualified | |

| | |
|---|---|
| Disqualified | 10.3% |
| Exempt | .9% |
| Excused | 33.6% |

| | |
|---|---|
| Mileage | 10.3% |
| Age | 8.3% |
| Small children | 6.3% |
| Teacher | 3.0% |
| Previous service | 2.0% |
| Lawyer | 1.1% |
| Dr. | .9% |
| Minister | .9% |
| Nurse | .4% |
| Student | .4% |
| | 33.6% |

*Summoning Process*
*1800 Summonses Sent*

| | |
|---|---|
| 1.3%<br>Undeliverable | |
| 1.6% No Show | |
| 47.0%<br>Exempt<br>Disqualified<br>Excused | |
| 20.1%<br>Postponed | |
| 30.0%<br>Serve | |

| | |
|---|---|
| Disqualified | 19.5% |
| Exempt | .1% |
| Excused | 27.4% |

| | |
|---|---|
| Mileage | 6.2% |
| Age | 2.7% |
| Small children | 3.7% |
| Teacher | 1.4% |
| Previous service | 6.0% |
| Lawyers | .4% |
| Religion | .5% |
| Student | 3.8% |
| Hardship | 2.7% |
| | 27.4% |

present the data in a helpful manner. For one thing the data is elusive. Nicholas Kozay, Jr., clerk of the Jury Selection Board in Philadelphia, expressed his jurisdiction's policy by saying, "Why should we keep a record? What purpose is served?"[4] Bernard J. Ward, jury commissioner for the San Francisco Superior and Municipal Courts, put it a somewhat different way when he said that his office does not keep statistics "to save the taxpayers a little money."[5] Some courts have difficulty keeping track of the excusing process because different judges on the same court have differing views on the proper procedure. Andrew D. Hiduke, court administrator in Lake County, Indiana, said that "The granting of excuses is a major problem due to the amount of personal requests that must be checked and the differing views for granting excuses of the ten judges within our system."[6]

But some courts do manage to maintain statistics, and the data that exist indicate wide variations among courts, with urban courts impaneling only a small percentage of those who originally receive questionnaires. To prepare its list of qualified jurors for 1975, the Superior Court in Los Angeles County mailed out 446,100 questionnaires and obtained only 113,574 qualified jurors, for a juror-per-questionnaire percent of 25.5. (A second summoning stage is used in this court, so the ultimate percentage that actually serves will be still lower.) In the Central District of Los Angeles County, which is heavily Hispanic and black (and poor), the Superior Court mailed out 131,000 questionnaires to obtain 25,078 qualified jurors, a juror-per-questionnaire percent of only 19.1.[7]

In the city of Baltimore, the qualified-juror-per-questionnaire (prior to actual summoning) fluctuated between 15.7 percent and 20.4 percent between 1971 and 1974.[8] In San Diego County, California, the percent prior to the summoning stage was 20.3 in 1971 and 19 in 1972.[9] In the county of Honolulu, Hawaii, the qualified-juror-per-questionnaire ranged from 26 to 35.2 percent between 1968 and 1973.[10] The local courts in New York City have an unusually difficult time assembling jurors. In New York County (Manhattan), questionnaires are sent to people whose names are taken from various lists, including telephone books and tax rolls as well as voter lists, but only about 10 percent of those receiving questionnaires are eventually deemed qualified.[11] The qualified jurors are then put on a permanent list and receive a summons to report as a juror every couple of years. Of those who receive their summons, however, only about 32 or 33 percent show up at the courthouse.[12] An enormous amount of slippage thus occurs.

The courts in states that have adopted the Uniform Jury Selection and Service Act—which lists no specific exemptions or excuses and says instead that excuses should be granted only in cases of "undue hardship, extreme inconvenience or public necessity"—seem to be able to obtain a higher juror-per-questionnaire percent, but most of these courts are in rural areas, so the comparison is not exact. Denver County, Colorado, is the only area in Colorado, Idaho, and North Dakota that is even somewhat urban, and its courts were able to qualify 68 percent of those who received questionnaires in 1972 and 56.4 percent in 1973 (prior to the summoning stage).[13] Virtually all the courts in those three states that I obtained information from had percentages at least this high, with many hitting 70 percent or more.

In all these courts, as previously mentioned, the prospective jurors receive a second chance to be excused at the time of summoning, and judges differ substantially in their attitude toward granting excuses at this stage.

One study on court efficiency—a report prepared by the Institute of Judicial Administration in 1971—suggesting ideas for reducing the time required to impanel a jury once the trial is ready to begin, *actually proposed that clerks should be more lenient* in granting excuses in order to facilitate the process at trial:

> The percentage of excuses for cause by the court is unusually high in the Eastern District of New York [Brooklyn & Long Island].... The larger panels and the added excuses in E.D.N.Y. cause the voir dires to take more time and require the payment of many prospective jurors who never sit on cases. The reasons for the large number of excuses are not clear. Pre-screening of prospective jurors would be contrary to the intent of the Jury Selection and Service Act of 1968, *but perhaps procedures could be derived to cut out some of the unsuitable jurors. One possibility is for the jury staff to be more lenient in granting excuses* requested by prospective jurors on the qualification questionnaires. The judge hearing requests for excuses and postponements on the Return Day could also be more lenient. When the jury clerk makes her welcoming speech on Return Day, she could ask if any jurors are hard of hearing or unable to understand English....[14]

Because so many different persons are using their individual discretion to decide who should be excused and who should serve, the possibility of individual prejudice influencing the process is great.

## THE DEMOGRAPHIC CONSEQUENCES OF THE EXCUSING PROCESS

The preceding data indicate that the qualfied jury wheel is generally a substantially smaller group than the master wheel from which names are originally drawn, and the qualified wheel is not likely to be a mirror image of the demographic composition of the master wheel because some demographic groups seek (and are granted) excuses much more frequently than others.

Perhaps the most dramatic example of underrepresentation-through-excuses is the case of women. Appendix I shows that of the *223* federal court surveys in which data is available for the master wheel and for the jury panels actually assembled, *185*—or an astounding *83 percent*—have a smaller pecentage of women on the jury panels than on the master wheel. In many of these cases, the rate of error is substantial—61 of the 223 surveys (27.4 percent) show a drop-off between 10 and 20 percent, and another 53 surveys (23.8 percent) show a decline of over 20 percent. Thus over half of all our federal courts (51.1 percent) lose more than 10 percent of the women on their master wheel, and women are usually underrepresented somewhat on the master wheel to begin with.

The young, and of course the old, also lose ground at the excusing stage, as shown in Tables K-5 through K-7. The young are excused in large numbers for several reasons—they have moved, they have gone away to school, they are in school and do not feel they can miss classes, they have young children at home they need to take care of, they are in an economically precarious position and will not receive

**Table K-5. Age Alteration**

| | U.S. *District Court for the Eastern District of Michigan* | | |
|---|---|---|---|
| *Age* | *Percent Sent Questionnaires* | *Percent Deemed Qualified for Jury Duty* | *Rate of Error* |
| 21-24 | 2.8 | 2.2 | −21.4 |
| 25-29 | 6.5 | 7.0 | + 7.7 |
| 30-34 | 8.5 | 8.3 | − 2.4 |
| 35-39 | 10.1 | 11.0 | + 8.9 |
| 40-44 | 12.2 | 14.3 | +17.2 |
| 45-49 | 12.8 | 16.7 | +30.5 |
| 50-54 | 12.7 | 14.9 | +17.3 |
| 55-59 | 10.1 | 11.6 | +14.9 |
| 60-64 | 8.3 | 7.6 | − 8.4 |
| 65 & Over | 16.0 | 6.3 | −60.6 |
| Number: | 6788 | 2544 | |

Source: Study of Juror Questionnaire by Attorney Neal Bush in 1970 for *United States Sinclair*, Crim. No. 44395 (E.D. Mich. 1970).

**Table K-6.  Age Alteration**

| | U.S. District Court for the District of New Jersey: Camden Division | | |
|---|---|---|---|
| Age | Percent Sent Questionnaires | Percent Deemed Qualified for Jury Duty | Rate of Error |
| 21-24 | 0 | 0 | – |
| 25-29 | 4.8 | 4.3 | –10.4 |
| 30-34 | 5.6 | 6.6 | +17.8 |
| 35-39 | 7.4 | 6.8 | – 8.1 |
| 40-44 | 11.4 | 15.1 | +32.4 |
| 45-49 | 14.5 | 17.2 | +18.6 |
| 50-54 | 14.9 | 18.0 | +20.8 |
| 55-59 | 9.3 | 12.2 | +31.2 |
| 60-64 | 9.2 | 10.1 | + 9.8 |
| 65-69 | 7.7 | 7.2 | – 6.5 |
| 70 & Over | 15.2 | 2.3 | –84.9 |
| Number: | 730 | | |

Source: Questionnaires examined by Attorney David Kairys, 1972 for *United States v. Anderson et al.*, Crim. No. 602-71 (D.N.J. 1973).

**Table K-7.  Age Alteration**

| | Arizona: Maricopa County (Phoenix) (Local Courts) | | |
|---|---|---|---|
| Age | Percent Sent Questionnaires | Percent Deemed Qualified for Jury Duty | Rate of Error |
| 18-24 | 10.3 | 6.9 | –33.0 |
| 25-34 | 22.6 | 23.6 | + 4.4 |
| 35-49 | 34.3 | 36.7 | + 7.0 |
| 50-64 | 25.3 | 28.3 | +11.9 |
| 65 & Over | 7.4 | 4.4 | –40.5 |
| Number: | 880 | 360 | |

Source: *Law & the Social Order* (1973): 188 (May 1972 survey).

any salary while on jury duty, they are in the military. Many jury commissioners are particularly receptive to excusing students.[15] Some try to postpone the student's service to some other time of year, but too often the student becomes lost in the administrative shuffle, or ignored because fewer trials occur in the summer.

Tables K-5 through K-7 all show that persons in the younger age categories lose some ground, or hold their own, but it is significant that persons in the middle-aged categories make a dramatic increase in their relative proportion of the jury panels. The young thus constitute a substantially smaller percent of the jury panels when compared to the middle-aged group. The older citizens, of course, are excused in droves, and they lose the most seats, with the middle-aged picking up most of them.

Persons in the lower socioeconomic groups almost always lose ground during the excusing process, because they can least afford to give up the time to serve. One illustration of this phenomenon can be found in a sample taken from the federal court in New Orleans (the Eastern District of Louisiana) in early 1974. Of 500 prospective jurors who returned questionnaires, 252 were deemed qualified after all questionnaires were returned. Of those returning their questionnaires, 35.4 percent had less than a high school education, but only 27.3 percent of those deemed qualified were in this category. Persons with a high school diploma composed 35.6 percent of those returning questionnaires, but were 42.8 percent of those found qualified. Persons with some college education made up 29 percent of those returning questionnaires and 29.8 percent of those deemed qualified.[16]

These examples are offered for illustrative purposes as presenting typical problems, but it should also be stated that each court's procedures are different and that they vary from year to year in the same court. Some clerks and judges try hard to prevent any prospective juror from obtaining an excuse in order to prevent a skewing of the cross-section obtained on the master wheel and to ensure that a jury that is truly representative of the community is impaneled. But many clerks and judges allow any and all to be excused on request, on the theory that a person who does not want to serve will not be a good juror. Such an attitude means that the resulting jury panel will really be a panel of volunteers, and they will not have the impartiality that only comes from a panel of disinterested persons who serve out of a sense of responsibility and duty, rather than out of desire for adventure or for relief from boredom.

The best way to ensure impartiality and the way to be fair to those who do serve is: (1) limit excuses to those of actual physical disability; (2) limit the time jurors must serve (and increase their pay) so that no one will suffer financial hardship; (3) allow prospective jurors to pick the days they want to serve to further reduce the possibility of hardship; and (4) insist that all persons whose names are picked do actually serve as jurors.

# NOTES

1. Hayward R. Alker, Jr., Carl Hosticka, and Michael Mitchell, "The Jury Selection Process in Eastern Massachusetts" (unpublished, 1973).

2. Interview with Mrs. Sandra Ferguson, May 7, 1973.

3. Interview with G. Thomas Munsterman, of Bird Engineering—Research Associates, Inc., April 2, 1975.

4. Interview, December 18, 1972.

5. Interview, May 8, 1972.

6. Letter to the author, November 14, 1974.

7. Letter from Judd L. Holtzendorff, assistant jury commissioner, December 2, 1974.

8. From statistics obtained from the court.

9. From statistics obtained from the court.

10. From statistics obtained from the court.

11. Letter from G. Thomas Munsterman, Bird Engineering—Research Associates, Inc., to the Law Enforcement Assistance Administration, March 10, 1975.

12. Interim Report of the Subcommittee on the Jury System, for the Appellate Division, First and Second Departments, November 13, 1972.

13. From statistics obtained from the court.

14. Institute of Judicial Administration, *Suggestions for Improving Juror Utilization in the United States District Court for the Eastern District of New York* (Mimeographed report, August 31, 1971), p. 16 (emphasis added).

15. Interview with Unwar J. Samaha, Rockingham County, N.H., June 10, 1974. Many other jury commissioners expressed this same sentiment in interviews.

16. From data provided by Janice K. Barden, jury commissioner for the Eastern District of Louisiana, dated February 5, 1974.

## Appendix L:
## U.S. Supreme Court
## Decisions Involving
## Jury Selection

*Strauder v. West Virginia*, 100 U.S. 303 (1880).
*Virginia v. Rives*, 100 U.S. 313 (1880).
*Ex Parta Virginia*, 100 U.S. 339 (1880).
*Neal v. Delaware*, 103 U.S. 370 (1881).
*Bush v. Kentucky*, 107 U.S. 110 (1883).
*Woods v. Brush*, 140 U.S. 278 (1891).
*Gibson v. Mississippi*, 162 U.S. 565 (1896).
*Smith v. Mississippi*, 162 U.S. 592 (1896).
*Carter v. Texas*, 177 U.S. 442 (1900).
*Tarrance v. Florida*, 188 U.S. 519 (1903).
*Brownfield v. South Carolina*, 189 U.S. 426 (1903).
*Rogers v. Alabama*, 192 U.S. 226 (1904).
*Martin v. Texas*, 200 U.S. 316 (1906).
*Rawlins v. Georgia*, 201 U.S. 638 (1906) (exemptions for professionals).
*Thomas v. Texas*, 212 U.S. 278 (1909).
*Norris v. Alabama*, 294 U.S. 587 (1935).
*Hollins v. Oklahoma*, 295 U.S. 394 (1935).
*Hale v. Kentucky*, 303 U.S. 613 (1938).
*Pierre v. Louisiana*, 306 U.S. 354 (1939).
*Smith v. Texas*, 311 U.S. 128 (1940).
*Glasser v. United States*, 315 U.S. 60 (1942).
*Hill v. Texas*, 316 U.S. 400 (1942).
*Akins v. Texas*, 325 U.S. 398 (1945).
*Thiel v. Southern Pacific Co.*, 328 U.S. 217 (1946) (daily wage-earners).

*Ballard v. United States*, 329 U.S. 173 (1946) (women).

*Fay v. New York*, 332 U.S. 261 (1947) (blue-ribbon juries).

*Patton v. Mississippi*, 332 U.S. 463 (1947).

*Moore v. New York*, 333 U.S. 565 (1948) (blue-ribbon juries).

*Cassell v. Texas*, 339 U.S. 282 (1950).

*Ross v. Texas*, 341 U.S. 918 (1951).

*Brown v. Allen*, 344 U.S. 443 (1953).

*Avery v. Georgia*, 345 U.S. 559 (1953).

*Hernandez v. Texas*, 347 U.S. 475 (1954) (Hispanic).

*Williams v. Georgia*, 349 U.S. 375 (1955).

*Reece v. Georgia*, 350 U.S. 85 (1955).

*Eubanks v. Louisiana*, 356 U.S. 584 (1958).

*Hoyt v. Florida*, 368 U.S. 57 (1961) (women).

*Arnold v. North Carolina*, 376 U.S. 773 (1964).

*Coleman v. Alabama*, 377 U.S. 129 (1964).

*Swain v. Alabama*, 380 U.S. 202 (1965).

*Whitus v. Georgia*, 385 U.S. 545 (1967).

*Coleman v. Alabama*, 389 U.S. 22 (1967).

*Jones v. Georgia*, 389 U.S. 24 (1967).

*Sims v. Georgia*, 389 U.S. 404 (1967).

*Duncan v. Louisiana*, 391 U.S. 145 (1968) (6th Amendment extended to states).

*Carter v. Jury Comm. of Greene County*, 396 U.S. 320 (1970).

*Turner v. Fouche*, 396 U.S. 346 (1970).

*Baldwin v. New York*, 399 U.S. 66 (1970) (6th Amendment extended to states).

*Williams v. Florida*, 399 U.S. 78 (1970) (6-person juries allowed).

*McKiever v. Pennsylvania*, 403 U.S. 528 (1971) (no right to jury trial for juveniles).

*Alexander v. Louisiana*, 405 U.S. 625 (1972).

*Johnson v. Louisiana*, 406 U.S. 356 (1972) (less-than-unanimous verdicts allowed).

*Apodaca v. Oregon*, 406 U.S. 404 (1972) (less-than-unanimous verdicts allowed).

*Peters v. Kiff*, 407 U.S. 493 (1972) (standing).

*Taylor v. Louisiana*, 419 U.S. 522 (1975) (women).

## Appendix M:
## The Federal and Uniform
## Jury Selection Statutes

*1968 Federal Jury Selection
and Service Act*

§ 1861. Declaration of policy. [*U.S. Code, Title 28*]

It is the policy of the United States that all litigants in Federal courts entitled to trial by jury shall have the right to grand and petit juries selected at random from a fair cross section of the community in the district or division wherein the court convenes. It is further the policy of the United States that all citizens shall have the opportunity to be considered for service on grand and petit juries in the district courts of the United States, and shall have an obligation to serve as jurors when summoned for that purpose.

§ 1862. Discrimination prohibited.

No citizen shall be excluded from service as a grand or petit juror in the district courts of the United States on account of race, color, religion, sex, national origin, or economic status.

§ 1863. Plan for random jury selection.

(a) Each United States district court shall devise and place into operation a written plan for random selection of grand and petit jurors that shall be designed to achieve the objectives of sections 1861 and 1862 of this title, and that shall otherwise comply with the provisions of this title. The plan shall be placed into operation after approval by a reviewing panel consisting of the members of the judicial council of the circuit and either the chief judge of the district whose plan is being reviewed or such other active district judge of that district as the chief judge of the district may designate. The panel shall examine the plan to ascertain that it complies with the provisions of this title. If the reviewing panel finds that the plan does not comply, the panel shall state the particulars in which the plan fails to comply and direct the district court to present within a reasonable time an alternative plan remedying the defect or defects. Separate plans may be adopted for each division or combination of divisions within a judicial district. The district court may modify a plan at any time and it shall modify the plan when so directed by the reviewing panel. The district court shall promptly notify the panel, the Administrative Office of the United States Courts, and the Attorney General of the United States, of the initial adoption and future modifications of the plan by filing copies therewith. Modifications of the plan made at the instance of the district court shall become effective after approval by the panel. Each district court shall submit a report on the jury selection process within its jurisdiction to the Administrative Office of the United States Courts in such form and at such times as the Judicial Conference of the United States may specify. The Judicial Conference of the United States may, from time to time, adopt rules and regulations governing the provisions and the operation of the plans formulated under this title.

(b) Among other things, such plan shall—

(1) either establish a jury commission, or authorize the clerk of the court, to manage the jury selection process. If the plan establishes a jury commission, the district court shall appoint one citizen to serve with the clerk of the court as the jury commission: *Provided, however*, That the plan for the District of Columbia may establish a jury commission consisting of three citizens. The citizen jury commissioner shall not belong to the same political party as the clerk serving with him. The clerk or the jury commission, as the case may be, shall act under the supervision and control of the chief judge of the district court or such other judge of the district court as the plan may provide. Each jury commissioner shall, during his tenure in office, reside in the judicial district or division for which he is appointed. Each citizen jury commissioner shall receive compensation to be fixed by the district court plan at a rate not to exceed $50 per day for each day necessarily employed in the performance of his duties, plus reimbursement for travel, subsistence, and other necessary expenses incurred by him in the performance of such duties. The Judicial Conference of the United States may establish standards for allowance of travel, subsistence, and other necessary expenses incurred by jury commissioners.

(2) specify whether the names of prospective jurors shall be selected from the voter registration lists or the lists of actual voters of the political subdivisions within the district or division. The plan shall prescribe some other source or sources of names in addition to

voter lists where necessary to foster the policy and protect the rights secured by sections 1861 and 1862 of this title. The plan for the District of Columbia may require the names of prospective jurors to be selected from the city directory rather than from voter lists. The plans for the districts of Puerto Rico and the Canal Zone may prescribe some other source or sources of names of prospective jurors in lieu of voter lists, the use of which shall be consistent with the policies declared and rights secured by sections 1861 and 1862 of this title.

(3) specify detailed procedures to be followed by the jury commission or clerk in selecting names from the sources specified in paragraph (2) of this subsection. These procedures shall be designed to ensure the random selection of a fair cross section of the persons residing in the community in the district or division wherein the court convenes. They shall ensure that names of persons residing in each of the counties, parishes, or similar political subdivisions with the judicial district or division are placed in a master jury wheel; and shall ensure that each county, parish, or similar political subdivision within the district or division is substantially proportionally represented in the master jury wheel for that judicial district, division, or combination of divisions. For the purposes of determining proportional representation in the master jury wheel, either the number of actual voters at the last general election in each county, parish, or similar political subdivision, or the number of registered voters if registration of voters is uniformly required throughout the district or division may be used.

(4) provide for a master jury wheel (or a device similar in purpose and function) into which the names of those randomly selected shall be placed. The plan shall fix a minimum number of names to be placed initially in the master jury wheel, which shall be at least one-half of 1 per centum of the total number of persons on the list used as a source of names for the district or division; but if this number of names is believed to be cumbersome and unnecessary, the plan may fix a smaller number of names to be placed in the master wheel, but in no event less than one thousand. The chief judge of the district court, or such other district court judge as the plan may provide, may order additional names to be placed in the master jury wheel from time to time as necessary. The plan shall provide for periodic emptying and refilling of the master jury wheel at specified times, the interval for which shall not exceed four years.

(5) specify those groups of persons or occupational classes whose members shall on individual request therefor, be excused from jury service. Such groups or classes shall be excused only if the district court finds, and the plan states, that jury service by such class or group would entail undue hardship or extreme inconvenience to

the members thereof, and excuse of members thereof would not be inconsistent with sections 1861 and 1862 of this title.

(6) specify those groups of persons or occupational classes whose members shall be barred from jury service on the ground that they are exempt. Such groups or classes shall be exempt only if the district court finds, and the plan states, that their exemption is in the public interest and would not be inconsistent with sections 1861 and 1862 of this title. The plan shall provide for exemption of the following persons: (i) members in active service in the Armed Forces of the United States; (ii) members of the fire or police departments of any State, district, territory, possession, or subdivision thereof; (iii) public officers in the executive, legislative, or judicial branches of the Government of the United States, or any State, district, territory, or possession or subdivision thereof, who are actively engaged in the performance of official duties.

(7) fix the distance, either in miles or in travel time, from each place of holding court beyond which prospective jurors residing shall, on individual request therefor, be excused from jury service on the ground of undue hardship in traveling to the place where court is held.

(8) fix the time when the names drawn from the qualified jury wheel shall be disclosed to parties and to the public. If the plan permits these names to be made public, it may nevertheless permit the chief judge of the district court, or such other district court judge as the plan may provide, to keep these names confidential in any case where the interests of justice so require.

(9) specify the procedures to be followed by the clerk or jury commission in assigning persons whose names have been drawn from the qualified jury wheel to grand and petit jury panels.

(c) The initial plan shall be devised by each district court and transmitted to the reviewing panel specified in subsection (a) of this section within one hundred and twenty days of the date of enactment of the Jury Selection and Service Act of 1968. The panel shall approve or direct the modification of each plan so submitted within sixty days thereafter. Each plan or modification made at the direction of the panel shall become effective after approval at such time thereafter as the panel directs, in no event to exceed ninety days from the date of approval. Modifications made at the instance of the district court under subsection (a) of this section shall be effective at such time thereafter as the panel directs, in no event to exceed ninety days from the date of modification.

(d) State, local, and Federal officials having custody, possession, or control of voter registration lists, lists of actual voters, or other appropriate records shall make such lists and records available to the jury commission or clerks for inspection, reproduction, and copying at all reasonable times as the commission or clerk may deem necessary and proper for the performance of duties under this title. The district courts shall have jurisdiction upon application by the Attorney General of the United States to compel compliance with this subsection by appropriate process.

§ 1864. Drawing of names from the master jury wheel; completion of juror qualification form.

(a) From time to time as directed by the district court, the clerk or a district judge shall publicly draw at random from the master jury wheel the names of as many persons as may be required for jury service. The clerk or jury commission shall prepare an alphabetical list of the names drawn, which list shall not be disclosed to any person except pursuant to the district court plan and to sections 1867 and 1868 of this title. The clerk or jury commission shall mail to every person whose name is drawn from the master wheel a juror qualification form accompanied by instructions to fill out and return the form, duly signed and sworn, to the clerk or jury commission by mail within ten days. If the person is unable to fill out the form, another shall do it for him, and shall indicate that he has done so and the reason therefor. In any case in which it appears that there is an omission, ambiguity, or error in a form, the clerk or jury commission shall return the form with instructions to the person to make such additions or corrections as may be necessary and to return the form to the clerk or jury commission within ten days. Any person who fails to return a completed juror qualification form as instructed may be summoned by the clerk or jury commission forthwith to appear before the clerk or jury commission to fill out a juror qualification form. A person summoned to appear because of failure to return a juror qualification form as instructed who personally appears and executes a juror qualification form before the clerk or jury commission may, at the discretion of the district court, except where his prior failure to execute and mail such form was willful, be entitled to receive for such appearance the same fees and travel allowances paid to jurors under section 1871 of this title. At the time of his appearance for jury service, any person may be required to fill out another juror qualification form in the presence of the jury commission or the clerk or the court, at which time, in such cases as it appears warranted, the person may be questioned, but only with regard to his responses to questions contained on the form. Any information thus acquired by the clerk or jury commission may be noted on the juror qualification form and transmitted to the chief judge or such district court judge as the plan may provide.

(b) Any person summoned pursuant to subsection (a) of this section who fails to appear as directed shall be ordered by the district court forthwith to appear and show cause for his failure to comply with the summons. Any person who fails to appear pursuant to such order or who fails to show good cause for noncompliance with the summons may be fined not more than $100 or imprisoned not more than three days, or both. Any person who willfully misrepresents a material fact on a juror qualification form for the purpose of avoiding or securing service as a juror may be fined not more than $100 or imprisoned not more than three days, or both.

## § 1865. Qualifications for jury service.

(a) The chief judge of the district court, or such other district court judge as the plan may provide, on his initiative or upon recommendation of the clerk or jury commission, shall determine solely on the basis of information provided on the juror qualification form and other competent evidence whether a person is unqualified for, or exempt, or to be excused from jury service. The clerk shall enter such determination in the space provided on the juror qualification form and the alphabetical list of names drawn from the master jury wheel. If a person did not appear in response to a summons, such fact shall be noted on said list.

(b) In making such determination the chief judge of the district court, or such other district court judge as the plan may provide, shall deem any person qualified to serve on grand and petit juries in the district court unless he—

(1) is not a citizen of the United States eighteen years old who has resided for a period of one year within the judicial district;

(2) is unable to read, write, and understand the English language with a degree of proficiency sufficient to fill out satisfactorily the juror qualification form;

(3) is unable to speak the English language;

(4) is incapable, by reason of mental or physical infirmity, to render satisfactory jury service; or

(5) has a charge pending against him for the commission of, or has been convicted in a State or Federal court of record of, a crime punishable by imprisonment for more than one year and his civil rights have not been restored by pardon or amnesty.

## § 1866. Selection and summoning of jury panels.

(a) The jury commission, or in the absence thereof the clerk, shall maintain a qualified jury wheel and shall place in such wheel names of all persons drawn from the master jury wheel who are determined to be qualified as jurors and not exempt or excused pursuant to the district court plan. From time to time, the jury commission or the clerk shall publicly draw at random from the qualified jury wheel such number of names of persons as may be required for assignment to grand and petit jury panels. The jury commission or the clerk shall prepare a separate list of names of persons assigned to each grand and petit jury panel.

(b) When the court orders a grand or petit jury to be drawn, the clerk or jury commission or their duly designated deputies shall issue summonses for the required number of jurors.

Each person drawn for jury service may be served personally, or by registered or certified mail addressed to such person at his usual residence or business address.

If such service is made personally, the summons shall be delivered by the clerk or the jury commission or their duly designated deputies to the marshal who shall make such service.

If such service is made by registered or certified mail, the summons may be served by the clerk or jury commission or their duly designated deputies who shall make affidavit of service and shall file with such affidavit the addressee's receipt for the registered or certified summons. If such service is made by the marshal, he shall attach to his return the addressee's receipt for the registered or certified mail.

(c) Except as provided in section 1865 of this title or in any jury selection plan provision adopted pursuant to paragraph (5), (6), or (7) of section 1863 (b) of this title, no person or class of persons shall be disqualified, excluded, excused, or exempt from service as jurors: *Provided*, That any person summoned for jury service may be (1) excused by the court, upon a showing of undue hardship or extreme inconvenience, for such period as the court deems necessary, at the conclusion of which such person shall be summoned again for jury service under subsections (b) and (c) of this section or (2) excluded by the court on the ground that such person may be unable to render impartial jury service or that his service as a juror would be likely to disrupt the proceedings, or (3) excluded upon peremptory challenge as provided by law, or (4) excluded pursuant to the procedure specified by law upon a challenge by any party for good cause shown, or (5) excluded upon determination by the court that his service as a juror would be likely to threaten the secrecy of the proceedings, or otherwise adversely affect the integrity of jury deliberations. No person shall be excluded under clause (5) of this subsection unless the judge, in open court, determines that such is warranted and that exclusion of the person will not be inconsistent with sections 1861 and 1862 of this title. The number of persons excluded under clause (5) of this subsection shall not exceed one percentum of the number of persons who return executed jury qualification forms during the period, specified in the plan, between two consecutive fillings of the master jury wheel. The names of persons excluded under clause (5) of this subsection, together with detailed explanations for the exclusions, shall be forwarded immediately to the judicial council of the circuit, which shall have the power to make any appropriate order, prospective or retroactive, to redress any misapplication of clause (5) of this subsection, but otherwise exclusions effectuated under such clause shall not be subject to challenge under the provisions of this title. Any person excluded from a particular jury under clause (2), (3), or (4) of this subsection shall be eligible to sit on another jury if the basis for his initial exclusion would not be relevant to his ability to serve on such other jury.

(d) Whenever a person is disqualified, excused, exempt, or excluded from jury service, the jury commission or clerk shall note in the space provided on his juror qualification form or on the juror's card drawn from the qualified jury wheel the specific reason therefore.

(e) In any two-year period, no person shall be required to (1) serve or attend court for prospective service as a petit juror for a total of more than thirty days, except when necessary to complete service in a particular case, or (2) serve on more than one grand jury, or (3) serve as both a grand and petit juror.

(f) When there is an unanticipated shortage of available petit jurors drawn from the qualified jury wheel, the court may require the marshal to summon a sufficient number of petit jurors selected at random from the voter registration lists, lists of actual voters, or other lists specified in the plan, in a manner ordered by the court consistent with sections 1861 and 1862 of this title.

(g) Any person summoned for jury service who fails to appear as directed shall be ordered by the district court to appear forthwith and show cause for his failure to comply with the summons. Any person who fails to show good cause for noncompliance with a summons may be fined not more than $100 or imprisoned not more than three days, or both.

## § 1867. Challenging compliance with selection procedures.

(a) In criminal cases, before the voir dire examination begins, or within seven days after the defendant discovered or could have discovered, by the exercise of diligence, the grounds therefor, whichever is earlier, the defendant may move to dismiss the indictment or stay the proceedings against him on the ground of substantial failure to comply with the provisions of this title in selecting the grand or petit jury.

(b) In criminal cases, before the voir dire examination begins, or within seven days after the Attorney General of the United States discovered or could have discovered, by the exercise of diligence, the grounds therefor, whichever is earlier, the Attorney General may move to dismiss the indictment or stay the proceedings on the ground of substantial failure to comply with the provisions of this title in selecting the grand or petit jury.

(c) In civil cases, before the voir dire examination begins, or within seven days after the party discovered or could have discovered, by the exercise of diligence, the grounds therefor, whichever is earlier, any party may move to stay the proceedings on the ground of substantial failure to comply with the provisions of this title in selecting the petit jury.

(d) Upon motion filed under subsection (a), (b), or (c) of this section, containing a sworn statement of facts which, if true, would constitute a substantial failure to comply with the provisions of this title, the moving party shall be entitled to present in support of such motion the testimony of the jury commission or clerk, if available, any relevant records and papers not public or otherwise available used by the jury commissioner or clerk, and any other relevant evidence. If the court determines that there has been a substantial failure to comply with the provisions of this title in selecting the grand jury, the court shall stay the proceedings pending the selection of a grand jury in conformity with this title or dismiss the indictment, whichever is appropriate. If the court determines that there has been a substantial failure to comply with the provisions of this title in selecting the petit jury, the court shall stay the proceedings pending the selection of a petit jury in conformity with this title.

(e) The procedures prescribed by this section shall be the exclusive means by which a person accused of a Federal crime, the Attorney General of the United States or a party in a civil case may challenge any jury on the ground that such jury was not selected in conformity with the provisions of this title. Nothing in this section shall preclude any person or the United States from pursuing any other remedy, civil or criminal, which may be available for the vindication or enforcement of any law prohibiting discrimination on account of race, color, religion, sex, national origin or economic status in the selection of persons for service on grand or petit juries.

(f) The contents of records or papers used by the jury commission or clerk in connection with the jury selection process shall not be disclosed, except pursuant to the district court plan or as may be necessary in the preparation or presentation of a motion under subsection (a), (b), or (c) of this section, until after the master jury wheel has been emptied and refilled pursuant to section 1863(b) (4) of this title and all persons selected to serve as jurors before the master wheel was emptied have completed such service. The parties in a case shall be allowed to inspect, reproduce, and copy such records or papers at all reasonable times during the preparation and pendency of such a motion. Any person who discloses the contents of any record or paper in violation of this subsection may be fined not more than $1,000 or imprisoned not more than one year, or both.

## § 1868. Maintenance and inspection of records.

After the master jury wheel is emptied and refilled pursuant to section 1863(b) (4) of this title, and after all persons selected to serve as jurors before the master wheel was emptied have completed such service, all records and papers compiled and maintained by the jury commission or clerk before the master wheel was emptied shall be preserved in the custody of the clerk for four years or for such longer period as may be ordered by a court, and shall be available for public inspection for the purpose of determining the validity of the selection of any jury.

## § 1869. Definitions.

For purposes of this chapter—

(a) "clerk" and "clerk of the court" shall mean the clerk of the district court of the United States or any authorized deputy clerk;

(b) "chief judge" shall mean the chief judge of any district court of the United States;

(c) "voter registration lists" shall mean the official records maintained by State or local election officials of persons registered to vote in either the most recent State or the most recent Federal general election, or, in the case of a State or political subdivision thereof that does not require registration as a prerequisite to voting, other official lists of persons qualified to vote in such election. The term shall also include the list of eligible voters maintained by any Federal examiners pursuant to the Voting Rights Act of 1965 where the names on such list have not been included on the official registration lists or other official lists maintained by the appropriate State or local officials. With respect to the districts of Guam and the Virgin Islands, "voter registration lists" shall mean the official records maintained by territorial election officials of persons registered to vote in the most recent territorial general election;

(d) "lists of actual voters" shall mean the official lists of persons actually voting in either the most recent State or the most recent Federal general election;

(e) "division" shall mean: (1) one or more statutory divisions of a judicial district; or (2) in statutory divisions that contain more than one place of holding court, or in judicial districts where there are no statutory divisions, such counties, parishes, or similar political subdivisions surrounding the places where court is held as the district court plan shall determine: *Provided*, That each county, parish, or similar political subdivision shall be included in some such division;

(f) "district court of the United States", "district court", and "court" shall mean courts constituted under chapter 5 of title 28, United States Code, section 22 of the Organic Act of Guam, as amended (64 Stat. 389; 48 U.S.C. 1424), section 21 of the Revised Organic Act of the Virgin Islands (68 Stat. 506; 48 U.S.C. 1611), and section 1 of title 3, Canal Zone Code; except that for purposes of sections 1861, 1862, 1866(c), 1866(d), and 1867 of this chapter such terms shall include the Superior Court of the District of Columbia;

(g) "jury wheel" shall include any device or system similar in purpose or function, such as a properly programmed electronic data processing system or device;

(h) "juror qualification form" shall mean a form prescribed by the Administrative Office of the United States Courts and approved by the Judicial Conference of the United States, which shall elicit the name, address, age, race, occupation, education, length of residence within the judicial district, distance from residence to place of holding court, prior jury service, and citizenship of a potential juror, and whether he should be excused or exempted from jury service, has any physical or mental infirmity impairing his capacity to serve as juror, is able to read, write, speak, and understand the English language, has pending against him any charge for the commission of a State or Federal criminal offense punishable by imprisonment for more than one year, or has been convicted in any State or Federal court of record of a crime punishable by imprisonment for more than one year and has not had his civil rights restored by pardon or amnesty. The form shall request, but not require, any other information not inconsistent with the provisions of this title and required by the district court plan in the interests of the sound administration of justice. The form shall also elicit the sworn statement that his responses are true to the best of his knowledge. Notarization shall not be required. The form shall contain words clearly informing the person that the furnishing of any information with respect to his religion, national origin, or economic status is not a prerequisite to his qualification for jury service, that such information need not be furnished if the person finds it objectionable to do so, and that information concerning race is required solely to enforce nondiscrimination in jury selection and has no bearing on an individual's qualification for jury service.

(i) "public officer" shall mean a person who is either elected to public office or who is directly appointed by a person elected to public office.

# Uniform Jury Selection and Service Act[1]

SECTION 1. [*Declaration of Policy.*] It is the policy of this state that all persons selected for jury service be selected at random from a fair cross section of the population of the area served by the court, and that all qualified citizens have the opportunity in accordance with this Act to be considered for jury service in this state and an obligation to serve as jurors when summoned for that purpose.

SECTION 2. [*Prohibition of Discrimination.*] A citizen shall not be excluded from jury service in this state on account of race, color, religion, sex, national origin, or economic status.

SECTION 3. [*Definitions.*] As used in this Act:

(1) "court" means the [_____] court[s] of this state, and includes, when the context requires, any [judge] [justice] of the court;

(2) "clerk" and "clerk of the court" include any deputy clerk;

(3) "master list" means the [voter registration lists] [lists of actual voters] for the [county] [district] which shall be supplemented with names from other sources prescribed pursuant to this Act (Section 5) in order to foster the policy and protect the rights secured by this Act (Sections 1 and 2);

---

[1]"Drafted by the National Conference of Commissioners on Uniform State Laws, and by it approved and recommended for enactment in all the states at its annual conference meeting in its seventy-ninth year at St. Louis, Missouri, August 1-7, 1970. 1971 edition, with preparatory note and comments."

[Alternative A]

[(4) "voter registration lists" means the official records of persons [registered] [qualified] to vote in the most recent general election;]

[Alternative B]

[(4) "lists of actual voters" means the official records of persons actually voting in the most recent general election;]

(5) "jury wheel" means any physical device or electronic system for the storage of the names or identifying numbers of prospective jurors;

(6) "master jury wheel" means the jury wheel in which are placed names or identifying numbers of prospective jurors taken from the master list (Section 6);

(7) "qualified jury wheel" means the jury wheel in which are placed the names or identifying numbers of prospective jurors whose names are drawn at random from the master jury wheel (Section 7) and who are not disqualified (Section 8).

SECTION 4. [*Jury Commission.*] A jury commission is established in each [county] [district] to manage the jury selection process under the supervision and control of the court. The jury commission shall be composed of the clerk of the court and a jury commissioner appointed for a term of [4] years by the [court] [chief justice of the Supreme Court] [chief administrative officer or board of the [county] [district] ]. The jury commissioner must be a citizen of the United States and a resident in the [county] [district] in which he serves. [The jury commissioner shall be reimbursed for travel, subsistence, and other necessary expenses incurred by him in the performance of his duties and shall receive compensation at a per diem rate fixed by the [chief justice of the] [Supreme Court] or as provided by [law].].

SECTION 5. [*Master List.*]

(a) The jury commission for each [county] [district] shall compile and maintain a master list consisting of all [voter registration lists] [lists of actual voters] for the [county] [district] supplemented with names from other lists of persons resident therein, such as lists of utility customers, property [and income] taxpayers, motor vehicle registrations, and drivers' licenses, which the [Supreme Court] [Attorney General] from time to time designates. The [Supreme Court] [Attorney General] shall initially designate the other lists within [90] days following the effective date of this Act and exercise the authority to designate from time to time in order to foster the policy and protect the rights secured by this Act (Sections 1 and 2). In compiling the master list the jury commission shall avoid duplication of names.

(b) Whoever has custody, possession, or control of any of the lists making up or used in compiling the master list, including those designated under subsection (a) by the [Supreme Court] [Attorney General] as supplementary sources of names, shall make the list available to the jury commission for inspection, reproduction, and copying at all reasonable times.

(c) The master list shall be open to the public for examination.

## Comment

The Federal Act, 28 U.S.C.A. § 1863(b) (2), uses the voter registration lists as the most inclusive list of names of potential jurors, providing, alternatively in those situations where registration lists are not maintained, that lists of actual voters will be used. The Federal Act leaves it up to the plan adopted in each federal district to "prescribe some other source or sources of names in addition to voter lists where necessary to foster the policy and protect the rights secured" by that Act. The Uniform Act leaves such responsibility for supplementing the voter lists to either the Supreme Court or the Attorney General, and it makes such supplementation mandatory.

Exclusive use of voter lists as the basis for selecting citizens to be called for jury service may have a chilling effect upon exercise of the franchise, particularly by wage-earners for whom jury service may be a particular economic hardship. Principally for that reason the Report of the President's Commission on Registration and Voting Participation (November, 1963) recommended that voter registration lists be used only for electoral purposes. Furthermore, voter lists typically constitute far from complete lists of the citizens qualified for jury service. Considerable filling out of the master list to be more inclusive than the voter lists is necessary to carry out the declaration of Section 1 that "all qualified citizens shall have the opportunity . . . to be considered for jury service." Despite these disadvantages of use of voter lists in jury selection, the Federal Act and a great many states now use voter lists for that purpose—undoubtedly because it is the most conveniently available public list.

In most instances the high court of the State should be the agency to prescribe the supplementary sources of names for the master list. Such would be consistent with the rulemaking power also granted to that court by Section 18. In some states, however, the legislature may conclude that the office of the Attorney General is better fitted to determine the availability and practicality of supplementary lists. Whichever agency is given the responsibility must act within 90 days of the effective date of the Act and must maintain a continuing watch over the matter to assure the adequacy of the supplementation. In particular the supplementary sources should be reviewed shortly before December each even-numbered year since pursuant to Section 6(a) the master jury wheel is refilled in that month by random selection from the master list.

It is frequently the case that no single voter registration list or list of actual voters is maintained for the county or judicial district but rather a separate list is kept for each voting precinct or municipality. In such case the starting point for the master list would be the aggregation of all the voter registration lists or lists of actual voters of the several political subdivisions. There is no need for the several lists to be put together into a single alphabetical list. It would, for example, be satisfactory for the lists simply to be put in alphabetical order by municipality. The exact method of putting together the several lists into the master list is left to the jury commission or may be prescribed by rule.

The sources of names for the master list may be public, such as voter lists and motor vehicle registration lists, or may be private, as lists of telephone subscribers or electric company customers. Section 5(b) requires such lists to be made available to the jury commission. If any expense beyond merely making the list available at reasonable times becomes involved, as for example the expense of producing a computer print-out, the owner of the private list can reasonably expect reimbursement of the actual cost thereof.

The master list is open to the public. In general other lists and papers used or produced in connection with the jury selection process, with the exception of the names of jurors drawn for jury service and the contents of their juror qualification forms (Section 9), are kept confidential, but even they can be opened up for examination by parties preparing, presenting or defending against motions for relief on the ground of a substantial failure to comply with this Act.

**SECTION 6.** [*Master Jury Wheel.*]

(a) The jury commission for each [county] [district] shall maintain a master jury wheel, into which the commission shall place the names or identifying numbers of prospective jurors taken from the master list. If the total number of prospective jurors on the master list is 1,000 or less, the names or identifying numbers of all of them shall be placed in the master jury wheel. In all other cases, the number of prospective jurors to be placed in the master jury wheel shall be 1,000 plus not less than [one] percent of the total number of names on the master list. From time to time a larger or additional number may be determined by the jury commission or ordered by the court to be placed in the master jury wheel. In December of each even-numbered year the wheel shall be emptied and refilled as prescribed in this Act.

(b) Unless all the names on the master list are to be placed in the master jury wheel pursuant to subsection (a) the names or identifying numbers of prospective jurors to be placed in the master jury wheel shall be selected by the jury commission at random from the master list in the following manner: The total number of names on the master list shall be divided by the number of names to be placed in the master jury wheel and the whole number next greater than the quotient shall be the "key number," except that the key number shall never be less than 2. A "starting number" for making the selection shall then be determined by a random method from the numbers from 1 to the key number, both inclusive. The required number of the names shall then be selected from the master list by taking in order the first name on the master list corresponding to the starting number and then successively the names appearing in the master list at intervals equal to the key number, recommencing if necessary at the start of the list until the required number of names has been selected. Upon recommencing at the start of the list, or if additional names are subsequently to be selected for the master jury wheel, names previously selected from the master list shall be disregarded in selecting the additional names. The jury commission may use an electronic or mechanical system or device in carrying out its duties.

**SECTION 7.** [*Drawings from Master Jury Wheel; Juror Qualification Form.*]

(a) From time to time and in a manner prescribed by the court, the jury commission publicly shall draw at random from the master jury wheel the names or identifying numbers of as many prospective jurors as the court by order requires. The clerk shall prepare an alphabetical list of the names drawn. Neither the names drawn nor the list shall be disclosed to any person other than pursuant to this Act or specific order of the court. The clerk shall mail to every prospective juror whose name is drawn from the master jury wheel a juror qualification form accompanied by instructions to fill out and return the form by mail to the clerk within 10 days after its receipt. The juror qualification form shall be subject to approval by the court as to matters of form and shall elicit the name, address of residence, and age of the prospective juror and whether he (1) is a citizen of the United States and a resident of the [county] [district], (2) is able to read, speak and understand the English language, (3) has any physical or mental disability impairing his capacity to render satisfactory jury service, and (4) has lost the right to vote because of a criminal conviction. The juror qualification form shall contain the prospective juror's declaration that his responses are true to the best of his knowledge and his acknowledgement that a wilful misrepresentation of a material fact may be punished by a fine of not more than [$500] or imprisonment for not more than [30] days, or both. Notarization of the juror qualification form shall not be required. If the prospective juror is unable to fill out the form, another person may do it for him and shall indicate that he has done so and the reason therefor. If it appears there is an omission, ambiguity, or error in a returned form, the clerk shall again send the form with instructions to the prospective juror to make the necessary addition, clarification, or correction and to return the form to the jury commission within 10 days after its second receipt.

(b) Any prospective juror who fails to return a completed juror qualification form as instructed shall be directed by the jury commission to appear forthwith before the clerk to fill out the juror qualification form. At the time of his appearance for jury service, or at the time of any interview before the court or clerk, any prospective juror may be required to fill out another juror qualification form in the presence of the court or clerk, at which time the prospective juror may be questioned, but only with regard to his responses to questions contained on the form and grounds for his excuse or disqualification. Any information thus acquired by the court or clerk shall be noted on the juror qualification form.

(c) A prospective juror who fails to appear as directed by the commission pursuant to subsection (a) shall be ordered by the court to appear and show cause for his failure to appear as directed. If the prospective juror fails to appear pursuant to the court's order or fails to show good cause for his failure to appear as directed by the jury commission, he is guilty of criminal contempt and upon conviction may be fined not more than [$100] or imprisoned not more than [3] days, or both.

(d) Any person who wilfully misrepresents a material fact on a juror qualification form for the purpose of avoiding or securing service as a juror is guilty of a misdemeanor and upon conviction may be fined not more than [$500] or imprisoned not more than [30] days, or both.

SECTION 8. [*Disqualifications from Jury Service.*]

(a) The court, upon request of the jury commission or a prospective juror or on its own initiative, shall determine on the basis of information provided on the juror qualification form or interview with the prospective juror or other competent evidence whether the prospective juror is disqualified for jury service. The clerk shall enter this determination in the space provided on the juror qualification form and on the alphabetical list of names drawn from the master jury wheel.

(b) A prospective juror is disqualified to serve on a jury if he:

(1) is not a citizen of the United States, [21] years old, and a resident of the [district] [county];

(2) is unable to read, speak, and understand the English language;

(3) is incapable, by reason of his physical or mental disability, of rendering satisfactory jury service; but a person claiming this disqualification may be required to submit a physicians's certificate as to the disability, and the certifying physician is subject to inquiry by the court at its discretion; or

(4) has lost the right to vote because of a criminal conviction.

## SECTION 9. [*Qualified Jury Wheel; Selection and Summoning of Jury Panels.*]

(a) The jury commission shall maintain a qualified jury wheel and shall place therein the names or identifying numbers of all prospective jurors drawn from the master jury wheel who are not disqualified (Section 8).

(b) [A judge] [The court administrator] or any court or any other state or [county] [district] official having authority to conduct a trial or hearing with a jury within the [county] [district] may direct the jury commission to draw and assign to that court or official the number of qualified jurors he deems necessary for one or more jury panels or as required by law for a grand jury. Upon receipt of the direction and in a manner prescribed by the court, the jury commission shall publicly draw at random from the qualified jury wheel the number of qualified jurors specified. The qualified jurors drawn for jury service shall be assigned at random by the clerk to each jury panel in a manner prescribed by the court.

(c) If a grand, petit, or other jury is ordered to be drawn, the clerk thereafter shall cause each person drawn for jury service to be served with a summons either personally or by registered or certified mail, return receipt requested, addressed to him at his usual residence, business, or post office address, requiring him to report for jury service at a specified time and place.

(d) If there is an unanticipated shortage of available petit jurors drawn from a qualified jury wheel, the court may require the sheriff to summon a sufficient number of petit jurors selected at random by the clerk from the qualified jury wheel in a manner prescribed by the court.

(e) The names of qualified jurors drawn from the qualified jury wheel and the contents of jury qualification forms completed by those jurors shall be made available to the public unless the court determines in any instance that this information in the interest of justice should be kept confidential or its use limited in whole or in part.

**SECTION 10.** [*No Exemption.*] No qualified prospective juror is exempt from jury service.

## Comment

The Federal Act, 28 U.S.C.A. § 1863(b) (6), permits the plan in each district to "specify those groups of persons or occupational classes whose members shall be barred from jury service on the ground that they are exempt" provided that "the district court finds, and the plan states, that their exemption is in the public interest and would not be inconsistent" with the policies declared in the first and second sections of the Act. The Federal Act goes on to require that exemption be provided for the following:

"(i) members in active service in the Armed Forces of the United States; (ii) members of the fire or police departments of any state, district, territory, possession or subdivision thereof; (iii) public officers in the executive, legislative, or judicial branches of the Government of the United States, or any State, district, territory, or possession or subdivision thereof, who are actively engaged in the performance of official duties." (*Ibid.*)

Many states also have a long list of exempt classes of persons. For example, Maine exempts all officers of the United States, officers of colleges, and cashiers of incorporated banks, as well as ministers, teachers, physicians, dentists, nurses and attorneys. 14 M.R.S.A. § 1201.

Exemption of particular classes by statute is believed inadvisable. The public policy declared in Section 1 is better achieved by individual excuses pursuant to Section 11 upon a showing in the individual case of undue hardship, extreme inconvenience, or public necessity. Moreover, since petit jury service, is except in the unusual case, limited by Section 15 of the Uniform Act to a specified number of court days in any two year period, the burden of jury service upon the individual is minimized. The individual should not be given an automatic exemption merely because he comes within a particular class, but rather should be required to make out a case of hardship to the court.

**SECTION 11.** [*Excuses from Jury Service.*]

(a) The court, upon request of a prospective juror or on its own initiative, shall determine on the basis of information provided on the juror qualification form or interview with the prospective juror or other competent evidence whether the prospective juror should be excused from jury service. The clerk shall enter this determination in the space provided on the juror qualification form.

(b) A person who is not disqualified for jury service (Section 8) may be excused from jury service by the court only upon a showing of undue hardship, extreme inconvenience, or public necessity, for a period the court deems necessary, at the conclusion of which the person shall reappear for jury service in accordance with the court's direction.

## Comment

The Federal Act permits the plan in each district to specify groups of persons or occupational classes whose members shall, on individual request therefor, be excused from jury service and also to fix the distance either in miles or travel time beyond which prospective jurors would not be required to travel to court. 28 U.S.C.A. § 1863(b) (5) and (7). Many plans adopted under the Federal Act give automatic excuse upon request to a long list of classes of groups, as, for example, the following list quoted from the plan for the District of Maine:

"(1) all persons over seventy years of age;

"(2) all ministers of the gospel and members of religious orders, actively so engaged;

"(3) all attorneys, physicians, surgeons, dentists, veterinarians, pharmacists, nurses, and funeral directors, actively so engaged;

"(4) all persons who have served as a grand or petit juror in a State or Federal court within the preceding two years;

"(5) all school teachers in public, parochial or private schools, actively so engaged;

"(6) all persons who do not have adequate means of transportation to the place of holding court;

"(7) all women who are caring for a child or children under the age of sixteen years;

"(8) all sole operators of businesses."

Other district plans have strictly limited the automatic excuses, as, for example, that for the Western District of North Carolina, which grants automatic excuse upon individual request only to the following:

"(1) persons over seventy-five years of age;

"(2) women who have legal custody of a child or children under the age of ten years;

"(3) any person who resides more than one hundred (100) miles from place of holding court."

Section 11 of the Uniform Act is based upon the same principle as Section 10, namely, that there should be no automatic exemptions or excuses from jury service, but rather that excuse should be only upon a showing of actual need or public reason therefor. The Uniform Act proceeds on the principle that jurors should be selected by random methods from the widest possible list of citizens. The corollary is that actual service on the jury should be shared as widely as possible and in particular that professional and business groups should be excused only in cases of demonstrated need. The so-called "blue ribbon jury" is outlawed by the Uniform Act. At the same time, business and professional groups within the community should not be permitted to avoid jury service. It is also believed that citizens in general will be more willing to perform jury service if it is known throughout the community that jury service is universal, barring only particular hardship in specific cases.

The Uniform Act does not refer to those other ways in which pursuant to other provisions of law prospective jurors may be excluded from service, namely, (i) exclusion upon peremptory challenge, (ii) exclusion for good cause; and (iii) exclusion because the requisite number of jurors, including alternate jurors, have already been impaneled in a particular case. Those other occasions for the exclusion of qualified jurors are well defined in the law. Otherwise than by exclusion under those circumstances, if a qualified juror is drawn from the qualified wheel and he is not excused upon a showing of undue hardship, extreme inconvenience, or public necessity, he has the obligation to serve and is guaranteed the opportunity to serve. See Section 1.

**SECTION 12.** [*Challenging Compliance with Selection Procedures.*]

(a) Within 7 days after the moving party discovered or by the exercise of diligence could have discovered the grounds therefor, and in any event before the petit jury is sworn to try the case, a party may move to stay the proceedings, and in a criminal case to quash the indictment, or for other appropriate relief, on the ground of substantial failure to comply with this Act in selecting the grand or petit jury.

(b) Upon motion filed under subsection (a) containing a sworn statement of facts which, if true would constitute a substantial failure to comply with this Act, the moving party is entitled to present in support of the motion the testimony of the jury commissioner or the clerk, any relevant records and papers not public or otherwise available used by the jury commissioner or the clerk, and any other relevant evidence. If the court determines that in selecting either a grand jury or a petit jury there has been a substantial failure to comply with this Act, the court shall stay the proceedings pending the selection of the jury in conformity with this Act, quash an indictment, or grant other appropriate relief.

(c) The procedures prescribed by this section are the exclusive means by which a person accused of a crime, the State, or a party in a civil case may challenge a jury on the ground that the jury was not selected in conformity with this Act.

(d) The contents of any records or papers used by the jury commissioner or the clerk in connection with the selection process and not made public under this Act (Section 5(c) and 9(e)) shall not be disclosed, except in connection with the preparation or presentation of a motion under subsection (a) until after the master jury wheel has been emptied and refilled (Section 6) and all persons selected to serve as jurors before the master jury wheel was emptied have been discharged. The parties in a case may inspect, reproduce, and copy the records or papers at all reasonable times during the preparation and pendency of a motion under subsection (a).

**SECTION 13.** [*Preservation of Records.*] All records and papers compiled and maintained by the jury commissioner or the clerk in connection with selection and service of jurors shall be preserved by the clerk for 4 years after the master jury wheel used in their selection is emptied and refilled (Section 6) and for any longer period ordered by the court.

SECTION 14. [*Mileage and Compensation of Jurors.*] A juror shall be paid mileage at the rate of [10] cents per mile for his travel expenses from his residence to the place of holding court and return and shall be compensated at the rate of [$20.00] for each day of required attendance at sessions of the court.

SECTION 15. [*Length of Service by Jurors.*] In any [2] year period a person shall not be required:

(1) to serve or attend court for prospective service as a petit juror more than [10] court days, except if necessary to complete service in a particular case;

(2) to serve on more than one grand jury; or

(3) to serve as both a grand and petit juror.

### Comment

This section is derived from the Federal Act, 28 U.S.C.A. § 1866(e), although a maximum of 10 days service on a petit jury is suggested as against the thirty-day limitation of the Federal Act. The purpose of the section is stated in the Senate Committee Report on the bill which became the Federal Act:

"This provision is designed to distribute the 'burden' of jury service and to enhance the representative quality of juries. Moreover, since jury service involves direct participation in the democratic process, as many citizens as possible ought to have the chance to serve."

SECTION 16. [*Penalties for Failure to Perform Jury Service.*] A person summoned for jury service who fails to appear or to complete jury service as directed shall be ordered by the court to appear forthwith and show cause for his failure to comply with the summons. If he fails to show good cause for noncompliance with the summons, he is guilty of criminal contempt and upon conviction may be fined not more than [$100] or imprisoned not more than [3] days, or both.

SECTION 17. [*Protection of Jurors' Employment.*]

(a) An employer shall not deprive an employee of his employment, or threaten or otherwise coerce him with respect thereto, because the employee receives a summons, responds thereto, serves as a juror, or attends court for prospective jury service.

(b) Any employer who violates subsection (a) is guilty of criminal contempt and upon conviction may be fined not more than [$500] or imprisoned not more than [6] months, or both.

(c) If an employer discharges an employee in violation of subsection (a) the employee within [ ] days may bring a civil action for recovery of wages lost as a result of the violation and for an order requiring the reinstatement of the employee. Damages recoverable shall not exceed lost wages for 6 weeks. If he prevails, the employee shall be allowed a reasonable attorney's fee fixed by the court.

**SECTION 18.** [*Court Rules.*] The [Supreme Court] may make and amend rules, not inconsistent with this Act, regulating the selection and service of jurors.

**SECTION 19.** [*Severability.*] If any provision of this Act or the application thereof to any person or circumstance is held invalid, the invalidity does not affect other provisions or applications of the Act which can be given effect without the invalid provision or application, and to this end the provisions of this Act are severable.

**SECTION 20.** [*Short Title.*] This Act may be cited as the Uniform Jury Selection and Service Act.

**SECTION 21.** [*Application and Construction.*] This Act shall be so applied and construed as to effectuate its general purpose to make uniform the law with respect to the subject of this Act among those states which enact it.

# Index

## About the Author

Jon Van Dyke is a Professor at the University of California's Hastings College of the Law (in San Francisco) and is currently a Visiting Professor at the new law school of the University of Hawaii (in Honolulu). Jon received his undergraduate degree from Yale University in 1964 and his law degree from Harvard Law School in 1967, and subsequently taught at the law school of Catholic University in Washington, D.C. (1967-69), served as law clerk to Roger J. Traynor, Chief Justice of the California Supreme Court (1969-70), and was a Visiting Fellow at the Center for the Study of Democratic Institutions, in Santa Barbara, California (1970-71). Since joining the Hastings faculty in 1971, Jon has been teaching Constitutional Law and International Law. He has written numerous articles on problems of social injustice and the need to reform our legal institutions. In 1972, his book *North Vietnam's Strategy for Survival*, describing the U.S. bombing of Vietnam and the Vietnamese response, was published by Pacific Books, Palo Alto, California.